Religion and the Global Politics of Human Rights

Religion and the Global Politics of Human Rights

EDITED BY
THOMAS BANCHOFF and
ROBERT WUTHNOW

OXFORD
UNIVERSITY PRESS

OXFORD
UNIVERSITY PRESS

Oxford University Press, Inc., publishes works that further
Oxford University's objective of excellence
in research, scholarship, and education.

Oxford   New York
Auckland   Cape Town   Dar es Salaam   Hong Kong   Karachi
Kuala Lumpur   Madrid   Melbourne   Mexico City   Nairobi
New Delhi   Shanghai   Taipei   Toronto

With offices in
Argentina   Austria   Brazil   Chile   Czech Republic   France   Greece
Guatemala   Hungary   Italy   Japan   Poland   Portugal   Singapore
South Korea   Switzerland   Thailand   Turkey   Ukraine   Vietnam

Published by Oxford University Press, Inc.
198 Madison Avenue, New York, New York 10016

www.oup.com

Oxford is a registered trademark of Oxford University Press

Library of Congress Cataloging-in-Publication Data
Religion and the global politics of human rights/edited by Thomas Banchoff and Robert Wuthnow.
     p.   cm.
Includes bibliographical references and index.
ISBN 978-0-19-534339-7; 978-0-19-534338-0 (pbk.)
   1. Human rights—Religious aspects. I. Banchoff, Thomas F., 1964–II. Wuthnow, Robert.
BL65.H78R47 2011
201'.723—dc22   2010021940

9 8 7 6 5 4 3 2 1

Printed in the United States of America
on acid-free paper

Contents

Acknowledgments

This book grew out of a conference held at Georgetown University's Berkley Center for Religion, Peace, and World Affairs in March 2007 on the topic "Religion and the Global Politics of Human Rights." The spirited discussions at the conference continued over the course of the following two years, as participants readied chapters for publication. We would like to thank the contributors for putting so much time, energy, and care into the case studies that make up this volume. A topic as broad as the intersection of religion, human rights, and world politics comes alive only through careful empirical research.

This is the third in a series of books published by Oxford University Press on religion and world affairs that have grown out of Berkley Center conferences. The first, *Democracy and the New Religious Pluralism* (2007), addressed the changing impact of religion on society and politics in the United States and Western Europe. The second, *Religious Pluralism, Globalization, and World Politics* (2008), extended the same themes in a more global direction. This third volume explores a critical global issue, human rights, in depth. Together, the three books are part of a wider, interdisciplinary effort to understand religion's changing role in world affairs. Like that literature as a whole, they pose key questions, try to answer them, but cannot begin to exhaust them.

This book's contribution to the wider debate would not have been possible without the wisdom and guidance of our editor, Theo Calderara. We would also like to thank Amy Vander Vliet for her research and editorial assistance, and the many colleagues at

Georgetown, Princeton, and elsewhere who provided feedback at different stages in this project.

Thomas Banchoff
Georgetown University
Robert Wuthnow
Princeton University

Contributors

Rogaia Mustafa Abusharaf is Visiting Associate Professor of Anthropology at the Georgetown University School of Foreign Service in Qatar.

Thomas Banchoff is Associate Professor, Department of Government and School of Foreign Service, and Director of the Berkley Center for Religion, Peace, and World Affairs, Georgetown University.

Marjorie Mandelstam Balzer is Research Professor in the Center for Eurasian, Russian and East European Studies and the Department of Anthropology, Georgetown University.

Paul Freston is Professor and CIGI Chair in Religion and Politics in Global Context at the Balsillie School of International Affairs and Wilfrid Laurier University in Ontario, Canada.

Yvonne Yazbeck Haddad is Professor of the History of Islam and Christian-Muslim Relations at the Prince Alwaleed bin Talal Center for Muslim-Christian Understanding, Georgetown University.

Robert W. Hefner is Professor of Anthropology and Director of the Institute on Culture, Religion, and World Affairs at Boston University.

Charles Keyes is Professor Emeritus of Anthropology and International Studies at the University of Washington.

Pratap Bhanu Mehta is President and Chief Executive of the Centre for Policy Research, New Delhi.

David Ownby is Professor of History and Director of the Centre for East Asian Studies at the Université de Montréal.

Robert Wuthnow is Gerhard R. Andlinger Professor of Sociology and Director of the Center for the Study of Religion at Princeton University.

Religion and the Global Politics of Human Rights

I

Introduction

Thomas Banchoff and Robert Wuthnow

The democratic revolution of the past century has heightened expectations in many parts of the world about human rights, including the right of representation and free speech, protection for women and children, and fair treatment for minorities. Political and ideological struggles over human rights in the global arena have centered on several questions: Are human rights universal or the product of specific cultures? How are generally accepted values about human dignity enacted in different social and political contexts? Is democracy a necessary condition for the achievement of human rights in practice? What are the social and political mechanisms through which claims about rights and responsibilities can be made? And when, if ever, is it legitimate for external actors to exert pressure for human rights upon particular countries?

Today these questions have a salient religious dimension. The last several decades have seen a remarkable mobilization of faith-inspired actors and organizations around diverse political, social, and economic human rights agendas. The end of the cold war in 1989–91 and democratization in Latin America and parts of Africa and Asia have reduced many political constraints on religious groups. Local and national faith communities have increasingly invoked and adapted international human rights norms to their particular social and political contexts. In pressing diverse human rights agendas at the local and national level they have encountered both support and resistance from the state and other social actors. Religion and the global politics of human rights are now more intertwined than ever.

In exploring this intersection, this book breaks with the focus of the established literature on the theoretical compatibility of different traditions with human rights. In that literature scriptures, tradition, and holy law are typically mined for references to prescriptions bearing on different spheres of life, including sexuality, community, and the economy. These ethical precepts are then juxtaposed with modern notions of human rights, as expressed in democratic political theory and in international legal instruments such as the 1948 United Nations Universal Declaration of Human Rights. Conclusions are then drawn about the compatibility or incompatibility of religious traditions with human rights in general.[1]

This book departs from that established approach in three ways. First, it regards traditions as internally diverse. The world's major religious communities are not monolithic; they are home to running debates about the value of human rights, their meaning, and practical implications. Second, it focuses less on traditions in the abstract than on their practical engagement in politics and society. Across a range of issue areas—including Islam and women's rights, Hinduism and religious liberty, Catholicism and the death penalty, and Buddhism and minority rights—the essays in this volume trace the mobilization of religious communities in practice. Third, the book emphasizes the state policies and institutions that constrain religious engagement around human rights from one national context to the next. The interplay of religion, politics, and human rights looks very different across world regions and key countries including the United States, China, and India.

The balance of this introductory chapter is divided into four parts. A first section explores two contrasting historical narratives of religion and human rights and their contemporary implications. A second section sketches the empirical chapters as they relate to three core questions: How are human rights understood in different traditions? How do religious communities mobilize around diverse human rights agendas? How do state institutions shape the religious politics of human rights in practice? A third section elaborates four main themes that cut across the individual chapters: the centrality of religious pluralism, diverse strategies of engagement, political constraints, and the framing effects of historical narrative. A concluding section reflects on the future impact of globalization and geopolitics on religion and the global politics of human rights.

Human Rights and Religion: Two Historical Narratives

Modern understandings of human rights assume that persons everywhere should enjoy the same rights; hence, the designation "universal." These rights include freedom from persecution, freedom to speak and assemble, and the expectation that individuals will be treated equally, regardless of race or gender, and that their need for food, housing, and other basic necessities will be respected. Human rights are also universal in a second sense: a near-global consensus that human rights are a good thing—that there should be clear limits on what the state can do to individuals and legitimate claims that individuals can make on the state. On this shared foundation, however, controversy rages. Rights are defined differently across the political spectrum. What rights mean and how to realize them are objects of contention. And governments insist, in different ways, that the exercise and promotion of human rights not endanger public safety, order, or morality.

The place of religion in this constellation is itself controversial. Some see religion, with its authority structures and truth claims, in fundamental tension with human rights. For others, religious actors and ideas often play a critical role in the articulation and advancement of human rights in practice. Each view of the religion/human rights nexus draws on a particular understanding of history.

The Dominant Narrative: Religion Opposes Human Rights

The still dominant story in Europe and North America goes something like this: once upon a time, long ago, humans everywhere were oppressed by cruel leaders and dictatorial ideologies that accorded little dignity to the individual and generally imposed duties on them. Slavery, exploitation, and general unhappiness resulted. Gradually, some enlightened leaders arose and some signs of hope emerged. Some basic rights were instituted—for example, in the practices of the Greek city-states and later in the Magna Carta. But ruthless monarchs continued to suppress the aspirations of ordinary people for liberty. Eventually, with the spread of markets and economic development, things began to change for the better. The American and French revolutions instituted new ideas of freedom that became beacons for people in other countries. Democracy began to spread, and while imperialism, fascism, and communism were serious setbacks, the free world prevailed during the latter half of the twentieth century. The forces of modernization were impossible to resist. Basic rights have increasingly been extended to encompass minorities, gender equality, and social and economic concerns. The struggle for human rights has been the long, upward trajectory of history.[2]

This familiar narrative has much to recommend it. But as a way of writing and talking about human rights it involves certain problematic assumptions about the past. Religion figures importantly among those assumptions. It is common for writers to argue that the modern conception of human rights triumphed only as traditional religious authorities eroded. These authorities and their ideologies, the argument goes, specified only duties to God and ignored or suppressed rights inherent in individuals. In this narrative the bloody European religious wars of the sixteenth and seventeenth centuries are best understood as clashes of opposing orthodoxies that engendered untold intolerance, cruelty, and suffering. The Enlightenment that followed eroded priestly power and superstition and enthroned human rights ideals. This story usually makes some acknowledgment that Judaism, Christianity, Islam, Buddhism, and other religions long before the modern era included ideas about respect, justice, mercy toward the poor, and so on. The idea of humanity being created in the image of God is recognized as a historical source of the idea of universal human dignity. But the dominant story is one of traditional religious authority opposed to the secular Enlightenment ideal of rational, autonomous individuals as bearers of universal rights.[3]

This *religion opposes human rights* narrative supports a particular way of thinking about the politics of human rights today. Against the historical backdrop of the religious wars and their fanaticism and destruction, citizens and their leaders are called to frame their arguments about human rights in secular, political, religion-free public language fully open to rational discussion. The closed-minded views of religionists who hear only the voice of God should be marginalized. Anyone familiar with recent discussions of human rights in the United States knows that this secularist perspective is very much alive. Students of American jurisprudence and political theory can be heard arguing that religion is traditional, thick, value-laden, and grounded in divine mandate, and as such is pitted against liberal understandings of human rights. The persistence of religion as a cultural force is acknowledged, but it is viewed mainly as an item of individual faith, on par with other beliefs adopted by autonomous individuals. Faith is not analytically distinct from other belief systems or culture more broadly. The authority claims of tradition and community are viewed with suspicion.[4]

This individualist and rationalist frame supports a narrow view of the politics of religion and human rights. Where religious communities are viewed as free associations of individuals, religious human rights become the rights of individuals who happen to share the same beliefs and practices. Such an individualized approach to human rights tends to approach religion through a narrow understanding of religious freedom. The freedom to have, practice, and change a religion is upheld, but the freedom of religious groups to engage in politics and push a wider human rights agenda is frowned upon. In this view it is legitimate for religious people to insist on freedom of belief and worship. But when they join with others of like mind about different policy agendas, they should do so as citizens and not as people of faith. To engage more broadly in the politics of human rights—to press their own ideas of what those rights mean and how they grow out of their traditions—is to inject religion where it does not belong and risk a sharp clash of orthodoxies that can promote intolerance, violence, and oppression.

An Alternative Narrative: Religion Engages Human Rights

An alternative historical narrative casts the contemporary religious politics of human rights in a different light. It does not deny the negative contribution of religious exclusivism and intolerance to violence and oppression through history and up to the present. And it does not insist on a direct connection between ideas about human dignity in ancient religious traditions and contemporary human rights. But the alternative narrative does take issue with the idea of an unwavering tension between religion and human rights throughout history. The movement from the Middle Ages to Modernity via the wars of religion and the Enlightenment was not a simple story of the eclipse of religious authority by a new discourse about individual freedom, self-determination, and human rights. It is better read as the story of struggles *within* and across religious and nonreligious communities about how to adapt to the rise of modernity, with its markets, laws, and individualist ethos. For centuries, scholars, leaders, and followers across traditions have differed on core issues, including whether democracy—the rule of the people—is compatible with God's rule, and whether respect for the rights of individuals is compatible with duties to the wider social and moral order.[5]

In this alternative narrative, religion is not the villain. That role is played by all ideologies, religious or secular, that deny the basic fundamental dignity of all human beings. The problem, then, is not religious tradition or authority. Rather, it is religious extremists who reject the idea that human beings are created equal and free and deploy state power or coercive force to impose their version of orthodoxy. Since the Enlightenment, the world's leading religious traditions have been home both to reactionaries of this stripe and to reformers who emphasize basic human dignity, respect for the rights for others, and the primacy of peaceful conflict resolution over war and violence. Since the middle of the twentieth century, in the wake of two world wars and the Holocaust, reform efforts to engage human rights discourse have been in ascendance. In this alternative narrative, the 1948 Universal Declaration appears in a different light. It does not represent an assertion of universal secular rationality over and against narrow religious views, but rather the outcome of deliberation among like-minded thinkers and activists from both religious and secular backgrounds, each drawing on the elements within their traditions that emphasize universal human dignity.[6]

This *religion engages human rights* narrative, by emphasizing the complexity of the relationship, suggests a more inclusive approach to the religious politics of human rights. In the dominant secularist story, the injection of religion displaces rational reflection with traditional authority. In the alternative narrative, religious traditions provide vital resources—most centrally the belief in the transcendent equality and dignity of all human beings—for reflection on the foundations of rights and how to secure them. Tradition, from this perspective, is a boon, not a hindrance. A source of collective identity and ethical orientation for a living community bound together by shared values, rituals, and experiences, it gives the belief in fundamental human dignity an emotional foundation it would otherwise not have. For extremists, of course, religion *is* a source of monolithic and irrational authority, a license to despise and attack outsiders. In the mainstream, however, at least since the middle of the twentieth century, and increasingly at the dawn of the twenty-first, faith traditions have become a space for a running debate on the challenges of modernity, including how to safeguard and advance human dignity amid the economic, social, and political transformations wrought by technological revolutions and globalization.[7]

This alternative narrative supports a greater legitimate scope for a religious politics of human rights. In the secularist narrative, religious freedom is understood as liberty of belief and worship; religious practice that spills over into political engagement is suspect. By contrast, where religion is acknowledged as a powerful source of ethical and emotional attachment to the idea of human dignity, one might expect—and even encourage—religious engagement in the public square. Religious communities are also political actors, and their freedom is political, and not just abstract or theological. Faith-inspired understanding of what human dignity demands of the state and its citizens shapes particular conceptions of economic, social, and political rights and how to pursue them. The threat of intolerance and extremism persists—for religious as for secular ideologies. But as long as the state retains its institutional autonomy from religious authorities, and faith communities seek to shape—and not dictate—politics and policy, fears that their human rights activism could encourage theocracy or sectarian violence are unfounded.

The essays in this volume are more in line with this second narrative, which highlights productive as well as contentious religious engagement with the politics of human rights. They reveal debates within and across religious traditions in which extremist advocates of theocracy and violence often play a subordinate role. They point to different patterns of practical involvement in the politics of human rights, within and across countries and regions. And they suggest that the scope and impact of religious engagement depends as much on the state and its structures as it does on the values and practices of the faith communities themselves.

THE CASE STUDIES. The nine core empirical chapters provide a global overview of the intersection of religion, politics, and human rights across four traditions (Islam, Christianity, Hinduism, and Buddhism) and major countries and world regions. A first section addresses Islam through a general overview of human rights controversies (Robert Hefner) and a specific focus on gender issues (Yvonne Haddad). A second section features regional analyses of Latin America (Paul Freston), sub-Saharan Africa (Rogaia Abusharaf), and Southeast Asia (Charles Keyes), while a final section centers on four key global powers: India

(Pratap Mehta), China (David Ownby), Russia (Marjorie Mandelstam Balzer), and the United States (Thomas Banchoff). Because the subject matter is vast, each of the chapters addresses a particular set of human rights challenges in a particular tradition, region, or country.

Islam and the Global Politics of Human Rights

In his chapter, "Human Rights and Democracy in Islam: The Indonesian Case in Global Perspective," Robert Hefner explores the connection between Islam, democracy, and human rights in theory and practice. The idea of shari`a, or divine law, remains a touchstone in internal Muslim debates about human rights. For most of Islamic history, Hefner points out, shari`a has served not as a basis for theocracy, but rather as a religious and moral frame of reference for secular authorities to both respect and protect. Recent global surveys suggest that significant majorities of Muslims around the world continue in this mainstream tradition, supporting the idea that law and politics should unfold in accordance with shari`a, while rejecting radical calls for a theocratic Islamic state in favor of democracy and human rights. On the question of what those rights mean in practice, however, Islam is home to a fervent debate. The right to religious freedom, the rights of religious minorities, the rights of women, and the legitimacy of traditional corporal punishments are all objects of ongoing contestation that often spills over into legislative and judicial conflicts that sometimes draw global media attention.

Indonesia, the world's most populous Muslim nation, serves to illustrate some of the ambiguities at the intersection of Islam and human rights in practice. Since the revolution of 1998, the country has seen a successful democratic experiment and the institutionalization of human rights to an unprecedented degree in its history. Within this context, education policy has emerged as a particular area of contestation. Hefner traces the evolution of government-supported efforts of the State Islamic Colleges to develop programs for civic education designed to deepen Muslims' commitment to democracy and human rights. The results of a survey of educators show overwhelming support both for democracy and human rights, on the one hand, and for shari`a, on the other. For Hefner, this dual affirmation is not a contradiction, but a sincere effort to maintain and combine two sets of deeply held value commitments. Low levels of support for Islamist parties suggest space for religion in public life short of full-scale Islamization. "Rather than rushing to support programs for far-reaching legal and political change," Hefner concludes, "most voters hedge their bets, deferring until some later moment the question of just how to accommodate God's law in a democratic state."

Yvonne Haddad's chapter titled "Muslims, Human Rights, and Women's Rights" takes a different approach to the intersection of Islam, politics, and human rights. She examines a contested issue—the status of women in

Islam—and parses its historical, social, and political dimensions. From the onset of colonialism through the current war in Afghanistan, she points out, the women's issue has been a focus both of Western criticism of Islam and of Muslim resistance. In the face of external demands for reform couched in terms of universal human rights, Islamic traditionalists have insisted that their emphasis on family, honor, and respect accords women more dignity than the West's obsession with individualism, materialism, and sexuality. The Islamization of culture, society, and politics in much of the Middle East since the late 1970s has exacerbated the global politics of the issue. Leaders have rolled back some of the gains of women in areas ranging from freedom of expression to access to education and political participation, while dismissing the protests of international human rights and women's groups as cultural imperialism. And the Organization of the Islamic Conference, a grouping of more than fifty Muslim-majority countries, has articulated a specifically Muslim understanding of human rights based on divine revelation that asserts the equality of women but also upholds traditional gender roles in the family and community.

As Haddad points out, these international and national human rights dynamics are not the whole story. Over the past two decades Muslim women themselves have increasingly seized upon the issue of rights as an object of critical reflection and social and political activism. An Islamic feminism has emerged that takes issue both with Islamic traditionalism and with secular human rights norms. A series of creative scholars have argued that both the Qur'an and other early Islamic sources provide a foundation for a full women's equality at odds with their traditional subservience to men, and that Western human rights norms are both alien to Islamic culture and an instrument of Western strategic dominance. Through an analysis of three groups—Women's Learning Partnership, Women Living under Muslim Laws, and Sisters in Islam—Haddad shows how these ideas are informing practical human rights activism on the ground. National and transnational women's groups anchored in a new understanding of the Islamic tradition are advancing the cultural, economic, social, and political rights of women in practice.

Three Regions: Latin America, Sub-Saharan Africa, and Southeast Asia

In his chapter titled "Religious Pluralism, Democracy, and Human Rights in Latin America," Paul Freston takes a "from below" perspective on the practical conduct of human rights issues among the continent's traditional Roman Catholic majority and its rapidly growing Pentecostal minority. Freston argues that the central debates about human rights that have emerged in response to Latin America's rising religious pluralism are not, as some observers anticipated, a concern over the role of international and foreign influences. They focus instead on the treatment of religious minorities. In its evolving relationships with the state, the Roman Catholic Church since the Second Vatican Council (1962–65) has embraced universal human rights and religious freedom but has sometimes reduced its emphasis on them in view of threats to its dominance from Pentecostal organizations. The situation varies from country to country but is compounded by historical legacies of dictatorship and close church-state ties, as well as by increasing urbanization and pervasive poverty and violence in many areas. Brazil, the largest country in Latin America in terms of size and population, is at the center of Freston's analysis.

Freston views Latin America as providing an important lesson in seeking generalizations about the relationship between religion and human rights. While the situation in the region is less complicated than in many parts of the world because of the dominance of Christianity, the relative weakness of Islam and other religious traditions, and the continent's lack of direct engagement in major international conflicts, it is also marked by diverse religious perspectives on human rights, ranging from progressive liberation theology to conservative social thought in the Catholic Church, and including a wide array of different currents among Pentecostals. While Latin America as a whole has made great strides toward stronger democratic institutions, Freston argues that commitments to religious liberty are not particularly strong. Neither the Catholic Church nor the most influential Pentecostal leaders appear eager to promote genuine religious freedom of the kind that would allow but also regulate proselytization. An unknown factor is whether Pentecostalism's emphasis on individual salvation may also encourage greater involvement in political efforts to protect individual human rights.

Taking up the question of "Gender Justice and Religion in Sub-Saharan Africa," Rogaia Abusharaf's chapter examines the impact of African cultural traditions on interpretations of human rights. Like other contributors she finds considerable tension between a Western-defined notion of universal human rights and the ways in which rights are understood within particular local contexts. She also observes how the intersection of globalization and local traditions is producing emergent and unexpected ways of thinking about gender equality. Religion is especially important, she suggests, not only because of its historic role in sub-Saharan Africa or the challenges it experienced during colonialism, but also because of the rapid growth in many areas of Islam and Pentecostal Christianity. Drawing on the work of Anthony Giddens, she argues that the changes taking place amid globalization represent a kind of "disembedding" of local traditions that yields new understandings of rights and how to secure them. Her focus on controversies surrounding women's rights and female genital mutilation (FGM) illustrates how different African societies have responded to this dynamic.

Female genital mutilation is, of course, a human rights issue with a global dimension that cuts across religious and secular perspectives. Abusharaf's analysis is especially instructive in showing how the authority of local religious leaders enables them to intervene in human rights discussions without appearing to be intrusive or interventionist. In more than one case, she finds that Muslim and Christian leaders have been able to work together across religious lines in opposition to FGM. Faith leaders, she suggests, can effectively "localize" international human rights by associating them with vernacular understandings and at the same time open these practices to "scrutiny in the light of ultimate values." Religious leaders are able to do this because they themselves are intimately familiar with local customs and because their authority within the community makes it possible for them to reframe and redefine the meanings of established practices, placing gender and sexuality in a new interpretive framework. A telling example is the Alternative Rights of Passage movement that developed in four predominantly Christian districts in Kenya.

In his chapter titled "Buddhism, Human Rights, and Non-Buddhist Minorities," Charles Keyes offers a rare empirical examination of the actual human rights practices of governments in societies in which Buddhism is the majority religion. These are Sri Lanka (formerly known as Ceylon), Burma (Myanmar), Thailand (formerly known as Siam), Cambodia, and Bhutan. Theravāda Buddhism is dominant in the first four, while Vajrayāna, a tradition particularly associated with Tibetan Buddhism, is dominant in Bhutan. Although Buddhist teachings that emphasize peace, harmony, and nonviolence are compatible with universal rights claims, Keyes finds that on the ground Buddhist-majority governments have been anything but favorable toward human rights. Historically, the politics of human rights in South and Southeast Asia has played out against a backdrop of colonialism and imposed Western cultural and religious patterns. In more recent decades since independence, the central questions have come to focus on the Buddhist majority's treatment of religious minorities. For example, in Sri Lanka the government's response toward uprisings among the Tamil Hindu and Muslim minorities has been a source of long-standing controversy.

The Buddhist cases Keyes examines provide an important cautionary note to arguments suggesting that religious teachings favorable to human rights necessarily shape governments' actions. As they do in other traditions, leaders find aspects of Buddhist teachings that can be used to suppress the interests of minorities in the name of social stability. Yet, on a more hopeful note, Keyes identifies groups of Buddhists within each of the societies he examines that are seeking to promote social justice in the name of Buddhism. He, too, emphasizes the importance of variations from country to country and even within regions and local areas. Rather than seeking broad generalizations about the relationship of religion to human rights, or focusing on religious texts and traditions, this chapter points to the need for fine-grained historical analysis. As Keyes points out, contextual variation does not mean that religion is unimportant. Both those he examines who wish to suppress the rights of minorities and those who work for social justice find legitimacy and mobilizing potential in appeals to Buddhist teachings.

Four Key Countries: India, China, Russia and the United States

In his chapter, "Hinduism and the Politics of Rights in India," Pratap Bhanu Mehta examines the articulation of Hinduism within the country's democratic institutions. Hinduism, it has often been pointed out, is pluralistic by nature. Even so, its relationship to democratic pluralism is not unproblematic. For centuries Hinduism in India coexisted with the social hierarchies of caste, and the experience of colonialism led many to construe Western insistence on human rights as hypocritical. In the decades since independence, however, both colonialism and caste have paradoxically reaffirmed the alignment of Hinduism with democracy and human rights. The legacy of British rule and its condescension toward Hinduism reinforced the desire of Hindu leaders to appear modern and to construct their tradition as compatible with evolving international standards. At the same time, Mohandas Gandhi and others sought to outlaw caste not just because it contradicted human rights, but also because it was a blight on Hinduism in the eyes of the world.

The politics of human rights in India cannot only be understood in terms of elites grappling with the colonial legacy and seeking to establish firm and respected democratic institutions. It has also been driven from below. A key exception to the Indian embrace of Western norms—an opposition to proselytism—has roots in local resistance grounded in Hinduism's understanding of pluralism, its opposition to the idea of orthodoxy, and its view of Christian and Muslim missionary efforts as the imposition of alien values. It is at the state level, where anxiety about inroads into local communities is strongest, that antiproselytism legislation has been instituted—and upheld, in most cases, by national courts. Mehta traces two more examples of politics from below. The agitation of the lower castes for an end to discrimination has sought to mobilize the resources of the Hindu tradition against inequality and to work through local movements and the courts. A second example is Hindu nationalism, which relies on a strong network of local organizations. Like the drive to establish India as a strong democracy, Mehta argues, the concern with a single, exclusive Hindu nationalism is part of a drive for international recognition. But in this case it is the recognition of national cohesiveness and power—and not of a democratic ethos—that is sought.

In his chapter, "Religion, State Power, and Human Rights in China," David Ownby argues that human rights discourse remains marginal to the politics of religion in China, despite the efforts of the United States and international organizations to bring it in. There has been a liberalization of religious practice in China since the Cultural Revolution (1966–1976) and the country's economic opening since 1979. By all accounts, the number of religious adherents in the country is surging, particularly within different forms of Protestant Christianity. While tolerating this development, the government has sought to carefully manage it. China recognizes freedom of belief as a human right, as well as religious practice—as long as the latter unfolds within a government-approved framework. Religious communities must be organized on a national basis, reflecting ongoing suspicion of external religious actors, a legacy of the involvement of missionaries in the colonial enterprise. And they must register with the Religious Affairs Bureau, which oversees the construction of new religious buildings, the printing of religious literature, and systems of seminaries and monasteries.

Within this structure, Ownby points out, local struggles for greater religious freedom have not focused on international human rights. The house church movement, in pressing its case for recognition, has tended to use theological rather than political arguments. And even the Dalai Lama, when discussing Tibet, is generally careful to pitch his arguments less in terms of international human rights than in terms of greater cultural autonomy. The most vocal proponents of human rights discourse are a group that faces the strongest government opposition, the Falun Gong—and it orchestrates its campaign from the West, not within China itself. Ownby argues that the ongoing dynamics of globalization, the growth of diaspora communities, and their links back to the mainland may alter these dynamics in years to come. This is particularly the case with Christianity, which is self-consciously global in its scope and aligned with international human rights movements. At the same time, he reminds us that the flowering of religion since the 1980s has gone hand in hand with the expectation that it would contribute to the stability of the country. Religious rights, like all human rights, remain subordinate to the prerogatives of state power.

Marjorie Mandelstam Balzer's chapter, "Religious Communities and Rights in the Russian Federation," provides a thorough examination of the human rights controversies centering on religion that have emerged in the former Soviet Union during the past two decades. The dominant factors influencing these controversies, she argues, are the diversity of ethnicities and administrative structures within the federation and the national government's efforts to maintain or reimpose a kind of centralized legal authority. The result is well expressed in the tension between "managed pluralism," as one rubric, and "managed nationalism," as another. Within this interplay of ethnic and political forces, the Russian Orthodox Church's relationship with the state and its dominant position in relation to other religious groups is the most important arena in which questions about religious freedom emerge. Highly symbolic gestures of respect for minority religions, such as the opening of a new synagogue or the inclusion of Muslims in a folk festival, occur against the backdrop of restrictions on religious freedom.

Like the Ownby chapter on China, Mandelstam Balzer's analysis of Russia underscores the role of state power and authority in curtailing the engagement of religious communities around human rights agendas. The Russian case presents an interesting location in which to consider the broader question of whether human rights are best conceived of as guarantees against incursions into the lives of individuals or whether a more communal understanding of human rights that acknowledges the rights of communities must be considered. As Mandelstam Balzer points out, communal rights are especially important in the post-Soviet era for Muslims, Jews, and members of religious groups with strong ethnic traditions. To impose Western definitions of human rights from the outside, she suggests, is likely to be ill-suited for the contemporary situation. She also argues that the most effective long-term guarantee of human rights is building a functioning civil society, a task to which religious groups can contribute.

In his chapter, "Human Rights, the Catholic Church, and the Death Penalty in the United States," Thomas Banchoff examines the intersection of religion and human rights within the West. For most Americans and Europeans the politics of human rights is about established democracies criticizing rights violations elsewhere. In the case of the death penalty, which has gradually and unevenly emerged as an international human rights issue since the late 1940s, the United States is an outlier. Since the Supreme Court reinstated the death penalty in 1976, more than 1,000 individuals have been executed. International condemnation of the United States has been led by European governments, which had almost all completely abolished the death penalty by the 1980s. But as Banchoff points out, human rights opposition has also emerged at a domestic level. Local chapters of the influential nongovernmental organization Amnesty International have campaigned actively against the practice across many states. But the most influential global critic of the death penalty—and a key actor in American domestic politics—has been the Roman Catholic Church.

The church, which includes some 20–25 percent of the U.S. population, gradually moved away from its traditional support for capital punishment in the decades after the Second Vatican Council of the 1960s. When Pope John Paul II came out strongly in favor of abolition in the mid-1990s, the American bishops fully integrated the issue into their human rights work. The U.S. trend away from capital punishment since the turn of the century, evident in public opinion and in successful abolition drives in New Jersey and New Mexico, has many national causes, including highly publicized cases of exoneration of death row inmates through DNA tests. It is significant, however, that a Supreme Court majority acknowledged international norms in two landmark cases that declared unconstitutional the execution of juvenile offenders and the mentally disabled. And Catholic leaders linked to global networks have been active participants in abolition drives in New Jersey, New Mexico, and elsewhere. U.S. opponents of capital punishment are still more likely to invoke a national civil rights rather than an international human rights frame. But through the opposition of the church, foreign governments, and transnational NGOs, the issue has taken on a greater global and human rights dimension.

Five Overarching Themes

Taken as a whole, the nine empirical chapters in this volume make five important contributions to the study of religion and the global politics of human rights. First, they point to the centrality of religious pluralism as an analytical starting point. Second, they illustrate a broad level of human rights engagement, well beyond a concern with religious freedom, narrowly defined. Third, the essays demonstrate the continued power of states and government institutions to define the human rights agenda domestically and constrain the activities of religious communities. Fourth, they point to the power of historical memory and competing narratives in shaping religion and the politics of human rights worldwide. And fifth, they suggest a continued role for globalization and geopolitics in shaping the intersection of religion, politics, and human rights into the future.

Religious Pluralism as a Point of Departure

Much work on religion and human rights begins with a purported opposition between the religious and the secular or with sharp distinctions among religious traditions and what they stand for. This can lead to sweeping statements about the compatibility of human rights with religion in general, or about their compatibility with a particular tradition. Such generalizations, whatever their merit as an abstract exercise, do not map onto the reality of pluralism within traditions. In the struggle over what counts as human rights and how to pursue them, the chapters in this volume point to a wide variety of views within Christianity, Islam, Hinduism, and Buddhism.

As the chapters by Hefner and Haddad point out, Muslims are engaged in a running debate about the shari`a and its implications for human rights. A principled affirmation both of God's law as revealed in Islam *and* of democracy and human rights leaves room for debate about how both should be combined in practice. Haddad illustrates this creative tension through an examination of women's rights within Islam, a theme that Hefner also addresses. Other chapters highlight the diversity of human rights perspectives within Christianity. Latin America has long been home to different Catholic views on economic and social rights, as Freston notes, and has more recently seen controversy over whether to try to limit the rights and freedoms of surging Pentecostal groups. Debates among Catholics about the death penalty recounted in Banchoff's chapter on the United States are another example of internal controversy. As in the case of Islam, there is a shared foundation—in this case, the idea of human dignity. But disagreement exists on whether capital punishment violates a human right or is the legitimate expression of a community's desire to punish transgressors.

In the case of Hinduism and Buddhism, religious pluralism and its effects are even more pronounced. If Christianity is the most hierarchical of the four traditions, and Islam is already considerably more decentralized, the varieties of Hinduism and Buddhism are even more pronounced. Mehta examines how Hinduism has historically been deployed both to legitimate tremendous social inequality in the form of the caste system and, in the hands of Mohandas Gandhi and other Hindu reformers, to emphasize the equal dignity and fundamental human rights of all human beings. In the case of Buddhism, the popular association is with passive contemplation or—through the example of the Dalai Lama and other well-known Buddhist leaders—social engagement for peace and justice. As Keyes points out, however, the relationship between Buddhism and human rights is far from simple. In the Buddhist-majority countries he surveys, secular leaders have often worked closely with officially recognized Buddhist authorities to discriminate against religious and ethnic minorities. Across all four religious traditions examined in this book, pluralism is a starting point for understanding the religious politics of human rights.

Engagement across Multiple Issues

Throughout the volume, the internal diversity of traditions in grappling with human rights goes hand in hand with the diversity of human rights agendas they engage, including women's rights, capital punishment, and economic and social rights. Not surprisingly, religious communities are often most concerned with religious freedom—with the liberty of their members to profess and practice their beliefs and participate fully in society. In several of the cases explored here, the struggle for religious freedom remains the human rights focus, including those of China, Russia, and the Buddhist-majority countries of Southeast Asia. The chapter on India and Hinduism raises the question of how and whether religious freedom can be limited to protect the identity of a majority religious community through an analysis of anticonversion laws designed to prevent the targeting of the lower castes by Indian Christians and foreign missionaries.

Other chapters focus on a broader range of human rights issues. Women's rights are among the most prominent. Haddad's survey of women's issues within the Islamic world demonstrates their complexity. It goes far beyond the question of civil equality to encompass the role of women in the family and the community on matters ranging from divorce to access to education. Islamic feminism is a broad agenda that invokes specific interpretations of the Qur'an and the life and sayings of Muhammad to challenge traditional views of women's subordination to men in Muslim-majority societies. In her chapter on women's issues in sub-Saharan Africa, Abusharaf extends the discussion of women's rights to female genital mutilation (FGM), and notes the role of religious leaders—both Muslim and Christian, and primarily male—whose condemnation of the practice has strengthened the human rights campaign against it. Of course most leadership positions in Islam—and in Christianity and Judaism—remain closed to women, itself a human rights concern. And Keyes reminds us that Buddhism in Asia has male-dominated leadership as well.

Religious advocacy of social and economic rights is most evident in the chapters by Freston and Keyes. In Latin America, campaigns for human rights have often been linked with concerns about poverty and social justice. As Freston notes, the Latin American local church produced liberation theology and grassroots organization through base communities as well as high-level interventions of the region's bishops around human rights questions, beginning with their 1968 Medellin Conference. Keyes relates the well-known examples of the peace activism of the Buddhist monk Mahā Ghosananda in Cambodia and monk-led protests in Burma, most recently in 2007. He also highlights the lesser known Sarvodaya Shramadana Movement in Sri Lanka, which grew from an early focus on Buddhist values in rural development in the 1950s into a major advocate for social justice, human rights, and inclusion. In opposition to Buddhist nationalists, Sarvodaya Shramadana has supported "a national identity that transcends ethnic or religious identity, and recognizes Sri Lanka's multi-ethnic, multi-religious character."

The Constraints of State Institutions

As the chapters make clear, the end of the cold war and globalization have not brought a much anticipated golden age for human rights around the world. The global trend toward liberalization and democratization that began in the 1980s has suffered setbacks in China and Russia, in much of the Middle East, and in the many dictatorships and failed states across the developing world. The idea that globalization would erode state power over time and usher in a transnational era marked by peace and the spread of democracy and human rights has also suffered a blow. While several of the chapters acknowledge the importance of transnational religious and human rights groups, they also underscore the centrality of the nation-state and the capacity of state institutions to both define human rights regimes and to constrain human rights activism within their borders.

China and Russia provide the two most telling examples of this trend. China's economic and cultural opening during the post-Mao era has not gone hand in hand with a parallel political liberalization. While religious groups have been allowed to exist and grow, they remain subject to state regulation and must recognize the leading role of the Communist Party in Chinese society.

Russia is no longer a one-party state, but it has reemerged as a centralized autocracy under the leadership of Vladimir Putin who, first as president and then as prime minister, enjoys considerable public support. The Russian approach to religious management is less rigorous than that of the Chinese, but it is also aimed at reducing the public role of religious communities–outside the officially favored Russian Orthodox Church–often in the name of national security. The potential threat posed by militant Islam is a particular concern of both regimes. In this setting, as both Ownby and Mandelstam Balzer point out, faith-inspired human rights activists have little room to maneuver. For example, the efforts of transnational human rights networks to press the concerns of Falun Gong members in China or of Baptist missionaries in Russia have little chance of success.

In many Muslim-majority countries, too, state power places strictures on both human rights and the political activism of religious communities. Haddad recounts how dictatorships in the Arab world have seized upon the idea of a specifically Islamic understanding of human rights to fend off Western criticism of their nondemocratic practices. Hefner points to some fault lines in the recent Muslim-majority democracies of Southeast Asia, such as Indonesia and Malaysia, where human rights norms officially endorsed by the state are in tension with traditionalist practices on issues such as apostasy and women's rights—practices sometimes tolerated by political and judicial elites. The Mehta chapter notes a similar trend in India, where Hindu nationalists identify with the country's democratic constitution but back legislation, including anticonversion laws, that constrains the rights of ethnic and religious minorities within the country.

The Force of Historical Narratives

An earlier section of this chapter discussed the contemporary salience of deep historical narratives about religion and human rights. The chapters themselves illustrate the force of historical memory at the national level as well. The politics of human rights is not just about whether a particular state should adopt an abstract rights catalog, and how it should do so. This politics is shaped on many levels by the historical associations of the concept. In North America and Western Europe, the association is generally positive; the turn to human rights coincided historically with the transition to democracy. Outside the Atlantic area, however, the idea of human rights is often associated with the era of colonialism, when human rights discourse was used both to denigrate non-Western cultures and to obscure the self-serving domination of colonial rule. If anything, the religious dimension of current human rights politics only strengthens negative associations for many for whom Western colonialism went hand in hand with missionary expansion, and the gospel of democracy, rights, and the rule of law was closely linked with the (foreign) gospel of Christ.

The actual historical role of missionaries in imperialism, in all its complexity, is largely beside the point. The narrative of colonial-Christian domination shapes today's politics at the intersection of religion and human rights.

China provides perhaps the most clear-cut example of this phenomenon. As Ownby demonstrates, the century of foreign domination from the Opium Wars through the Communist revolution left a strong association of colonialism with foreign mission activity. Concern about foreign involvement and political instability, rooted in historical memory, sheds light on the reasons why Western human rights and religious freedom criticisms are rejected as unwarranted interference in Chinese domestic affairs. It also explains the caution with which religious communities in China have sought to press their rights claims. House church leaders, Ownby points out, have often defended their opposition to state registration on theological, not political grounds. The Buddhist-majority autocracies that Keyes describes also justify their repression of religious and ethnic minorities with a historical narrative of resistance to colonialism. As early as the 1920s, he argues, a Buddhist nationalism emerged "predicated less on traditional Buddhist ideas about the sociopolitical order than on reforms of Buddhist thought in response to Western religious and cultural influence."

The colonial legacy has had a different impact in India and Latin America. While it explains the defensive Indian reaction to foreign criticism of caste and anticonversion laws as human rights violations, the colonial legacy has also strengthened overall identification with democracy in the country. Over time, exposure to Western ideas of human rights and individual freedoms has sparked a desire to endorse and even embrace the Western human rights regime. As Mehta argues, "Hinduism became aware that if it failed to claim as its own certain values identified with progressive modernity, it would always remain vulnerable to both criticism by outsiders and inner defections by its own adherents." In Latin America, Freston points out, the historical association of autocracy with the Catholic Church and Western economic and security presence initially generated opposition to the idea of human rights. Leading liberation theologians, for example, viewed human rights "as a kind of Trojan Horse for imperialism or an individualistic First World luxury that should be corrected by a stress on economic rights." Over time, however, "much of the hostility to the concept of human rights dissipated as increasingly brutal dictatorships mobilized broad-based opposition."

The most powerful evidence of a postcolonial legacy may be the Muslim world, particularly in North Africa and the Middle East, where efforts to advance human rights are often discredited through their widespread association with the United States and its allies. As Yvonne Haddad points out in her chapter, efforts to advance women's rights in Muslim-majority countries are often dismissed as an assault on Islam itself and part of a historical trend that can be traced back more than a century. Abusharaf gives examples of defenders of

FGM in Muslim-majority countries invoking time-honored "national traditions" against human rights advocates they associate with external imperialism. In Hefner's chapter, which combines an overview of human rights
controversies within Islam and an examination of the Indonesian case in particular, the legacy of colonial rule continues to shape the politics of human
rights as well.

Looking Forward: Globalization and Geopolitics

Taken together, the empirical studies in this volume make the case for an understanding of religion and the global politics of human rights that is attentive
to pluralism within traditions, diverse human rights agendas, state structures
and policies, and the political force of historical narratives. The idea that globalization, with its flows of ideas and people and its individualist ethos, would
smoothly transmit human rights discourses around the world and drive their
adoption, as if by popular acclaim, has proved illusory. Human rights remain
contested; what they mean, which are decisive, and how they are to be implemented are objects of ongoing struggle within national contexts. Religious actors, ideas, and issues have shaped the politics of human rights in varied ways,
often on both sides of a particular controversy. But they, too, have had mainly a
country-level impact.

Still, as the chapters make clear, international context matters. Competition for economic and security advantage among states—the geopolitical dimension of globalization—has shaped the global politics of human rights in
significant ways. Efforts of the world's only superpower, the United States, to
spread democracy to Afghanistan and then Iraq by force of arms, has both
strengthened national advocates of human rights in both societies and made
them vulnerable to charges of collaborating with a foreign occupier. U.S. criticism of the human rights and religious freedom records of states like China
and Russia, even when not backed by credible threats, has sometimes had an
effect on those governments' policies—if not always the one intended. And an
upsurge of Hindu and Buddhist nationalism in South and Southeast Asia over
the last two decades shows that a desire to project a cohesive religious and cultural national identity in international competition can have a negative impact
on human rights domestically.

As the global balance of power shifts away from U.S. predominance toward
multipolarity in the years to come, the national and international politics of
religion and human rights may take a different turn. With U.S. and European
power receding in relative terms, new rising powers may more self-confidently
proclaim their own conceptions of human rights as universally valid. An individualist emphasis on political freedoms on the U.S. model may be challenged
by a neo-Confucian emphasis on family and community emanating from
China or Buddhist-majority countries. More independent Muslim-majority

countries may further develop the idea of a specifically Islamic understanding of human rights, partly in response to domestic pressures and partly to signal their greater political independence from the West. And the United States and Western Europe, their relative power in decline, may show less interest in the fate of their human rights discourse abroad and draw less on the idea of universal human rights in seeking to improve their own societies.

In all these scenarios, the global politics of human rights will persist, even as it pushes in new directions. One reason is institutional. While globalization has not seen the automatic spread of the idea and reality of human rights around the world, it has seen the gradual emergence of an international human rights regime—a series of declarations and conventions that develop human rights as part of international law. This regime, which can be traced back to the 1948 Universal Declaration of Human Rights, cannot be imposed on sovereign states. But it does provide a vital resource for supporters of human rights, religious and secular, struggling to advance their agendas at the national and local level. Because it is institutionalized on the global level, the idea of universal human rights is unlikely to fade. We can expect members of the world's faith communities, like nonreligious leaders and citizens, to continue to invoke the international human rights regime as a political resource in their national struggles. As a backdrop for the empirical studies that follow, a second introductory chapter traces the emergence and evolution of that regime as a framework for the global politics of human rights.

NOTES

1. For overviews of the literature on religion and human rights, see John Witte and Johan D. Van Der Vyver, eds., *Religious Human Rights in Global Perspective: Religious Perspectives* (Grand Rapids, MI: Eerdmans, 2000); Irene Cohen, J. Paul Martin, and Wayne Proudfoot, *Religious Diversity and Human Rights* (New York: Columbia University Press, 1996); and Michael J. Perry, *The Idea of Human Rights: Four Inquiries* (New York: Oxford University Press, 2000). For approaches to Islam that acknowledge its diversity with respect to human rights, see Abdullahi An-Na'im, *Islam and Human Rights*, ed. Mashood A. Baderin (Farnham, UK: Ashgate, 2010) and Abdulaziz Sachedina, *Islam and the Challenge of Human Rights* (New York: Oxford University Press, 2009).

2. On the narrative of rationalist progress and its roots in the Enlightenment, see Carl L. Becker, *The Heavenly City of the Eighteenth-century Philosophers* (New Haven, CT: Yale University Press, 1962).

3. This line of thought can be traced from Voltaire to Jacob Burckhardt. Exemplary is Jacob Burckhardt, *The Civilization of the Renaissance in Italy* (New York: Harper and Row, 1958). See also Owen Chadwick, *The Secularization of the European Mind in the Nineteenth Century* (New York: Cambridge University Press, 1976).

4. The work of John Rawls has been most influential here. See, in particular, his *A Theory of Justice* (New York: Oxford University Press, 1973).

5. Charles Taylor has emphasized the diversity of religious responses to modernity in his *A Secular Age* (Cambridge, MA: Harvard University Press, 2007).

6. Mary Ann Glendon, *A World Made New: Eleanor Roosevelt and the Universal Declaration of Human Rights* (New York: Random House, 2002).

7. For a discussion of diverse religious responses to the constraints and opportunities of globalization, see Thomas Banchoff, ed., *Globalization, Religious Pluralism, and World Politics* (New York: Oxford University Press, 2008).

BIBLIOGRAPHY

An-Na'im, Abdullahi. *Islam and Human Rights*. ed. Mashood A. Baderin. Farnham, UK: Ashgate, 2010.

Banchoff, Thomas, ed. *Globalization, Religious Pluralism, and World Politics*. New York: Oxford University Press, 2008.

Becker, Carl L. *The Heavenly City of the Eighteenth-century Philosophers*. New Haven, CT: Yale University Press, 1962.

Burckhardt, Jacob. *The Civilization of the Renaissance in Italy*. New York: Harper and Row, 1958.

Chadwick, Owen. *The Secularization of the European Mind in the Nineteenth Century*. New York: Cambridge University Press, 1976.

Cohen, Irene, J. Paul Martin, and Wayne Proudfoot. *Religious Diversity and Human Rights*. New York: Columbia University Press, 1996.

Glendon, Mary Ann. *A World Made New: Eleanor Roosevelt and the Universal Declaration of Human Rights*. New York: Random House, 2002.

Perry, Michael J. *The Idea of Human Rights: Four Inquiries*. New York: Oxford University Press, 2000.

Rawls, John. *A Theory of Justice*. New York: Oxford University Press, 1973.

Sachedina, Abdulaziz. *Islam and the Challenge of Human Rights*. New York: Oxford University Press, 2009.

Taylor, Charles. *A Secular Age*. Cambridge, MA: Harvard University Press, 2007.

Van Der Vyver, Johan D., and John Witte, eds. *Religious Human Rights in Global Perspective: Legal Perspectives*. Grand Rapids, MI: Eerdmans, 2000.

Witte, John, and Johan D. Van Der Vyver, eds. *Religious Human Rights in Global Perspective: Religious Perspectives*. Grand Rapids: Eerdmans, 2000.

2

The International Human Rights Regime

Thomas Banchoff

The global politics of human rights is not new.[1] Since the American and French revolutions, struggles within states and societies over political and social rights have seldom taken place in national isolation. The idea embedded in the first article of the 1789 Declaration of the Rights of Man and of the Citizen—"Men are born and remain free and equal in rights"—polarized politics across Europe through the nineteenth century. Human rights, as a cause to be championed or crushed, animated struggles between postrevolutionary France and the Holy Alliance, between transnational socialism and Europe's autocracies, and between national liberalism and an international papacy. During the first half of the twentieth century, opponents of fascism and communism invoked universal human rights—a concept both totalitarian ideologies rejected. On a global scale, human rights informed anticolonial struggles in Latin America in the nineteenth century and in Africa and Asia into the twentieth.

If the global politics of human rights goes back two centuries, World War II and the Holocaust marked a critical juncture. The decades after 1945 saw the emergence of an international human rights regime with two related components. The first was normative. The international community, in the shape of the United Nations, endorsed the universal validity of human rights at a declaratory level. The second component was legal. Through a series of treaties or conventions, international law—since the seventeenth century a framework for relations among states—began to incorporate the rights of individuals. During the second half of the twentieth century, the combination of UN declarations and international conventions bearing on human rights constituted a new, global human rights regime. At the dawn of the twenty-first century, state sovereignty remains the foundation of the international system and the politics of human rights still plays out mainly on a national stage. But more than at any previous point in history, that politics and its religions dimension are now framed by international norms and rules—a common, if contested, frame of reference.[2]

To grasp the contemporary nexus between religion and the global politics of human rights and its various manifestations across states and regions, one must first understand the main outlines of the international human rights regime and its postwar evolution. That evolution went through three broad phases: the height of the cold war (1945–69), the trend toward détente (1969–89), and the end of the postwar order (1989–). Each phase saw institutional innovation—normative and legal—that shaped, and was shaped by, the broader geopolitical context. In each of the three phases, the United States proved the most important driver of a global politics of human rights and the role of religious issues and religious actors took on new forms. And during each phase, tensions among key state and nonstate actors and between human rights norms and the principle of national sovereignty influenced the global politics of human rights in practice.[3]

The Height of the Cold War: 1945–1969

The origins of the global human rights regime go back to the end of World War II, the founding of the United Nations (1945), and the Universal Declaration of Human Rights (1948). Previous efforts to ground rights for individuals in international norms and law had largely failed. The UN's predecessor, the League of Nations, was conceived mainly as an antiwar organization, a means of collective defense against aggression. The idea of fundamental human rights did inform the work of various League committees and commissions, including the Health Committee, the Commission for Refugees, and the Slavery Commission. Some of this work would be later folded into the UN system. But during its short and ineffective history the League did not develop a catalog of universal rights. The most vocal exponent of those rights, the United States, opted not to join the League, and Italian and German aggression effectively destroyed it. The brutality of World War II overshadowed those provisions of the Geneva and Hague Conventions designed to protect noncombatants—the only semblance of a human rights regime at the time.

The horrific legacy of Nazism and the Holocaust provided the political impetus for the institutionalization of human rights on a global scale after the war. The national delegations that convened in San Francisco from April to October 1945 were determined to make a break with the past. Like the League of Nations, the UN was conceived as an organization of sovereign states created mainly to prevent war and foster peace. But in contrast to the League, ideals of justice and human dignity—and not just a concern with interstate violence—animated the UN project from the beginning. The preamble to the UN Charter referenced the "scourge of war" and then moved to "reaffirm faith in fundamental human rights, in the dignity and worth of the human person." Article 55 refers to the goal of "universal respect for, and observance of, human rights and fundamental freedoms for all without distinction as to race, sex, language, or religion." The Charter laid the foundations for an international human rights regime, even if it emphasized rights mainly as a means to the end of world peace. It deemed human rights crucial "to the creation of conditions of stability and well-being which are necessary for peaceful and friendly relations among nations based on respect for the principle of equal rights and self-determination of peoples."

The Universal Declaration of Human Rights (1948) marked a further critical juncture in the evolution and institutionalization of human rights norms.[4] Adopted by the General Assembly in December 1948, the Declaration did not have the legal status of a treaty. Rather, it intended to forge "a common understanding of [the] rights and freedoms" set out in the Charter. Its preamble asserted that "recognition of the inherent dignity and of the equal and inalienable rights of all members of the human family is the foundation of freedom, justice and peace in the world." According to Article 1, "All human beings are born free and equal in dignity and rights. They are endowed with reason and conscience and should act towards one another in a spirit of brotherhood." Article 2 insists that "no distinction shall be made on the basis of the political, jurisdictional or international status of the country or territory to which a person belongs." Subsequent articles enumerate rights including equality before the law (Article 7), freedom of movement (Article 13), expression (Article 19), association (Article 20), and democratic participation (Article 21), as well as social rights including a right to work and form unions (Article 23) and a standard of living adequate for "health and well-being . . . including food, clothing, housing and medical care and necessary social services" (Article 25).

The Universal Declaration did not, in itself, constitute a robust international human rights regime. As a Declaration it had normative but not legal force. Moreover, while it set out an impressive rights catalog, the Declaration did not define those rights and their scope in any detail or outline mechanisms for their enforcement. States were granted tremendous leeway in interpretation and application. Most notably, Article 29 underscored the authority of states to limit human rights in practice: "In the exercise of his rights and freedoms, everyone shall be subject only to such limitations as are determined by law solely for the purpose of securing due recognition and respect for the rights and freedoms of others and of meeting the just requirements of morality, public order and the general welfare in a democratic society." With key terms

such as "public order," "general welfare," and "democratic society" left unde-
fined, dictatorships in Stalin's Russia and elsewhere were free to suppress
human rights in the name of national sovereignty—while still aligning themselves with the Declaration and its principles.

Amid the geopolitical tensions of the cold war, the international human
rights regime remained weak. Ironically, the passage of the Declaration in the
General Assembly by a vote of 40 to 0 in favor, with 8 abstentions, coincided
with the Berlin Blockade that brought the United States and the Soviet Union
to the brink of armed conflict. As the cold war continued, the Universal Declaration served as a cudgel with which to beat the other camp over the head. The
United States and its allies condemned political repression and religious persecution in the Soviet Union, China, and other socialist countries, while Moscow
and Beijing lambasted violations of social rights in the capitalist West in the
form of economic inequality, homelessness, and unemployment. The breakup
of colonial empires in the 1950s and 1960s extended East-West rivalry to Africa
and Asia, where ideological charges and countercharges undermined the normative force of the Declaration and impeded efforts to anchor human rights
norms in international law.

Religious rights and religious actors figured prominently in this ideological struggle. Article 18 of the Declaration had placed religion within the broader
context of freedom of conscience: "Everyone has the right to freedom of
thought, conscience and religion; this right includes freedom to change his
religion or belief, and freedom, either alone or in community with others and
in public or private, to manifest his religion or belief in teaching, practice, worship and observance." Both elements of religious freedom—to have and change
beliefs and to practice one's faith—were evoked in Western criticisms of religious repression in the Soviet Union, China, and other socialist countries. Attacks on "Godless communism," a staple of cold war rhetoric in the United
States in particular, were met in Moscow and Beijing with accusations of unwarranted interference in other countries' internal affairs. At the same time,
Muslim-majority states, mainly aligned with the United States during the cold
war, tended to distance themselves from the Declaration and Article 18, which
clashed with the traditional Muslim prohibition against apostasy. Saudi Arabia
was among the states that abstained in the General Assembly vote on the Declaration.

A key religious actor in the cold war constellation was the Roman Catholic
Church. Staunchly anticommunist, the church vocally criticized religious persecution behind the Iron Curtain at the height of the cold war, even as it upheld
its own traditional opposition to full religious freedom in favor of privileged
legal status for itself and its teachings within a given state order. Here the Second Vatican Council (1962–65) marked a historic break. Pope John XXIII
(1958–63) inaugurated an opening to the modern world that incorporated a full
embrace of the concept of universal human rights, including religious freedom.

In authoritative documents including *Pacem in Terris* (1963) and *Dignitatis Humanae* (1965), the church aligned itself with the civil and social rights articulated in the Universal Declaration of 1948, even as it espoused them in its own religious idiom, invoking both scripture and tradition. This newfound enthusiasm for human rights meshed with the views already articulated by the Protestant World Council of Churches and leading Jewish organizations, marking a critical juncture in religious support for an emergent international human rights regime.

The first signs of détente that followed the 1962 Cuban Missile Crisis saw progress in anchoring human rights norms in international law. Two landmark conventions were signed in 1966 and entered into force in 1976: the International Covenant on Civil and Political Rights (ICCPR) and the International Covenant on Economic, Social, and Cultural Rights (ICESCR).[5] UN member states that signed and ratified the ICCPR committed to uphold basic civil and political rights outlined in the 1948 Declaration and strengthened the UN Human Rights Commission to monitor compliance (the Commission was replaced by a reconstituted Human Rights Council in 2006.) Two significant modifications to the language of the Declaration deserve mention. The first was the incorporation of group rights—the rights of ethnic, religious, and linguistic minorities to "to enjoy their own culture, to profess and practise their own religion, or to use their own language" (Article 27). Another was a tempering of the religious freedom provisions of the Declaration. The ICCPR now referred to the freedom to "have or adopt a religious belief" (Article 18). The word "change" was dropped largely in order to secure support from China, India, and Muslim-majority countries that restricted proselytism within their borders.

The ICESCR placed the social rights enumerated in the Declaration on a legal foundation. Key articles enjoined states to promote rights including work (Article 6), fair wages (Article 7), trade union membership (Article 8), and "an adequate standard of living" (Article 11). Like the ICCPR, the text placed human rights within the context of growing cultural and religious pluralism. Education, it insisted, should "enable all persons to participate effectively in a free society, promote understanding, tolerance and friendship among all nations and all racial, ethnic or religious groups." In contrast to the ICCPR, however, the text recognized the existence of constraints on the achievement of these goals. Each signatory was called upon not to realize them but to "undertake to take steps . . . to the maximum of its available resources" for their realization. A Committee on Economic, Social and Cultural Rights was set up in 1985 to monitor progress within and across countries.

The adoption of both covenants did not mark the full institutionalization of an international human rights regime. Like other treaties in international law they bind only those states that sign and ratify them. Key states could and did exclude themselves from both conventions. The United States, for example, only ratified the ICCPR in 1992, and then with significant reservations; it has yet to ratify the ICESCR. Moreover, while UN bodies are empowered to monitor compliance and criticize violations they cannot enforce any sanctions. And when member states do come under human rights criticism they can invoke the values of "national security" and "public order" to justify their policies. Despite these limitations, the twin covenants of 1966 and subsequent protocols marked an important advance toward an international human rights regime. Together with the Declaration they constituted an "International Bill of Rights," a common point of reference for human rights struggles at the national and regional level.

The Trend Toward Détente: 1969–1989

A second phase in the evolution of the international human rights regime can be dated from the late 1960s through the collapse of the Berlin Wall two decades later. The U.S. opening to China and the Soviet Union that began under President Richard Nixon in 1969 changed the geopolitical context for the global politics of human rights. Détente marked a reduction of cold war rhetoric and pragmatic steps toward deeper economic cooperation and more stable security arrangements. At the same time, it created political space for reformers within socialist states who—supported by international organizations, NGOs, and other governments—sought to hold their governments to emergent international human rights standards. This political dynamic flagged in the late 1970s and early 1980s, when crises in Afghanistan and Poland and the nuclear arms race renewed superpower tension. But it picked up again once Mikhail Gorbachev took power in 1985 and initiated a series of reforms that eventually—and unexpectedly—unraveled the Soviet bloc.

Europe was the main arena for the global politics of human rights over this period. Western European countries had embraced human rights after World War II through the creation of the Council of Europe in 1949, the core of a robust human rights regime with its own treaties and monitoring mechanisms. Only with U.S.-Soviet détente in the early 1970s, however, did an all-European human rights regime begin to take shape. In 1973 the Conference on Cooperation and Security in Europe (CSCE) convened in Helsinki for two years of deliberation that culminated in a far-reaching accord. The Helsinki Final Act, signed by North Atlantic Treaty Organization (NATO) and Warsaw Pact members, outlined areas for security and economic cooperation, and included a strong endorsement of human rights. For Soviet leaders and their allies, the Final Act meant Western recognition of the postwar political status quo, including the border between the two German states, and of the principle of nonintervention in the internal affairs of sovereign states. The United States and its allies, for their part, highlighted the Soviet Union's acknowledgment of the binding force of human rights.

The human rights provisions, included in the Final Act's Paragraph 7, enjoined signatories to "promote and encourage the effective exercise of civil, political, economic, social, cultural and other rights and freedoms all of which derive from the inherent dignity of the human person and are essential for his free and full development."[6] It included a strong assertion of religious freedom, calling on states to "recognize and respect the freedom of the individual to profess and practice, alone or in community with others, religion or belief acting in accordance with the dictates of his own conscience." As the CSCE process continued in the years after 1975, all-European human rights norms constituted a political resource for dissidents including Václav Havel and the Charter 77 movement in Czechoslovakia and Lech Walesa and Solidarity in Poland. Pro-democratic forces across the Soviet bloc could and did charge their governments with not living up to their European responsibilities—and they helped to undermine the legitimacy of socialist regimes in the process.

During the presidency of Jimmy Carter (1977–81), human rights controversy moved beyond Europe. More than his predecessors, Carter was willing to place human rights alongside security and economic interests as a motive force in U.S. foreign policy. In 1977 Carter received Soviet dissident Vladimir Bukovsky in the White House—from the Soviet perspective, a throwback to the ideological warfare of the 1950s. At the same time, however, Carter criticized U.S. allies including Nicaragua and the Philippines for their failure to live up to human rights norms, even tying foreign economic and military assistance to their domestic behavior. Carter's successor Ronald Reagan, determined to redress the perceived military superiority of the Soviet Union, toned down criticism of human rights abuses committed by U.S.-friendly governments and stepped up attacks on violations committed by the Soviet Union and its allies. Only during his second term (1985–89) did Reagan downplay ideological differences, engage Gorbachev's diplomatic offensive, and throw his full support behind the CSCE process in Europe.

At a global level, the most visible and powerful transnational force for human rights during the 1980s was the Roman Catholic Church. Building on the opening of Vatican II, Pope John Paul II (1978–2005) articulated a strong commitment to human rights—both political and social—on his many trips to advanced industrialized nations and developing countries. In Europe, John Paul II aligned himself with Walesa and the Solidarity movement in his native Poland, further undercutting the legitimacy of the regime. In the Philippines, the critical stance of Cardinal Jaime Sin helped to bring down the Ferdinand Marcos regime. In Latin America, too, the pope and local church leaders, historically identified with the interests of the ruling elites, encouraged democratization and called for more social justice. While the hierarchy condemned liberation theology for its proximity to Marxism and disciplined those clergy engaged in revolutionary politics, it increasingly emerged as a vocal and effective supporter of human rights in Latin America and around the world.

During the 1970s and 1980s the Catholic Church was not the only transnational religious force pressing a human rights agenda. Protestant and Orthodox churches and affiliated NGOs took public stances against human rights violations, particularly infringements on religious freedom, in the Soviet bloc, China, and throughout the developing world. Jewish organizations highlighted the repression of minorities and pressed for the freedom of Soviet Jews to emigrate to Israel and the West. During this period, secular nongovernmental organizations, too, took advantage of global communications networks to mobilize public support and lobby governments around human rights agendas. Among the most important were Amnesty International, which focused on political prisoners, and Helsinki Watch, which grew out of efforts to monitor the Final Act but became more global in its orientation during the 1980s.

During the two decades after 1969, the overall relaxation of East-West tensions and the increasing engagement of transnational actors, both religious and secular, created a political atmosphere conducive to a stronger international human rights regime. At the normative level, a series of prominent UN General Assembly declarations elaborated different sets of rights and the international community's commitment to uphold them. Among the most important was the 1981 Declaration on the Elimination of All Forms of Intolerance and of Discrimination Based on Religion or Belief. Other milestones included the 1979 Convention on the Elimination of All Forms of Discrimination against Women; the 1984 Convention against Torture or Other Cruel, Inhuman or Degrading Treatment and Punishment; the 1989 Protocol to the ICCPR on Capital Punishment; and the 1989 Convention on the Rights of the Child. The willingness of a growing number of governments to bind themselves with these accords and to submit to monitoring (if not enforcement) from UN bodies marked a key further step in the evolution of the postwar international human rights regime.

Within this institutional constellation, religious freedom remained contested. China, India, and Muslim-majority countries, increasingly influential within the UN, helped to turn back efforts to make religious freedom binding international law. While Article 1 of the 1981 Declaration on the Elimination of All Forms of Intolerance and of Discrimination Based on Religion or Belief affirmed that "Everyone shall have the right to freedom of thought, conscience and religion," it did not echo key earlier formulations, including a "freedom to change" beliefs (Declaration, 1948) or to "have or adopt" beliefs (ICCPR, 1966) but referred only to the freedom to "have a religion or whatever belief of his choice." Article 1 strengthened the traditional sovereignty provisions: the freedom to manifest religion was made potentially subject to limitations "necessary to protect public safety, order, health or morals or the fundamental rights and freedoms of others." In the wake of the Iranian revolution of 1979, Muslim leaders began to articulate human rights perspectives more prominently beyond issues of religious freedom, apostasy, and conversion. The Universal

Islamic Declaration of Human Rights, presented by Muslim-majority states at the UN in 1981, rejected secular reason in favor of God's sovereignty as a point of departure. This resulted in different approaches to a variety of rights, including freedom of expression. Paragraph 12, for example, held that "No one shall hold in contempt or ridicule the religious beliefs of others or incite public hostility against them."

The Collapse of the Postwar Order: 1989–

As long as the postwar bipolar order persisted, religious freedom and West-Islamic divisions had limited international political salience. Political and media attention in the late 1980s focused on reform dynamics within the communist world. In China, Deng Xiaoping's economic liberalization, inaugurated in 1979, spawned pressure for political reform a decade later. The military suppression of pro-democracy protests in Tiananmen Square in June 1989 sparked international condemnation from Western governments and human rights organizations. In Europe, the unexpected collapse of the Berlin Wall in November 1989 signaled an end to Gorbachev's efforts to reform socialism from within. The entire Soviet bloc collapsed through national and democratic revolutions, and the Soviet Union itself dissolved in 1991. If the Chinese experience suggested the limits of democratic reform in a key country, the collapse of the Soviet empire unleashed a wave of optimism about a new era of democracy and human rights.

This human rights optimism, reinforced by the end of apartheid in South Africa and the spread of democracy in Latin America in the late 1980s and early 1990s, did not last long. The collapse of communism left ethnic and religious strife in its wake, particularly in the former Yugoslavia. The civil war in Bosnia and Kosovo revived old hostilities between Orthodox Christians and Muslims. Territorial tensions between Armenia and Azerbaijan pitted Muslims against Christians, and ethnic and religious differences fed the conflict in Chechnya. Sectarian violence between Hindus and Muslims flared in India after the destruction of a mosque in 1992. In Africa, a Hutu minority in Rwanda perpetrated genocide against the Tutsi majority in 1994, and ethnic and religious strife in Somalia, Sudan, and Nigeria took a toll on the civilian population. Autocratic dictatorships persisted across the Middle East, and the Oslo Accords signed in 1993 did not lead to an Israeli-Palestinian peace. By the late 1990s, these trends, along with faltering democracy in Russia and robust authoritarianism in China, had undermined the human rights optimism of a decade earlier.

The United Nations sought to counter this upsurge in violence, disorder, and human rights violations, with limited results. Peacekeeping forces in Bosnia and Kosovo helped to stabilize the situation in the Balkans only after US-led military intervention had put an end to ethnic and religious violence there. Similar multinational forces were deployed in Somalia, the Central African Republic, and other regions marked by civil strife, with very mixed results. But while the UN proved powerless to stop violence and protect human rights in these and other crisis areas, the institutionalization of a normative and legal human rights regime did make progress during these years. The creation of the International Criminal Court in 1998, a tribunal to try individuals for crimes against humanity, marked a further critical juncture in the construction of an international human rights regime—even if the United States, jealous of its sovereignty, declined to partici- pate. A succession of further legal instruments was created, including an optional protocol to the ICESCR in 2008 that allows individuals to lodge official human rights complaints. And the endorsement of the Millennium Development Goals by the General Assembly in 2000 positioned the UN as an advocate for economic and social rights on a global scale.

As in previous decades, the United States charted its own human rights course in the 1990s. Upon taking office in 1993, President Bill Clinton was supportive of the UN and its efforts to deepen the international human rights regime. The failure of the UN to curtail religious and ethnic strife in the Bal- kans and in Africa as well as the emergence of the Republican majority in Congress after 1994 changed the political constellation. The persecution of religious minorities abroad gained broader salience in U.S. politics, particu- larly the fate of Christians in southern Sudan under attack from the Muslim- dominated government in the North. In 1998 the Congress unanimously passed the International Religious Freedom Act, legislation that created an independent, bipartisan commission to monitor violations of religious free- dom worldwide and instructed the State Department to make religious free- dom an issue in bilateral relations with other countries. This special emphasis on religious freedom as a particularly salient human right resonated within American political culture, but created diplomatic problems. China, Russia, and other countries singled out for criticism attacked the U.S. policy as inter- ference in their domestic affairs. And critics pointed to the selective applica- tion of the law, especially the long absence of sharp criticisms or sanctions against violators aligned with the United States, most notably Saudi Arabia.

In the aftermath of September 11, 2001, the global politics of human rights took a new turn. The administration of George W. Bush construed the attacks on the World Trade Center and the Pentagon as an assault on the values of human dignity and freedom. The subsequent U.S.-led invasions of Afghani- stan (2001) and Iraq (2003) were designed not only to destroy Al-Qaeda and eliminate the purported threat posed by weapons of mass destruction but also to create a foothold for democracy and human rights in the Middle East. In the years that followed, the conduct of the "war on terror" and the war in Iraq led to accusations that the United States itself was violating basic human rights through its detention and interrogation policies. The bigger question raised by September 11, 2001—relations between the West and Islam—remained at the forefront of world politics in the years that followed. Controversies around the case of an Afghan convert to Christianity threatened with the death penalty in 2004, the publication of Muhammad cartoons in 2005, and Pope Benedict XVI's 2006 remarks critical of Islam underscored different understandings of basic human rights across the Islam-West divide, but also within Islam and the West, broadly conceived but difficult to define entities.

Overall, the path of the international human rights regime took an ambiguous turn after the collapse of the postwar order in 1989. Two key trends of previous decades continued: the multiplication of international declarations and legal conventions designed to safeguard and extend the basic rights first cataloged in the 1948 Declaration, and the mobilization of national and transnational political forces around them. At the same time, the end of bipolarity created a global politics of human rights with three new features. First, it generated greater global consensus about the importance of those rights and their incorporation into national constitutional and political arrangements—a consensus that now encompassed most of the former Soviet bloc but still did not extend to China, other parts of Asia, or much of Africa and the Middle East. Nor did that consensus necessarily prove stable, as the resurgence of autocracy in Vladimir Putin's Russia made clear. But it nevertheless marked a more broadly shared framework for international affairs, a point of reference for the politics of human rights at the national and regional levels.

A second transformation of the global politics of human rights after 1989—new patterns of transnational mobilization—was largely a byproduct of globalization. Increasing migration flows created transnational communities supportive of human rights agendas in both their countries of origin and destination—a dynamic evident, for example, among Muslim minorities in Europe and Hispanic minorities in the United States. Global communications media—especially television and the Internet—publicized human rights violations in places like Bosnia and Rwanda, helping to mobilize public opinion across state boundaries. Humanitarian disasters such as the Asian tsunami of December 2005, highlighted in the global media, sparked unprecedented outpourings of solidarity and support. The technologies of globalization did not only have salutary effects. Transnational terrorist networks such as Al-Qaeda could and did make use of them to organize their campaigns and disseminate propaganda. And states including China and Russia could manipulate them in an effort to quell dissent and control public opinion. But overall, globalization had the effect of reinforcing the international human rights regime.

The third post-1989 transformation, closely linked to the first two, was the growing intersection between religion and the global politics of human rights. With the collapse of bipolarity, religion emerged as a more important marker of identity in world politics, particularly in relations between the West and Muslim-majority countries. At the same time, technologies of globalization contributed to the dissemination of religious ideas and the linking of communities on a

worldwide scale, promoting an upsurge of evangelical Christianity internationally, and of Catholicism and Islam, particularly in Africa and Asia. As these and
other religious communities pressed their human rights agendas—and other
forces in state and society mobilized alongside or against them—they interacted
with the international human rights regime in two related ways. On the one
hand, they appealed to international norms in efforts to hold their governments
accountable. On the other hand, they adapted those norms in light of their national circumstances, reading them through their own particular faith traditions,
and pressing them across a variety of policy agendas. The nine chapters that
follow illustrate the diversity of religious approaches to human rights, the broad
range of political engagement around them, and the ongoing constraints posed
by state power. They suggest that the future of religion and the global politics of
human rights will depend as much on the outcome of national political struggles as on the evolution of the international human rights regime.

NOTES

1. Lynn Hunt, *Inventing Human Rights: A History* (New York: Norton, 2007);
Micheline Ishay, *The History of Human Rights: From Ancient Times to the Globalization
Era* (Berkeley: University of California Press, 2004).

2. For overviews of the global politics of human rights, Jack Donnelly, *Universal
Human Rights in Theory and Practice* (Ithaca: Cornell University Press, 2002); Paul
Gordon Lauren, *The Evolution of International Human Rights: Visions Seen* (Philadel-
phia: University of Pennsylvania Press, 2003); Henry Steiner and Philip Alston,
International Human Rights in Context: Law, Politics, Morals (Oxford: Oxford University
Press, 2000); and Margaret E. Keck and Kathryn Sikkink, *Activists beyond Borders:
Advocacy Networks in International Politics* (Ithaca, NY: Cornell University Press, 1998).

3. On religion and global human rights see, in particular, Johan D. Van Der Vyver
and John Witte, eds., *Religious Human Rights in Global Perspective: Legal Perspectives*
(Grand Rapids, MI: Eerdmans, 2000).

4. For the text of the UN Charter and the Universal Declaration, see http://www.
un.org/en/documents/.

5. The text of the two covenants and the other international legal instruments
mentioned in this chapter are available through the Web site of the Office of the High
Commissioner for Human Rights, http://www2.ohchr.org/english/law/.

6. The text of the Helsinki Final Act and other agreements signed under the
rubric of what became the Organization on Security and Co-operation in Europe can
be accessed on the OSCE Web site, http://www.OSCE.org/library.

BIBLIOGRAPHY

Donnelly, Jack. *Universal Human Rights in Theory and Practice*. Ithaca, NY: Cornell
    University Press, 2002.
Keck, Margaret E., and Kathryn Sikkink. *Activists beyond Borders: Advocacy Networks in
    International Politics*. Ithaca, NY: Cornell University Press, 1998.

Hunt, Lynn. *Inventing Human Rights: A History*. New York: Norton, 2007.

Ishay, Micheline. *The History of Human Rights: From Ancient Times to the Globalization Era*. Berkeley: University of California Press, 2004.

Lauren, Paul Gordon. *The Evolution of International Human Rights: Visions Seen*. Philadelphia: University of Pennsylvania Press, 2003.

Steiner, Henry, and Philip Alston. *International Human Rights in Context: Law, Politics, Morals*. Oxford: Oxford University Press, 2000.

Witte, John, and Johan D. Van Der Vyver, eds. *Religious Human Rights in Global Perspective: Religious Perspectives*. Grand Rapids, MI: Eerdmans, 2000.

PART I

Islam and the Global Politics of Human Rights

3

Human Rights and Democracy in Islam

The Indonesian Case in Global Perspective

Robert W. Hefner

Of all of today's globalized religions, Islam provokes the most questions concerning its compatibility with modern concepts of democracy and human rights. Samuel Huntington's well-known thesis on Islam and the "clash of civilizations" no doubt contributed to the questioning, since a key premise of Huntington's argument was that Islamic civilization lacks the sanctions for freedom, individual rights, and a separation of powers on which modern ideas of human rights and democracy depend.[1] From the other side of the civilizational divide, Huntington's views have been endorsed by a host of conservative Muslim commentators, only too happy to agree that modern human rights are not universal but peculiar to Judeo-Christianity. More recently, militants in groups like al-Qaeda have indicated that they share this skepticism, and, not surprisingly, their views have received greater attention in global media than have those of Muslim democrats.

It is not just radicals, however, who have expressed doubts about the compatibility of Islam with democracy and liberal understandings of human rights. In 1981, representatives from Egypt, Saudi Arabia, Pakistan, and other Muslim countries, working under the sponsorship of a London-based affiliate of the Muslim World League, prepared a Universal Islamic Declaration of Human Rights (UIDHR) for presentation to the United Nations Educational, Scientific, and Cultural Organization (UNESCO). Significantly, the declaration made clear that the general concept of human rights is compatible with Islam. However, on matters of women, non-Muslims, and freedom of religion, the

UIDHR also indicated that many Muslim scholars and leaders take exception to conceptions of human rights based on liberal notions of individual rights and autonomy. Since the issuance of the UIDHR, other governmental and nongovernmental groups have come forward to express similar reservations.[2] Indeed, compared with the 1950s and 1960s, opposition in conservative Muslim circles to internationalized notions of human rights seems louder and better orchestrated than ever. Equally important, in Sudan, Pakistan, and revolutionary Iran the rejectionists have managed to enshrine their views in constitutional legislation. Indeed, even the constitutions forged in Iraq and Afghanistan under U.S. sponsorship have formalized ideals of citizens' rights at variance with Western liberalism's notions of individual freedom.

Muslim politics today is nothing if not varied, however, and other evidence suggests that most Muslims are favorably inclined toward democracy and human rights. Data from the World Values Survey, the Gallup World Poll, and other sources show that in all but a few Muslim-majority countries most of the public feels that democracy and human rights are compatible with Islam.[3] Indeed, from a political-cultural perspective, the biggest news from the Muslim world over the past generation is not terrorism, which remains the preserve of a tiny fringe, but the Muslim majority's shift toward pro-democracy views. No less significant, a number of Muslim-majority countries, including Senegal, Mali, Turkey, Indonesia, and Bangladesh, have developed political systems based on constitutions and relatively competitive elections. It goes without saying that several parts of the Muslim world, especially the Arab Middle East, have remained aloof from some of these democratizing trends.[4] But these exceptions do not negate the basic fact that citizens in many Muslim-majority societies have embraced key elements of the democracy and human rights formula.

This mixed state of affairs acknowledged, however, the fact is that there is no single consensus in the Muslim world on human rights issues. Indeed, it is no exaggeration to suggest that debate over human rights and democracy is today a central issue in a broader "culture war" now raging in Muslim-majority countries. In this chapter, I examine the cultural and political background to this debate as well as future prospects for democracy and human rights in the Muslim world. As my earlier remarks imply, this is not an easy task because Muslim politics from Morocco to Indonesia is multifarious, considerably more so, in fact, than politics in the modern West. There is no single Muslim approach to the question of human rights, and the precise balance of opinion in any national setting reflects a complex interplay of local authorities, translocal networks, and religio-intellectual currents.

Beyond modern Islam's civilizational diversity, however, common themes appear whenever Muslim publics debate democracy and human rights. At the heart of most of these debates lies one recurring question: Are modern notions of democracy and human rights compatible with Islam's divine law, the shari`a?

Opponents of democracy and human rights insist that these notions are Western constructs contrary to the spirit of God's law. Supporters of human rights express a contrary view. Any effort to understand the prospects for democracy and human rights in the Muslim world must begin, then, by determining just what the shari`a entails, how it has been interpreted, and what its varied understandings mean for modern Muslim politics and culture around the world.

Having examined this broader background, I will in the latter portion of this chapter use ethnographic, survey, and historical materials from the Southeast Asian country of Indonesia, the world's most populous Muslim-majority nation, to examine the conditions that might favor democratic and human rights–friendly interpretations of the shari`a. I then compare the Indonesia data with findings from other studies, including those conducted by the World Values Survey and the Gallup World Poll. On the basis of this rich comparative data, I conclude that the prospects for some kind of accommodation of democracy and human rights in the Muslim world look promising. At the same time, however, I suggest that, even where these ideals are given institutional form, on several key points the concept of human rights and the balance struck between public interests and individual rights may differ from that currently favored in Western liberal democracies. In other words, while diminishing some differences between the West and the Muslim world, the diffusion of democratic and rights discourses into Muslim lands may make other value-differences more salient. Rather than being a deformation of the democratic process, this localization testifies to the inevitable and necessary accommodation of democratic and human rights ideals to different sociocultural landscapes. The reality of localization highlights the need for analysts to approach the study of human rights not by way of abstract and unchanging principles, but through the examination of the way in which generalized discourses interact with particular cultures, powers, and practices when migrating across countries and cultures.

Shari`a as Ideal and Practice

Commonly translated as "Islamic law," the shari`a is at once vaster and less specific than Western secular understandings of positive law imply. As the anthropologist Brinkley Messick has observed, adapting a phrase from the French sociologist Marcel Mauss, the shari`a is a "total discourse," one in which "all kinds of institutions find simultaneous expression: religious, legal, moral and economic."[5] Much like Jewish law, the shari`a provides guidance on matters of prayer, diet, dress, and sexual purity as well as economic justice and political organization.[6] Rather than positive law in the Western sense, then, the shari`a is perhaps better understood as God's injunctions for an entire way of life, of which one part, and a rather small part at that, includes regulations and sanctions of the sort associated in the West with law.[7]

Although some of the historical shari`a's prescriptions provide details as to their precise range and application, many do not. Equally important, as with any legal tradition, new questions constantly arise, and there are many areas where the law provides little prefigured guidance. Of its 6,200 verses, the Qur'an contains just 500 of a broadly legal nature.[8] However, as Wael Hallaq has observed, "these cover a relatively limited number of legal issues and, furthermore, treat of them selectively."[9] The jurists involved in the early development of Islamic law, then, had to look beyond the Qur'an to find the building blocks for a more comprehensive legal system. As accounts of the actions and sayings of the Prophet known as *hadith* were collected and recorded during the first two centuries of the Islamic era, legal rulings came increasingly to be grounded on either a binding passage from the Qur'an or hadith. Known collectively as the *Sunna* ("exemplary conduct," in this instance of the Prophet Muhammad), the hadith came to be a second canonical source for the law. Although Shi'ism adopted a formula that left greater room for independent reasoning, in Sunni Islam the sources of the law eventually came to consist of the Qur'an; the Sunna; the consensus of religious scholars, known as *ijma'* (a consensus assumed to have been reached on the basis of revelation); and analogic reasoning (*qiyas*) from binding passages in the Qur'an and Sunna.[10]

For most of Islamic history, of course, ordinary Muslims knew little if anything of the details of the law. Like their counterparts in other Old World civilizations, the great majority of believers were unschooled, illiterate, and more likely to become familiar with the tenets of their religion through participation in rites of passage, devotional orders, and public worship than through detailed legal exegeses. From the perspective of the lay public, then, the significance of the law lay less in its specific prescriptions than in the generalized ethical sensibility it inspired: that God has enjoined the creation of a social order based on His law, and that abiding by these commandments is the first duty of all believers.

The idealization of the law in this manner, placing the commitment to God's commands at the heart of the pious life, has sound scriptural precedents. In the Qur'an, God commands, "Judge in accordance with what God has revealed" and "We have revealed unto you the Book with the truth, confirming whatever Scripture was before it . . . we have made for each of you a law and a normative way to follow" (Qur. 5:48).[11] Across the great expanse of Muslim civilization, however, it was and is still today this generalized idealization, rather than agreement on the details of ethico-legal rules, that became the most salient feature of public religious culture. As Marshall Hodgson has noted, there was in the idea of the law an "aspiration . . . to form all ordinary life in its own mould."[12] The aspiration was not compromised by the fact that on many key points Muslim scholars and laypersons might not agree on just what, practically speaking, the law prescribed.

Even for those trained as scholars of the law, the shari`a's distinctive conjunction of idealized comprehensiveness and practical generality presented daunting epistemological challenges. To have faith in the all-encompassing nature of God's law is not the same as having settled understandings of its instructions for living in the world. In the absence of an ecclesiastical hierarchy or a centralized church like that of Western Christianity, Muslim jurists, the *fuqaha*, came to play a pivotal role in the deciphering of the law's meanings. Acting independently of state officials and without the benefit of ecclesiastical councils (like those in Western Christianity), jurists during the first centuries of the Muslim era responded to the shari`a's unfinished specification by developing legal and ethical commentaries known as *fiqh* (jurisprudence, lit., "understanding"), which extended the reach of God's law into new fields. Although during its first centuries Islam had dozens of legal schools, from the ninth century onward the number recognized by Sunnis gradually diminished, until by the thirteenth or fourteenth century the four major Sunni schools (*madhahib*) that exist today prevailed.[13]

No matter the legal tradition invoked, the development of fiqh did not dispel the epistemological tension between the presumed comprehensiveness of the law and the less-than-specific nature of its practical stipulations. More vexing yet for modern heirs to the Islamic legal tradition, the tension between the ideal of comprehensiveness and the reality of unspecificity happens to be especially pronounced in matters of politics and public law. By comparison with the law's detailed commentaries on ritual and family matters, on matters of state and politics the shari`a tends to be general and underdeveloped. For Western readers unfamiliar with the historical development of Islamic law, this fact may occasion surprise. After all, modern Islamist activists often claim that Islam differs from Christianity in having comprehensive plans for how state and society should be organized. Although it is true that Islam has a different perspective on the state from that of the Jesus movement and early Christianity, on many critical matters of state and governance the shari`a remains theoretical.

There are sound historical reasons for the underspecified nature of the shari`a in matters of governance. The composition of the historical shari`a began toward the end of the Umayyad dynasty (661–750 C.E.) and during the early years of its Abbasid successor (750–1258 C.E.). The Abbasid leadership had taken up arms against the Umayyads, rallying supporters by inveighing against the impiety and corruption of their rivals. Once in power, the Abbasids took pains to demonstrate their piety by, among other things, lavishing favors on the emerging class of religious jurists. In matters of state administration, the Abbasids differed from the Umayyads in their extensive reliance on Persian models of governance. These were more systematic and bureaucratic than the political system the Arabs had brought to Persia a century earlier.

The Abbasid accommodation to Persian political culture had two consequences for the elaboration of the historical shari`a. The first was that, faced with a powerful state, Muslim legal scholars confined their pronouncements on politics to well-established and largely uncontroversial matters, such as the procedures for war and the division of booty. On most other practical political matters, the jurists deferred to Abbasid authorities. As the sociologist Sami Zubaida has observed, this implicit division of legislative labor meant that "The shariah developed historically to rule mostly on the private affairs of the community, dealing with commercial and property transactions and family matters, as well as ritual performances. The public law provisions of the shariah have remained largely theoretical."[14]

The second consequence of the religious scholars' tacit agreement with the Abbasids was that early on state officials began to issue edicts to cover those aspects of governance on which the shari`a was silent, unspecific, or too cumbersome to allow for effective enforcement. Specialists of Islamic law today talk about this legal bifurcation by distinguishing shari`a from rulers' edicts and statute law, much of which came to be known in the later Ottoman period as *qanun*.[15] Statute law played a central role in all of the great Islamic empires of the Middle Ages and Early Modern Period. In principle, and notwithstanding claims that the ruler's edicts were inspired by God's law, these statutes remained separate from the shari`a, with the result that the legislation achieved a considerable measure of discursive and institutional autonomy. Because the ideal of the shari`a as unchanging and all-encompassing remained in place, however, Islam's legal scholars were unable to draw on this parallel legislation to revisit or enrich the divinely revealed legal tradition to which they were heir. Scholars of law were also reluctant to provide this statutory legislation with any but general sanction, for to do so would have been to create the impression that on some points the shari`a is in fact *not* comprehensive in a specific or detailed manner.[16]

A similar pattern of discursive differentiation was seen in other areas of political and intellectual life in premodern times. For example, although most Islamic empires encouraged the development of Islamic courts under the jurisdiction of Islamic judges (*qadi*), from the Abbasid period on there also developed a system of *mazalim* tribunals in which rulers and their aides provided a setting in which subjects could petition for the righting of some wrong.[17] Although some of these tribunals were advised by Muslim jurists, many were not. Most rulers also did not feel obliged to follow the strict procedures of evidence required in Islamic courts; nor did most feel that they had to justify their judgments in terms of shari`a principles. "We may say that its [the *mazalim*'s] standards of justice were ad hoc and 'common sense' based on common ethics and customary standards."[18]

A similar ships-passing-in-the-night pattern prevailed in the political manuals prepared by advisors to Muslim rulers, known today as "mirrors for princes." Whereas the historical shari`a provided general principles but little specific guidance for day-to-day governance, the mirrors for princes were packed with level-headed counsel. As Carl Brown has observed, however, to play this practical role the mirrors had to steer clear of anything that might be seen as challenging the claims of the shari'a or the authority of religious scholars. Inasmuch as most scholars avoided practical politics, the latter tack was easy enough. But this intellectual segregation had serious consequences for the long-term development of Islamic political theory. The dual economy of political knowledge meant that there was less of the "continuing dialectic of ideas and experience" required for the development of an intellectually inte-grated political tradition, one that draws on the lessons of history to enrich and concretize its formal legal corpus.[19] Instead, in its formal expression Muslim political thought remained dualized between the abstract and (in principle if not practice) normatively unchanging ideals of the shari'a, on one hand, and the richly empirical but theoretically quarantined knowledge of political philos-ophers and practitioners, on the other.

None of this is to say, of course, that there was a "separation of mosque and state," comparable to the so-called separation of church and state authority in Christian Europe. To whatever degree they operated independently of state con-trol (and this varied in classical Muslim societies, and declined dramatically under the Ottomans), the qadis who officiated in Islamic courts held to the idea that their authority and their rulings were based firmly on the shari'a. Equally important, both popular and juristic opinion subscribed to the notion that it was the responsibility of the ruler to uphold Islam and support scholars in their efforts to implement the shari'a. Inasmuch as in most Muslim societies the practical scope of the historical shari'a had been circumscribed so as to leave princes free to devise their own governance procedures, however, it is clear that there *was* a practical differentiation of rulers' and scholarly authority. The sep-aration preserved the purity of shari'a while providing Ottoman, Mughal, and Safavid rulers with the running room they required to develop a flexible and effective system of government.

The fact remained, however, that Islam's jurists, the fuqaha, were unable to acknowledge this differentiation in an explicit and discursively expansive manner. The ideal of the shari'a as all-encompassing survived even in the his-torical breach. It is important to note, however, that many religious scholars responded to the discrepancy, not with righteous indignation but with a sober and measured resignation. They saw the discrepancy between normative ideal and practical reality as proof of the inevitable degeneracy of the age in which they lived compared to the age of the Prophet. In other words, and not surpris-ingly, they concluded that the shari'a was an ideal of such moral excellence that it was unthinkable that its terms could be realized as fully as they had been in the age of the Prophet.

At various times in Islamic history, however, a few scholars took exception to this devolutionist view of Muslim civilization. Perhaps the best known of these figures is Ibn Taimiyya (d. 1328), a late medieval scholar whose writings have achieved canonical status in Saudi Arabia and among Sunni Islamists.[20] In his *al-Siyasa al-Shar`iya* (statecraft according to the shari`a), Ibn Taimiyya rejected the idea that the shari`a could be confined to commercial, ritual, and private affairs. The state too, Taimiyya insisted, must be brought under the jurisdiction of God's law. No more than a ripple on the surface of the medieval Muslim ocean, this idea was to become a powerful current at the end of the twentieth century.

Women, Apostates, and Non-Muslims

Although the historical shari`a offered only select details on matters of practical governance, it provided a clear message on the relationship of private ethics to the public good, which I discuss in the next section of this chapter, and on certain categories of actors who in modern times have become an object of concern for Muslim human rights activists: women, non-Muslims, and religious dissidents. The situation of women is discussed by Yvonne Haddad in her contribution to this volume. However, to make the point quickly, the status of women in the historical shari`a was handled primarily through family law, touching on matters of marriage, divorce, property, and inheritance. In all of these fields, women were accorded far broader rights than they are thought to have enjoyed in pre-Islamic Arabia.[21] Indeed, in these areas, the rights accorded Muslim women were greater than those given their counterparts in medieval Europe. Although women did not play a central role in mosque services or religious education, they did sponsor the establishment of religious schools. And while they were barred from the madrasas, some could, through private study, become respected scholars.

Notwithstanding these generous provisions, on a number of points the historical shari`a seemed to put women at a significant disadvantage relative to men. In principle if not always in practice, women's testimony in courts counted as just half that of men. A woman's right to initiate divorce was severely restricted compared to her husband's. A girl's inherited share of her parents' properties was one-half her brother's. Perhaps most problematic for modern notions of citizenship, classical commentaries stipulated that in both family and public affairs women were not to exercise authority over men. Citing Qur'an 4:34, classical jurists assigned men guardianship (*qawama*) over women. Later commentators went further, limiting the rights of women to appear in public or to associate with men, thereby blocking women's access to male-dominated political spheres.[22]

The actual rulings and actions of judges in Islamic courts were often more flexible than these formal provisions imply. Indeed, as a number of recent studies have shown, court rulings were often informed by local notions of equity, fairness, and gender identity, in addition to shari`a prescriptions.[23]

Nonetheless, in modern times, Islamist appeals for the implementation of shari`a have typically referenced not the situated practices of real-and-existing Muslim jurists but the formal provisions of the historical shari`a, elements of which are at variance with gender-equitable understandings of citizenship.[24]

The law's stipulations with regard to non-Muslims show a similarly differentiating disposition, one that both its Muslim defenders and critics trace back to Qur'anic precedents. Revelations dating from the Medina period (622–632 C.E.) distinguish sharply between Muslims and non-Muslims. Qur'an 9:29, for example, urges believers to fight against and humble those to whom God has given revelation, that is, Jews and Christians, but who no longer forbid what God has forbidden. Passages like these have led modern Muslim reformists to argue that the passages in question apply only to heated contests taking place in seventh-century Medina, not to Muslim relations with Christians and Jews for all time. The well-known Muslim democrats, Abdullahi Ahmed an-Na'im and his teacher Muhammad Taha, go even further. They suggest that the earlier Meccan, and not the Medinan, revelations should be used as the basis for a reformulation of the shari`a in line with modern notions of citizenship and human rights.[25] Taha and an-Na'im's proposal has its supporters, but most Muslim jurists regard it as an unacceptable departure from the established methodologies of Qur'anic scholarship.

From the classical period onward, the main stream of jurisprudential opinion interpreted passages like Sura 29 as evidence of enduring tension, if not hostility, between Muslims and non-Muslims. During Islam's middle ages, jurists extended the distinction into an elaborate set of prescriptions concerning the political standing of non-Muslim "peoples of the book" (*ahl al-kitab*). As recipients of earlier divine revelations, and as the demographic majority in most of the newly conquered lands during the first 150 years of the Muslim era, the peoples of the book were accorded a "protected" status known as dhimmi-hood.[26] *Dhimmas* were tolerated and given social autonomy on the condition that they submit to Muslim rule and pay a special capitation tax, the *jizya*. However, the shari`a imposed other restrictions on dhimmas, the effect of which was to underscore their subordination, sometimes quite starkly. For example, dhimmas were barred from serving in the military, forbidden to mount horses, obliged to wear clothing that marked them as non-Muslims, and, in general, excluded from positions of executive authority over Muslims. In legal principle, polytheists like Hindus, who were not included among peoples of the book, were subject to even more draconian restrictions.

In historical practice, many Muslim rulers took a pragmatic approach to the governance of their multireligious societies and set aside the shari`a's restrictions on polytheists and people of the book. For most of their history, for example, India's great Mughal rulers chose to dispense with the shari`a's provisions with respect to non-Muslims, although at first they did apply the jizya tax.[27] Muslim rulers in premodern Southeast Asia were also casual with regard to the shari`a's guidelines for dealing with non-Muslims.[28] Nonetheless, although often set aside in practice, the principle of religiously differentiated citizenship was never formally effaced from Muslim jurisprudence. Its lingering presence has posed special problems for modern Muslim jurists supportive of international models of human rights and democratic citizenship.

A similar tension has emerged in modern times on questions of religious freedom, not least of all with regard to apostasy from Islam. Historically, Islam had no counterpart to the inquisitional arrest, torture, and execution of tens of thousands of heretics, witches, and unconventional thinkers that occurred in early modern Europe. Indeed, Muslim rulers tolerated or even supported a variety of what today would be regarded as mildly heterodox brotherhoods, many of them pantheistic varieties of Sufism. Nonetheless, throughout Muslim history, there were occasional prosecutions for apostasy, some of which resulted in capital punishment.[29] At times rulers mounted full-blown campaigns against Sufis and others deemed heterodox, particularly where followers of the mystic path acquired a mass following and threatened central authority.

Again, however, by comparison with the legal stipulations of medieval Christianity, Islamic jurisprudence took care not to apply the accusation of apostasy broadly and to require high standards of proof for a conviction. Those accused of apostasy were given repeated opportunities to revert back to a proper profession of Islam. However, if the accused chose not to recant, the shari`a stipulated that he or she was to be stripped of all civil rights, including rights of inheritance and the right to marry a Muslim; an already married apostate would see his or her marriage dissolved. If the offender persisted in his or her ways, the penalty was death or, in the case of women, indefinite imprisonment. On these points, the historical shari`a developed a legal vigilance on matters of the faith that, to some commentators, contradicts the oft-cited injunction in Qur'an 2:26 that there is no compulsion in Islam.[30]

On all of these issues—women, non-Muslims, and Muslim non-conformists or apostates—the historical shari`a prescribed ethical strictures that stand in tension with the liberal principles enshrined in documents like the 1948 Universal Declaration of Human Rights. In modern times, Islamist political thinkers like Sayyid Qutb of Egypt and Abdu'l A'la Mawdudi of Pakistan have taken strong exception to liberal formulations of human rights.[31] Documents like the Universal Islamic Declaration of Human Rights (UIDHR) and the constitutions of the Islamic Republics of Iran and the Sudan have tended to be more restrained in their objections to UN-promoted human rights proposals, but their basic position is similar. As with the UIDHR, most of these declarations begin by affirming two key principles: that God has provided humanity with comprehensive legal and moral guidelines, and that human-made regulations must not contradict these divine commands.[32]

Although such a principle might seem to open the floodgates to Islamic exceptionalism with regard to human rights concerns, the main points of disagreement typically center on the same issues of women, non-Muslims, and freedom of religious expression. Documents like the Constitution of the Islamic Republic of 1979 dedicate great space to affirming the dignity and equality of women, rejecting anything and everything that might use women "as an instrument in the service of promoting consumerism and exploitation." But the constitution also emphasizes women's "momentous and precious function" as mothers, and stipulates that "since the family is the fundamental unit of Islamic society, all laws must . . . safeguard its sanctity and the stability of family relations on the basis of the law and ethics of Islam."[33]

When referring to non-Muslims, the Iranian constitution also extends rights of religious expression only to Zoroastrians, Jews, and Christians. The constitution makes no provisions for freedom of religion as such, and groups like the Baha'i, who once flourished in Iran, have been systematically denied rights of religious expression, on the grounds that they are actually apostates from Islam.[34]

There is one other point of tension between liberal notions of human rights and their Muslim critics. Focused as it is on the defense of individual freedoms, the Universal Declaration of Human Rights says little about the need for individuals or institutions to uphold any specific idea of the good. Although some Western political philosophers of communitarian persuasion have taken exception to this feature of liberal philosophy, the general tendency in liberal and human rights circles has been to promote neutrality with regard to ethical issues other than human rights themselves, on the grounds that ethical matters are best left to the private deliberations of individual citizens. By contrast, the 1979 constitution of the Islamic Republic of Iran, the Universal Islamic Declaration of Human Rights, and the 1993 Cairo Declaration on Human Rights in Islam all make clear that affirmations of individual rights must be linked to the upholding of ethical norms, including most importantly the obligations of believers to God. As we shall see, the theme of not merely defending individual rights but commanding the good runs through contemporary Muslim commentaries on human rights, including some that are otherwise sympathetic to liberal understandings.

Commanding Right and Creating the Public Good

Although a few individuals and groups took exception from early on, during the 1950s and 1960s most Muslim countries adopted official positions that were either favorable to the Universal Declaration of Human Rights or silent on its more controversial provisions. Nonetheless, in the aftermath of the Islamic resurgence that swept most of the Muslim world in the 1970s and 1980s, once-latent tensions became apparent, as growing numbers of religious scholars and activists pressed their governments to bring national law into conformity with elements of the shari`a. These campaigns sought to respond to the Muslim public's growing piety, and the widespread conviction that the most fitting expression of piety is conformity to God's law. The first wave of these campaigns, which stretched from North Africa to Southeast Asia, focused on bringing family law into line with the perceived ideals of the shari`a.[35] More recently, however, the supporters of shari`a have extended their campaigns into two additional domains: religious expression, where activists have demanded tighter controls against those they see as deviating from Islam; and public morals, where activists have demanded proactive measures to "command right and forbid wrong."

The much discussed case of Nasr Hamid Abu Zayd in Egypt provides a striking example of the way in which strict-constructionist supporters of shari`a have pressed for limits on fellow Muslims' freedom of religious expression. Abu Zayd is a liberal-minded specialist of religious studies who, in 1990, was brought to court by Islamist lawyers on charges of apostasy. The charges were related to a book that Abu Zayd had published, in which, among other things, he expressed doubts about the existence of angels and jinns (a category of spirit acknowledged in the Qur'an). Although Egyptian statutory law does not actually have provisions for prosecuting apostasy, Islamist lawyers took advantage of other provisions in state law to petition that Abu Zayd be declared an apostate and his marriage dissolved. Egypt is unusual among Muslim-majority countries in that in recent years its supreme court has managed to achieve a significant measure of autonomy from the government. Having done so, however, the court has used its authority to bring portions of Egyptian law into line with conventional understandings of the shari`a.[36] In 1994, a court of appeal ruled in the plaintiff's favor. After the ruling was upheld in 1996, Abu Zayd and his wife had to flee Egypt for Europe so as to save their marriage.[37]

In other countries, campaigns to implement shari`a have focused on combating vice and promoting a vigorously interventionist approach to public morality. In several countries these efforts have assumed the form of "antivice" militias that take the enforcement of the shari`a into their own hands, sometimes in defiance of state authorities. For example, in Indonesia after the fall of the authoritarian Soeharto government in May 1998, there was a rash of militia formation in cities and towns around the country. The largest militias were organized into quasi-military formations, complete with commanders, officers, and named battalions. One of the best known of the big militias was the Islamic Defenders Front or FPI (Front Pembela Islam), founded in the capital city of Jakarta in August 1998 by Habib Muhammad Rizieq ibn Hussein Shihab, popularly known as Habib Rizieq.[38]

Rizieq cited three reasons for establishing his antivice militia: the growing availability of drugs; a tidal wave of illicit pornography that had swept Indonesia during the early post-Soeharto period; and the alleged influence of Marxists in the country's booming democracy movement. In the two years following its establishment in 1998, Rizieq turned the Front into the most potent paramilitary force in the nation's capital, commanding 50,000 part-time troops and striking fear into the hearts of mainstream Muslims. The Front ransacked bars, brothels, and gambling houses, alleging, not implausibly, that these were centers of vice. With the backing of a well-known general close to former president Soeharto, a number of groups with ties to the Front provided protection for the November 1998 meeting of the Special Session of the People's Representative Assembly, which met to lay the ground rules for the first elections to be held after Soeharto's resignation. Tellingly, the main groups against which the Assembly was to be "protected" were pro-democracy activists and secular nationalists opposed to Soeharto's hand-picked successor, B. J. Habibie, a political reformist who, because of his reputation for piety, enjoyed the support of many in the Islamist community. In June 2000, Front activists ransacked the headquarters of the National Commission on Human Rights when the latter body implicated members of the army command in the 1999 violence in East Timor. In March and April 2001, the Front launched a campaign that targeted leftist students, union organizers, and bookstores selling Marxist literature.[39] In the run-up to the U.S. intervention in Afghanistan, the Front organized the largest of Jakarta's anti-American demonstrations.

In interviews, Rizieq justified his actions by citing the well-known Islamic ethical principle that it is the duty of pious believers to "command right and forbid wrong" (al-amr bi'l-ma'rûf wa'-nahy 'an al munkr). As the Princeton historian of Islam, Michael Cook, has explained, this first principle of Islamic public ethics, known as hisba, is deeply rooted in Qur'anic tradition. Its modern political sociology is interesting as well, not least of all because it has the potential to challenge conventional human rights regimes, dependent as they are on state-enforced law. To quote Cook, the hisba principle implies "that an executive power of the law of God is vested in each and every Muslim." As a result, "the individual believer as such has not only the right, but also the duty, to issue orders pursuant to God's law, and to do what he can to see that they are obeyed."[40]

Perhaps no principle captures the spirit of classical Islamic public ethics better than this one. None too better illustrates just why efforts to promote notions of civil and human rights premised on the idea that ethical decisions are above all matters of individual choice meets with skepticism on the part of many Islamic scholars and even the lay public. The shari`a and popular ethical traditions to which most of the Muslim world is heir do not segregate the affirmation of individual rights from the moral obligation to uphold the public good. On the contrary, the legacy of hisba merges the two concerns into a joint ethical project. It is this ethos that is so clearly expressed in Article 3 of the constitution of the Islamic Republic of Iran, which states that "the government of the Islamic Republic has the duty of directing all its resources to . . . the creation of a favorable environment for the growth of moral virtues based on faith and piety and the struggle against all forms of vice and corruption."[41]

Although vividly expressed in passages like these, the principle of commanding right and forbidding wrong is not easily operationalized. For centuries, Muslim jurists have grappled with just this issue, recognizing that "the virtuous performance of the duty can degenerate into vice."[42] After all, just *who* has the right to command right and forbid wrong? Efforts to uphold public morality can easily degenerate into anarchy and unilateral preemptive strikes— unless the principle is tethered to some agreed notion of the public good and practical measures for its implementation. Without these, the principle may tempt nonstate actors to usurp the state's putative monopoly over legal violence.

In modern times, the hisba's potential to challenge state authority and spark controversy has prompted reform-minded scholars to argue that democracy and the rule of law are the best way to enact hisba today. However, even among those who conclude that democracy can best realize hisba's aims, the "good" that is to be promoted is typically perceived in ways subtly different from Western liberal notions. Typically the idea of the good is less individualized and privatized than its counterpart in liberal human rights schemes. Thus, in his recent book on Islam and the secular state, the much-respected Sudanese-American scholar Abdullahi Ahmed An-Na'im—a staunch defender of universal human rights—remarks that the shari`a "will always remain the total obligation of Muslims to observe in their daily lives," and even secular democracy "needs religion to provide a widely accepted source of moral guidance for the political community."[43]

As noted above, recent survey data, like that provided by the World Values Survey and the Gallup World Poll, make clear that there is broad support for democracy and some features of human rights in Muslim-majority countries.[44] These survey findings provide evidence of a cultural shift under way in Muslim lands that is both real and politically momentous. However nuanced its meanings, the idea of human rights has captured the imagination of modern Muslims. Much of the idea's appeal has to do with the notion that there are limits to what a government can do to its citizens, limits defined in relation to social assets with which citizens are putatively endowed.

All this suggests that there is a real, if unfinished, convergence of political-cultural currents taking place between Muslim publics and Western proponents of human rights. At the same time, however, survey and interview data also indicate that the commitment to human rights is not stand-alone, but is inflected by Muslim notions of public ethics, as well as shari`a commentaries on women, non-Muslims, and religious freedom. This is not surprising. After all, the diffusion of modern notions of human rights to Muslim lands has taken place at roughly the same time that most countries have also felt the effects of an enormous revitalization in Islamic learning and piety.

In the next section, I want to draw on survey data and in-depth interviews from Indonesia to explore the interaction between these two transcultural currents. As in the World Values and Gallup surveys, my data indicate strong support for human rights and democracy. But they also show that that subscription is cross-cut by an equally strong commitment to the notion that, for Muslims, citizen rights cannot be neatly separated from shari`a or ideas of the good. The interplay of these ideas has serious implications for the reception and implementation of human rights in Muslim-majority countries, not least of all with regard to the management of public morals and the rights of women, non-Muslims, and non-conformist Muslims.

Indonesia and the Dual Economy of Political Virtue

By most measures, Indonesia is a country where one would expect the Muslim public's support for human rights to be strong. During the 1990s, Indonesia gave birth to the largest democracy movement the Muslim world has ever seen.[45] Since the fall of the country's authoritarian "New Order" regime in May 1998, the country has held three free and fair national elections (in 1999, 2004, and 2009), as well as several subsequent rounds of regional elections, the results of which have been notable for their moderation. One among Muslim Indonesia's many impressive democratic achievements has been the effort of its State Islamic Colleges (known by the acronym UIN or IAIN) to develop programs for civic education to deepen Muslims' commitment to democracy and human rights.

At the center of the State Islamic Colleges' effort has been a program that, since 2004, has required all students entering the State Islamic system to take a civics course on just these topics. The curriculum for this program was developed during 2001–2002 in collaboration with the Asia Foundation. The significance of this program for democracy and human rights is that the primary purpose of the State Islamic College system is to train Muslim educators who go on to work in Islamic madrasas and boarding schools (known locally as *pesantren*), and to train Muslim professionals climbing the social ladder from rural and poor backgrounds into the middle class. In other words, the State Islamic system serves as a cultural broker for all manner of values, including in this case understandings of democracy and human rights.

The State Islamic system also acts as an institutional mentor to Indonesia's 46,000 Islamic schools, which provide primary and secondary school education for 15 percent of the country's students, and informal religious instruction to twice that number.[46] One development that has enhanced the colleges' role is that over the past fifteen years the state Islamic system has become the preferred higher educational venue for graduates of the country's Islamic schools. Rather than going to the Middle East for higher education, as they used to, most Muslim educators now attend Indonesia's State Islamic Colleges. (Of course, most still jump at the chance to travel to the Middle East if given the opportunity.) There they are introduced to courses in contextual hermeneutics and democratic theory for which there are few counterparts in the Middle East.[47]

Is this shift in Islamic higher education likely to strengthen democratic and human rights awareness in Muslim schools? The editors of a 2002 report on the State Islamic Colleges were decidedly optimistic on this point.[48]

> The large number of IAIN [State Islamic College] alumni who go on to become *kyai* [directors] or religious teachers [*ustadz*] in *pesantren* certainly gives rise to the hope that they will bring with them a new Islamic culture that is modern, contextual, liberal, and rational, like that which is being developed in the IAIN. . . . With the model of understanding developed at the IAIN, Muslim Indonesians, who of course represent the majority of Indonesians, will be educated so as to be able to understand the important meaning of modernity, progress (*the idea of progress*), societal pluralism, and tolerance toward people who profess other religions.

Notwithstanding the report's optimism, the precise impact of the State Islamic College programs on Muslim public opinion remains unclear. It is not that there is much opposition to instruction on human rights and democracy. Indeed, interviews I conducted with 100 faculty and administrators at four Islamic university campuses during July and December 2006 indicated that the overwhelming majority (87%) support the civic education program. But the long-term impact of these programs will depend on the outcome of an as yet unfinished shift in Indonesian Muslim understandings of public ethics and human rights.

As discussed earlier, there is a tension in modern Muslim political thought between democratic and human rights ideals, with their emphasis on equality and individualist privacy, and conventional understandings of the shari`a.[49] In an effort to gauge Muslim educators' views on these matters, in January 2006 I worked with staff at the Center for the Study of Islam and Society (PPIM) at the Hidayatullah National Islamic University in Jakarta to carry out a survey of 940 Muslim educators in 100 madrasas and Islamic boarding schools in eight provinces in Indonesia. The survey was coordinated by eight PPIM staffers. The survey had 184 questions, the aggregate results of which are too complex to present here. Table 3.1 summarizes the data concerning Muslim educators' attitudes toward democracy, Islamism, and pluralism.

As one might expect, the most interesting feature of the survey data concerns educators' views on democracy, human rights, and the shari`a. On one hand, an impressive 85.9 percent of Muslim educators agree that democracy is the best form of government for Indonesia. Moreover, when we look more closely we see that the educators' support is neither formalistic nor crudely majoritarian. Rather, their views extend to subtle aspects of civil and human rights, including support for the idea of equality before the law (94.2%),

TABLE 3.1.   Indonesia Madrasa and Islamic Boarding School Teachers' Views on Democracy, Islamism, Pluralism, and Gender (1/2006 Survey of 940 Teachers in 8 Provinces): Percentage of Respondents Agreeing with Statements

A. Support for Democracy	
Democracy, compared to other forms of governance, is the best form of government for a country like ours	85.9%
Democracy is a source of political disorder	8.1%
Every citizen is equal before the law regardless of his or her political views	94.2%
Every citizen must be allowed to join any political organization	82.5%
Mass media must by protected by law to protect them from arbitrary actions of government	92.8%
Our economy will be better if the government gives more freedom to each citizen to do as he or she wishes	73.4%
Free and fair contestation between political parties improves the performance of government of this country	80%

B. Islam and State	
Islamic governance, i.e., governance based on the Qur'an and Sunna and under the leadership of Islamic authorities like ulama, is the best for this nation	72.2%
The state should enforce the obligation to implement Islamic law (shari`a) for all Muslims	82.8%
The amputation of the hand of a thief as prescribed in the Qur'an should be enforced by the government	59.1%
General elections should be limited to candidates who understand and agree to fight for the implementation of Islamic teachings in the polity	63.9%
Only Islamic parties should be allowed to participate in general elections	24.3%
The Muslims who do not perform their religious duties should not be allowed to serve as members in the National Assembly	74.3%
The ideals and practices of Islamist organizations, like the Darul Islam, Negara Islam Indonesia, Front Pembela Islam, Laskar Jihad, etc., to implement Islamic law (shari`a) in the society and polity should be supported	64.4%
The government (police) should close restaurants during days of the month Ramadan	82.9%
The government and police should intervene to question mixed-sex couples walking in public to make sure that they are married or relatives	66.6%
The government should engage in surveillance so as to insure that Muslims perform the Ramadan fasting.	49.9%

C. Pluralism: Views on Muslims and non-Muslims	
Non-Muslims should be allowed to become President of this country	6.5%
Non-Muslims should not be allowed to be a teacher in public school	19.9%
Non-Muslims should be allowed to perform their religious rites in this area	20.1%
Non-Muslims should be allowed to build places of worship in this area	39.8%
Islam is the best umma (religious community)	92.5%
We are not supposed to cooperate with non-Muslims in anything	10.5%
We are not allowed to say greetings like "assalamu'alaikum" or "Merry Christmas" to non-Muslims [Christians]	73.5%
Islam is the only true religion and therefore non-Muslims should convert to Islam	58.7%

(continued)

TABLE 3.1. (continued)

D. Gender Issues	
Generally speaking, males are superior to females	61.3%
Like males, females have the right to run for membership in the legislature	81.6%
It is best that women not be allowed to run for president	55.8%
Women are too weak to serve as judges in court	51.3%
The practice of polygamy should be legal and allowed in Indonesia	75.7%
Females should not be allowed to take distant trips without the accompaniment of a close family member or relative	79.6%

freedom to join political organizations (82.5%), protections for the media from arbitrary government action (92.8%), and the notion that party competition improves government performance (80%). These figures are as high as survey data on similar issues from Western Europe and the United States. They are also consistent with findings from other parts of the Muslim world, which indicate that with a few notable exceptions, the majority of people subscribe to the idea that democracy and citizen rights are compatible with Islam.[50]

If this were all there was to educators' attitudes on democracy and human rights, it would be smooth sailing indeed. However, educators' views on democracy are not self-contained. The Muslim community has become familiar with democracy and human rights issues over a two-decade period that roughly coincides with a far-reaching resurgence in Islamic learning and piety. Against this historical backdrop, then, it is perhaps not surprising that the educators' enthusiasm for democracy is complemented by an equally strong commitment to God's law. For example, notwithstanding the strength of their commitment to democracy, 72.2 percent of the educators believe the state should be based on the Qur'an and Sunna and to some degree advised by religious experts. A full 82.8 percent of educators think the state should work to implement the shari`a. Support for the shari`a wobbles on a few points. For example, it drops to 59.1 percent when the regulation in question concerns the amputation of thieves' hands, or government efforts to compel performance of the Ramadan fast (only 49.9% agree). On these matters, at least, some educators seem to have second thoughts about a too-literalist implementation of the law. Nonetheless, when asked whether inobservant Muslims should be allowed to serve in the National Assembly, 74.3 percent of educators feel they should not. A full 64.4 percent agree with Muslim militants' campaigns to implement Islamic law.

On matters of women and non-Muslims, the tension between educators' enthusiasm for democracy and civil rights, on one hand, and their understanding of the shari`a, on the other, is even more striking. Some 93.5 percent of the educators believe that a non-Muslim should not be allowed to assume the presidency. A full 55.8 percent feel that women should not run for office. Some 51.3 percent feel that women should not serve as judges. About 20 percent would bar non-Muslims from teaching in public schools; a similar percentage want to prohibit non-Muslims from performing religious services in Muslim areas. Twice that percentage would bar non-Muslims from erecting houses of worship nearby. In short, on these three matters—gender, non-Muslims, and the place of Islamic law in government—the educators' enthusiasm for democracy is qualified by shari`a commitments that seem at odds with liberal notions of individualist ethics, as well as some dimensions of human rights.

These data point to what is in fact a political and ethical disposition widespread in Muslim-majority societies. The disposition goes against the liberal philosophical preference for separating religion from politics and characterizing religious affairs as personal and private. Indonesian educators' stated commitments to democracy are about as strong as among any sample population in the democratic West. However, where a democratic or human rights principle runs up against an issue on which the shari`a is seen as having something to say, most educators feel obliged to defer to the shari`a. This deference results in judgments that many observers, including most Muslim democrats, would regard as potentially problematic, especially on matters related to equal rights for women and non-Muslims, as well as protection for dissident or nonconformist Muslims' rights of religious expression.

In actual political practice, however, this latter sensibility is more nuanced than the survey data indicate. It is telling in this regard that notwithstanding polls showing most Indonesian Muslims support the implementation of Islamic law, in the national elections of 1999 and 2004 no more than 22 percent of the electorate cast its vote for parties that support such programs. In conjunction with this survey, during August and December of 2006 I put a related question to about 200 Muslim educators, asking them about their choices in the national elections. Although in my larger survey, 72.2 percent of respondents had expressed support for establishing a state based on the Qur'an and Sunna, fewer than 30 percent indicated that they had actually voted for a party advocating the implementation of Islamic law. And the great majority of these respondents had voted for a party (the PKS, or "Prosperous Justice Party") which wants a gradual and "ethicalized" rather than immediate implementation of the law. Indeed, the party's success in the elections had more to do with its promotion of clean government and public services than shari`a.[51]

Asked in open-ended interviews why they chose not to make implementation of the law their top voting priority, most respondents explained that they felt that the Indonesian people were not "ready" for the full implementation of shari`a, and that any steps in such a direction had to be gradual. Others confided that they worried that handing authority for the shari`a to state officials might make God's law vulnerable to political manipulation.

Survey and interview findings like these are not unique to Indonesia. They suggest that in many societies the Muslim public's views on democracy and Islamic law are in dynamic tension, but often in flexibly creative ways. In Indonesia, the public seems to be subtly aware of the tension between its general commitment to the shari`a and its desire for democratic and just government. Rather than rushing to support programs for far-reaching legal and political change, most voters hedge their bets, deferring until some later moment the question of just how to accommodate God's law in a democratic state.

Democracy and Shari`a in Global Perspective

Survey research from other Muslim-majority countries indicates that these Indonesian findings are not at all exceptional but reflect public-ethical tensions common to many Muslim societies. Pippa Norris and Ronald Inglehart's recent (2004) analysis of World Values Survey data provides one of the strongest gauges of the breadth of popular support for democratic principles in Muslim-majority countries. Working from data gathered in eleven Muslim-majority countries, Norris and Inglehart report that the majority of respondents view democracy as a good form of government and one to which they aspire. Comparing these data with comparable surveys conducted in the West, the authors note, "There were no significant differences between the publics living in the West and in Muslim religious cultures in approval of how democracy works in practice, in support for democratic ideals, and in approval of strong leadership."[52]

However, when they turn their investigative gaze toward gender issues, Norris and Inglehart find a significant difference in values, similar to that apparent in the Indonesian data. Muslim publics are far more likely than their Western counterparts to have what Western analysts would regard as conservative views on gender equality, abortion, divorce, and women's leadership. Norris and Inglehart conclude: "Any deep seated-divisions between Islam and the West will revolve far more strongly around social rather than political values, especially concerning the issues of sexual liberalization and gender equality."[53]

Oriented as they are to the analysis of public opinion around the world rather than in Muslim-majority societies alone, Norris and Inglehart's surveys did not touch on some of the more vexing questions with regard to Islamic ethics and the shari`a. Analyzing data from Gallup World Poll surveys conducted between 2001 and 2007 in thirty-five Muslim-majority countries, John L. Esposito and Dalia Mogahed take on these latter issues more directly. Their conclusions illustrate the complex way in which democratic and religious commitments interact in making Muslim public opinion.

The authors first note that in most countries the majority of respondents "value a number of democratic principles" and "see no contradiction between democratic values and religious principles."[54] However, just as in Indonesia, most respondents do not neatly segregate their private religious convictions from their public political views. "Along with indicating strong support for Islam and democracy," Esposito and Mogahed remark, "poll responses also reveal widespread support for Sharia."[55] As in Indonesia, the interweaving of the two convictions is particularly subtle when respondents are invited to comment on political matters that the respondents hear as falling under the authority of religious law. Thus, "The majority of those surveyed want religious leaders to have no direct role in crafting a constitution." Nonetheless, most "favor religious law as a source of legislation."[56] In five of the thirty-five countries, "majorities want Sharia as the 'only source' of legislation."[57] Indeed, Esposito and Mogahed conclude, most Muslim respondents aver that democratic politics "does not require a separation of religion and state"; most "want neither a theocracy nor a secular democracy and would opt for a third model in which religious principles and democratic values coexist."[58]

Not just in Indonesia, then, but in most Muslim-majority countries the public embraces broad portions of the democracy and human rights formula, but appears reluctant to consign religion to the realm of private personal ethics. Of course, if we take Western variants of "unsecular politics"—like Christian democracy in early twentieth-century Europe—as our point of reference, this reluctance does not appear exceptional. At least during its first half-century of existence, Christian democracy also subscribed to a politics in which "religious ideas, symbols, and rituals . . . [were] used as the primary (though not exclusive) instrument of mobilization."[59] Moreover, in early Christian democracy as with its Muslim cousin today, religious discourses were used not merely for the purposes of mobilization, but for imagining the way in which public morals should be upheld in an erstwhile democratic order. Although there are clear precedents for such arrangements in Western as well as Muslim countries, such religious collaborations across the state-society divide stand in tension with the more individualistic formulations enshrined in the 1948 Universal Declaration of Human Rights.

Conclusion

In an essay a few years back on Islam and the challenge of democracy, Khaled Abou El Fadl argued that the prospects for a *sustainable* accommodation of Islam and democracy will remain slim until sound religious arguments in support of democracy and human rights are formulated by leading Islamic jurists and then accepted by the broader Muslim public.[60] In his remarks, El Fadl also implied that at present no such systematic integration of Islam and democracy has been attempted. This latter assessment is almost certainly too dire. Indonesia's state Islamic universities, Iran's dissident democrats, and scholars like Abdullahi Ahmed An-Na'im, Abdulaziz Sachedina, and Abdolkarim Soroush, among others, have made impressive efforts to provide systematic Islamic rationales for democracy and civic freedom.[61] More generally, surveys of Muslim public opinion like those discussed in this chapter indicate that citizens in most (but not all) Muslim-majority countries embrace democratic principles while still grappling with the question of how to accommodate those principles to Islam.

In a more limited sense, however, El Fadl's basic intuition seems correct. Sustainable democracy and the strengthening of human rights in the Muslim world will not just depend on the usual balances of power in state and civil society highlighted in Western theories of democratization. The accommodation of democracy and human rights schemes in the Muslim world will also involve something more specifically religious and cultural: a new and no doubt variegated accommodation of those democratic schemes to Muslim notions of the shari`a and public ethics.

As noted at the beginning of this chapter, for most of Muslim history, the general public was unfamiliar with all but the general outlines of the shari`a. Unlettered Muslims often assumed that their customs were consistent with the shari`a and left the matter there. Some even mocked religious scholars for their allegedly arid approach to the divine.[62] Rulers issued edicts in such a way that they effectively circumscribed any detailed extension of the law to matters of governance. Religious scholars resigned themselves to the fact either by assuming that the edicts were consistent with the spirit of God's law or that the contemporary age was such that the law's brilliance could never again fully shine. Under these circumstances, the law's comprehensiveness was piously affirmed but, in matters of everyday governance, kept conveniently theoretical.

During the first years of the postcolonial era, the circumscription of the law remained the rule rather than the exception, as secular nationalist polities prevailed in most Muslim lands. However, in the aftermath of the great urbanization, mass education, and Islamic resurgence of the late twentieth century, the overwhelming majority of citizens in Muslim-majority lands concluded that "religion is an important part of their daily lives."[63] Many also concluded that the shari`a happens to be an important part of religion.

By remarkable historical coincidence, the Islamic resurgence got under way just a decade or two prior to the diffusion of human rights and democratic discourses into Muslim lands in the 1980s and 1990s. The coincidence assured that inasmuch as those latter ideals took root, they did so in soils recently enriched by religious idealism and organizations. For a few conservative Islamists, Islam and the shari`a were understood as so fixed and complete as to obviate any need for democracy and human rights. Some among these conservative activists launched campaigns similar to those seen in Egypt, Indonesia, or post-Saddam Iraq, in which calls for the implementation of the shari`a have been used to silence those who aspire to civic and democratic rights.

As the broader historical overview provided in this chapter makes clear, however, these activists understand shari`a in a manner profoundly different from that of classical Islam. The neoconservatives identify Islam as an objective "system" (*minhaj*) that contains specific, positive, and practical prescriptions intended to cover all aspects of life.[64] Their vision of the law is not that of Islamic tradition but modeled on Western positive law, complete with canons, casebooks, and state-administered courts. The old idea of the law's comprehensiveness has been fused with a new *étatizing* modernism to create a model for a totalizing state and legal culture unlike any ever seen in Islamic history.[65]

As in today's Iraq, Iran, and Afghanistan, among other countries, neoconservative proponents of the shari`a may try to assail the supporters of democracy and human rights, alleging that the democrats' views on women, non-Muslims, and religious freedom are antithetical to Islam. However, the neoconservatives are but one current in the broader Muslim world, and in most countries they remain a minority. As surveys and ethnographic studies have shown, the populace in most countries sees democracy and human rights as compatible with Islam. At the same time, most of these Muslim democrats are not secular liberals. Although they have not yet reached an "overlapping consensus"[66] on just how government should accommodate God's law, most seem committed to a third way between theocracy and secular democracy, in which "religious principles and democratic values coexist."[67] The coexistence will no doubt continue to generate heated debates for many years to come, especially on matters related to religious freedom, women and non-Muslims, and the role of the state in the promotion of ethico-religious values.[68]

What, then, does all this mean for the future of human rights and democratization in the Muslim world? On one hand, support for democracy and some features of human rights schemes may continue to grow. Where this occurs, it will be the result not of Western hegemony but of the simple social fact that many Muslims see democracy and human rights as useful instruments for constraining an otherwise aggressive state or "uncivil" elements in society. At the same time, a conservative minority will continue to challenge the legitimacy of democracy and human rights schemes. The resulting contest will not pit neoconservative Islamists against secularist liberals intent on the privatization of religion. The Muslim world's democrats are for the most part *religious* democrats, not secularists. The more common contest, then, will pit those who believe God's law is fixed, comprehensive, and specific against ethical substantivists who, although not denying the shari`a's urgency, insist that it is best understood in terms of its higher principles (*maqasid al-shari`a*) and general ethical guidance.[69]

Where Muslim-majority countries take steps toward a fuller embrace of democracy and human rights, we should not be surprised to see that issues relating to women, non-Muslims, and freedom of religion remain points of contention. More generally, even where democratic views prevail, we are likely to see significant public support for the "un-liberal" idea that religious ethics are not purely private matters, and the state should not be neutral on the promotion of the public good, not least of all as it relates to Islam. In terms of public culture, religion, and state, the Muslim world's emerging democracies are likely to be *religious* democracies.

The idea of nonsecular democracy, of course, alarms some proponents of human rights and Western liberal democracy. However, rather than contradicting democracy, the accommodation reached in such a Muslim polity is perhaps better viewed as a consequence of the deepening reach of democratization into Muslim societies. Contrary to some earlier theories of modernization, the globalization of democracy and human rights schemes does not augur a homogenizing end of history. It is instead inaugurating a new and more differentiated phase in modern democracy's cross-cultural development.

NOTES

I want to thank Thomas Banchoff, Robert Wuthnow, and Andrée Feillard for comments on early drafts of this paper. Responsibility for its content is, of course, my own.

1. Samuel P. Huntington, *The Clash of Civilizations and the Remaking of the World Order* (New York: Simon & Schuster, 1996).

2. Ann Elizabeth Mayer, *Islam and Human Rights*, 4th ed. (Boulder: Westview, 2007), 77–97.

3. See Pippa Norris and Ronald Inglehart, *Sacred and Secular: Religion and Politics Worldwide* (Cambridge: Cambridge University Press, 2004), 134; John L. Esposito and Dalia Mogahed, *Who Speaks for Islam: What a Billion Muslims Really Think* (New York: Gallup Press, 2007); cf. Moataz A. Fattah, *Democratic Values in the Muslim World* (Boulder: Lynne Reinner, 2006), 3–4; and Riaz Hassan, *Faithlines: Muslim Conceptions of Islam and Society* (Karachi: Oxford University Press, 2002).

4. For an overview of democratic trends in the Middle East, see Larry Diamond, Marc F. Plattner, and Daniel Brumberg, eds., *Islam and Democracy in the Middle East* (Baltimore and London: Johns Hopkins University Press, 2003). For a comparative study that demonstrates that although there may be a "democracy deficit" in Arab-majority countries, there is none in the thirty-one non-Arab Muslim-majority countries; see Alfred Stepan and Graeme B. Robertson, "An 'Arab' More than a 'Muslim' Electoral Gap," *Journal of Democracy* 14:3 (July 2003): 30–44.

5. Brinkley Messick, *The Calligraphic State: Textual Domination and History in a Muslim Society* (Berkeley and London: University of California Press, 1993), 3.

6. Cf. Marshall G. S. Hodgson, *The Venture of Islam*, 3 vols. (Chicago: University of Chicago Press), 1: 315–58.

7. For a comparison of the Islamic legal tradition with the Western common law and civil law traditions, see H. Patrick Glenn, *Legal Traditions of the World* (New York: Oxford University Press, 2000).

8. The figure of 500 is itself a matter of dispute. Other scholars of the law put the number of verses with legally relevant commentary at just 350.

9. Wael B. Hallaq, *A History of Islamic Legal Theories: An Introduction to Sunnî usûl al-fiqh* (Cambridge: Cambridge University Press, 1997), 10.

10. On Shi'ism see, for example, Moojan Momen, *An Introduction to Shi'i Islam: The History and Doctrines of Twelver Shi'ism* (New Haven and London: Yale University Press, 1985), 185–89.

11. Hallaq, *A History of Islamic Legal Theories*, 5.

12. Hodgson, *The Venture of Islam*, Vol. 1, 315.

13. See George Makdisi, *The Rise of Colleges: Institutions of Learning in Islam and the West* (Edinburgh: University of Edinburgh Press, 1981), 2–4.

14. Sami Zubaida, *Law and Power in the Muslim World* (London: I. B. Tauris, 2003), 2. Not all analysts subscribe to Zubaida's characterization of the shari`a and governance. Noah Feldman has recently suggested that in classical times the scholars' commitment to the law and rulers' willingness to implement the law created an effective "constitutional arrangement" in which the law was "supreme." See Feldman, *The Fall and Rise of the Islamic State* (Princeton: Princeton University Press, 2008), 35.

15. Haim Gerber, *Islamic Law and Culture: 1600–1840* (Leiden: Brill, 1999); Jonathan Berkey, *The Formation of Islam* (Cambridge: Cambridge University Press, 2003), 21; Colin Imber, *The Ottoman Empire, 1300–1600: The Structure of Power* (New York: Palgrave Macmillan, 2002); Zubaida, *Law and Power*, 11.

16. According to the doctrine of *siyasa shar`iyya* ("governance consistent with shari`a"), non-shari`a legislation of this sort was often conceived as having been authorized by religious scholars on the condition that it was based on shari`a principles. In political reality, however, the degree to which religious scholars supervised and authorized such state legislation varied significantly, in a manner that reflected the oscillating balance of power between the state and the scholarly establishment. See Knut S. Vikor, *Between God and the Sultan: A History of Islamic Law* (Oxford: Oxford University Press, 2005), 189–205.

17. Berkey, *The Formation of Islam*, 23; Vikor, *Between God and the Sultan*, 189–93; Zubaida, *Law and Power*, 51–52.

18. Zubaida, *Law and Power*, 52. Vikor adds, however, that this non-shari`a court was nonetheless justified in the public mind as Islamic, on the grounds that the ruler's decisions were "'inspired' by . . . the Shari`a," even if they did not follow the letter of the law. Vikor, *Between God and the Sultan*, 192.

19. Carl Brown, *Religion and State: The Muslim Approach to Politics* (New York: Columbia University Press, 2000), 57.

20. See Henri Laoust, *Essai sur les doctrines sociales et politiques de Taki-d-din Ahmad b. Taimiya* (Cairo: Institut Francais d'Archéologie Orientale, 1939); Emmanuel Sivan, *Radical Islam: Medieval Theology and Modern Politics* (New Haven: Yale University Press, 1985), 94–102.

21. Leila Ahmed, *Women and Gender in Islam: Historical Roots of a Modern Debate* (New Haven: Yale University Press, 1992), 9–25.

22. See Fatima Mernissi, *Women in Islam: An Historical and Theological Enquiry* (Oxford: Basil Blackwell, 1991), 151–53.

23. For examples of the way in which judges' rulings can be informed by local notions of gender, justice, and equity, see Michael G. Peletz, *Islamic Modern: Religious Courts and Cultural Politics in Malaysia* (Princeton: Princeton University Press, 2002), 84–97; and Susan F. Hirsch, *Pronouncing and Persevering: Gender and the Discourses of Disputing in an African Islamic Court* (Chicago: University of Chicago Press, 1998).

24. See Ahmed, *Women and Gender*, 89–207; Yohanan Friedmann Yohanan, *Tolerance and Coercion in Islam: Interfaith Relations in the Muslim Tradition* (Cambridge: Cambridge University Press, 2003); Norani Othman, "Grounding Human Rights

Arguments in Non-Western Cultural Terms: Shari`a and the Citizenship Rights of Women in a Modern Nation-State," IKMAS Working Paper Series, No 10 (Bangi, Malaysia: Malaysian National University, 1997).

25. See Abdullahi Ahmed An-Na'im, *Toward an Islamic Reformation: Civil Liberties, Human Rights, and International Law* (Syracuse: Syracuse University Press, 1990), as well as his more recent, *Islam and the Secular State: Negotiating the Future of Shari`a* (Cambridge: Harvard University Press, 2008); and Mahmoud Mohamed Taha, *The Second Message of Islam* (Syracuse: Syracuse University Press, 1987). On Taha's thought, see Mohamed A. Mahmoud, *Quest for Divinity: A Critical Examination of the Thought of Mahmud Muhammad Taha* (Syracuse: Syracuse University Press, 2007).

26. See Richard W. Bulliet, *Islam: The View from the Edge* (New York: Columbia University Press, 1994), 39; and Friedmann, *Tolerance and Coercion*, 58–74.

27. John F. Richards, *The Mughal Empire* (Cambridge: Cambridge University Press, 1995), 39; Douglas E. Streusand, *The Formation of the Mughal Empire* (Delhi: Oxford University Press, 1989), 28.

28. Anthony Reid, *Southeast Asia in the Age of Commerce, 1450–1680, vol. 2, Expansion and Crisis* (New Haven: Yale University Press, 1993).

29. Friedmann, *Tolerance and Coercion*, 121–59. A particularly infamous incident of antiheretical repression was the execution of the tenth-century mystic al-Hallaj. See Louis Massignon, *Al-Hallâj: Mystic and Martyr*, trans., ed., and abr. Herbert Mason (Princeton: Princeton University Press, 1994).

30. According to some commentators, the capital penalty for apostates did not contradict the Qur'anic injunction against coercion, because apostasy was in fact a matter of political treason, not religion.

31. See Adnan A. Musallam, *From Secularism to Jihad: Sayyid Qutb and the Foundations of Radical Islamism* (Westport: Praeger, 2005); and Vali Seyyed Reza Nasr, *Mawdudi and the Making of Islamic Revivalism* (Oxford: Oxford University Press, 1996).

32. Mayer, *Islam and Human Rights*, 123–24.

33. See "Excerpts from the Constitution of the Islamic Republic of Iran," Appendix A in Ann Elizabeth Mayer, *Islam and Human Rights: Tradition and Politics*, 4th ed. (Boulder: Westview 2007), 206, 209.

34. Mayer, *Islam and Human Rights*, 181–84.

35. See, for example, Abdullahi Ahmed An-Na'im, "Shari`a and Islamic Family Law: Transition and Transformation," in *Islamic Family Law in a Changing World: A Global Resource Book*, ed. Abdullahi Ahmed An-Na'im (London: Zed Books), 1–22; John R. Bowen, *Islam, Law and Equality in Indonesia: An Anthropology of Public Reasoning* (Cambridge: Cambridge University Press, 2003), esp. 200–28; and Othman, "Grounding Human Rights Arguments."

36. On the recent but growing incorporation of shari`a into Egyptian state law, see Clark B. Lombardi, *State Law as Islamic Law in Modern Egypt: The Incorporation of the Shari`a into Egyptian Constitutional Law* (Leiden: Brill, 2006).

37. Zubaida, *Law and Power*, 169.

38. See Jamhari and Jajang Jahroni, *Gerakan Salafi Radikal di Indonesia* [Radical Salafi Movements in Indonesia] (Jakarta: Rajawali Press, 2004), 129–60.

39. Robert W. Hefner, "Muslim Democrats and Islamist Violence in Post-Soeharto Indonesia," in *Remaking Muslim Politics: Pluralism, Contestation, Democratization*, ed. Robert W. Hefner (Princeton: Princeton University Press, 2004), 273–301.

40. Michael Cook, *Commanding Right and Forbidding Wrong in Islamic Thought* (Cambridge: Cambridge University Press, 2000), 9.

41. The translated text is from Mayer, *Islam and Human Rights*, Appendix A, 207.

42. Cook, *Commanding Right*, 12.

43. Abdullahi Ahmed An-Na'im, *Islam and the Secular State*, 2, 276.

44. Norris and Inglehart, *Sacred and Secular*; Esposito and Mogahed, *Who Speaks for Islam?*

45. Robert W. Hefner, *Civil Islam: Muslims and Democratization in Indonesia* (Princeton: Princeton University Press, 2000).

46. See Azyumardi Azra, Dina Afrianty, and Robert W. Hefner, "Pesantren and Madrasa: Muslim Schools and National Ideals in Indonesia," in *Schooling Islam: The Culture and Politics of Modern Muslim Education*, ed. Robert W. Hefner and Muhammad Qasim Zaman (Princeton: Princeton University Press, 2007), 172–98.

47. See Azyumardi Azra et al., "Pesantren and Madrasa"; cf. Kusmana and Yudhi Munadi, *Proses Perubahan IAIN Menjadi UIN Syarif Hidayatullah Jakarta: Rekaman Media Massa* [The process of changing the IAIN into a National Islamic University] (Jakarta: UIN Jakarta Press, 2002).

48. See Fuad Jabali and Jamhari, *IAIN dan Modernisasi Islam di Indonesia* [State Islamic Institutes and the Modernization of Islam in Indonesia] (Jakarta: UIN Jakarta Press, 2002), 114.

49. See An-Na'im *Toward an Islamic Reformation*; and Khaled Abou El Fadl, *Islam and the Challenge of Democracy* (Princeton: Princeton University Press, 2004).

50. Norris and Inglehart, *Sacred and Secular*, 146.

51. On the PKS's appeal, see Edward Aspinall, "Elections and the Normalization of Politics in Indonesia," *South East Asia Research* 13.2 (2005): 117–56.

52. Norris and Inglehart, *Sacred and Secular*, 146.

53. Norris and Inglehart, *Sacred and Secular*, 139.

54. Esposito and Mogahed, *Who Speaks for Islam?* 63.

55. Esposito and Mogahed, *Who Speaks for Islam?* 35.

56. Esposito and Mogahed, *Who Speaks for Islam?* xiii.

57. Esposito and Mogahed, *Who Speaks for Islam?* 48.

58. Esposito and Mogahed, *Who Speaks for Islam?* 35, 63.

59. The quotation is from Stathis N. Kalyvas, "Unsecular Politics and Religious Mobilization: Beyond Christian Democracy," in *European Christian Democracy: Historical Legacies and Comparative Perspectives*, ed. Thomas Kselman and Joseph A. Buttigieg (Notre Dame: University of Notre Dame Press, 2003), 294.

60. Khaled Abou El Fadl, *Islam and the Challenge*.

61. Abdullahi Ahmed An-Na'im, *Islam and the Secular State*; Ziba Mir-Hosseini and Richard Tapper, *Islam and Democracy in Iran: Eshkevari and the Quest for Reform* (London: I. B. Tauris, 2006); Abdolkarim Soroush, *Reason, Freedom, and Democracy in Islam* (Oxford: Oxford University Press, 2000); Abdulaziz Sachedina, *The Islamic Roots of Democratic Pluralism* (Oxford: Oxford University Press, 2001).

62. For a late medieval case in point, see Jonathan Berkey, *The Transmission of Knowledge in Medieval Cairo: A Social History of Islamic Education* (Princeton: Princeton University Press, 1992), 244.

63. Esposito and Mogahed, *Who Speaks for Islam?* 47.

64. See Dale F. Eickelman and James Piscatori, *Muslim Politics* (Princeton: Princeton University Press, 1996), 42.

65. On the postcolonial origins of the idea of the Islamic state, see also Abdullahi Ahmed An-Na'im, *Islam and the Secular State*, 20.

66. The phrase is John Rawls's; see his *The Law of Peoples, with "The Idea of Public Reason Revisited"* (Cambridge: Harvard University Press, 1999), 144.

67. Esposito and Mogahed, *Who Speaks for Islam?* 63.

68. Hallaq, *A History*, 207–54; Knut S. Vikor, *Between God and the Sultan: A History of Islamic Law* (Oxford: Oxford University Press, 2005), 257–79.

69. For examples of democratic substantivism, see Sachedina, *The Islamic Roots*; Khaled Abou El Fadl, *The Place of Tolerance in Islam* (Boston: Beacon Press, 2002); Nurcholish Madjid, "Islamic Roots of Modern Pluralism: Indonesian Experience," *Studia Islamika: Indonesian Journal for Islamic Studies* 1:1 (1994): 55–77; Soroush, *Reason, Freedom, and Democracy in Islam*; and Greg Barton, "Neo-Modernism: A Vital Synthesis of Traditionalist and Modernist Islamic Thought in Indonesia," *Studia Islamika: Indonesian Journal for Islamic Studies* 2:3 (1995): 1–71.

BIBLIOGRAPHY

Ahmed, Leila. *Women and Gender in Islam: Historical Roots of a Modern Debate*. New Haven: Yale University Press, 1992.

An-Na'im, Abdullahi Ahmed. *Toward an Islamic Reformation: Civil Liberties, Human Rights, and International Law*. Syracuse: Syracuse University Press, 1990.

———. "Shari'a and Islamic Family Law: Transition and Transformation." In *Islamic Family Law in a Changing World: A Global Resource Book*, ed. Abdullahi Ahmed An-Na'im, 1–22. London: Zed Books, 2002.

———. *Islam and the Secular State: Negotiating the Future of Shari'a*. Cambridge: Harvard University Press, 2008.

Aspinall, Edward. "Elections and the Normalization of Politics in Indonesia." *South East Asia Research* 13:2 (2005): 117–56.

Azra, Azyumardi, Dina Afrianty, and Robert W. Hefner. "Pesantren and Madrasa: Muslim Schools and National Ideals in Indonesia." In *Schooling Islam: The Culture and Politics of Modern Muslim Education*, ed. Robert W. Hefner and Muhammad Qasim Zaman, 172–98. Princeton: Princeton University Press, 2007.

Barton, Greg. "Neo-Modernism: A Vital Synthesis of Traditionalist and Modernist Islamic Thought in Indonesia." *Studia Islamika: Indonesian Journal for Islamic Studies* 2:3 (1995): 1–71.

Berkey, Jonathan. *The Transmission of Knowledge in Medieval Cairo: A Social History of Islamic Education*. Princeton: Princeton University Press, 1992.

———. *The Formation of Islam*. Cambridge: Cambridge University Press, 2003.

Bowen, John R. *Islam, Law and Equality in Indonesia: An Anthropology of Public Reasoning*. Cambridge: Cambridge University Press, 2003.

Brown, Carl. *Religion and State: The Muslim Approach to Politics.* New York: Columbia University Press, 2000.

Bulliet, Richard W. *Islam: The View from the Edge.* New York: Columbia University Press, 1994.

Cook, Michael. *Commanding Right and Forbidding Wrong in Islamic Thought.* Cambridge: Cambridge University Press, 2000.

Diamond, Larry, Marc F. Plattner, and Daniel Brumberg, eds. *Islam and Democracy in the Middle East.* Baltimore and London: Johns Hopkins University Press, 2003.

Eickelman, Dale F. "Mass Higher Education and the Religious Imagination in Contemporary Arab Societies." *American Ethnologist* 19:4 (1992): 1–13.

Eickelman, Dale F. and James Piscatori. *Muslim Politics.* Princeton: Princeton University Press, 1996.

El Fadl, Khaled Abou. *Islam and the Challenge of Democracy.* Princeton: Princeton University Press, 2004.

———. *The Place of Tolerance in Islam.* Boston: Beacon Press, 2002.

Esposito, John L. and Dalia Mogahed. *Who Speaks for Islam? What a Billion Muslims Really Think.* New York: Gallup Press, 2007.

Fattah, Moataz A. *Democratic Values in the Muslim World.* Boulder: Lynne Reinner, 2006.

Feldman, Noah. *The Fall and Rise of the Islamic State.* Princeton: Princeton University Press, 2008.

Friedmann, Yohanan. *Tolerance and Coercion in Islam: Interfaith Relations in the Muslim Tradition.* Cambridge: Cambridge University Press, 2003.

Gerber, Haim. *Islamic Law and Culture: 1600–1840.* Leiden: Brill, 1999.

Glenn, H. Patrick. *Legal Traditions of the World: Sustainable Diversity in Law.* New York: Oxford University Press, 2000.

Hallaq, Wael B. *A History of Islamic Legal Theories: An Introduction to Sunnî usul al fiqh.* Cambridge: Cambridge University Press, 1997.

Hassan, Riaz. *Faithlines: Muslim Conceptions of Islam and Society.* Karachi: Oxford University Press, 2002.

Hefner, Robert W. *Civil Islam: Muslims and Democratization in Indonesia.* Princeton: Princeton University Press, 2000.

———. "Civic Pluralism Denied? The New Media and Jihadi Violence in Indonesia." In *New Media in the Muslim World: The Emerging Public Sphere,* ed. Dale F. Eickelman and Jon W. Anderson, 158–79. Bloomington: Indiana University Press, 2003.

———. "Muslim Democrats and Islamist Violence in Post-Soeharto Indonesia." In *Remaking Muslim Politics: Pluralism, Contestation, Democratization,* ed. Robert W. Hefner, 273–301. Princeton: Princeton University Press, 2005.

Hefner, Robert W. and Muhammad Qasim Zaman, eds. *Schooling Islam: The Culture and Politics of Modern Muslim Education.* Princeton: Princeton University Press, 2007.

Hirsch, Susan F. *Pronouncing and Persevering: Gender and the Discourses of Disputing in an African Islamic Court.* Chicago: University of Chicago Press, 1998.

Hodgson, Marshall G. S. *The Venture of Islam.* 3 vols. Chicago: University of Chicago Press, 1974.

Huntington, Samuel P. *The Clash of Civilizations and the Remaking of the World Order.* New York: Simon & Schuster, 1996.

Imber, Colin. *The Ottoman Empire, 1300–1600: The Structure of Power*. New York: Palgrave Macmillan, 2002.

Jabali, Fuad and Jamhari. *IAIN dan Modernisasi Islam di Indonesia* [State Islamic Institutes and the Modernization of Islam in Indonesia]. Jakarta: UIN Jakarta Press, 2002.

Jamhari and Jajang Jahroni. *Gerakan Salafi Radikal di Indonesia* [Radical Salafi Movements in Indonesia]. Jakarta: Rajawali Press, 2004.

Kalyvas, Stathis N. "Unsecular Politics and Religious Mobilization: Beyond Christian Democracy." In *European Christian Democracy: Historical Legacies and Comparative Perspectives*, ed. Thomas Kselman and Joseph A. Buttigieg, 293–320. Notre Dame: University of Notre Dame Press, 2003.

Kusmana and Yudhi Munadi. *Proses Perubahan IAIN Menjadi UIN Syarif Hidayatullah Jakarta: Rekaman Media Massa* [The Process of Changing the IAIN into a National Islamic University]. Jakarta: UIN Jakarta Press, 2002.

Laoust, Henri. *Éssai sur les doctrines sociales et politiques de Taki-d-din Ahmad b. Taimiya*. Cairo: Institut Francais d'Archéologie Orientale, 1939.

Lombardi, Clark B. *State Law as Islamic Law in Modern Egypt: The Incorporation of the Sharî'a into Egyptian Constitutional Law*. Leiden: Brill, 2006.

Madjid, Nurcholish. "Islamic Roots of Modern Pluralism: Indonesian Experience." *Studia Islamika: Indonesian Journal for Islamic Studies* 1:1 (1994): 55–77.

Mahmoud, Mohamed A. *Quest for Divinity: A Critical Examination of the Thought of Mahmud Muhammad Taha*. Syracuse: Syracuse University Press, 2007.

Makdisi, George. *The Rise of Colleges: Institutions of Learning in Islam and the West*. Edinburgh: University of Edinburgh Press, 1981.

Massignon, Louis. *Al-Hallâj: Mystic and Martyr*, trans., ed., and abr. Herbert Mason. Princeton: Princeton University Press, 1994.

Mayer, Ann Elizabeth. *Islam and Human Rights*. 4th ed. Boulder: Westview, 2007.

Meeker Michael E. "The New Muslim Intellectuals in the Republic of Turkey." In *Islam in Modern Turkey: Religion, Politics and Literature in a Secular State*, ed. Richard Tapper, 189–219. London: I. B. Tauris, 1991.

Mernissi, Fatima. *Women in Islam: An Historical and Theological Enquiry*. Oxford: Basil Blackwell, 1991.

Messick, Brinkley. *The Calligraphic State: Textual Domination and History in a Muslim Society*. Berkeley: University of California Press, 1993.

Mir-Hosseini, Ziba and Richard Tapper. *Islam and Democracy in Iran: Eshkevari and the Quest for Reform*. London: I. B. Tauris, 2006.

Musallam, Adnan A. *From Secularism to Jihad: Sayyid Qutb and the Foundations of Radical Islamism*. Westport: Praeger, 2005.

Nasr, Seyyed Vali Reza. *Mawdudi and the Making of Islamic Revivalism*. Oxford: Oxford University Press, 1996.

Norris, Pippa and Ronald Inglehart. *Sacred and Secular: Religion and Politics Worldwide*. Cambridge: Cambridge University Press, 2004.

Othman, Norani. "Grounding Human Rights Arguments in Non-Western Cultural Terms: Shari`a and the Citizenship Rights of Women in a Modern Nation-State." IKMAS Working Paper Series, No 10. Bangi, Malaysia: Malaysian National University, 1997.

Peletz, Michael G. *Islamic Modern: Religious Courts and Cultural Politics in Malaysia*. Princeton: Princeton University Press, 2003.

Rawls, John. *The Law of Peoples, with "The Idea of Public Reason Revisited."* Cambridge: Harvard University Press, 1999.

Reid, Anthony. *Southeast Asia in the Age of Commerce, 1450–1680, Vol. 2, Expansion and Crisis*. New Haven: Yale University Press, 1993.

Richards, John F. *The Mughal Empire*. Cambridge: Cambridge University Press, 1995.

Sachedina, Abdulaziz. *The Islamic Roots of Democratic Pluralism*. Oxford: Oxford University Press, 2001.

Schacht, Joseph. *An Introduction to Islamic Law*. Oxford: Oxford University Press, 1964.

Shamsul A.B. "Identity Construction, Nation Formation, and Islamic Revivalism in Malaysia." In *Islam in an Era of Nation-States: Politics and Religious Renewal in Muslim Southeast Asia*, ed. Robert W. Hefner and Patricia W. Horvatich, 207–27. Honolulu: University of Hawaii Press, 1997.

Sivan, Emmanuel. *Radical Islam: Medieval Theology and Modern Politics*. New Haven: Yale University Press, 1985.

Soroush, Abdolkarim. *Reason, Freedom, and Democracy in Islam*. Oxford: Oxford University Press, 2000.

Stepan, Alfred and Graeme B. Robertson. "An 'Arab' More than a 'Muslim' Electoral Gap." *Journal of Democracy* 14:3 (July 2003): 30–44.

Streusand, Douglas E. *The Formation of the Mughal Empire*. Delhi: Oxford University Press, 1989.

Taha, Mahmoud Mohamed. *The Second Message of Islam*. Syracuse: Syracuse University Press, 1987.

Tamimi, Azzam S. *Rachid Ghannouchi: A Democrat within Islamism*. Oxford: Oxford University Press, 2001.

Vikor, Knut S. *Between God and the Sultan: A History of Islamic Law*. Oxford: Oxford University Press, 2005.

Zubaida, Sami. *Law and Power in the Islamic World*. London: I. B. Tauris, 2003

4

Muslims, Human Rights, and Women's Rights

Yvonne Yazbeck Haddad

In the aftermath of September 11, 2001, the administration of President George W. Bush utilized the concept of the "miserable" condition of Muslim women as part of the propaganda for war. It highlighted the oppression of women by the Taliban, a particularly pernicious interpretation of Islam, in justifying a military intervention that would liberate Afghani women from their degrading condition. The war was cast as an effort to bring both democracy and civilization to a despotic and uncivilized Muslim nation—and to free its women in the process. As First Lady Laura Bush put it in a November 2001 radio address, "the fight against terrorism is also a fight for the rights and dignity of women."[1] Over the decade that followed, U.S. leaders, media, and public opinion continually identified the oppression of women and the denial of their human rights with Islamic militancy, extremism, jihadism, and "Islamofascism."

The widespread view that the war in Afghanistan had a righteous cause—namely, the liberation or "empowerment" of Muslim women—harkened back to the justification of the Barbary Wars of the early nineteenth century. It also conjured up images of the French invasion of Algeria, which was justified as a "civilizing mission," and the British colonization of Asia and Africa under the banner of the "white man's burden." For over a century, Orientalist scholars, Christian missionaries, and colonial bureaucrats had tended to fault Islam as the cause of the backwardness of Muslim societies, affirming the importance of emulating European models of political, cultural, economic, and social organization, including more "enlightened" attitudes toward women.[2]

Over the past century, this condescending attitude toward Islam in general and its treatment of women in particular has sparked a defensive reaction. An extensive literature declares Islam innocent of all accusations of complicity in the decline of Muslim-majority nations and attacks the discourse of universal human rights as an extension of centuries-old stereotypes nurtured in the West that ascribe superiority to Western over Islamic values, particularly with regard to women.[3] While some Muslim secularists have appropriated and advocated Western values, traditionalist scholars teaching at Islamic schools of higher learning, as well as Islamist members of the Muslim Brotherhood of the Arab world and the Jamaati Islami of South Asia, have produced literature affirming that Islam itself pioneered many of the values and virtues touted by the West. In defending Islam against its detractors, they have turned the accusations on their head. If Muslim-majority nations are weak and cannot defend themselves against an intrusive and violent West, according to this literature, it is because they have deviated from the true path of Islam. If their societies are underdeveloped, it is because the secularists have led them away from the source of their strength. Only a return to the core values of the faith can guarantee their revival.[4]

The fact that Western political, religious, and scholarly leaders have for over a century championed change in Muslim women's lives is the backdrop for the wary Muslim response to Western conceptions of human rights and women's rights. For every criticism of Islam voiced by Westerners, Muslims have fashioned a counter-argument in defense of Muslim womanhood. For every stereotype spun by Orientalists and Christian missionaries, Muslims created an Islamic prototype. The Islamic literature varies in approach: it is apologetic, dialogical, defensive, or combative in nature. It includes traditional voices and a new range of feminist perspectives. Overall, it rejects the Western paradigm of the "Muslim woman" and posits a positive counter-model, one that affirms that Western norms debase women while Islam has liberated them.

This chapter analyzes Muslim responses to Western discourse on human rights and women's rights in Muslim societies, with a particular emphasis on the enduring legacy of colonialism and its effects. It first examines debates about the role of women among Muslim scholars, moving from secular modernizers to their opponents among traditionalists and to a new generation of Islamic feminists. The chapter then traces the status of women in post-independence Muslim-majority nations, with a focus on the Arab world. It describes the causes and consequences of Islamization from the 1980s onward and the articulation of Muslim understanding of human rights through official declarations. A final section provides examples of three prominent national and transnational Muslim women's organizations engaged in the struggle for practical improvements of the status of women in the contemporary context of globalization.

Muslim Human Rights and Women's Rights

The Western concept of human rights does not accord automatically with the traditional interpretation of the Qur'an, the premodern Islamic juridical and theological discourse, or the Islamic cultural worldview. The Qur'an has no concept of human rights. The word *haqq*, close to the English "duty," is one of the names of God. It connotes ultimate reality, truth, justice, duty, and obligation to God. The Western idea of individual human entitlement to rights is alien to traditional Islamic thought, since Islam recognizes human responsibilities and duties rather than rights. The individual has duties toward God, *haqq Allah*, and to the community, *haqq al-nas*.[5] Legal rights, *al-huquq al-shar`iya*, are derived from the shari`a, or divine law. They are considered religious rights to be guaranteed by the state.[6] Rights are not the prerogatives of individuals, although all Muslims are obliged to take into consideration the rights of others. Man, from this perspective, is not born free but, as Ahmad Moussali puts it, "is born to be free from whims, instincts, and desires through proper shouldering of responsibility toward himself, the community and humankind."[7] The struggle to balance the discrepancies between the culture of duties and the culture of rights has challenged individual scholars to attempt to locate human rights in the Qur'an and the Hadith (sayings and narratives by and about the Prophet Muhammad).

The issue of women's rights has long been a focus of efforts to think through the meaning of human rights within the Muslim tradition. Women's liberation has been a topic of contention between Western nations and Muslims since the outset of the colonial era. It became the battleground for the hearts and minds of Muslims at the turn of the twentieth century, when it was used by colonial rulers in collusion with Christian missionaries as the means of transforming Islamic society. Women were selected as the primary instrument of change, the vulnerable point through which to penetrate the edifice of Islam. Many in the West believed that if transformed, Muslim women would help bring the system down.

The Western challenge generated a profound sense of dissatisfaction among Muslim intellectuals who began to promote change in the conditions that obtained in traditional Islamic societies, including the condition of women. In contrast to the West, however, regardless of the ideological commitment of the defender of women's rights (whether nationalist, socialist, or Islamist) and regardless of the gender, the liberation of women was generally seen as part of a general struggle against colonial oppression.[8] By 1919, Muslim women were marching in the streets of Cairo, Damascus, and Jerusalem against foreign occupation. Some even joined in the war of resistance in Syria, Palestine, and Algeria. As one Egyptian author argued, promoting the liberation of women "was out of the desire to elevate the level of the nation and to place it in its respective place among the nations." He told women, "Your goal in your efforts must be the same goal we strove for the day we called for liberation: to work for Egypt, not for men alone and not for women alone."[9]

Among the early promoters of women's rights at the turn of the twentieth century was Qasim Amin, who posited European culture and American women in particular as worthy of emulation. He described the situation that prevailed in Egypt as

the disease which we must proceed to remedy; there is no medicine but that we teach our children about western civilization, its sources, branches and heritage. When the time comes—and we hope that it isn't too far off—the truth will be manifested before our eyes, shining brightly as the sun. Then we will know the value of western civilization and will realize that it is impossible to reform what is around us if it is not founded on modern scientific knowledge.[10]

Amin's books *The Liberation of Woman* (1899) and *The New Woman* (1900) generated heated intellectual debates in the Egyptian press that focused on the issue of change and whether the laws regulating society are to be conceived as part of culture and therefore subject to change or whether they are the core of teachings on the foundation of an Islamic order.[11] Participants to the debate tended to agree that the Islamic message is immutable and valid for all time and place. They differed on whether the social teachings of Islam are to be adapted to fit the time and the place—a position of socialists and nationalists—or whether the teachings of the Qur'an and the Hadith as interpreted by the early Islamic schools of law remain prototypes valid for eternity, not subject to any change, and therefore must be imposed on society—the Islamist position.[12]

Amin's work generated a sustained critical response among the traditionalists. They argued that while Islam affirms gender equality, there are verses in the Qur'an that have historically been seen as legislating gender relationships in marriage, assigning to the husband the right to demand sex, initiate divorce, and to restrict his wife's activities outside the home. Traditionalists insisted that the husband should have the authority in the family unit, arguing that the issue is not equality, which is affirmed in the Qur'an, but one of equity based on the biologically determined roles each plays in the family unit. In the process they invented a new model of the "Muslim woman," one that confirms traditional teachings that women are innately lacking in intellectual capacity or are contrarian. At the same time, other traditionalists ascribed to women a new role, one that has been embraced by Islamists: that of preservers and maintainers of Islamic culture. This model was promoted as one that Muslims can be proud of and one that they would have to strive to realize as the way to successfully realize true Islamic norms. This ideal of womanhood was not formulated by authors who are eager to emulate Western norms; it is based on a reinterpretation of the foundational principles of Islam, posited as the initial intent of the Qur'an.

These and other responses to Amin's writings have often extolled the Islamic approach to women and women's rights as superior to that of the West. This literature affirms that Islam pioneered the elevation of the status of women by guaranteeing her the right to live, to be educated, to inherit, to own and dispose of her property, to maintain her maiden name, and to carry out business transactions.[13] The authors generally affirm that there is no fundamental distinction in the Qur'an between women and men before Allah, that both will be held accountable and punished or rewarded on the Day of Judgment, and that many verses address both sexes together. However, when it comes to the family code, the several verses that have been traditionally interpreted as sanctioning gender hierarchies and legitimating a treatment that recognized gender distinction are to be respected.[14]

Islamic feminism represents a further development in the debate over the religious grounds for women's equality in the Muslim world. The term was coined in the 1990s, in the wake of the Fourth United Nations World Conference on Women in Beijing held in 1995, with its emphasis on women's rights as human rights. Islamic feminism is led by urban educated women who in the age of communication are able to disseminate information to each another and to read each others' work, despite the fact that some live in diaspora in the West while others live in Muslim-majority states. None of these women has traditional training in Islamic sciences. All are Western-educated. They are all fighting patriarchal and misogynistic interpretations of the Qur'an.

The Western media tend to ascribe Islamic feminism to secular women from Muslim backgrounds who attack Islam as a religion that subjugates and abuses women. They are delighted to feature the works of Wafa Sultan; Tasleema Nasreen; Ayaan Hirsi Ali, author of *Infidel*; and Irshad Manji, author of the provocative book, *The Trouble with Islam: A Muslim's Call to Reform in Her Faith*, in which she contends that the Qur'an may not be completely "God-authored."[15] While other Muslim women may agree with their assessment of current conditions of women in certain countries, they reject buying into the Western critique and blaming the religion for the shortcomings of Muslim society. The overt attack on Islam and Muslims put forward by outspoken secular feminist Muslims sends traditionalists and Islamists into a defensive mode. They particularly dislike the assumption that to levy a critique on Islam means that one has renounced her faith. These women are then portrayed as the product of liberation, a prototype of what more freedom for women would produce—namely self-flagellating, self-hating Muslims.

Used by its detractors as an epithet, Islamic feminism refers to thinkers who advocate women's rights from within the Islamic tradition but depart from the conservative traditionalist discourse. Leading Islamic feminist scholars include Asma Barlas, Amina Wadud, Nimat Hafiz Barazngi, and Riffat Hassan in the United States and Jawad and Mona Siddiqi in the United Kingdom. They are engaged in fashioning an attractive twenty-first century, Islamically validated, modern way of life as an alternative to secular liberal feminism that they see subordinate to the changing whims and values of a West that has declared war on Islamic cultural values and traditions. They attempt to ground their gender paradigms of equality and liberation in the Qur'an, the Hadith, and the example of the first women of Islam. They address social issues from within the heritage and seek to reconcile Islam and feminism, examining the traditional narratives of Islamic history, legal precedents, and court decisions in order to make this history accessible to the general public.

Haifaa Jawad of the University of Birmingham, for example, contends that Islam grants women "broad social, political and economic rights, education and training rights and work opportunity rights." These include the right to independent ownership, the right to respect, the right to marry whoever one likes and to end an unsuccessful marriage, the right to education, the right to inherit, and the right to keep one's own identity.[16] It also includes the right to sexual pleasure.[17] Islam also grants women political rights: the right to vote, to run for political office, and to participate more broadly in public affairs.[18] According to Jawad, at the time of Prophet Muhammad women were allowed to pray with the men in congregational prayers at the mosque and to act as *imams* for women (and sometimes for both sexes in their household). They participated in military campaigns and had the authority to grant protection and asylum to fugitives. They were also allowed to devote themselves to the study of religious sciences, theology, the Qur'an, and the traditions.[19]

Other Islamic feminist scholars have echoed these themes, countering the traditional subordinate view of a woman's role with a strong case for full equality based on the Qur'an and the sayings of the Prophet.[20] They, too, have scoured the narratives of the life of the Prophet Muhammad for parallels to be promoted as models of liberation, challenging patriarchal exegesis and in the process reconciling the religion with feminism. In the process, these scholars offer new interpretations of the verses that have historically been used by traditionalists to affirm gender hierarchies. They insist on the core teaching of the Qur'an that justice and compassion are the essential characteristics of God and thus are incumbent on human beings. God's justice would not tolerate unjust (and unequal) treatment of women. They point to the fact that the Qur'an clearly states that man and woman were created from one soul, and they maintain that therefore the Qur'an does not sanction the submission of one gender to the other.[21] Some argue that equality is the essential core of the Islamic faith; it is the essence of *tawhid*, the oneness of God and the oneness of the *umma*, the worldwide community of Muslims.[22] Still others ground equality in the concept of *khilafa*, God's commission to humans, both male and female, to be his agents on earth, to nurture creation, to construct a civilization, and to bring forth a just society.[23]

Muslim feminists have not restricted their criticism to traditional and conservative male Muslim interpretations of their role. They also criticize Muslim secularists who are perceived as having surrendered Islamic values and embraced Western definitions of human rights. Secularists are accused of being so eager for change that they have decided to break away from tradition and fully embrace Western ideals. According to Jawad, their conviction of the superiority of Western values leads them to espouse an untenable position that sees the Western model as the only viable way "to the extent that they believe that to be Western is to be free and to be Muslim is to be a slave." The West is depicted as having launched a "crusade against anything to do with Islam." Secularists are accused of being complicit in the bitter Western attacks and of ridiculing the very foundations of Islam. They have mocked its principles and culture, in the process alienating themselves from their culture. They have become self-righteous and set themselves as "superior to 'ordinary' Muslim women."[24]

Women's Rights and the Nation-State

These three waves of reflection on human rights and women's rights—Amin's pro-Western approach, traditionalist responses, and Islamic feminism—developed in the context of far-reaching national and international political changes that have shaped the rights and condition of Muslim women in practice.

The liberation from colonial rule in the Arab Middle East brought about major changes in the role of Muslim women and their status in society. The most important area of change has been the phenomenal growth in the number of girls attending schools. While colonial bureaucrats criticized traditional Islamic education wherever they ruled, they opened a limited number of modern educational institutions in key cities to provide a cadre of male employees to sustain the colonial bureaucracies. It is only after independence that Muslim-majority nations initiated universal education and made it available to girls at all levels. The governments also became the primary employers of educated women. However, despite these advances, a 1999 United Nations Development Program (UNDP) Human Development Report found that most women continue to be subject to inequality, discrimination, violence, and abuse at home and in the labor force. A subsequent UNDP 2005 report on women's development in the Arab world recognized some progress but noted that Arab countries continue to lag behind other nations.[25]

Another change that came with independence was the growth in the number of women interested in women's rights. The leadership of the early women's organizations had been predominantly from upper and middle-class women focused on philanthropy and social work and the importance of education for women and lifting the face veil. With independence and the opening up of educational opportunities, a new generation of women from the middle and lower middle classes began to seek recognition as leaders. The focus was on Arab unity now that the colonial powers had carved nation-states out of the Arab world. As early as 1944, when the first Arab Feminist Congress met, it had demanded social, political, and economic rights. With the transition to independence, the struggle turned to achieving the right to vote and run for office, to work and receive equal pay for equal work, and to pass their citizenship to their husbands and children.

Governments caught up in the struggle for Arab unity and the consolidation of domestic rule did not ignore women and their interests. Burdened with social, political, and economic problems, festering in the wake of liberation from occupation, they co-opted the existing women's organizations or sponsored new ones. They determined the ideology, chose the leadership, and set the agenda. Such organizations became part of the national development projects but were generally placed under the Ministry of Culture. By 1975, the Year of the Woman, fifteen out of twenty-one Arab nations had an official feminist movement whose goals, agenda, and activities were planned and supervised by the state. "Woman's liberation" had become part of official state bureaucracy.[26] Meanwhile, the international forums on women's rights continued to demand change in women's status, which the governments generally ignored. To agitate for additional rights was to potentially threaten the hegemony of the state and its security—especially when causes were backed not just by domestic groups but also by nongovernmental organizations (NGOs), international organizations, and governments.

There were some real gains for women as early as the 1960s. For example, women in Sudan won the right to vote in 1964 and the Sudanese Women's Union turned its focus to laws that affect working women, seeking equal pay, maternity leave, and pensions. Women in other countries, however, generally had less success. The Yemeni Women's Union was organized in 1968 in the south but had no presence in the north. In Palestine in 1967 Fatah formed the General Union of Palestine Women to work in the resistance movement, concentrating on health, political education, and covert operations.[27] Women's gains in Turkey, Tunisia, and Iran came by decree of the ruling autocrats. In Iran, for example, women got the vote in 1963 and soon thereafter some successfully ran for political office.

One hurdle to further advancement in many countries was constitutional; most post-independence constitutions restricted some rights available to women in Islam under the shari`a. Relying on Western models brought a further patriarchal infusion of gender discrimination in certain areas of the law as European constitutions banned discrimination based on race, language, and religious affiliation, but not gender. The Turkish constitution, for example, affirms the equality of all citizens but prohibits women from becoming judges or performing military service. In this case, legal discrimination was derived from the civil code adopted from Switzerland in 1926 and based also on the Italian penal code of 1889.

Jordan also provides another example of legal constraints and evolution. Under Muslim law, a husband's absence for over a year without providing for his wife gives her the right to seek the dissolution of the marriage. Jordan's constitution, modeled after European law, does not allow for such a right. In 1985, the feminists of Jordan sought a change in the law citing the fact that many young men marry and leave their wives behind to work in the Gulf countries. There many get married and raise a family while ignoring the wife left behind. The Jordanian feminists sought the implementation of Islamic law in these cases. The chief Muslim authority of Jordan retorted that he was willing to implement changes only if the feminists accepted all the regulations of the shari`a. They were not allowed to pick and choose. For its part, the Jordanian government has been very supportive of women's issues. It has weighed in against customary law that allows honor killing and resisted the implementation of Islamic law as demanded by Islamist parliamentarians who wanted sex segregation in higher education. The constitution was altered in 1991 to incorporate a guarantee against gender discrimination.[28]

Feminists have not shied away from criticizing Muslim governments for affirming equal rights while in reality the personal status laws enforce inequality between males and females. In most Muslim-majority states, girls continue to be married off with no say in the matter. Polygyny is allowed except in Tunisia and Turkey, although in rural Turkey men have been known to contract additional marriages not sanctioned by the state but performed by the village imam. These wives and their children are not recognized by the state. Feminists argue that the rights of the first wife are violated when a husband is allowed to marry a second wife without the permission of the first. All Arab states allow the husband to divorce his wife for no cause. However, if the wife wants a divorce, she needs to seek permission from the court. The Muslim husband can forbid his wife to work, to leave the house, or to travel, while the wife has no such rights over him. The woman inherits half the man's portion.[29]

Not surprisingly, many Muslim-majority countries that have ratified the 1979 UN Convention on the Elimination of All Forms of Discrimination against Women (CEDAW) have also expressed reservations concerning some of its articles perceived to be in conflict with the shari`a. These reservations are used as a shield against criticism. However, Muslim women members of the committee that oversees the application of CEDAW have not refrained from raising probing questions when investigating the records of Muslim governments. They accuse them of hypocrisy because in many cases while constitutions guarantee equality, in reality local governments support discrimination in matters of personal status law.[30]

Islamization and Islamic Human Rights Declarations

Efforts by human rights advocates to invoke international law in support of women's rights in Muslim-majority nations are complicated by two related developments of the past two decades: the Islamization of society and the emergence of state-sponsored international accords outlining an alternative, Islamic conception of human rights.

Since the 1967 Arab-Israeli War, Islamists have been campaigning under the slogan: "Islam is the solution." Islam is promoted as the answer to the creeping decadence of Muslim societies. This approach, widely supported by traditionalists, includes a gender agenda that relegates women to the home. This has been the first order of business wherever Islamists have taken over rule from secularist or leftist countries, as has happened in Iran, Sudan, and Pakistan. Islamizing society appears to bring about setbacks to individual rights as well as gender segregation, head covering, and restrictions on women entering public space. It is worth noting that gender restrictions under such circumstances and the repression of human rights and women's rights in the name of Islam has been rejected as un-Islamic not only by feminists but, more importantly, by prominent male religious leaders, as was the case in Sudan in 1977 and in Iran in 1980.[31]

The Iranian revolution of 1979 had a great impact on Islamization of the Muslim world. It was perceived as demonstrating that belief in Islam can defeat the greatest of tyrants and their American supporters. It heralded a setback for Westernized and liberal women. The government dismissed professional women so as to eradicate "Western" influence; they imposed the veil, which has become the symbol of Islam. They repealed the Family Protection Act of 1967 and barred women from majoring in certain concentrations in higher education. They restored the male right to arbitrary divorce, polygyny, and temporary marriage, and reduced alimony obligations.

With increased Islamization, those who had called for the liberation of women to achieve parity with Western societies and adhere to international norms found themselves increasingly marginalized and dismissed as agents of Western interests or as self-hating Muslims. A few began to question the secular strategies being used to achieve national liberation, especially since the nation-states began to accommodate Islamist demands to maintain their own power. The Islamization of society spurred the growth of Islamic feminism, outlined earlier, that opposed both traditional restrictions on women and a secular, Western approach to human rights. For example, anthropologist Fatima Mernissi, one of the most important feminists of the 1980s and a founding member of the Moroccan Organization for Human Rights, noted that it was necessary for women to revise their strategy and personally engage the Islamic texts that for centuries have been the prerogative of male interpretation. She began to study and write about the traditions to bring about change from within.[32] Mernissi has influenced other scholars who have become convinced that it is crucial for women to participate in the creation of Islamic knowledge.

Coteries of female scholars throughout the Muslim world are currently engaged in similar activist scholarship. They are affirming women's right to define themselves with full awareness that any attempt to change the patriarchal structure and the traditionalist interpretations made in the name of Islam has to come from within and not simply be adopted from the West. This work, informed both by reflection on the Islamic tradition and on the exigencies of women's struggles for equality in Muslim societies, encompasses scholar-activists at colleges and universities in the West. For example, Amira al-Azhari Sonbol at Georgetown University has focused her research on court documents and archives, demonstrating that Islamic law was flexible and in many cases favored women's full participation in the economy. Her research challenges the dogmatic interpretations of jurists by documenting the legal opinions of judges and how they organized and supervised the implementation of Islamic law in society. She demonstrated that legal reforms initiated during the colonial period were inspired by nineteenth-century Western views of gender. Her scholarship as well as that of other Muslim women challenges Western presuppositions that modernization and Westernization are necessarily good for women, while Islamic law is archaic, repressive, and impedes progress. In the process, it makes room for a progressive interpretation of Islamic law.[33]

Islamization has sparked a further development that has also complicated efforts to develop a women's rights agenda within Islam: the emergence of an official state-sponsored and international discourse about Islamic human rights. When the United Nations first issued the Universal Declaration of Human Rights (UNDH) in 1948, most Muslim-majority nations had not gained their independence and thus were not members of the organization. Of those who were, Saudi Arabia did not endorse the Declaration on the grounds that it was against the shari`a as it gave the right to an individual to change his or her religion. These reservations have not, however, kept forty-eight out of the fifty-seven nations that now constitute the Organization of the Islamic Conference (OIC) from ratifying many of the international human rights instruments issued by the United Nations. In so doing they have registered their reservations about specific articles that are not in agreement with the shari`a, dismissing them as "manifestations of cultural imperialism and Euro-centrism."[34]

Much Islamic literature regarding United Nations conventions assesses human rights as a Western, secular concept grounded in the European philosophical heritage and inspired by the French and American revolutions. It also takes note of the Marxist challenge to these rights on the grounds that they are capitalist in conception and do not guarantee social and economic rights. Over the postwar period, Muslims began to reflect and search for Islamic alternatives. These Muslim writings point to inconsistencies in the Western claim to universal validity for its understanding of human rights, seeing it as part of cold war propaganda. Islam has its own system of rights, they argued, one that is neither Western nor Eastern, but grounded in the revelation of God valid for all humanity throughout time.[35]

A major impediment to the general acceptance, adoption, and implementation of the Universal Declaration of Human Rights in the Muslim world is the fact that the West has used human rights and democracy as a wedge to interfere and control the politics as well as the economies of the third world.[36] The weakness of the indigenous movement for human rights can also be attributed to the fact that the membership of these organizations is elitist, Western oriented, and generally funded by foreign agencies or governments. In some cases, foreign funding has led to unhealthy competition among organizations and individuals, which at times has bred dependency. Local groups begin to serve the interests of the funding agencies, promoting their goals, ideas, and programs, and therefore failing to engage the majority of the population. Furthermore, at times foreign organizations have funded individuals who have no credentials in conducting the research, thus raising questions about the whole endeavor. It is also true that politicians who are out of favor with national governments have joined the ranks of human rights organizations and use these organizations as a way to continue their political activity, resulting in some cases in competition and rivalry.[37]

Some Muslim observers have also noted that the deterioration in the human rights situation in Muslim-majority countries and the growth of interest in specifically Islamic approaches to human rights can be traced to the 1967 Israeli preemptive strike against Egypt, Jordan, and Syria. The Arab defeat marked the beginning of the retreat from liberal policies, including modernization and Westernization. The defeat sparked a self-assessment of the causes of Arab failure and raised questions about political, economic, and social developments as well as cultural and intellectual production, a trend reinforced by the string of crises that followed, including the 1973 October War, the controversy surrounding the 1978 Camp David Accords, the Iranian Revolution of 1979, the failed Olso Accords of 1993, the Gulf War of 1991 and the U.S.-led invasions of Afghanistan and Iraq in the new century.[38]

By the 1980s, with the growth of Islamic identity in various parts of the Muslim world, the formation of the Islamic Republic of Iran, and the rise in the importance and wealth of Gulf nations, the various Islamic governments felt it necessary to issue the Universal Islamic Declaration of Human Rights (UIDHR) at a United Nations Educational, Scientific, and Cultural Organization (UNESCO) meeting in 1981. Its Islamic legitimacy was bolstered by the fact that each of its twenty-three articles was supported by reference to Qur'anic verses or the Hadith, demonstrating not only that Islam has its own foundation for human rights but also that it pioneered such rights. The Foreword to the Declaration states:

> Islam gave humanity an ideal code of human rights 1400 hundred years ago. The purpose of these rights is to confer honor on humanity and to eliminate exploitation, oppression and injustice. Human rights in Islam are deeply rooted in the conviction that God, and God alone, is the author of Law and the source of all human rights. Given the divine origin, no leader, no government, no assembly or other authority can restrict, abrogate or violate in any manner the rights conferred by God.[39]

The end of the cold war reinforced these efforts to articulate an Islamic understanding of human rights at the global level. With the fall of the Soviet Union, some policy makers in the United States began to proclaim the United States as the unipolar power in the world. At the same time, a growing number of American leaders were associating Islam with terrorism. The pressure on Muslim-majority nations to accept Western hegemony increased, as their ability to maneuver between the two powers seeking to dominate the world during the cold war ended. Leaders began to respond to the growing Islamization of their populations, raising hopes that Islamic civilization might be a viable alternative to that of the West. In 1990, the Cairo Declaration of Human Rights in Islam (CDHRI) was signed by forty-five Muslim-majority nations.

The American intervention in the "liberation of Kuwait" (the Gulf War of 1991), gave a further impetus to this growing wave of Islamization. In the two decades since, Western nations have been seen as hijacking the Security Council to make it an instrument of American policy, particularly under the presidency of George W. Bush, whose invasions of Afghanistan and Iraq and "war on terror" were widely perceived as an assault on the Muslim world. Many see the politicization of human rights as manifested in the double standards of the Security Council resolutions, the muffled criticism of the United States and Israel, and the uneven implementation of UN resolutions. According to Nader Fergany, a founding member of both the Arab and the Egyptian Organizations for Human Rights, this "blatant hypocrisy is a serious obstacle to the respect of human rights in the Arab world."[40]

For Islamic feminists, successive international Islamic human rights instruments were a mixed blessing. While the Cairo declaration asserted the equality of all human beings, it also affirmed the supremacy of the shari`a and thus reiterated the traditional role of women as dependents of their husbands. The declaration recognizes a woman as a "civil entity" who has rights and duties, but identifies men as responsible for "the support and welfare of the family."[41] At the dawn of a new century, Islamic feminists find themselves caught between a traditionalist discourse that subordinates women and a

Western human rights discourse viewed as alien and discredited. For many, the way out of this dilemma is not deeper theological and philosophical reflection as much as broader social and political engagement. Islam informs both their broad vision of human rights and the passion with which they seek to remedy abuses in practices.

Islamic Feminism in the Age of Globalization

In the age of globalization, Islamic feminism has become a transnational endeavor of individuals as well as local, national, and international organizations engaged in the effort to create a more just and equal Islamic society. Taking advantage of foreign and international funds available for development as well as the Internet and other means of instant communication, women have stepped up to try to create a corps of Muslim activists in various parts of the Muslim world. Their goal is also to put pressure on the various governments to uphold the values they espouse about equality. They emphasize that women should be full participants in the public sphere, contributing to the betterment of society and rejecting their relegation to the traditional status of dependents in the family context. They have generally abandoned the efforts of the secular feminists to promote Western values as normative, out of a fear of losing credibility through association with "degenerate Western women" seen daily on television and in the movies.

Several international organizations that support women's rights in Muslim societies have come into existence. Three of the most effective organizations are Women's Learning Partnership for Rights, Development and Peace (WLP); Women Living under Muslim Laws (WLUML); and Sisters in Islam (SIS). These organizations work with local and national groups in creative ways to empower women and change the conditions that obtain in various Muslim-majority nations. Some of the strategies and accomplishments of each are elaborated below.

Women's Learning Partnership (WLP)

The Women's Learning Partnership was founded by Mahnaz Afkhami in 1995; its headquarters are in Bethesda, Maryland, but it operates in eighteen Muslim-majority countries in partnership with autonomous and independent organizations.[42] It takes the Platform for Action of the Fourth World Conference on Women in Beijing as its main point of reference. Afkhami, who had an illustrious career in pre-revolutionary Iran serving as secretary general of the Women's Organization of Iran and as minister of state for Women's Affairs, seeks to enable grassroots populations to understand the universal concepts developed in international forums and incorporate them with indigenous ideas, traditions, myths, and texts. The goal of WLP is to create a generation of women leaders in the global South and teach them the necessary skills to work for human rights and to increase the number of women who participate in decision making in the family. Using the international frameworks for guidance, the organization has a leadership development curriculum available in sixteen languages that is used in training sessions that teach advocacy and networking for NGO leaders. Afkhami is optimistic about the progress that can be made through education. By directing a great deal of effort and attention toward educational institutions, especially for the young, she believes that society can begin to foster open-mindedness and respect for women.[43]

Afkhami also believes that for Muslim societies to accept the changes conceived in international law, they must see them as demonstrably in agreement with and supported by Islamic teachings. She argues that the Qur'an is eternal and mystical and that humans can at best attempt to understand it, but can never comprehend it in its essential form. Therefore, all of historical Islam is mere interpretation. Hierarchical and patriarchal societies have interpreted the Qur'an without women's input. She cites the Qur'an and the Hadith as well as the early heroines of Islam (the Prophet's wives Aisha and Khadija, and his daughter Fatima) to assert that Islam and women's equal rights are not mutually exclusive. On the contrary, she argues that Islam recognizes women as human beings and individuals worthy of all earthly goods and respect.[44]

Afkhami insists that women must work nationally and internationally to foster greater support for their rights within local and transnational organizations. She qualifies her statements by saying that free and open political settings are necessary for such activities to be carried out, that "ideas, structures, and actions that enhance democracy and promote civil society" are needed.[45] Afkhami has been at the forefront in producing important human rights literature to guide activists throughout the Muslim world in their work.[46] She envisions the process of promoting women's human rights to include activities such as legal reform, resistance to extremism, and building an egalitarian civil society. With a methodology informed by cultural sensitivity, she writes that the people to whom the message is addressed "must be able to operate and effect change within the existing cultural, political, and technological environments."[47]

Women's Learning Partnership is involved with national as well as regional networks in Africa, Asia, and the Middle East. The organization supports groups seeking legislative and policy change at the national level. Members are engaged in advocacy networking, raising consciousness, education, and leadership development.[48] They also provide support through alerts regarding issues of human rights in an attempt to focus international attention and garner global support for women who are arrested or harassed because of their commitment to human rights or women's rights. An example of their collaborative efforts is their support of the initiative, "Claiming Equal

Citizenship: The Campaign for Arab Women's Rights to Nationality," aimed at gaining rights for citizenship for nonnational spouses and their children. WLP has also condemned the Iranian government's crackdown on civil society and women's rights organizations, and has supported a women's rights advocate in Jordan, as well as the plight of Afghan women and children.[49]

Women Living under Muslim Laws (WLUML)

Women Living under Muslim Laws is a transnational organization with offices in London, Lahore, and Dakar that "provides information, support and a collective space for women whose lives are shaped, conditioned or governed by laws and customs said to derive from Islam." Present in more than seventy countries, the organization has focused its energies on the project of reforming the laws of Muslim-majority states to make them accord with the "spirit of the Qur'an." The organization was founded in 1984 in an effort to preserve women's rights instituted by governments that were increasingly being threatened by the rising tide of Islamization. Nine women from Algeria, Bangladesh, Iran, Morocco, Mauritius, Pakistan, and Tanzania met and decided to oppose Islamic fundamentalism that threatens to revoke gains women have achieved over the years. At the time they were particularly concerned about the efforts of the newly established Islamic regimes in Iran, Pakistan, and Sudan that were eager to put an Islamic stamp on society by repealing laws favoring women's rights and instituting new restrictions in the name of Islam.

In the decades since, WLUML has opposed the streamlining of laws as promoted by Islamists, maintaining that laws in Muslim-majority countries vary and come from various sources besides religion, such as customary, colonial, and secular law. Challenging the myth of a homogenous "Muslim world," the organization seeks to deconstruct the patriarchal and legal dictates of the *fiqh*, Islamic jurisprudence. Its members are not satisfied with simply making proclamations about the egalitarian and ethical nature of Islam. They back legislation that guards the rights of women as equal citizens in all fields.[50]

At its London conference in 2002 entitled "Warning Signs of Fundamentalism," two leaders, Ayesha Imam and Nira Yuval-Davis, noted that when the conference was first being planned in 1997, they were hoping to issue a warning about fundamentalism and its repercussions for women's rights. By the time it took place in 2002, they were reflecting on an "ongoing" situation.

> Not only had religious and ethnic "fundamentalist" politics recognizably gained power in many more countries (including Nigeria and India), but also, under the guise of a 'global war against terrorism' a new leadership in Washington, DC, controlled by a fundamentalist Christian and nationalist movement, was taking social and political license around the world. Globally the period since 2000 has seen

civil and political rights taken away from larger and larger numbers of people, while the popular appeal of fundamentalist leaders everywhere has been growing.[51]

Particular areas of concern included India, where Hindu women watched with no apparent concern as Muslim women were raped and killed in March 2002, and Rwanda, where Hutu militias were incited by women politicians and journalists to go on their killing rampage. For WLUML leaders, fundamentalist movements, whether through emulation, collaboration, or confrontation, "stoke each other's fires." Whether in Afghanistan or the United States, fundamentalists share a vision that sees women's sexuality as the underlying cause of immorality and press for "patriarchal controls over women and their sexuality, with women constructed primarily as the domestic mother and wife, subordinate to men."[52] Based on their various experiences, the women at the London conference identified spheres of resistance to encroaching fundamentalisms, including the utilization of education, law, media, and political organizations.

The conference also underscored the importance of collaboration with other organizations and the identification of best practices. One example was BAOBAB for Women's Human Rights in Nigeria, a grassroots organization that reported that while working within the Muslim discourse is important, it is also crucial to work with other communities and build solidarity. Its membership includes Christians who work together with Muslims to negotiate women's rights in a shari`a environment, especially after it was instituted in the northern areas of Nigeria in 1999. In the *zina* (adultery) cases of Safiyya Husseini and Amina Lawal, who had been sentenced to death by stoning by the lower court, BAOBAB's lawyers were able to marshal arguments culled from the vast sources of Islamic law and gain their acquittal. In the process, they demonstrated "the capacity of Islamic jurisprudence to protect the rights of the accused, including women."[53] They considered Western pressures counterproductive.

Sisters in Islam

Founded by Zainah Anwar, a member of the Malaysian Human Rights Commission and the author of *Islamic Revivalism in Malaysia*, Sisters in Islam (SIS) was organized as a response to the Islamization policies of the 1990s that increased segregation in society.[54] Under political pressure, the Malaysian government sought to appease Islamic groups such as Parti Islam Se Malaysia (PAS) by reintroducing Islamic laws. SIS literature takes note that part of the Islamization project was a retrogression in which women were restricted to the traditional roles of wife and mother. As a consequence, Malaysian society began to experience an "erosion of women's freedom and rights in the areas of law and access to justice in the Shari`a system, social rights in the family, dress, public participation and socialization between the sexes."[55]

SIS membership is composed primarily of professional women who are committed to the promotion of the rights of women within the framework of Islam "based on the principles of equality, justice and freedom enjoined in the Qur'an."[56] They believe that the Qur'an revolutionized the role of women fourteen centuries ago. The models they aspire to follow are the Mothers of the Believers: the wives of the Prophet and the first converts to Islam. The goal is to "promote and develop a framework of women's rights in Islam, which takes into consideration women's experiences and realities; to eliminate injustice and discrimination against women by changing practices and values that regard women as inferior to men; to create public awareness, and reform laws and policies, on issues of equality, justice, freedom, dignity and democracy in Islam."[57] They believe that "Islam does not enforce the oppression of women and denial of their basic rights of equality and human dignity." Oppression has occurred because men have had exclusive control of interpreting the Qur'anic texts, and they have used religion to "justify cultural practices and values that regard women as inferior and subordinate to men."[58]

Sisters in Islam has campaigned with support from other women's groups against the revision of Malaysian law which relegalized polygyny for Muslims. Countering the view that polygyny would help "reduce social ills such as illicit affairs, prostitution and the birth of illegitimate children," SIS argued that polygyny would aggravate social ills, especially among children who grow up in such households. They further maintained that the question that should be addressed is whether polygyny should still be continued under the Islamic family law for Muslims, bearing in mind that the true purpose of the Qur'anic injunctions relating to polygyny is "clearly restrictive rather than permissive." Aware that there is a mistaken belief that polygyny is "a sacred male right guaranteed by Islam," they quote Muslim male authorities that support their arguments.[59]

In support of this campaign, SIS published a sample marriage contract in the hope that young people contemplating marriage would take it as a model. The contract recognizes that marriage is between two individuals (not parents or guardians), that it is based on love, and that the relationship should be free from abuse and be sustained by mutual respect, openness, and honesty. It asserts that both partners have the right to seek employment, to maintain individual banking accounts, and to share domestic responsibilities and that it "will not be the sole duty of either spouse to maintain an attractive domestic environment or to provide meals and, in general, to maintain the household." Furthermore, "Sexual relations will be consensual at all times and will, like all other relations in the marriage be based on mutual trust and respect." The man allows his wife the right to seek divorce and both have the right to apply *faskh* (annulment) in case of physical abuse, infidelity, and verbal and emotional abuse. The framework is put forward as a model for Islamic family law in Malaysia.[60]

Advocacy work of Sisters in Islam includes submitting memoranda to government officials and agencies seeking the appointment of women judges in shari`a courts, as well as an emphasis on "the right of women to equal guardianship" on issues pertaining to domestic violence, polygamy, and reform of Islamic law. SIS also seeks a public airing of the issues by engaging the media and alerting the public to the alternate interpretations available to Muslims. Its members are not afraid to speak out on issues including Islamist efforts to institute traditional *hudud* laws, which do not accept women as witnesses in the case of rape. One result has been withering attacks from the PAS party, which has demanded—unsuccessfully—that SIS drop the term "Islam" from its title. For the Sisters of Islam, in order to combine Muslim ideas and practices with human rights, "Muslims must first accept equality for women and not see women as second class citizens."[61]

Conclusion

Contradictory trends have shaped the global politics of human rights as it pertains to the status of women in the Muslim world. The policies of the Bush administration, including its "war on terror" and wars in Afghanistan and Iraq, have discredited American and international campaigns for human rights and democratization in the eyes of most Muslims around the world. At the same time, in an era of globalization, advocacy for human rights by individuals and organizations—local, national, and transnational—has increased the consciousness of human rights in the Muslim world. In poll after poll, Muslims favor the principles of democracy and protection for human rights by wide majorities. A 2002 report by well-known Arab intellectuals acknowledged deep-seated human rights deficits in many Muslim-majority nations, pointing to the gap between discourse that upholds the sacredness of human rights and the silence about their violation in the shadow of the "autocratic power of the state."[62]

The relationship between women's rights and Islam, this chapter has argued, cannot be understood apart from this broader historical, geopolitical, and political context. Many Muslims see the Western push for the liberation of women from Islam in Afghanistan and elsewhere as a hypocritical effort to undermine Islamic civilization and assert strategic dominance. For traditionalists, a response that reiterates a conservative understanding of women's roles is appropriate. For Islamic feminists, who share the critique of Western imperialism, the Qur'an and the early Muslim tradition provide strong support, both for human rights and for full women's equality. In the context of Islamization of society and politics over the last two decades, the cause of women's rights has suffered some setbacks in Muslim-majority countries. But a resurgence of Islam in society has also spurred a creative rethinking of women's rights as human rights independent of—but not necessarily opposed to—the international human rights norms sustained and promoted by the West.

The strongest evidence for the vitality of the Islamic feminist response is the activity of nongovernmental organizations working at the national and transnational level to secure greater economic, cultural, and social rights for women. The examples of Women's Learning Partnership, Women Living under Muslim Laws, and Sisters in Islam underscore the importance of mobilization at the grass roots, which takes the ideas of Islamic feminism as a starting point for the formation of coalitions for social change. Through outreach to the media and the public and concerted lobbying efforts, these groups have been able to achieve greater social protections for women and to broaden the scope for women's political participation. They have pressed the case for women's rights as human rights, drawing creatively on the resources of their tradition.

The fact that foreign governments and organizations continue to monitor human rights and women's rights violations is a double-edged sword. While such monitoring has been important in alleviating injustice in high-visibility cases, it has also generated a backlash. The Western concern for women under Islam, whether through programs and projects sponsored by the United States Agency for International Development, the United Nations Development Program, European agencies, or the World Bank, remains widely perceived as part of a centuries-old Western obsession to liberate Muslim women *from* Islam. The onus has fallen on the women of Islam to continue to strive to gain their rights without appearing to be ventriloquists of Western values or stooges of Western interests.

Looking to the future, the questions raised by Islamic feminists will shape the intersection of religion and the global politics of human rights in decisive ways. Why should Western feminism serve as the universal model of what it means to be a liberated woman? Will Muslim women be allowed to have a genuine Muslim model of women's rights and human rights? What would such a model look like given the great cultural, political, and ideological diversity among Muslims? Could this model be celebrated? And are international women's organizations willing to make room for the kind of real pluralism that such different understandings of human rights and women's rights must entail?

NOTES

1. Laura Bush, "Radio Address by Laura Bush to the Nation" (radio address, Crawford, Texas, November 17, 2001), http://avalon.law.yale.edu/september11/fl_001.asp.

2. See, for example, Bernard Lewis, *What Went Wrong? The Clash between Islam and Modernity in the Middle East* (New York: HarperCollins, 2005); Maina Chawla

Singh, *Gender, Religion, and "Heathen Lands"—American Missionary Woman in South Asia (1860–1940s)* (New York: Garland, 2000); and Annie Van Summer and Samuel M. Zwemer, *Our Moslem Sisters: A Cry in Need from Lands of Darkness Interpreted by Those Who Heard It* (New York: F. H. Revell, 1907).

3. For critical overviews of Western depictions of women under Islam, see Linda Steet, *Veils and Daggers: A Century of National Geographic's Representation of the Arab World* (Philadelphia: Temple University Press, 1998); Mohja Kahf, *Western Representations of the Muslim Woman: From Termagant to Odalisque* (Austin: University of Texas Press, 1999); Rana Kabbani, *Imperial Fictions—Europe's Myths of the Orient* (Bloomington: University of Indiana Press, 1994); and Lamia Ben Youssef Zayzafoon, *The Production of the Muslim Woman: Negotiating Text, History and Ideology* (Lanham: Lexington Books, 2005).

4. See, for example, Ahmad `Abd al-`Aziz al-Hasin, *al-Mar'ah al-Muslimah Amam al-Tahaddiyat* (al-Qasim: Daar al-Bukhari, 1406H [1985]); Al-Sayid Ahmad Faraj, *al-Mu'amarah `Ala al-Mar'ah al-Muslimah* (al-Mansura: Dar al-Wafa', 1411H [1990]); `Abd al-Qadir Ahmad `Abd al-Qadir, *al-Gharah `Ala al-Usrah al-Muslimah* (Cairo: al-Mukhtar al-Islami, 1991).

5. Bassam Tibi, "Islamic Sharia, Human Rights and International Relations," in *Islamic Law Reform and Human Rights: Challenges and Rejoinders*, ed. T. Lundholm and K. Vogt (Copenhagen: Nordic Human Rights Publications, 1993), 86–87. See also Muhammad Fathi `Uthman, *Huquq Allah bayn al-Shari`a al-Islamiyah wa al-Fikr al-Qanuni al-Gharbi* (Beirut: Dar al-Shuruq, 1982), 29–36.

6. Ahmad S. Moussalli, *The Islamic Quest for Democracy, Pluralism and Human Rights* (Gainesville: University Press of Florida, 2001), 126; `Abd al-Latif bin Sa`id al-Ghamidi, *Huquq al-Insan fi al-Islam* (Riyad: Nayif Arab Academy, 2000), 36–44.

7. Moussalli, *The Islamic Quest*, 127. See also *Huquq al-Insan fi al-Mamlakah al-`Arabiyyah al-Su`udiyyah* (Cairo: Gulf Center for Strategic Studies, 2001), 25–27.

8. Yvonne Yazbeck Haddad, "Islam, Women and Revolution in Twentieth-Century Arab Thought," in *Women, Religion and Social Change*, ed. Yvonne Yazbeck Haddad and Ellison Banks Findley (Albany: State University of New York Press, 1985), 279.

9. `Abd al-Hamid Hamdi, "Al-Yawm Ja'a Dawrukum," *Bint al-Nil* 7 (June 1946): 4, quoted in Haddad, "Islam, Women and Revolution," 279.

10. Qasim Amin, *al-Mar'ah al-Jadidah*, quoted in Muhammad `Abd al-Hakim and Mahmud Muhammad al-Jawhari, *Al-Akhawat al-Muslimat was Bina' al-Usrah al-Qur'aniyah* (Alexandria: Dar al-Da'wa, 1980), 250–51.

11. Qasim Amin, *The Liberation of Women and The New Woman*, trans. Samiha Sidhom Peterson (Cairo: American University in Cairo Press, 2000); *al-Mar'ah al-Jadidah* (Cairo: al-Majlis al-A'la li'l-Thaqafah, 1999).

12. For a look at some of the debates on the issue of the liberation of women, see Mukhtar al-Tuhami, *Thalath Ma`arik Fikriyah* (Cairo: Dar Ma'mun li al-Tiba'ah, 1976), 5–50.

13. See, for example, Muhammad `Izzat Darwazah, *al-Mar'ah fi al-Qur'an wa al-Sunnah* (Beirut: Dar al-Fikr, 1967), 15ff; Muhammad `Atiyyah al-Abrashi, *Makanat al-Mar'ah fi al-Islam* (Cairo: Dar al-Ma`arif, 1970), 7–35; Al-Bahi al-Khuli, *al-Islam wa Qadaya al-Mar'ah al-Mu`asirah* (Kuwait: Dar al-Tawzi' `wa'l-Nashr, 1970), 10–27;

Abu Radwan b. al-Sanusi Zaghlul, *al-Mar'ah bayn al-hijab wa al-Sufur* (Beirut: Dar al-Qalam, 1967), 13–16.

14. Abdullahi Ahmed An-Naim, *Towards an Islamic Reformation: Civil Liberties, Human Rights, and International Law* (Syracuse: Syracuse University Press, 1990), 39.

15. See, for example, Ayaan Hirsi Ali, *Infidel* (New York: Simon and Schuster Adult Publishing Group, 2008); and Irshad Manji, *The Trouble with Islam: A Muslim's Call to Reform in Her Faith* (New York: St. Martin's Press, 2005).

16. Haifaa A. Jawad, *The Rights of Women in Islam* (London: Macmillan, 1998), 7.

17. The Prophet Muhammad is reported to have taught: "When one of you copulates with his wife, let him not rush away from her, having attained his own climax, until she is satisfied." Ibid., 10.

18. Ibid., 10.

19. Ibid., 14.

20. Riffat Hassan, "Human Rights in the Qur'anic Perspective," in *Windows of Faith: Muslim Women Scholar-Activists in North America*, ed. Gisela Webb (Syracuse: Syracuse University Press, 2000), 241–48; Riffat Hassan, "Muslim Feminist Hermeneutics," in *In Our Own Voices*, ed. Rosemary Skinner Keller and Rosemary Radford Reuthe (San Francisco: Harper, 1995), 455–59; Hassan, "On Human Rights and the Qur'anic Perspective," in *Human Rights in Religious Traditions*, ed. Arlene Swidler (New York: Pilgrim Press, 1982); Asma Barlas, *Believing Women in Islam. Understanding Patriarchal Interpretations of the Qur'an* (Austin: University of Texas Press, 2002); Amina Wadud, *Qur'an and Woman: Reading the Sacred Text from a Woman's Perspective*, 2nd edition (New York: Oxford University Press, 1999); Nimat Hafez Barazangi, *Woman's Identity and the Qur'an: A New Reading* (Gainesville: University Press of Florida, 2004).

21. Hassan, "Muslim Feminist Hermeneutics," 455–59.

22. Azizah al-Hibri, "An Introduction to Muslim Women's Rights," in *Windows of Faith: Muslim Women Scholars Activists in North America*, ed. Gisela Webb (Syracuse: Syracuse University Press, 2000), 51–71; Barlas, *Believing Women in Islam*.

23. Barazangi, *Woman's Identity and the Qur'an: A New Reading*.

24. Jawad, *The Rights of Women in Islam*, 98.

25. United Nations Development Program, *The Arab Human Development Report 2005: Towards the Rise of Women in the Arab World* (New York: UNDP Regional Bureau for Arab Studies, 2006).

26. For a detailed study, see Haddad, "Islam, Women and Revolution," 275–306.

27. Carolyn Fluehr-Lobban, "The Political Mobilization of Women in the Arab World," in *Women in Contemporary Muslim Societies*, ed. Jane Smith (Lewisburg: Bucknell University Press, 1980), 235–52, quotation on 241.

28. Laurie A. Brand, "Women and State in Jordan: Inclusion or Exclusion?" in *Islam, Gender and Social Change*, ed. Yvonne Yazbeck Haddad and John L. Esposito (New York: Oxford University Press, 1998), 106.

29. Sami Awad al-Dhib, *Huquq al-Insan `Ind al-Muslimin wa-al-Masihiyin wa-al-Yahud* (Kuwait: Sharikat al-Rubay`an li'l Nashr wa'l Tawzi', 1998), 24–25.

30. For more information on the reservations entered by Muslim-majority states, see Shaheen Sardar Ali, *A Comparative Study of the United Nations Convention on the Elimination of All Forms of Discrimination against Women: Islamic Laws and the Laws of*

Pakistan (Peshawar: Shaheen, 1995); and J. Connors, "The Women's Convention in the Muslim World," in *Feminism and Islam*, ed. Mai Yamani (Reading: Ithaca Press, 1996), 351–66.

31. Ann Elizabeth Mayer, *Islam and Human Rights: Tradition and Politics* (Boulder: Westview, 2007), 34.

32. Fatima Mernissi, *Women and Islam*, trans. M. J. Lakeland (Oxford: Basil Blackwell, 1991).

33. Amira El-Azhary Sonbol, *Beyond the Exotic: Women's Histories in Islamic Societies* (Syracuse, NY: Syracuse University Press, 2005); Sonbol, "Rethinking Women and Islam," in *Daughters of Abraham: Feminist Thought in Judaism, Christianity, and Islam*, ed. Yvonne Yazbeck Haddad and John L. Esposito (Gainesville, Fl: University Press of Florida, 2002), 108–46.

34. Ali, *A Comparative Study*, 1.

35. Muhammad Fathi ʿUthman, *Huquq al-Insan bayna al-Shariʿa al-Islamiyah wa al Fikr al-Qanuni al-Gharbi* (Beirut: Dar al-Shuruq, 1982), 13.

36. Nader Fergany, "Hawl Maʿuqat Intishar Mabadi' Huquq al-Insan wa-Siyanatiha fi al-Watan al-ʿArabi," in *Huquq al-Insan wa Taʾakhur Misr*, ed. Amir Salem (Cairo: Markaz al-Dirasat wa al-Maʿlumat al-Qanuniyah li-Huquq al-Insan, 1993), 150.

37. Ibid., 141–52; Nader Fergany, "The Human Rights Movement in Arab Countries: Problems of Concept, Context and Practice," *Human Rights: Egypt and the Arab World, Cairo Papers in Social Science* 17, no. 3 (Fall 1994): 28–31.

38. Nasr Hamid Abu Zaid, "Huquq al-Mar'ah fi al-Islam," in *Huquq al-Insan fi al-Fikr al-ʿArabi: Dirasat fi al-Nusus*, ed. Salma al-Khadra' al-Jayyusi (Beirut: Markaz Dirasat al-Wahdah al-'Arabiyah, 2002), 222.

39. For a copy of the declaration, see Appendix 1 in Shaheen Sardar Ali, *Gender and Human Rights in Islam and International Law* (The Hague: Kluwer Law International, 2000). See also legal consultant in the Arabic and Islamic Section of the Swiss Institute on Comparative Law, Sami Awad al-Dhib, *Huquq al-Insan 'Ind al-Muslimin wa-al-Masihiyin wa-al-Yahud.*

40. Ibid., 28.

41. The text is available at http://www1.umn.edu/humanrts/instree/cairodeclaration.html.

42. For background, visit Women's Learning Partnership, "About Us," *Women's Learning Partnership homepage*, http://learningpartnership.org/en/about.

43. Mahnaz Afkhami, et al., *Claiming Our Rights: A Manual for Women's Human Rights* (Bethesda, MD: Sisterhood Is Global Institute, 2001).

44. Ibid., 8.

45. Ibid., 5.

46. Mahnaz Afkhami, *Women in Exile* (Charlottesville: University of Virginia Press, 1994); Mahnaz Afkhami and Erika Friedl, eds., *Muslim Women and the Politics of Participation: Implementing the Beijing Platform* (Syracuse: Syracuse University Press, 1997); Mahnaz Afkhami, Ann Eisenberg, and Haleh Vaziri, *Leading to Choices: A Leadership Training Handbook for Women* (Bethesda, MD: Women's Learning Partenership for Rights, Development, and Peace, 2003); Afkhami, ed., *Faith and Freedom: Women's Human Rights in the Middle East* (Syracuse: Syracuse University Press, 1995).

47. Ibid.

48. Ibid.

49. For a list of various alerts, see Women's Learning Partnership, "Advocacy and Networking," *Women's Learning Partnership homepage*, http://www.learningpartner-ship.org/advocacy.

50. For background, see Women Living under Muslim Laws, "About WLUML," *Women Living under Muslim Laws homepage*, http://www.wluml.org/node/5408.

51. Ayesha Imam and Nira Yuval-Davis, "Introduction," in *Warning Signs of Fundamentalism*, ed. Ayesha Imam, Jenny Morgan, and Nira Yuval-Davis (London: WLUML Publications, 2004), ix–xviii.

52. Ibid.

53. Margot Badran, *Feminism beyond East and West: New Gender Talk and Practice in Global Islam* (New Delhi: Global Media Publications, 2007), 73.

54. Zainah Anwar, *Islamic Revivalism in Malysia: Dakwah among the Students*, ed. Pataling Jaya and Selangor Darul Ehsan (Kuala Lumpur: Pelanduk Publications, 1987).

55. Nora Murat, "Advocacy for Change within the Religious Framework," in *Warning Signs of Fundamentalisms: Papers from a Meeting Held by the International Solidarity Network Women Living Under Muslim Laws* (London: WLUML Publications, London 2002), 1.

56. Sisters in Islam, "Mission," *Sisters in Islam homepage*, http://www.sistersinislam.org.my/mission.htm.

57. Ibid.

58. Ibid.

59. Sisters in Islam, "Misunderstanding the Prophet's Sunnah on Polygamy," *Sisters in Islam homepage*, http://www.sistersinislam.org/.

60. Sisters in Islam, "Research," *Sisters in Islam homepage*, http://www.sistersinislam.org.my/research.htm.

61. Ibid.

62. Salma al-Khadra al-Jayyusi, *Huquq al-Insan fi al-Fikr al-`Arabi: Dirasat fi al-Nusus* (Beirut: Markaz Dirasat al-Wahdah al-'Arabiyah, 2002), 11–13.

BIBLIOGRAPHY

`Abd al-Hakim, Muhammad and Mahmud Muhammad al-Jawhari. *Al-Akhawat al-Muslimat was Bina' al-Usrah al-Qur'aniyah*. Alexandria: Dar al-Da`wa, 1980.

`Abd al-Hamid, Hamdi. "Al-Yawm Ja'a Dawrukum." *Bint al-Nil* 7 (June 1946): 4, quoted in Yvonne Yazbeck Haddad, "Islam, Women and Revolution in Twentieth-Century Arab Thought." In *Women, Religion and Social Change*, ed. Yvonne Yazbeck Haddad and Ellison Banks Findley, 275–306. Albany: State University of New York Press, 1985.

`Abd al-Qadir. `Abd al-Qadir Ahmad. *Al-Gharah 'Ala al-Usrah al-Muslimah*. Cairo: al-Mukhtar al-Islami, 1991.

al-Abrashi, Muhammad `Atiyyah. *Makanat al-Mar'ah fi al-Islam*. Cairo: Dar al-Ma`arif, 1970.

Abu Zaid, Nasr Hamid. "Huquq al-Mar'ah fi al-Islam." In *Huquq al-Insan fi al-Fikr al-`Arabi: Dirasat fi al-Nusus*, ed. Salma al-Khadra al-Jayyusi, 221–56. Beirut: Markaz Dirasat al-Wahdah al-`Arabiyah, 2002.

Afkhami, Mahnaz. *Women in Exile*. Charlottesville: University of Virginia Press, 1994.

————, ed. *Faith and Freedom: Women's Human Rights in the Middle East*. Syracuse: Syracuse University Press, 1995.

———— and Erika Friedl, eds. *Muslim Women and the Politics of Participation: Implementing the Beijing Platform*. Syracuse: Syracuse University Press, 1997.

————, Haleh Vaziri, and Yollande Amzallag. *Claiming Our Rights: A Manual for Women's Human Rights*. Bethesda, MD: Sisterhood Is Global Institute, 2001.

Ali, Ayaan Hirsi. *Infidel*. New York: Simon and Schuster Adult Publishing Group, 2008.

Ali, Shaheen Sardar. *A Comparative Study of the United Nations Convention on the Elimination of All Forms of Discrimination against Women: Islamic Laws and the Laws of Pakistan*. Peshawar: Shaheen Printing Press, 1995.

————. *Gender and Human Rights in Islam and International Law*. The Hague: Kluwer Law International, 2000.

Amin, Qasim. "Al-Mar'a al-Jadida." In *Al-Akhawat al-Muslimat wa Bina' al-Usrah al-Qur'aniyyah*, ed. Muhammad 'Abd al-Hakim and Mahmud Muhammad al-Jawhari, 250–51. Alexandria: Dar al-Da'wah, 1980.

————. *al-Mar'ah al-Jadidah*. Cairo: al-Majlis al-A`la li'l-Thaqafah, 1999.

Anwar, Zainah. *Islamic Revivalism in Malaysia: Dakwah among the Students*. Pataling Jaya, Selangor Darul Ehsan, Malaysia: Pelanduk Publications, 1987.

Badran, Margot. *Feminists, Islam, and Nation: Gender and the Making of Modern Egypt*. Princeton: Princeton University Press, 1995.

Barazangi, Nimat Hafez. *Woman's Identity and the Qur'an: A New Reading*. Gainesville: University Press of Florida, 2004.

Barlas, Asma. *"Believing Women" in Islam: Unreading Patriarchal Interpretations of the Qur'an*. Austin: University of Texas Press, 2002.

Brand, Laurie A. "Women and State in Jordan: Inclusion or Exclusion?" In *Islam, Gender and Social Change*, ed. Yvonne Yazbeck Haddad and John L. Esposito, 100–23. New York: Oxford University Press, 1998.

Bush, Laura. "Radio Address by Laura Bush to the Nation." Radio address, Crawford, TX, November 17, 2002, http://avalon.law.yale.edu/sept11/fl_001.asp.

Connors, J. "The Women's Convention in the Muslim World." In *Feminism and Islam*, ed. Mai Yamani, 351–66. Reading: Ithaca Press, 1996.

Darwazah, Muhammad `Izzat. *Al-Mar'ah fi al-Qur'an wa al-Sunnah*. Beirut: Dar al-Fikr, 1967.

al-Dhib, Sami Awad. *Huquq al-Insan `Ind al-Muslimin wa-al-Masihiyin wa-al-Yahud*. Kuwait: Sharikat al-Rubay`an li'l Nashr wa'l Tawzi', 1998.

Faraj, Al-Sayid Ahmad. *Al-Mu'amarah `Ala al-Mar'ah al-Muslimah*. al-Mansurah: Dar al-Wafa', 1411H.

Fergany, Nader. "The Human Rights Movement in Arab Countries: Problems of Concept, Context and Practice." *Human Rights: Egypt and the Arab World, Cairo Papers in Social Science* 17, no. 3 (Fall 1994).

Fluehr-Lobban, Carolyn. "The Political Mobilization of Women in the Arab World." In *Women in Contemporary Muslim Societies*, ed. Jane Smith, 235–52. Lewisburg: Bucknell University Press, 1980.

al-Ghamidi, 'Abd al-Latif bin Sa'id. *Huquq al-Insan fi al-Islam*. Riyad: Nayif Arab Academy, 2000.

Haddad, Yvonne Yazbeck. "Islam, Women and Revolution in Twentieth-Century Arab Thought." In *Women, Religion and Social Change*, ed. Yvonne Yazbeck Haddad and Ellison Banks Findley, 275–306. Albany: State University of New York Press, 1985.

al-Hasin, Ahmad `Abd al-`Aziz. *Al-Mar'ah al-Muslimah Amam al-Tahaddiyat*. Al-Qasim: Daar al-Bukhari, 1006H.

Hassan, Riffat. "Human Rights in the Qur'anic Perspective." In *Windows of Faith: Muslim Women Scholar-Activists in North America*, ed. Gisela Webb, 241–48. Syracuse: Syracuse University Press, 2000.

———. "Muslim Feminist Hermeneutics." In *In Our Own Voices*, ed. Rosemary Skinner Keller and Rosemary Radford Reuther, 455–59. San Francisco: Harper, 1995.

———. "On Human Rights and the Qur'anic Perspective." In *Human Rights in Religious Traditions*, ed. Arlene Swidler. New York: Pilgrim Press, 1982.

al-Hibri, Azizah. "An Introduction to Muslim Women's Rights." In *Windows of Faith: Muslim Women Scholar Activists in North America*, ed. Gisela Webb, 51–71. Syracuse: Syracuse University Press, 2000.

Huquq al-Insan fi al-`Iraq: Min Taqarir al-Munazammah al-`Arabiyah li-Huquq al-Insan. Cairo: al-Zahra' li-al-i'lam, 1990.

Imam, Ayesha and Nira Yuval-Davis. "Introduction." In *Warning Signs of Fundamentalism*, ed. Ayesha Imam, Jenny Morgan, and Nira Yuval-Davis, ix–xviii. London: WLUML Publications, 2004.

Jawad, Haifaa A. *The Rights of Women in Islam*. London: Macmillan, 1998.

al-Jayyusi, Salma al-Khadra, ed. *Huquq al-Insan fi al-Fikr al-`Arabi: Dirasat fi al-Nusus.* Beirut: Markaz Dirasat al-Wahdah al-'Arabiyah, 2002.

Kabbani, Rana. *Imperial Fictions—Europe's Myths of the Orient*. Bloomington: University of Indiana Press, 1994.

Kahf, Mohja. *Western Representations of the Muslim Woman: From Termagant to Odalisque*. Austin: University of Texas Press, 1999.

al-Khuli, Al-Bahi. *Al-Islam wa Qadaya al-Mar'ah al-Mu'asirah*. Kuwait: Dar al-Tawzi` wa'l-Nashr, 1970.

Lewis, Bernard. *What Went Wrong?: The Clash between Islam and Modernity in the Middle East*. New York: HarperCollins, 2005.

Manji, Irshad. *The Trouble with Islam: A Muslim's Call to Reform in Her Faith*. New York: St. Martin's Press, 2005.

Mayer, Ann Elizabeth. *Islam and Human Rights: Tradition and Politics*. Boulder: Westview, 2007.

Mernissi, Fatima. *Women and Islam*, trans. M. J. Lakeland. Oxford: Basil Blackwell, 1991.

Moussalli, Ahmad S. *The Islamic Quest for Democracy, Pluralism and Human Rights*. Gainesville: University Press of Florida, 2001.

Murat, Nora. "Sisters in Islam: Advocacy for Change within the Religious Framework." WHR institutional profiles, 2003, www.whrnet.org/fundamentalisms/docs/doc-wsf-murat-sis-0311.rtf.

An-Naim, Abdullahi Ahmed. *Towards an Islamic Reformation: Civil Liberties, Human Rights, and International Law*. Syracuse: Syracuse University Press, 1990.

Singh, Maina Chawla. *Gender, Religion, and "Heathen Lands"—American Missionary Woman in South Asia (1860–1940s)*. New York: Garland, 2000.

Sonbol, Amira El-Azhary. "Rethinking Women and Islam." In *Daughters of Abraham: Feminist Thought in Judaism, Christianity, and Islam*, ed. Yvonne Yazbeck Haddad and John L. Esposito, 108–46. Gainesville: University Press of Florida, 2002.

Steet, Linda. *Veils and Daggers: A Century of National Geographic's Representation of the Arab World*. Philadelphia: Temple University Press, 1998.

Tibi, Bassam. "Islamic Sharia, Human Rights and International Relations." In *Islamic Law Reform and Human Rights: Challenges and Rejoinders*, ed. T. Lundholm and K. Vogt, 86–87. Copenhagen: Nordic Human Rights Publications, 1993.

United Nations Development Program. *The Arab Human Development Report 2005: Towards the Rise of Women in the Arab World*. New York: UNDP Regional Bureau for Arab States, 2006. http://books.google.com/books?id=bW3dz2EdjzwC&lpg=P P1&dq=Towards%20the%20Rise%20of%20Women%20in%20the%20Arab%20 World&pg=PP2#v=onepage&q=&f=false.

al-Tuhami, Mukhtar. *Thalath Ma`arik Fikriyah*. Cairo: Dar Ma'mun li al-Tiba`ah, 1976.

'Uthman, Muhammad Fathi. *Huquq al-Insan bayna al-Shari`a al-Islamiyah wa al-Fikr al-Qanuni al-Gharbi*. Beirut: Dar al-Shuruq, 1982.

Van Summer, Annie and Samuel M. Zwemer. *Our Moslem Sisters: A Cry in Need from Lands of Darkness Interpreted by Those Who Heard It*. New York: F. H. Revell, 1907.

Wadud, Amina. *Qur'an and Woman: Reading the Sacred Text from a Woman's Perspective*, 2nd edition. New York: Oxford University Press, 1999.

Zayzafoon, Lamia Ben Youssef. *The Production of the Muslim Woman: Negotiating Text, History and Ideology*. Lanham: Lexington Books, 2005.

Zaghlul, Abu Radwan b. al-Sanusi. *Al-Mar'ah bayn al-hijab wa al-Sufur*. Beirut: Dar al-Qalam, 1967.

PART II

Three Regions: Latin America, Sub-Saharan Africa, and Southeast Asia

5

Religious Pluralism, Democracy, and Human Rights in Latin America

Paul Freston

While Latin America is often mentioned as a violator of human rights, it is not usually the focus of discussions regarding the universality or otherwise of such rights and their relationship to diverse religious concepts. If human rights are alleged by some to be an imposition of Christian understandings, that is surely no problem in a region born under the sign of Christendom. In the numerical heartland of Roman Catholicism, there can surely be no concern about whether democracy, wholeheartedly endorsed by the Second Vatican Council, is compatible with God's law. And yet, John Witte tells us that the human rights revolution has triggered an explosion of evangelical and Pentecostal movements and "a new war for souls between indigenous and foreign religious groups" in parts of Latin America.[1] If this were so, it would lead us directly to one of the questions at the center of this volume: whether the religious freedom claims of religious groups with strong transnational and international ties can be construed as the imposition of particular understandings of rights from without. But the indigenous-versus-foreign dimension in Pentecostal growth in the region is minimal. Rather, Pentecostal movements allow us to examine another dimension of human rights: how the growing pluralism of Latin American Christianity affects the relationship of religion to dictatorships, to other religions, and to the escalating problem of urban violence.

Latin America permits an examination of two major Christian traditions, Catholicism and Pentecostalism, in their practical relationship to human rights rather than in their abstract stances. If this approach "from below" is advisable even for the Catholic Church, it is a necessity for Pentecostalism, an often local and lower class phenomenon. Straddling the gap between these two traditions are the historical Protestant churches, including Lutherans, Presbyterians, and Baptists. Taken as a whole, Latin America presents us with a paradox: the apparent inversion of the roles that Catholicism and Protestantism have historically had in relation to human rights in other contexts. But all churches are in flux in the region, including Catholicism which, having made Latin America a major site for implementing the new rights emphasis emanating from Vatican II, has had to adjust to the more complex world of formal democracy and growing religious pluralism that characterize the very unequal and increasingly violent societies of the region.

Latin America has the disadvantages, from the standpoint of human rights, of poverty, massive inequality, and a legacy as a Cold War battleground where rights were often subordinated to geopolitics. The political trajectory of the region is well known—a wave of military regimes in the 1960s and 1970s, followed by a trend to democratization in the 1980s, accompanied by economic liberalization and, in recent years, by the election of a growing number of left or center-left governments. The religious trends are often less familiar. The religious field is fast-changing, resulting in more pluralism within Christianity and a growing pluralism beyond it. For example, the latest census data from Brazil and Chile is remarkably similar: Catholicism in sharp decline at just over 70 percent of the population, Protestants around 15 percent and climbing, and "nonreligious" at 7 percent or 8 percent. The great majority of Protestants are Pentecostals disproportionately concentrated among the lower classes. Catholic-Protestant tension remains high. But this is not a replay of Europe's national reformations; it is the grassroots erosion of a Catholic Christendom by voluntarist evangelicalism.

In the face of the Pentecostal challenge, a tension has emerged between the Catholic Church's support for religious freedom and its desire to hold on to its privileged position in traditionally Catholic areas of the world. This basic tension intersects with a range of other political and social issues with a human rights dimension, including the shape of democratic institutions, and problems of corruption, inequality, and violence. In exploring religion and the politics of human rights in Latin America, this chapter focuses on Brazil, the largest country in the region.

Catholicism and Human Rights: Background to a Great Transformation

In one of the great revolutions of the twentieth century, the Roman Catholic Church at the global level was transformed in the early 1960s into a leading institutional defender of human rights.[2] This culminated a decades-long shift from positions such as that of the Fourth Lateran Council of 1215 that secular authorities ought to exterminate all heretics, and of the encyclical *Singulari Nos* of 1834 which spoke of the "false and absurd maxim, freedom of conscience." In response to the positive experience of the church in the United States and the negative experience under European totalitarianisms, a series of encyclicals between 1961 and 1965 affirmed democracy, human rights, and religious liberty as ideals to be promoted by the church. Since then, official Catholic social teaching has leaned heavily on a rights-based analysis, encompassing both civil-political and socioeconomic dimensions. From a standpoint within the human community rather than the Catholic subculture, this teaching has reopened the gates to full participation in pluralist societies. Although still in tension with more church-centered theologies and political strategies concerned with ecclesiastical privileges and sexual ethics, it has made the promotion of human dignity central to the church's mission, as symbolized by Pope John Paul II's comment during a visit to Latin America in 1987, that "to the Gospel message belong all the problems of human rights."[3] As a result, says Witte, the Roman church, which led a first rights movement of its own a thousand years ago—the struggle for freedom of the church against the authority of secular rulers—now stands poised to lead the global human rights movement, with its unique combination of local, national, and global capacity, and confessional and universal strategies.[4]

Justice and Peace Commissions, established after Vatican II within the Curia and replicated at national and diocesan levels, have translated the concern into practical action. While national episcopacies have reacted in a variety of ways, in Latin America and elsewhere, Brian Hehir stresses that on human rights the Latin American local church led the way for the whole church, producing an authentically local theology (Liberation Theology), a grassroots pastoral method (the Base Ecclesial Communities), and episcopal leadership symbolized in the regional gatherings of bishops at Medellin (1968), Puebla (1979), and Santo Domingo (1992).[5]

Not only was Latin America central for the new global Catholic strategy; the church was also central to the emergence of a strong human rights movement in Latin America. Notwithstanding precursors, human rights as such only emerged as an issue in world politics in the middle third of the twentieth century, with the Holocaust as the catalyst. But even though Latin American governments were signatories to the UN Universal Declaration in 1948, it was a long time before "human rights" entered the vocabulary of most Latin Americans.[6] When it did, it was largely out of the simultaneous transformation in global Catholicism and as a response to a range of secular developments: the increase in state violence perpetrated by military regimes during the Cold War, to the Cuban Revolution and its aftermath, the rise of guerrilla movements in many countries, and the electoral success of some left-wing political parties.

At the outset, Liberation Theology was initially far from enamored with rights talk. Many of its prominent exponents viewed human rights as a kind of Trojan Horse for imperialism or an individualistic First World luxury that should be corrected by a stress on economic rights and the God-given "rights of the poor." Gustavo Gutiérrez's classic *A Theology of Liberation*, for example, contains not a single reference to the concept of human rights, and the term appears only twice in his work on the great early defender of the Indians, Bartolomé de las Casas.[7] Over time, much of the hostility to the concept of human rights dissipated as increasingly brutal dictatorships mobilized broad-based opposition.

Thus, despite inconsistencies from one country to another during the military period; despite the perceived gap between what the church has demanded of governments and its own internal life; and despite blemishes on its record with regard to religious freedom—despite all this, the Catholic contribution to human rights in Latin America has been indispensable since around 1970, when clergy and laypeople began to apply the ideas of Vatican II in the context of an increasing number of military dictatorships.

Catholicism and Human Rights under Military Regimes

Existing trends in Latin America helped the churches pick up enthusiastically on the new orientations of the Vatican Council. Some Catholic Action movements had been transformed by French Catholic intellectual influences from writers like Emmanuel Mounier over previous decades. And the regional bishops' conference known as CELAM (Consejo Episcopal Latinoamericano) and the national bishops' conferences were well placed to implement changes. The 1968 Medellin conference applied Vatican II to regional reality, stressing work for justice and peace, and what came to be known as base communities and the preferential option for the poor. Latin American underdevelopment was seen as "an unjust situation" requiring a "total change of Latin American structures" and a church that defended "the rights of the poor and oppressed."[8]

However, the international dimension is also vital for understanding Catholic reactions. The Vatican was able, from 1968 onward, to monitor new patterns of systematic rights violations, and publicize them internationally. Foreign clergy in Latin America had an important role in stimulating and staffing human rights initiatives. Church-related organizations, often energized by ex-missionaries, also played a role, including the Washington Office on Latin America. The religious moblization for human rights and against dictatorship also encompassed smaller Protestant communities and ecumenical efforts throughout the region. And it enjoyed the support of international Catholic and Protestant organizations as well.

The reasons for the political transformation of Latin American Catholicism in the 1960s and 1970s are much debated, with authors placing varying weight on factors such as grassroots pressure, institutional considerations, and religious rivalry. But clearly global Catholic changes and the shock of state-sanctioned torture and disappearance of clergy and laypeople were important in causing several national churches to become key defenders of human rights. This was especially so in Brazil, where the church had welcomed the 1964 coup that inaugurated a military dictatorship and only moved gradually into opposition after 1968.

But this change happened in varying degrees in different countries, and in some countries not at all. Military dictatorships were a "necessary but not sufficient condition to bring the progressive church into being."[9] In Brazil, Chile, and El Salvador the church forcefully advocated human rights, economic justice, and redemocratization. But in Argentina, Paraguay, Uruguay, and (until 1983) Guatemala, it continued to support dictators. Options were constrained by multiple factors, including papal diplomacy, church disunity, internal tensions, leadership preferences, the political context, and foreign influence.[10] For example, the papacy never reproached the Argentine episcopate for its silence and complicity during the military-led "dirty war" of the late 1970s and the early 1980s. Around the same time, the murder of six Jesuits at the Central American University spurred initiatives, including one led by Georgetown University, to have the crime investigated and American military aid to El Salvador suspended.[11]

The most striking example of an untransformed national church was that of Argentina, which from 1976 to 1983 experienced perhaps the most brutal of all "national security" regimes. Not only did the hierarchy not denounce the dirty war against anyone suspected of sympathy with "subversives," but it enjoyed a close relationship with the regime. Almost the whole episcopacy supported the dictatorship, priests were attached to interrogation centers, and Archbishop Quarracino affirmed in 1983 that all the "disappeared" were in gilded exile.[12] Into the breach stepped unofficial initiatives such as the Ecumenical Movement for Human Rights and SERPAJ (Servicio Paz y Justicia). The latter's leader, Adolfo Pérez Esquivel, won the Nobel Peace Prize, but the hierarchy pointedly refrained from congratulating him.

Outside of Argentina, many other human rights initiatives in the region were very much under official church patronage, the best known being the Vicariate of Solidarity in Santiago, the Tutela Legal in El Salvador, and the Justice and Peace Commission of the Archdiocese of São Paulo. These centers gathered information, denounced abuses, visited prisons, succored families of victims, and generally pressured governments to change course. The two best-documented cases of church defense of human rights were those of Chile and Brazil.

The brutal Chilean coup of 1973 came as a shock in one of the most stable democracies of the region. Church reaction was neither immediately nor uniformly condemnatory, but Cardinal Raúl Silva Henríquez was soon involved in creating the Committee of Cooperation for Peace (Copachi), with the support of some Protestants and Jews and co-chaired by himself and Lutheran Bishop Helmut Frenz. Copachi helped the persecuted leave the country, visited prisons, and gave legal counsel, breaking the almost total silence in Chile's cowed civil society. When the government moved against Copachi in 1975, preventing Frenz from reentering the country, Cardinal Silva created the Vicariate of Solidarity. The Vicariate functioned at the diocesan level in Santiago, allowing Silva to ignore objections from conservative bishops. Unlike Copachi, it was not ecumenical, although it did receive funding from external Protestant sources. Some Protestant churches formed the Foundation for Social Help of the Christian Churches (Fasic), which also substituted for the Vicariate where the local bishop was antagonistic.[13]

In Brazil, the military regime established in 1964 with considerable church support became even more repressive from 1968, affecting church personnel. Between 1968 and 1973, around 100 priests were detained for political reasons.[14] At the same time, a new generation of progressive bishops appeared, supplementing the historic efforts of older bishops such as Dom Hélder Câmara. The best known was the archbishop of São Paulo, Dom Paulo Evaristo Arns. From 1973, the bishops' conference and some regional conferences published bold statements on human rights, and Arns established a local Justice and Peace Commission which incarnated the church's new role as "voice of the voiceless." Arns was subsequently named a cardinal. The culmination of the Commission's work came with its role in the 1985 publication of *Brasil: Nunca Mais*, an exposé of the abuses reconstructed secretly out of the military's own files. This was an ecumenical initiative under the Reverend Jaime Wright, a Presbyterian minister, with funding from the World Council of Churches.

The Brazilian Catholic Church's opposition to the regime had public and private faces, made feasible by its historic position in Brazil, the personal ties of its leaders in society, and the support of the global church. The private side has been written about only in more recent times.[15] It was expressed through the Bipartite Commission, a secret committee of bishops and generals that met from 1970 to 1974. Its architects were a devout Catholic general, a Catholic philosopher from the military's Superior War School, and the secretary-general of the Justice and Peace Commission from Rio de Janeiro. The main themes of the meetings were development, church-state relations, and human rights. In Serbin's interpretation, while the bishops publicly radicalized their opposition, they privately temporized to safeguard institutional influence. But at no time, says Serbin, did the church's private voice contradict its public positions. On human rights, there was no compromise.

However, the bishops also brought other concerns to the Bipartite meetings, including divorce, birth control, state financial assistance, and competition from other religions. They pushed for continued recognition of Catholicism as Brazil's semi-official religion. The military had shattered the compact of Brazil's elites and tried to reduce the church's own political status; the Bipartite thus functioned as an attempt at elite settlement.[16] Clearly, this was a role that only Catholicism among Brazil's religions could play, since only it had the mix of historical roots, transnational networks, and elite connections.

Catholicism and Human Rights after Redemocratization

Much has changed since the era of military dictatorships, and many changes have limited the capacity or disposition of the Catholic Church to have such a prominent human rights role. Nevertheless, as Serbin asserts, human rights are now part of the political landscape, thanks to the church's campaign during the authoritarian era.[17]

With democratization, both civil society and the religious landscape have fragmented. Democracy and religious pluralism have reinforced each other as challenges to the church's position.[18] Growing pluralism weakens the church's capacity to present itself as the conscience of society or the voice of the marginalized. As for civil society, much of it is now mobilized in organizations beyond ecclesiastical authority, and it manages a discourse that challenges the church's agenda on certain prominent issues, including reproduction and the family.

The church has also undergone internal changes. Liberation Theology and the Base Communities have declined, and the most vital movement now is the more conservative Charismatic Renewal. And the official Catholic project is the New Evangelization, which aims not at a Christian social order through concordats or Christian political parties, and still less at a left-wing revolution, but at an evangelization of culture through the penetration of civil society. But recent analyses (e.g., Hagopian) are pessimistic about the church's capacity to do that, especially in view of its weakening vitality as a religion of personal salvation among Latin Americans.

Relative withdrawal from direct political involvement has led to varied outcomes. In Chile, the Vicariate was closed in 1992 and the episcopate has deemphasized human rights. A similar trend has occurred in El Salvador and Guatemala.[19] But in Brazil the episcopate has retained a progressive posture on many issues, helped by the fact that its radicals did not become isolated from the mainstream. In the mid-1990s, 60 percent of the groups in the National Movement for Human Rights were tied to churches, mainly the Catholic Church.[20] The church has carried out campaigns on the civil, social, and economic dimensions of human rights. Its Pastoral Letters have been prominent defenders of agrarian reform and indigenous rights and have denounced violence and enslavement in the countryside. In keeping with an expanded definition of human rights, the high concentration of landholding which has encouraged massive migration to the cities, immense urban problems, and the continued erosion of indigenous land rights and cultural autonomy are regarded as serious human rights issues in the Latin American context.

While the big difference between the authoritarian era and today is the rule of law, human rights concerns have since broadened. From the social costs of neoliberal policies to combating enclaves of authoritarianism; from support to victims of past repression to denouncing the torture of common criminals; from the street children's movement to Indian rights; from fraudulent elections to corruption—on all these issues, hierarchies or church-related movements have been active. CELAM has come out against the proposal for a Free Trade Area of the Americas, as have ecumenical institutions composed largely of the Catholic and some historical Protestant churches. The Brazilian episcopate sponsored an unofficial "plebiscite" on the issue in 2002. In this way the church has connected with large popular movements fearful of the economic, social, and cultural consequences of such an agreement with the United States.

Religious Freedom in Latin America

We have already mentioned Witte's comment on the "explosion of new evangelical and pentecostal movements." But his concern is mainly with countries where new freedoms have brought an influx of *foreign* movements. In Latin America, however, the controversy is not really about foreign proselytism; the threat to Catholicism is local. And in any case the Catholic Church, while occasionally still resentful of "the participation in the marketplace of religious ideas that democracy assumes," is constrained by its own post-conciliar global discourse in favor of religious freedom.[21] This is unlike many parts of the world where the traditional religion faces no such constraint in attempts to delegitimize its proselytizing rivals.

A pioneer of modern social science and of the analysis of democracy, Alexis de Tocqueville viewed concepts of universal human rights and the Christian proselytizing impulse, neither of which are "natural to man," as two sides of the same coin. As he put it, "proselytism does not arise simply from sincerity of belief, but from the idea of the equality of men and especially the unity of the human race."[22] This point is important, since many discussions of human rights seem to presuppose stable religious identities, whereas in some parts of the world there is much conversion going on. The right to convert is related to the right to "be proselytized," that is, to make informed religious choices. There is a class component to this: middle-class people can often "convert themselves" by taking advantage of religious freedom in self-starting ways, whereas people with fewer economic and cultural resources are more dependent on proselytizers appearing on their cultural horizon. Those who change religion in Latin America are disproportionately the latter. In Brazil, for example, conversion—from one religion to another, or to "no religion"—is now similar to that of the United States: 26 percent in Brazil as compared to 29 percent of the U.S. population, according to the 2006 Pew Survey.[23] The expansion of Pentecostalism has been fastest in "the most dynamic spaces in terms of the economy and of migratory movements"—the metropolitan areas of the south-east and the agricultural frontiers of the north and center-west.[24] In metropolitan regions, Pentecostals are located heavily in the poor periphery, where they account for as much as 30 percent of the population. In the more central areas of São Paulo, the figure is less than 5 percent.

Of the countries examined in Paul Marshall's *Religious Freedom in the World*, Latin America ranks level with sub-Saharan Africa as the second-freest region of the world (behind "Western Europe and the North Atlantic"), and Catholic-majority countries rank second only to Protestant-majority ones.[25] What this means in practice can be exemplified by a recent report on Peru. On the one hand, "the constitution guarantees religious freedom and the government generally respects this right." All religions have freedom to "train their clergy and to proselytize," and there are "generally amicable relations" between religions. Nevertheless, a concordat confers special status on the Catholic Church, which translates into educational, fiscal, and bureaucratic privileges.[26] Thus, while only three countries in Latin America still have an official religion, there are several where non-Catholic religions do not enjoy the same legal rights as the Catholic Church. One still finds in some countries, for example, state subsidies to the Catholic Church, state funding only to Catholic and not to other private universities, and restrictions on non-Catholic missions in indigenous areas. In practice, the Catholic Church's commitment to human rights coexists with continued institutional privileges.

But it is not always the state that has caused concern for non-Catholic groups; sometimes the Catholic Church itself has been less than a bold defender of religious freedom, even in post-Vatican II times. As the percentage of declared adherents to Catholicism has declined sharply—down by 10 percent of the population between the Brazilian censuses of 1991 and 2000, a greater decline than in the other countries of the region, taken as a whole—post-conciliar ecumenical initiatives have come to coexist with denunciations of "sects" by Catholic leaders. Such denunciations were especially common in the early 1990s. One Catholic publication wrote of the "evangelical offensive" which relies on the "ignorance of the people." The "Catholic counter-offensive" includes the "appeal to legal protection. . . . A bit shame-facedly, but more openly elsewhere—including amongst some progressives—the repressive intervention of governments is desired" in the name of a "threat to the fundamental values of our nationality."[27] A Latin American report to the Vatican in 1991 affirmed that "the sects are being promoted by interests distant from our own life. . . . The idea grows that it is not necessary to be Catholic . . . to maintain the greatness of our national identity." As Mexico was debating the 1992 reform of laws on religion, the hierarchy pressed for preferential space vis-à-vis other groups. In the words of the Vatican representative, "an elephant does not eat the same way as an ant." There was a spate of statements regarding evangelical churches: "you do not have dialogue with bandits" (Bishop Lozano); "the sects, like flies, have to be removed" (the Vatican representative); "we will defend ourselves from these imposters who wish to root out the faith and buy it with dollars" (the Bishop of Cuernavaca).[28] Indeed, with regard to dialog, Edward Cleary, himself a former Catholic missionary, observes that the Catholic-Pentecostal dialog that the Vatican has co-sponsored since 1972 goes unnoticed in the region, and "the Latin American church has almost no intellectual resources to enter into a dialogue with indigenous pentecostalism."[29]

In a few parts of Latin America, notably indigenous areas of southern Mexico, conversion can still be dangerous. Thousands of Protestant converts among highland Indians in Chiapas have faced hostility from local Catholic caciques for over thirty years, ranging from social pressure, through ostracism and threats, to expulsion and murder.[30] However, local Catholic bishops have repudiated such expulsions, and local Catholics supportive of the Protestants have also suffered violence.

Thus, we see that the Catholic Church has had a vital role in the defense of human rights in Latin America, but its own behavior with regard to religious freedom in the region has been somewhat ambiguous in the more democratic atmosphere of recent years. This ambiguity is related largely to the sharp numerical growth of Protestantism in Latin America.

Protestantism and Human Rights in Latin America: Background to a Great Disappointment?

Protestantism's recent expansion in Latin America has transformed the region into a significant global center of that Christian tradition. But we cannot talk of its regional role in relation to human rights without mentioning Protestantism's historical role in its traditional strongholds. Protestantism has historically had a closer relationship to human rights than any other religion. Jellinek's classic study of 1895 already argued that declarations of human rights had historically centered on the demand for religious freedom heralded through the Reformation and claimed by religious minorities in the English-speaking world.[31] Recent authors have also affirmed Protestantism's historical centrality in the human rights context. Johnson avers that "a principled position of toleration and freedom happened more quickly in the Protestant camp," if, he adds, eventually more systematically in Catholicism.[32] For Witte, the right to choose and change religion was "patristic, pragmatic and Protestant in initial inspiration."[33]

It was, of course, hard to discern the seeds of religious liberty in Luther's idea of the tasks of the godly prince or Calvin's defense of the execution of Servetus, which is why many authors attribute Protestantism's positive role in the development of human rights to the unintended fracturing of the religious landscape and stalemate in the wars of religion.[34] But that is to neglect the contribution of the radical Reformation, and especially of early seventeenth-century voices who made a principled defense of religious freedom on theological grounds. An early English Baptist, Thomas Helwys, wrote in 1614: "Let them be heretics, Turks, Jews or whatsoever it appertains not to the earthly power to punish them."[35] In the English North American colonies, Rhode Island implemented this principle, and its founder Roger Williams stated in 1644 that it is the command of God that since the coming of Christ "a permission of the most Paganish, Jewish, Turkish or Antichristian consciences and worships be granted to all men in all nations," a position echoed by the Levellers during the English Civil War of the 1640s.[36]

Freedom of conscience was the basis for the broader principle of freedom of association. Even Calvinism, as Ernst Troeltsch argued, later evolved into nontheocratic neo-Calvinism which "extends the principle of . . . [free] association to every relationship in life" and "develops a pacifist international spirit and pacifist propaganda, champions the right of humanity, encourages the antislavery movement, and allies itself with philanthropic and humanitarian movements. The feminist movement also found some support here, long before other denominations dared to broach the subject."[37] Out of such stables came the antislavery activists and missionaries who engaged in human rights campaigns, connecting humanitarianism with a rights frame focused on empowering individual citizens.[38] Their evangelical focus on the individual may have blinded them to structural issues such as "wage slavery" but did not stop them from campaigning for causes that could be understood in an individualistic framework.

Protestantism's connection with the modern human rights movement is also well documented.[39] The emerging ecumenical movement made clear affirmations of religious freedom and human rights, which led to the involvement of the Commission of the Churches in International Affairs in campaigning for the UN Charter of 1945 and the Universal Declaration of Human Rights of 1948. By then the Protestant world in the West was divided between ecumenical and evangelical currents, but by the late twentieth century Traer could speak of a growing consensus: "liberal and conservative Protestants, Catholics, Orthodox and evangelicals are remarkably unified on their understanding of the importance of human rights advocacy."[40]

Nevertheless, Witte concludes that an irony of the contemporary human rights movement is the relative silence of the Protestant churches. While the practical efforts of the largely Protestant World Council of Churches have been important, neither it nor the main denominations have developed a systematic theory or program.[41] Perhaps one can say that Protestantism has run into two problems in this respect. One is that, from its position of historical smugness vis-à-vis Catholicism regarding its pioneer contributions to the development of human rights, the standard of comparison is now with post-conciliar Catholicism, with its sophisticated theological statements, official magisterium, and global articulation. Protestantism's divisions, which once put it in the vanguard, now work to its disadvantage, ruling out the equivalent of a single magisterium and minimizing the capacity for transnational articulation and political reach. And the second problem is Protestantism's recent and massive relocation to the global South in a largely autonomous process of appropriation. This new grassroots Protestantism is generally concentrated among the poorer and less educated sectors in Third World countries, and is often unconnected to organizations in the traditional Protestant heartlands. Growth in the developing world has coincided with considerable decline elsewhere.

Thus, if there have always been *Protestantisms* in the plural, that is even more the case today. Historical contributions to the idea of universal rights are unassailable. At the same time, strands of Protestantism have often been unfavorable to human rights, not only in their internal life but also in their attitudes toward other religions and in their association with undemocratic regimes or with undemocratic political actors. Those strands would seem to constitute a growing segment of today's increasingly global Protestantism, and Latin America is no exception.

Protestantism and Human Rights in Latin America: What There Is and Why So Little

Latin America has recently been marked by rapid Protestant and especially Pentecostal growth in a traditionally Catholic region. While largely dependent on the existence of freedom of religion, this growth has raised new human rights concerns. While Catholic-Protestant tension has significantly decreased in Europe and North America, it is probably greater now in Latin America than anywhere else. But this does not mean that Latin America is replaying the European trajectory which, according to standard historiography, resulted in toleration only after exhaustion had set in. On the contrary, since the Latin American process is erosion of Catholic allegiance "from below" through individual conversion rather than through political decisions, most of the conflict lacks an explicitly political dimension.

Protestant success is due largely to Pentecostalism, a highly expressive form of religiosity which emphasizes experience of "gifts of the Holy Spirit" such as speaking in tongues, prophecy, healing, and exorcism, some of it in imported denominations such as the Assemblies of God, but increasingly in denominations founded within Latin America. Diversity among Pentecostal denominations is now as great as that of non-Pentecostal Presbyterians, Methodists, Baptists, and Lutherans, collectively referred to in Latin America as "historical Protestants." And the preponderance of Pentecostal churches within Protestantism has grown markedly. In Brazil, members of Pentecostal churches now account for over two-thirds of all Protestants, and their average social level, as measured by income level and years of education, is markedly lower than that of historical Protestants. Differences in social composition and style of worship and propagation have significantly changed the way Protestantism as a whole is perceived in the region.

Brazil makes a useful case study of religious reactions to military dictatorship. Historical Protestantism arrived in the nineteenth century, both through German Lutheran immigrants and through missionaries. The latter were largely from the southern United States and brought a tradition of individualistic thought centered on individual change as a way to transform society. In addition, organizational forms were largely synodal or congregational, allowing adaptation to local interests. This flexibility, with its distance from transnational ecclesiastical pressures, facilitated the transformation of apolitical theology into support for the state.

Presbyterianism in Brazil illustrates this "local captivity" of the church into the postwar period. In the 1960s it went through internal purges that paralleled those of the country under the post-1964 military regime. It left the World Alliance of Reformed Churches, and its leaders were invited by the government to take courses at the Superior War School. Baptist leaders were equally responsive to government overtures; their pro-regime stance became so notorious that President Carter, a Baptist deacon, avoided meeting with them when he visited the country in the late 1970s.[42]

There were, of course, dissidents in the Presbyterian, Methodist, and Baptist churches, and the Catholic hierarchy was also initially favorable to the 1964 military coup. But differences emerged after more severe repression began in 1968. In the Catholic case, the regime's strategy to isolate the radicals ceased functioning, but in the Protestant churches the radicals were left isolated. Catholic change was also aided by its international structure, which provided a greater measure of protection in defending human rights than the Protestant churches had.

Greater vulnerability may explain why Protestant churches did not wish to expose themselves to the full fury of repression. But it does not explain why they identified so fully with the regime. For that we must look to the role of religious rivalry—the desire to weaken or even replace Catholicism—and the Cold War context. Inasmuch as the Brazilian churches, although autonomous, were still responsive to ideological inputs from abroad, they were influenced by the influx of American missionaries fearful of communism after the fall of China and Cuba.

The Pentecostal churches, which at that time accounted for less than half of all Protestants in Brazil, were more national, but given their lower class nature, even more vulnerable to repression and hungry for any crumbs of status the regime might throw at them. It is significant that the few counter-examples within the Pentecostal or historical Protestant world involved connection with international and/or ecumenical organizations. One Pentecostal church, Brazil for Christ, founded by a working-class Brazilian in the 1950s, joined the World Council of Churches in 1968 and made mildly critical pronouncements about the regime, largely for external consumption. Similarly, Jaime Wright, the Brazilian son of American missionaries who collaborated with Cardinal Arns on the influential book *Brazil: Never Again*, had strong ties with the missions of the U.S.-based Presbyterian Church.

The fundamental role of foreign contacts can be seen also in the Lutheran Church, which was still largely an enclave of German-Brazilians. The catalyst for its transformation was the 1970 assembly of the Lutheran World Federation; scheduled for Brazil, it was transferred to France in protest at the silence of the Brazilian church on human rights violations. The leadership realized with surprise that it was regarded by its sister churches abroad as responsible for the country in which it was located. It then produced a public declaration claiming the role of "conscience of the nation" and cautiously questioning the regime. This case exemplifies the role of international forces in shaping national articulation of human rights concerns by religious groups.[43]

In Latin America as a whole, Protestant groups (and not just individuals) committed to the human rights cause generally sought ecumenical affiliations, either with international associations or with the Catholic Church. Starting in 1976, for example, the Human Rights Office for Latin America of the World Council of Churches (WCC) worked closely with the Latin American Council of Churches. Cleary regards the WCC as "exceptional in the creativity and magnitude of its response to human rights organizing" in the region.[44] In more recent times, the Mennonite Central Committee has emerged as a key actor. A church of Anabaptist origin with only a small ecclesiastical presence in Latin America, the Mennonites have nevertheless carried on significant human rights work, especially in Guatemala and Colombia.

What of the Protestant world not linked with ecumenical organizations, which in Latin America is the vast majority? A key organization has been World Vision, of American evangelical origin but within Latin America now heavily Latin American in staff and increasingly in ethos. In more recent post-authoritarian times it has provided a context for socially concerned evangelicals, bereft of denominational initiatives, to express their activism. Basically involved in relief and development, World Vision has acted locally on human rights issues and has raised awareness in evangelical churches, especially regarding children's rights and global economic justice.

Given evangelical divisions and traditional apoliticism, effective human rights advocacy usually depends heavily on trans-denominational representative organizations at the national level, which are usually weak in Latin America. By Latin American standards an exceptionally strong and long-lasting representative organization is the National Evangelical Council of Peru (Conep), which incorporates the majority of historical and Pentecostal churches. Its strength helped it to develop a Peace and Hope Commission that defended evangelicals against human rights abuses in zones affected by the Shining Path guerrilla insurgency and the increasingly violent army counter-insurgency in the 1980s and early 1990s. The Peace and Hope Commission was largely the initiative of university-educated evangelicals. As often with Catholic initiatives, violence against one's own religion was the catalyst. In addition, the conservative nature of Peruvian Catholicism meant it had not preempted the theme of human rights to the point of making anti-Catholic evangelicals steer clear of it.[45] This exemplifies the important role of local religious rivalries in helping to shape responses to human rights and other political issues. A change in the position of one's rival can often lead to a change in one's own position, without any profound theological rethinking.

The Peruvian situation was also unique in that outside the emergency zones there was a functioning democracy. This unusual conjunction of abuses and democracy encouraged the involvement of a fairly poor religious minority in politically risky human rights activism. Peace and Hope was an observer in the National Coordinating Committee on Human Rights. Together with Catholics, it published a booklet, "Campaign of Prayer and Solidarity for Those Unjustly Detained for Terrorism," that contained graphic testimonies of torture. Resources for this human rights work came largely from European ecumenical and evangelical organizations. But in contrast to the Brazilian cases already outlined, the foreign role was one of financial support rather than of ideological impulse.

Starting in 1992, Peace and Hope's freedom of maneuver became more restricted within Conep. Most human rights movements are led by middle-class intellectuals, and the acceptance of this emphasis as part of the mission of the church thus provides space for such people to achieve leadership within the evangelical community. Resistance to a continued emphasis on such aspects could be seen as a fight for turf. If a broader concept of "the mission of the church" were admitted, more traditional leaders would see their preeminence jeopardized. This is especially the case where transnational ecumenical movements do not have a fundamental role in initiating human rights work. Such ecumenical contacts thus seem to be the most favorable context for overcoming the traditional weakness of Latin American Protestantism's rights activism.

Pentecostalism and Religious Freedom

In the case of Pentecostal denominations, the difficulty of incorporation into formal human rights activities is related partly to the apolitical, individualistic, and eschatological tendencies in their theology, but also to two other characteristics: a proselytizing impulse and a heavily lower class character. Both characteristics of Pentecostalism tend to distance it from the social environments in which rights discourse is most widely disseminated. Nevertheless, as we shall see, in informal settings Pentecostalism is widely recognized as making a significant contribution to dignifying and protecting the most vulnerable in Latin American society.

The perceived aggressiveness of much Pentecostal proselytizing vis-à-vis other religions creates some social tension in Brazil. Undoubtedly, many churches have often shown a lack of proper respect for other religions and often participate in a demonizing discourse. Yet it should be stressed that the clash between Pentecostalism and Afro-Brazilian religions has very rarely been violent. Rather, it usually plays out as a verbal dispute between social equals at the grassroots level.

The Universal Church of the Kingdom of God (UCKG), a Brazilian church founded in 1977, illustrates this side of Pentecostalism. It has been embroiled in multiple controversies and subject to criticism, including from other Pentecostal groups. In the most famous controversy, in 1995 a UCKG bishop kicked an image of Our Lady of Aparecida, patron saint of Brazil, in a live television program, to show it could not answer prayers. The bishop was given a two-years suspended sentence. As Eric Kramer points out, contrasting interpretations of religious freedom came into play in the trial: legitimate expression of convictions versus the right to be free from the incursions of others upon one's beliefs. In Kramer's view, the concept of religious pluralism adopted by the judge ignores claims to moral superiority asserted by many religions. From the judge's perspective, it was criminal to disturb the religious *convictions* of others—in contrast to their *observances*. The defense might have countered that the Brazilian state, in sponsoring a federal holiday in honor of Aparecida, also offends the convictions of many of its citizens.[46]

Ted Stahnke stresses that it is necessary not only to respect other religions but also to protect them from ridicule and contempt. Yet he also insists that the substance of a message must generally be tolerated by the state; it is the manner, not the content, that may justify some restriction.[47] The UCKG has not ceased portraying Afro-Brazilian religions as demonic but has evolved somewhat in the direction of a more "civilized" proselytizing style. One of its politicians made an interesting defense when the church's media was sued by Afro-Brazilian religious groups. "The Catholic Church adores images. This offends us. The sacrifices [in Afro-Brazilian religions] offend us. But we do not take legal action against these religions. We respect people's right to profess their faith, but we do not need to respect their gods."[48]

The questions of proselytization and of class location represent a Brazilian refraction of an international tension between religion and human rights movements. As Rosalind Hackett puts it, human rights movements often present the face of a "worldwide secular religion" governed by an internationalized elite.[49] For Martin Marty, the post-Enlightenment assumption was that "philosophy, anthropology and politics would provide the new language of rights," whatever religion's past contribution might have been, and that "any religion that survived would be tolerant and philosophically enlightened." On the other hand, Marty argues, "the religions of the world regard Enlightenment reasoners to be one more set of competitors."[50] In relation to Latin American Pentecostalism, an example of this can be seen in a brochure called "Religious Diversity and Human Rights," produced by the Brazilian National Program on Human Rights, a governmental body.[51] The aim of the document is "to encourage dialogue between religious movements." To this end, there are quotes from various movements, including evangelical churches. But instead of seeking a basis for human rights in the teaching of each confession, the document tries to construct a common creed which, in effect, approves of the teaching of certain religions and disapproves of others. "God, Allah, Yahweh, Olorum, the Great Spirit, the Goddess, Brahman . . . there are many names by which human beings call the Creator." The document links itself to an "inter-religious" lineage, speaking of the 1893 World's Parliament of Religions in Chicago and its 2004 successor meeting in Barcelona. There is no inkling in the document that the "inter-religious" movement is itself a very particular and not necessarily generalizable manifestation of the religious impulse. The authors would have done well to read Harvey Cox's brilliant contrast between the World's Parliament of 1893, with its "learned and accomplished delegates from the religious and educational elite" and the origins of Pentecostalism in a 1906 revival, a "breakthrough of primal spirituality" among the disenfranchised.[52]

All the behaviors referred to with disapproval by the Brazilian document are clearly aimed at real or supposed activities of Pentecostals: "invasion of umbanda and candomblé temples"; "disrespect for the spirituality of indigenous peoples, or trying to impose on them the view that their religion is false"; "Wicca rituals called 'Satanic.'" The Afro-Brazilian religions are mentioned as the main victims of intolerance, with references to cultic objects destroyed, celebrations interrupted, and followers referred to as "devil worshippers." But this is not a calm analysis of actual incidents of cases of Pentecostal intolerance in relation to Afro-Brazilian and indigenous religions; instead, there is a lengthy recounting of an Afro-Brazilian religious myth regarding the broken mirror: "Olorum said: everyone . . . from now on will be finding only one part of the truth." The redactors of the document then conclude: there is no longer one truth. "Therefore, in order to follow the will of the Creator, it is necessary . . . to accept . . . that the Truth belongs to no-one."

This is a specific example of the hijacking of the prestigious language of "human rights" by a particular approach to religion. Although based on real incidents of reprehensible Pentecostal behavior, the underlying problem seems to be Pentecostalism's proselytistic success. The document goes far beyond a calm analysis of those incidents and endorses a religiously specific view of the relationship of "the Creator" to human beings. The irony, of course, is that (disapproved) proselytism is the root of (approved) diversity, in the sense that freedom to propagate other religious views underlies the plurality of religions coexisting in Brazilian social space. But, as Scott Appleby stresses, to be effective, human rights discourse cannot glide over what individuals and communities hold sacred, but instead needs fluent "translators" who comprehend believers' sensibilities while weighing their conduct against universal norms.[53] It is the absence of an attempt to "translate" rights discourse in terms of Pentecostal sensibilities that makes the document ineffective.

With regard to the key Brazilian religious tension between Pentecostalism and the Afro-Brazilian religions, John Burdick points out that the *movimento negro* in Brazil responded to incidents between Pentecostals and Afro-Brazilian religions (which are, in fact, far from limited to blacks) by asking the Ministry of Justice to apply antiracism laws against the "violence of the Nazi-pentecostal churches against the African worldview."[54] The irony, of course, is that Africa itself is now full of churches that critique the same practices that Brazilian Pentecostals rail against. In addition, Pentecostalism is critiqued by the *movimento negro* for being a religion of ethnic assimilation whose mix of individualism and universalism is supposedly antipathetic to a strong racial identity. Whether it is actually antipathetic is questioned by Burdick, and in fact Pentecostalism is very "dark" in composition.

James Spickard stresses that the veneration of rights and the rise of fundamentalisms that seek to overturn them are simultaneous global phenomena. He refers, for example, to Muslim and Confucianist attempts at alternative rights philosophies, as well as to movements based on ethnic consciousness.[55] Is Latin American Pentecostalism part of this? Does it, as Spickard says of these counter-movements, place the group above humanity? Does it refuse to treat as equals those whom it opposes, and would it like to deny them political, civil, economic, and social rights? Would it, if it had the intellectual resources, construct an alternative rights philosophy? Or is it basically in agreement with mainstream human rights ideas, albeit hampered in its own articulation of those ideas by poverty and lack of educational and cultural resources, and marginalized by insensitive approaches from the human rights movement itself?

In its origins in popular Western Christianity, Pentecostalism is part of the very culture that developed the dominant international concepts of rights and subsequently diverged. It questions liberal understandings without going as far as the questioning of the whole idea of universal rights that is found among some communitarians. It stands within the dissenting Protestant tradition that generally refers neither to the modern liberal "individual" nor to stable "ascriptive communities," but to "achieved communities" peopled by accountable individuals.

The 2006 Pew survey of Pentecostals (*Spirit and Power*) including Brazil, Guatemala, and Chile, helps evaluate Latin American Pentecostalism's relationship to questions of human rights. On the whole, results suggest that Pentecostalism is not a barrier to the advance of human rights in the region. To the question of whether it is important that there be freedom for religions other than one's own, Pentecostals everywhere were at least as affirmative as the general population of their countries—94 percent of Brazilian Pentecostals, for example, compared to a national average of 95 percent. Notwithstanding a relatively small number of violations of the rights of other traditions, the statistical data do not corroborate the idea that Pentecostal beliefs and practice are, in themselves, problems for the acceptance of religious freedom and the promotion of tolerance.

With regard to social rights, the "prosperity gospel" characteristic of many though not all more recent Pentecostal tendencies is often presumed to be favorable to neoliberal economic policies. Nevertheless, in the Pew survey question on welfare, Pentecostals in Latin America are slightly more favorable than their general populations. When asked whether government should guarantee food and shelter to every citizen, 95 percent of Pentecostals in Brazil responded in the affirmative, in contrast to 93 percent of the overall population.

Similarly, the view that Pentecostals' liking for charismatic leaders renders them more favorable to authoritarian political systems is challenged by the Pew data. When asked whether, to solve the country's problems, it would be better to have a more participatory government or a strong leader, a majority of Latin American Pentecostals always prefer a participatory government. Pentecostal attitudes, it seems, are not at odds with democracy and human rights in the region. And when asked whether government should make their country a Christian country or whether there should be separation of church and state, Pentecostals reject the "Christian country" idea, notably in Chile (23% to 62%) and Brazil (32% to 50%). It is worth noting, however, that everywhere except Chile, Pentecostals are more favorable to the Christian country idea than are other religious believers.

Pentecostalism and Violence

The violence that troubles most Latin Americans today is not the occasional exacerbation of religious rivalries; it is the everyday violence of the big cities. Over the past two decades urban violence has worsened dramatically, especially in the poor peripheries. Pentecostalism is disproportionately concentrated in such areas, and therefore its relationship to violence is key for understanding its relationship to human rights. In these marginal areas virtually untouched by other sectors of civil society or the state, the Pentecostal presence is generally perceived as vital. Pentecostalism's "civilizing" mission is to provide ways of escape from criminality, prostitution, and drug addiction. In the Rio de Janeiro slum called Cidade de Deus, Zaluar says that "the few stories of regeneration I heard involved healing in Pentecostal churches or a radical conversion."[56] Regina Novaes argues along similar lines that mothers in the shanties see only two alternatives for their sons, either to become criminals or "believers."[57] Two other scholars suggest that "the myth that there is no way back from the world of crime finds a clear exception in criminals' conversion to evangelical churches."[58] Astonishingly, a recent study of a shantytown in Rio claims that the strong Pentecostal presence extends even to a monument erected by the local drug lords: "A Bible sculpted in stone, the monument represents a homage by the [drug lords] to the faith professed by their relatives and friends."[59] Stories abound of would-be muggers letting their victims go—and even apologizing to them—after discovering that they were "believers." Thus, we see that Pentecostalism's emphasis on individual piety does not preclude and may in fact favor practical, unostentatious support for the Universal Declaration of Human Rights' insistence that "everyone has the right to . . . security of person" (article 3) and to a "social . . . order in which the rights and freedoms set forth in this Declaration can be fully realized" (article 28), and where "the family is the natural and fundamental group unit of society and is entitled to protection by society and the State" (article 16).

In their examination of the relationship of urban violence and religion, Patricia Birman and Marcia Leite analyze how certain religious interpretations have lost credibility and others, particularly those of Pentecostals, have gained plausibility. The Catholic Church is perceived as at best helpless to deal with the causes of urban violence. Pentecostal pastors, on the other hand, are widely regarded as possessing more power and effectiveness than Catholic priests. They interrupt the flow of violence with the word of God and rituals of exorcism. Indeed, exorcism has become one of the most significant methods of dealing with evil in the shantytowns.[60] While the transnational and hierarchical Catholic Church was better at combating state violence, the individual transformative power of Pentecostalism seems to do better against privatized violence, whether by dissuading young males from becoming criminals, converting prisoners, or providing "spiritual protection" for potential victims of violence.

For many Latin Americans the concept of human rights surfaces most often in discussions that touch on this violence. In 2007, the particularly sadistic murder of a seven-year-old boy in Rio de Janeiro led to an acrid public debate in which, for perhaps the first time, some left-wing intellectuals seemed to abandon the discourse that the criminal is the victim of society. This discourse has always been difficult for the law-abiding poor, an increasing proportion of whom are Pentecostals, to accept, since they share precisely the social characteristics that allegedly make the criminals victims of society, but without becoming criminals themselves. Pentecostalism, immersed in the everyday challenges of grassroots existence in the megacities of Latin America, thus provides an alternative approach to human rights and dignity. This Pentecostal discourse of the discovery of personal agency, of empowerment through personal transformation, sits uneasily with a concept of human rights that appears to rob people of personal agency and transform them into victims of social processes that, although supposedly changeable through mobilization, seem always to remain as intractable as ever.

How does evangelical growth in Latin America relate to forms of geopolitical violence such as the war on terror? The question arises because just as the region's Catholics are influenced by changes in the Church's global magisterium, so its evangelicals are often assumed to reflect trends among evangelicals in the United States. Allen Hertzke claims that American evangelicals are now increasingly engaged in human rights causes, one of the reasons being the southward shift of global Christianity. Hertzke believes the globalization of Christianity ensures "a new constituency for international human rights."[61] But this is probably overly optimistic. The process might not lead to global fellow-feeling and mutual learning, but to a balkanization of Christian perspectives. The latter seems prefigured in the global evangelical rift over Iraq and the war on terror.[62] The paradox of a human rights constituency arising in one of the most nationalistic, militaristic, and anti-UN segments of American society could only be resolved by self-criticism of American foreign policy. Significantly, the Pew global survey asked whether respondents favored "the U.S.-led efforts to fight terrorism." In Latin America only about one-third of Pentecostals support the war on terror, as compared to 72 percent of American Pentecostals. Latin American Pentecostals are actually slightly less favorable toward U.S. policy than their general populations. The growth of Pentecostalism in Latin America, therefore, does not necessarily mean a strengthening of American soft power and imitation of American evangelical geopolitical attitudes.

Conclusion

Current global debates on religion and human rights often revolve around two themes. One is the relationship of Islam to human rights discourse. The other is the rights and wrongs of religious proselytization. While Islam's presence is small in Latin America, the region has become a major locus of controversies surrounding proselytization, courtesy of Pentecostalism. The division of the religious field in Latin America between a slimmer but more committed Catholic community led by a hierarchy with a less proprietary relationship to its flock and a growing and hopefully maturing Pentecostal community may bode well for human rights in the region. Post-conciliar Catholicism has much to teach the Protestants, if the latter have ears to hear. And Pentecostalism, if engaged on its own terms, can be seen to play an important role in a world where human rights concerns encompass not only national institutions but also local violence and lawlessness. The success of Pentecostalism in preaching personal salvation may have further, unanticipated impacts on the politics of human rights in Latin America—for example, the conversion of more and more left-wing militants still committed to their causes might eventually change Pentecostalism's overall political complexion.

The current moment, however, may be the worst of both worlds. On the one hand, the Catholic Church no longer enjoys unchallenged hegemony but has yet to adjust to the new situation. It still often clings to its institutional privileges, resisting efforts to grant other traditions—and Pentecostals in particular—equal treatment in their interactions with the state. If it had to combat a new round of repressive regimes, the old methods would be less effective, since it represents an ever-diminishing proportion of the population. At the same time, Pentecostalism is still largely alienated by the culture of the human rights movement, which has difficulty incorporating a lower class religious movement successful at proselytizing under conditions of pluralism. Human rights activists in Europe and North America might find sympathy for the Pentecostal creed of individual empowerment through the discovery of personal agency. But they are unlikely to endorse exorcism as a progressive strategy! Cultural differences inform very different approaches to religion and human rights in practice.

Our exploration of the diversity of Catholic and Protestant responses to human rights questions in Latin America in the last three or four decades has shown the importance of local political and religious factors in framing such responses, including the struggle for democratization, the presence of indigenous populations, the rise of urban violence, and the growth in religious competition. These local concerns will continue to frame Latin American responses to the interplay of religion and human rights for the foreseeable future.

NOTES

1. John Witte, *God's Joust, God's Justice* (Grand Rapids: Eerdmans, 2006), 66.

2. John Coleman, ed., *One Hundred Years of Catholic Social Thought*, 2nd ed. (Maryknoll: Orbis, 1991); Bryan J. Hehir, "Religious Activism for Human Rights: A Christian Case Study," in *Religious Human Rights in Global Perspective: Religious Perspectives*, ed. John Witte and Johan van der Vyver (The Hague: Martinus Nijhoff, 1996), 97–120.

3. Edward Cleary, *The Struggle for Human Rights in Latin America* (Westport: Praeger, 1997), 132.

4. Witte, *God's Joust, God's Justice*, 83.

5. Hehir, "Religious Activism for Human Rights: A Christian Case Study," 112.

6. Cleary, *The Struggle for Human Rights in Latin America*, 64.

7. Cleary, *The Struggle for Human Rights in Latin America*, 94.

8. Citations from the Medellín documents online: http://www.providence.edu/las/documents.htm.

9. Frances Hagopian, "Religious Pluralism, Democracy, and the Catholic Church in Latin America in the Twenty-First Century," paper presented at the conference "Contemporary Catholicism, Religious Pluralism, and Democracy in Latin America: Challenges, Responses, and Impact," University of Notre Dame, March 31–April 1, 2005, 44.

10. Jeffrey Klaiber, *The Church, Dictatorships, and Democracy in Latin America* (Maryknoll: Orbis, 1998), 11–16.

11. Klaiber, *The Church, Dictatorships, and Democracy in Latin America*, 18.

12. Kevin Boyle and Juliet Sheen, eds., *Freedom of Religion and Belief* (London: Routledge, 1997).

13. Klaiber, *The Church, Dictatorships, and Democracy in Latin America*, 50–54; Cleary, *The Struggle for Human Rights in Latin America*, 8.

14. Klaiber, *The Church, Dictatorships, and Democracy in Latin America*, 29.

15. Kenneth Serbin, *Secret Dialogues* (Pittsburgh, PA: University of Pittsburgh Press, 2000).

16. Serbin, *Secret Dialogues*, 16.

17. Kenneth Serbin, "Brazil," in *Religious Freedom and Evangelization in Latin America*, ed. Paul Sigmund (Maryknoll: Orbis, 1999), 212.

18. Hagopian, "Religious Pluralism, Democracy, and the Catholic Church in Latin America in the Twenty-First Century," 1.

19. Hagopian, "Religious Pluralism," 60.

20. Edward Cleary, "The Brazilian Catholic Church and Church-State Relations: Nation-Building," *Journal of Church and State* 39.2 (Spring 1997): 253–72.

21. Witte, *God's Joust, God's Justice*, 66.

22. In Larry Siedentop, *Tocqueville* (Oxford, Oxford University Press, 1994), 108.

23. *Spirit and Power* (Washington: Pew Forum on Religion and Public Life, 2006), 125.

24. Cesar Romero Jacob et al., *Atlas da Filiação Religiosa e Indicadores Sociais no Brasil* (Rio de Janeiro: Ed. PUC-Rio/São Paulo: Loyola, 2003), 39.

25. Paul Marshall, ed., *Religious Freedom in the World* (Nashville: Broadman and Holman, 2000), 26–27.

26. "Informe sobre Libertad Religiosa 2007," http://spanish.peru.usembassy.gov/relfreedom.html.

27. *30 Dias*, October (1990): 48–55.

28. Allan Metz, "Protestantism in Mexico: Contemporary Contextual Developments," *Journal of Church and State* 36.1 (1994): 72–73; *Revista del Instituto Rutherford*, 8 (1993): 7; Kurt Bowen, *Evangelism and Apostasy: The Evolution and Impact of Evangelicals in Modern Mexico* (Montreal and Kingston: McGill-Queen's University Press, 1996), 164, 249.

29. Edward Cleary, "The Catholic Church," in *Religious Freedom and Evangelization in Latin America*, ed. Paul Sigmund (Maryknoll: Orbis, 1999), 26.

30. Francisco Limón and Abel Clemente, "Iglesias Históricas y Pentecostales: espíritu de lucha social y participación política en México: el caso de Chiapas," in *En la Fuerza del Espíritu: Los Pentecostales en América Latina: un desafío a las iglesias históricas*, ed. Benjamín Gutiérrez (Mexico City: Aipral/Guatemala City: Celep, 1995), 189.

31. Wolfgang Huber, "Human Rights and Biblical Legal Thought," in *Religious Human Rights in Global Perspective: Religious Perspectives*, ed. John Witte and Johan van der Vyver (The Hague: Martinus Nijhoff, 1996), 58.

32. Luke Timothy Johnson, "Religious Rights and Christian Texts," in *Religious Human Rights in Global Perspective: Religious Perspectives*, ed. John Witte and Johan van der Vyver (The Hague: Martinus Nijhoff, 1996), 69.

33. John Witte, *God's Joust, God's Justice*, 105.

34. Brian Tierney, "Religious Rights: An Historical Perspective," in *Religious Human Rights in Global Perspective: Religious Perspectives*, ed. John Witte and Johan van der Vyver (The Hague: Martinus Nijhoff, 1996), 34.

35. In James E. Wood, "An Apologia for Religious Human Rights," in *Religious Human Rights in Global Perspective: Religious Perspectives*, ed. John Witte and Johan van der Vyver (The Hague: Martinus Nijhoff, 1996), 465.

36. In Edwin Gaustad, *Liberty of Conscience: Roger Williams in America* (Grand Rapids: Eerdmans, 1991), 70.

37. Ernst Troeltsch, *The Social Teaching of the Christian Churches* (Chicago: University of Chicago Press, 1931), 675.

38. Margaret Keck and Kathryn Sikkink, *Activists beyond Borders* (Ithaca: Cornell University Press, 1998), 76.

39. Max Stackhouse and Deirdre King Hainsworth, "Deciding for God: The Right to Convert in Protestant Perspectives," in *Sharing the Book*, eds. John Witte and Richard Martin (Maryknoll: Orbis, 1999), 201–30; John Nurser, *For All Peoples and All Nations* (Geneva: WCC Publications, 2005).

40. Robert Traer, *Faith in Human Rights* (Washington: Georgetown University Press, 1991), 85–92.

41. John Witte, *God's Joust, God's Justice*, 84.

42. Paul Freston, *Evangelicals in Asia, Africa and Latin America* (Cambridge, Cambridge University Press, 2001), 15.

43. Freston, *Evangelicals in Asia, Africa and Latin America*, 19.

44. Cleary, *The Struggle for Human Rights in Latin America*, 130.

45. Freston, *Evangelicals in Asia, Africa and Latin America*, 238–41.

46. Eric Kramer, "Law and the Image of a Nation: Religious Conflict and Religious Freedom in a Brazilian Criminal Case," *Law and Social Inquiry* 26.1 (2001): 35–62.

47. Ted Stahnke, "Proselytism and the Freedom to Change Religion in International Human Rights Law," 1995. www.irla.org/documents/articles/stahnke-proselytism.html.

48. *Folha de S. Paulo*, December 14, 2003.

49. Rosalind Hackett, "Human Rights: An Important and Challenging New Field for the Study of Religion," in *New Approaches to the Study of Religion*, ed. Peter Antes, Armin Geertz, and Randi Warne (Berlin: Walter de Gruyter, 2004), 190.

50. Martin Marty, "Religious Dimensions of Human Rights," in *Religious Human Rights in Global Perspective: Religious Perspectives*, ed. John Witte and Johan van der Vyver (The Hague: Martinus Nijhoff, 1996), 1, 15.

51. *Diversidade Religiosa e Direitos Humanos*. n/d. http://www.mj.gov.br/sedh/documentos/cartilha.pdf.

52. Harvey Cox, *Fire from Heaven* (London: Cassell, 1996).

53. R. Scott Appleby, *The Ambivalence of the Sacred* (Lanham: Rowman and Littlefield, 2000), 280.

54. John Burdick, *Blessed Anastácia* (New York: Routledge, 1998), 119.

55. James Spickard, "Human Rights, Religious Conflict, and Globalization: Ultimate Values in a New World Order," *Management of Social Transformations (MOST)* 1.1 (1999): 2–19.

56. In Regina Reyes Novaes, "Pentecostalismo, política, mídia e favela," in *Religião e Cultura Popular*, ed. Victor Vincent Valla (Rio de Janeiro: DP&A, 2001), 70.

57. Novaes, "Pentecostalismo," 71.

58. Paulo Lins and Maria de Lourdes da Silva, "Bandidos e Evangélicos: Extremos que se Tocam," *Religião e Sociedade* 15.1 (1990): 172.

59. Bianca Freire-Medeiros and Filippina Chinelli, "Favela e Redes Solidárias: Formas Contemporâneas de Mobilização e Organização Popular no Rio de Janeiro," CSUIM Working Paper # 2-BRA-01, 2003, 32.

60. Patrícia Birman and Marcia Leite, "Whatever Happened to What Used to Be the Largest Catholic Country in the World?" *Daedalus* 129.2 (Spring 2000), 271–90.

61. Allen Hertzke, *Freeing God's Children* (Lanham: Rowman and Littlefield, 2004), 16.

62. Paul Freston, "Evangelicalism and Fundamentalism: The Politics of Global Popular Protestantism," in *The Sage Handbook of the Sociology of Religion*, ed. James Beckford and N. J. Demerath III (London: Sage, 2007), 217–20.

BIBLIOGRAPHY

Appleby, R. Scott. *The Ambivalence of the Sacred*. Lanham: Rowman and Littlefield, 2000.

Birman, Patrícia, and Marcia Leite. "Whatever Happened to What Used to Be the Largest Catholic Country in the World?" *Daedalus* 129.2 (Spring 2000): 271–90.

Bowen, Kurt. *Evangelism and Apostasy: The Evolution and Impact of Evangelicals in Modern Mexico*. Montreal and Kingston: McGill-Queen's University Press, 1996.

Boyle, Kevin, and Juliet Sheen, eds. *Freedom of Religion and Belief*. London: Routledge, 1997.

Burdick, John. *Blessed Anastácia*. New York: Routledge, 1998.

Cleary, Edward. *The Struggle for Human Rights in Latin America*. Westport: Praeger, 1997.

Cleary, Edward. "The Brazilian Catholic Church and Church State Relations: Nation-Building." *Journal of Church and State* 39.2 (Spring 1997): 253–72.

Cleary, Edward. "The Catholic Church." In *Religious Freedom and Evangelization in Latin America*, ed. Paul Sigmund, 11–27. Maryknoll: Orbis, 1999.

Coleman, John A., ed. *One Hundred Years of Catholic Social Thought*. 2nd ed. Maryknoll: Orbis, 1991.

Cox, Harvey. *Fire from Heaven*. London: Cassell, 1996.

Diversidade Religiosa e Direitos Humanos. n/d. http://www.mj.gov.br/sedh/documentos/cartilha.pdf.

Freire-Medeiros, Bianca, and Filippina Chinelli. "Favela e Redes Solidárias: Formas Contemporâneas de Mobilização e Organização Popular no Rio de Janeiro." CSUIM Working Paper # 2-BRA-01, 2003.

Freston, Paul. *Evangelicals in Asia, Africa and Latin America*. Cambridge University Press, Cambridge, 2001.

———. "Evangelicalism and Fundamentalism: The Politics of Global Popular Protestantism." In *The Sage Handbook of the Sociology of Religion*, ed. James Beckford and N. J. Demerath III, 205–26. London: Sage, 2007.

Gaustad, Edwin. *Liberty of Conscience: Roger Williams in America.* Grand Rapids: Eerdmans, 1991.

Hackett, Rosalind. "Human Rights: An Important and Challenging New Field for the Study of Religion." In *New Approaches to the Study of Religion,* ed. Peter Antes, Armin Geertz, and Randi Warne, 165–93. Berlin: Walter de Gruyter, 2004.

Hagopian, Frances. "Religious Pluralism, Democracy, and the Catholic Church in Latin America in the Twenty-First Century." Paper presented at the conference "Contemporary Catholicism, Religious Pluralism, and Democracy in Latin America: Challenges, Responses, and Impact," University of Notre Dame, March 31–April 1, 2005.

Hehir, J. Bryan. "Religious Activism for Human Rights: A Christian Case Study." In *Religious Human Rights in Global Perspective: Religious Perspectives,* ed. John Witte and Johan van der Vyver, 97–120. The Hague: Martinus Nijhoff, 1996.

Hertzke, Allen. *Freeing God's Children.* Lanham: Rowman and Littlefield, 2004.

Huber, Wolfgang. "Human Rights and Biblical Legal Thought." In *Religious Human Rights in Global Perspective: Religious Perspectives,* ed. John Witte and Johan van der Vyver, 47–64. The Hague: Martinus Nijhoff, 1996.

Informe sobre Libertad Religiosa. 2005. Department of State (Spanish version). www.marcohuaco.com/mh.

Jacob, Cesar Romero, Dora Rodrigues Hees, Philippe Waniez, and Violette Brustlein. *Atlas da Filiação Religiosa e Indicadores Sociais no Brasil.* Rio de Janeiro: Ed. PUC-Rio/São Paulo: Loyola, 2003.

Johnson, Luke Timothy. "Religious Rights and Christian Texts." In *Religious Human Rights in Global Perspective: Religious Perspectives,* ed. John Witte and Johan van der Vyver, 65–95. The Hague: Martinus Nijhoff, 1996.

Keck, Margaret, and Kathryn Sikkink. *Activists beyond Borders.* Ithaca: Cornell University Press, 1998.

Klaiber, Jeffrey. *The Church, Dictatorships, and Democracy in Latin America.* Maryknoll: Orbis, 1998.

Kramer, Eric. "Law and the Image of a Nation: Religious Conflict and Religious Freedom in a Brazilian Criminal Case." *Law and Social Inquiry* 26.1 (2001): 35–62.

Limón, Francisco, and Abel Clemente. "Iglesias Históricas y Pentecostales: espíritu de lucha social y participación política en México: el caso de Chiapas." In *En la Fuerza del Espíritu: Los Pentecostales en América Latina: un desafío a las iglesias históricas,* ed. Benjamín Gutiérrez, 175–97. Mexico City: Aipral/Guatemala City: Celep, 1995.

Lins, Paulo, and Maria de Lourdes da Silva. "Bandidos e Evangélicos: Extremos que se Tocam." *Religião e Sociedade* 15.1 (1990): 166–73.

Marshall, Paul, ed. *Religious Freedom in the World.* Nashville: Broadman and Holman, 2000.

Marty, Martin. "Religious Dimensions of Human Rights." In *Religious Human Rights in Global Perspective: Religious Perspectives,* ed. John Witte and Johan van der Vyver, 1–16. The Hague: Martinus Nijhoff, 1996.

Metz, Allan. "Protestantism in Mexico: Contemporary Contextual Developments." *Journal of Church and State* 36.1 (1994): 57–78.

Novaes, Regina Reyes. "Pentecostalismo, política, mídia e favela." In *Religião e Cultura Popular,* ed. Victor Vincent Valla, 41–74. Rio de Janeiro: DP&A, 2001.

Nurser, John. *For All Peoples and All Nations*. Geneva: WCC Publications, 2005.

Serbin, Kenneth. "Brazil." In *Religious Freedom and Evangelization in Latin America*, ed. Paul Sigmund, 204–19. Maryknoll: Orbis, 1999.

———. *Secret Dialogues*. Pittsburgh: University of Pittsburgh Press, 2000.

Siedentop, Larry. *Tocqueville*. Oxford, Oxford University Press, 1994.

Spickard, James. "Human Rights, Religious Conflict, and Globalization: Ultimate Values in a New World Order." *Management of Social Transformations (MOST)* 1.1 (1999): 2–19.

Spirit and Power. Washington: Pew Forum on Religion and Public Life, 2006.

Stackhouse, Max, and Deirdre King Hainsworth. "Deciding for God: The Right to Convert in Protestant Perspectives." In *Sharing the Book*, ed. John Witte and Richard Martin, 201–30. Maryknoll: Orbis, 1999.

Stahnke, Ted. "Proselytism and the Freedom to Change Religion in International Human Rights Law." 1995. www.irla.org/documents/articles/stahnke-proselytism. html.

Tierney, Brian. "Religious Rights: An Historical Perspective." In *Religious Human Rights in Global Perspective: Religious Perspectives*, ed. John Witte and Johan van der Vyver, 17–46. The Hague: Martinus Nijhoff, 1996.

Traer, Robert. *Faith in Human Rights*. Washington: Georgetown University Press, 1991.

Troeltsch, Ernst. *The Social Teaching of the Christian Churches*. Chicago: University of Chicago Press, 1931.

Witte, John. *God's Joust, God's Justice*. Grand Rapids: Eerdmans, 2006.

Wood, James E. "An Apologia for Religious Human Rights." In *Religious Human Rights in Global Perspective: Religious Perspectives*, ed. John Witte and Johan van der Vyver, 455–84. The Hague: Martinus Nijhoff, 1996.

6

Gender Justice and Religion in Sub-Saharan Africa

Rogaia Mustafa Abusharaf

Are global human rights and particular cultural outlooks mutually exclusive categories, or can they be understood as reciprocally interrelated and negotiable matters that, when grasped in their dynamic totality, can serve as critical resources of empowerment? What spaces can be created for individuals and communities to critique and alter structures of power in their societies and nations, if the local and the global are reimagined in nonbinary terms? How do the local struggles of religious leaders advance our understanding of the advocacy of women's rights at the intersection of religion and the global politics of human rights?

To respond to these pressing questions, I begin by arguing that a comprehensive understanding of the burgeoning role of religion and its functioning as a significant force for social change must be linked to its engagements with the state as a "modern institution." When situated squarely within broader sociopolitical framings and processes, other binaries, especially that of tradition embodied in religious edicts versus modernity as a secularizing force, become less pronounced and more complex. Anthony Giddens, whose theory informs my effort to grapple with various ways of interrogating binary oppositions, defines "the essential element and nature and impact of modern institutions" as "the lifting out of social relations from local contexts and their rearticulation across indefinite tracts of time-space."[1] Giddens argues that this dissociation is accomplished through "disembedding mechanisms," which separate "interactions from the particularities of locales" and bring about "distanciation between the mutability of local circumstances and local engagements."[2] This perspective provides a powerful

theoretical tool for examining the ways in which local traditions are being transformed. It highlights the constant recalibration and metamorphosis of tradition
as it is subject to ongoing processes of redefinition and reassessment across
time and space.

Following Giddens, this chapter focuses on the struggle to end the practice of female genital mutilation (FGM) and specifically examines the convergence of local and global arguments around a subject deemed central to the
promotion of women's rights. It examines policy statements, public declarations, nongovernmental organization (NGO) activism, testimonials, sermons,
and other sources that connect religious beliefs and practices with human
rights principles. It begins with a theoretical discussion of gender politics,
religion, and the global discourse of human rights and of the seeming conflict
that exists between universalistic and particularistic claims. It then provides
background on the extent of FGM in Africa and the traditional religious and
cultural justifications for it. A discussion of specific local initiatives against
FGM follows, focusing on the role of religious leaders alongside women's
rights activists and in interaction with international and regional campaigns.
The analysis does not encompass South Africa and other states in which the
practice is not an accepted tradition, although these nations, like the United
Kingdom, Canada, Australia, France, and the United States, do deal with FGM
among immigrants.

Theoretical Positions

Patterns and processes of "disembedding," particularly when positioned
within a rapidly changing political universe, require serious reckoning with
the local and the global. Recognition of their multifarious forms of interrelatedness sharpens our ideas regarding the indivisibility and inalienability of
rights and the dynamics and politics of culture. Both emerge as fields of
knowledge and praxis that must be accounted for theoretically and empiri-
cally. Dissolving the assumed discontinuity between the global and the local
leads me to engage several other arguments drawn from comparative perspectives on culture, law, and society. Sally Merry identifies the localization
and vernacularization of international human rights as constructive processes that expand the compass of human rights within different cultural
perspectives. Accordingly, she has suggested building a human rights regime
"in a transnational social space where actors come together as locally embedded people and as participants in a transnational setting that has its own
norms, values, and cultural practices."[3] In a similar vein, Henrietta Moore
argues: "When we write of cultures being mobile and unbounded, or selves
as contingent and multiply positioned, or communities as being dispersed
and global, we need to be certain that we are not unintentionally cutting

people off their aspirations to the universal within their own particularities."[4] In an essay on "Islam and Human Rights in Sahelian Africa," the legal scholar and human rights advocate Abdullahi Ahmed an-Na'im comments: "The cultural diversity of any human society, and availability of different options within each culture, should make it possible to mobilize existing cultural resources in order to promote a particular objective in a given society, such as the legitimating and effectuation of international human rights norms. Appropriate strategies for such a project must be grounded on a clear understanding of the nature, dynamics and prospects of cultural transformation in the particular society."[5]

Current debates on the shifting contexts of religion in a globalized world necessitate new ways of thinking about resources for cultural change, particularly in situations where transformative politics seem impossible to institutionalize. Instead of compartmentalizing human rights, religion, and cultural processes, we must understand them as dynamic and mutually inclusive categories that take into account local and supra-local needs and interests. I take these positions on human rights, cultural particularity, religion, and the modern state to be fundamental to my analysis of the role of religious leaders in obliterating the old tradition of female genital surgeries in sub-Saharan Africa. In specific contexts, these leaders have been and continue to be indispensable partners to other community organizers and activists. Elsewhere, I have discussed how efforts to end female circumcision in colonial Sudan were backed by strong religious leaders who created significant solidarities and served as brokers and interlocutors in a campaign that addressed some of the most momentous issues regarding cultural practices and women's rights.[6] The examples discussed in this chapter demonstrate that although some commentators denounce religion as playing a reactionary role with regard to women's rights, it has been one of the most valuable tools in the localization of rights. Without vernacularization, rights discourse remains tightly linked to liberal Western traditions and rejected as distant, alien, and utterly untranslatable. Theorizing connections between the local and the global within a larger framework of culture and politics is an important tool for understanding the complex meanings and expressions surrounding the vocabulary and language of rights that are often cast as expressions of Western notions of individuality and agency. Taken together, these arguments can remove doubts about the presuppositions of rights discourse that have beleaguered local activists for decades. When they are presumed to be "universal," notions of human rights are often rejected as ethnocentric and homogenizing attacks on cultural difference.

To localize the concept of rights, the ways people think about the societies in which they live must be identified, explored in their nuanced articulations, and explicated in their varied layers of significance. In so doing, we can come to understand how human rights are understood, expressed, and utilized in specific sociocultural contexts. This interactive way of thinking about religion and human rights helps reveal creative strategies that are mobilized by diverse communities to counteract prevalent forms of violence. It requires "thick description" of societies riven by culturally sanctioned discriminatory practices. I unfold these epistemological positions in relation to a specific case on the ground in order to show that local struggles for gender justice and women's rights cannot be grasped in isolation from national, regional, and international human rights.

Contexts of Female Genital Mutilation

Female circumcision, also known as female genital mutilation (FGM), is a common practice in at least twenty-eight African countries, cutting a brutal swath through the center of the continent from Mauritania and the Ivory Coast in the west to Egypt, Somalia, and Tanzania in the east. Where it is practiced, female circumcision is passionately perpetuated and closely safeguarded; it is regarded as an essential coming-of-age ritual that ensures chastity, promotes cleanliness and fertility, and enhances the beauty of the woman's body. In Arabic the colloquial word for circumcision is *tahara*, which means to "purify." It is estimated that 100–130 million women living today have undergone genital surgeries, and each year two million more—mostly girls from four to twelve years old—will be cut.

The practice comprises a variety of ritualized surgeries, including clitoridectomy, excision, and infibulation, all of which have been performed for thousands of years. These operations are performed on girls ranging in age from infancy through puberty. Trained or untrained midwives, traditional healers, barbers, and occasionally doctors perform the surgeries. For males, ritual circumcision is a source of joyous celebration and elaborate festivities. For females, the practice is more often shrouded in secrecy, though in some settings girls are feted and given gifts after the operation. Even within the same geographic locality, the nature of the practice, its justifications, and the age at which it is performed differ vastly by ethnicity and class. There are also wide variations in its prevalence, in the type of surgery practiced, and in the rituals associated with it. For instance, the Yoruba of southwestern Nigeria remain committed to the perpetuation of female circumcision, while the Ijebus, another section of the same ethnic group, have rejected it unreservedly, although this tradition was formerly widespread in the community.

The origins of current practices in sub-Saharan Africa are impossible to ascertain, given the marked sociocultural and religious diversity of these societies. Justifications for FGM vary vastly across the continent.[7] In studying the practice among the Yoruba of southwestern Nigeria, Orbuloye, Caldwell, and Caldwell chronicled significant steps in the direction of change and offered an original interpretation of the meanings of this tradition. "The Yoruba have no great emotional investment in retaining female 'circumcision.' It is not a pillar of Yoruba culture or their new religions, and it does not distinguish them from neighboring groups. When they answer that it is their tradition, most mean that they do not want their daughters to be innovators, to be regarded as 'unnatural' and perhaps to be unmarriageable."[8] In Ethiopia, where FGM is practiced across all religious groups, the Adere and Oromo Muslims perform the practice for religious reasons, while the Christian Amhara see it as guaranteeing chastity and marriageability. The key to change in these groups, then, is to ensure that uncut daughters are regarded as marriageable and to generate social solidarity among families that refuse to have their daughters cut. The consequences of not undergoing the ritual are equally powerful: teasing, disrespect, and ostracism.[9]

In most African societies, religion is widely regarded as one of the major reasons behind the propagation of FGM as well as one of the active forces working toward its obliteration. This paradox is illuminated in Somalia, where Maryan Abdulle Qawane of the Coalition of Grassroots Women Organizations (COGWO) reports that in 2004,

> in Mogadishu alone more than 10,000 women came out to protest
> against the practice and urged the population to save their daughters,
> reminding them that it was not a religious obligation. It is estimated
> that 98% of Somali women have been subject to FGM. The majority
> of these who mostly endured the severe form of FGM (infibulation)
> were mistakenly responding to a religious obligation which they were
> led to believe existed.

Religious opposition to the practice can be traced to the precolonial era, when indigenous efforts attempted to eradicate it. But the popular belief that religious dogma endorses or even requires female circumcision is a notion that only religious authorities can contradict effectively. In Chad, where "religion is not a factor as all groups (Muslim, Christian and others) practice it, Muslims believe that it is a religious obligation and [it] is preached as such by the local sheikhs."[10] Clerics and scholars who offer alternative interpretations of key texts and practices lend religious authority to campaigns in support of women's right to bodily integrity.

Interpretations of the meanings of FGM are so abundant and various that combating or refuting any one of them in isolation is bound to be ineffective. Fully cognizant of the urgency of collaborative and holistic approaches to change, organizations have adopted strategies to persuade people to abandon the practice by articulating culturally acceptable terminology and by employing legal, medical, religious, and economic means to foster women's political representation and ability to partake in decision-making processes. Because religion is taken as authoritative by adherents, it serves as a potent counterpoint to other traditions. Its moral dimensions in particular address the perceived connections between FGM and women's purity, chastity, virtue, and honor. Religiously based programs that seek to combat FGM often inculcate the view that women's sexual morality is achieved by their own choices and values, not guaranteed by any surgical procedure. Religious leaders play a paramount role in dissociating notions of ritual purity and sexual morality from FGM and translating human rights messages to the communities in which they live.

On Religion and Gender Politics

Not only is religion important in relation to other social institutions, but its complex symbolic significances exercise a powerful influence on cultural attitudes, public policy, and overall visions of self and society. As Lamin Sanneh puts it, religion "falls like a shaft of light across the entire spectrum of life, fused and undifferentiated at one end, and refracted and highly refined at the other. From casual, daily, and spontaneous incidents to somber, highly structured, public occasions, it is the focus of elaborate and detailed interest."[11] Whether enacted in the rituals of daily life or codified in formal teachings and legal rulings, religion saturates African cultures and shapes social relationships. Religious elements help to constitute gender, from the materiality of female genital cutting to the symbolic meanings of purity and fertility it carries.

The African religious landscape is pluralistic, as cultural cosmologies and belief systems are formed by what Ali Mazrui has identified as "a triple heritage." The dynamic interaction of indigenous beliefs, Christianity, and Islam continues to sculpt Africans' political and cultural identities.[12] Mazrui emphasizes the "improvisatory and creative ways" in which Africans draw upon this multidimensional religious repertoire.[13] Most do not feel compelled to follow the dictates of one religious system exclusively but incorporate aspects of various traditions in their encounters with the most painful and joyful passages of human life. In a powerful ethnography, El-Sayed El-Aswad observes a folk cosmology within major religions, which is visible in "discursive and nondiscursive actions . . . varied arrays of similes, practices, rituals and ceremonies . . . and concepts of the person and the body."[14] The perpetual intermingling of these religions and cosmologies mirrors the dynamism and malleability of African societies, their responsiveness to change, and their active engagement in world affairs.

Religious beliefs and practices are among the most deeply rooted dimensions of cultures, and movements for human rights are more effective when they gain the support of religious authorities and mobilize the resources of religious organizations. In contemporary sub-Saharan Africa, despite the prevalent assumption among commentators outside of Africa that both indigenous and foreign religions are patriarchal and that Islam in particular is hostile to women's rights, religious leaders are also playing a positive role in the cultural transformation that the realization of gender justice entails. In sub-Saharan Africa, religion is an important force for distanciation, enabling adherents to reconsider traditions and disavow those they deem harmful. It is this capacity to disembed practices that surgically alter women's bodies from local traditions that gives religion its peculiarly subversive, even transformative power.

In elucidating the convergences of African politics with religion and human rights, anthropologist James Ferguson warns: "To take seriously African experiences of the global requires that any discussion of globalization and new world orders must first of all be a discussion of social relations of membership, responsibility, and inequality on a truly planetary scale."[15] The rising significance of grassroots campaigns for change cannot be detached from transnational constellations of forces that include the flow of capital and information across borders. African scholars and political activists have recognized the urgency of ameliorating pervasive forms of human rights violations that are legitimized through religion, gender politics, and cultural tradition.

Gender Politics in Religion

As a major source of social regulation, religion is employed to demarcate public and private, configuring situations that may buttress the subordination of women by excluding them from the exercise of formal or ritual authority and relegating them to supportive, gender-specific positions.[16] The religious traditions extending from the ancient Near East regarded women as impure and polluting; female bodies' connections with the mysterious forces of fertility made them both powerful and dangerous. In all three world religions that have influenced Africa over the millennia, women were excluded from positions of power, decision making, and authoritative interpretation of the faith. Historically, the invention and reinvention of tradition have strengthened the exclusionary practices employed to control women's bodies. Gender discrimination has routinely been justified by religious edicts, and nowhere has the exploitation of religion been so damaging to women as in matters relating to sexuality.

Within the principal faith traditions of sub-Saharan Africa, discourses on women's rights are fraught with competing explanations. According to Berger and White, less orthodox forms of Christianity often were more appealing than the mission churches because of their gendered practices and beliefs. In the Kigezi district of Southwestern Uganda, for example, the highly successful Balokole revival movement responded to women's tensions over issues of family life and sexuality and to individual difficulties in meeting the rigid standards of mission churches.[17] Because gender inequality is deeply engraved in religious and ritual practices throughout the region, these controversies and debates exemplify ongoing attitudinal changes and processes of transformation with respect to women's right to bodily integrity. In a comparative study coordinated by the International Reproductive Rights Research Action Group, Rosalind Petshskey argues that religious authorities still wield great power over women's ability to realize their sense of reproductive as well as sexual entitlement.[18] In the West and Africa alike, religious organizations have a direct influence on the provision of reproductive health services to women, as well as on public and personal opinions. In Africa, Thoraya Obaid explains: "Faith-based organizations provide 50% or more of the social services, in particular education and health services, in the poor communities."[19]

The increasingly significant role that religion plays in the global discourse of rights illustrates current efforts at unearthing what Mahnaz Afkhami calls "an epistemology of rights" within local faith traditions. "Rights are related to the changing properties of political culture, values, beliefs, and aesthetics that have to do with the dispositions of power."[20] African leaders' commitment to continental and national efforts to institutionalize reproductive and sexual rights as indivisible rights was coupled with the call for gender justice as a fundamental element in the struggle for human rights.[21] Understanding the intricacies of local, national, and regional agitation for advancing reproductive rights necessitates that we recognize the cultural embeddedness of women's bodies, sexuality, and fertility. In her important study of anthropological demography in rural Gambia, Caroline Bledsoe argues that reproductive decisions are not seen as matters of individual choice.[22] Notions of the fertile feminine body are deeply rooted in patriarchal structures of kinship and family, and gender equality cannot be attained unless human rights activists take up matters of kinship as well as sexuality.

Women's right to health is one of the most productive fields for exploring the specificities as well as the commonalities of human rights discourses relative to gender. Proponents of sexual rights in sub-Saharan Africa are well aware of the possibilities and challenges they face as they forge strategic approaches to attaining social justice and subverting previously unquestioned hierarchies and relations of power. While these rights are surrounded with profound ambivalence, their protection cannot be regarded, and therefore rejected, as a Western dictate. This ambivalence was expressed a decade ago by Aja Tounkara Dialo Fatimata, who was praised for sparing thousands of girls in her native Guinea-Bissau by staging fake operations rather than conducting surgery on their genitals. Fatimata was especially disapproving of interventionist programs aimed at ending FGM: "Western activists seem less concerned with the negative effects circumcision can have on African women's health and more concerned about their own agenda—raising issues of women's rights and sexual repression."[23]

Michelle Johnson makes three crucial observations about the situation in Guinea-Bissau. First, "Muslim women explained to me that non-Muslims oppose the practice because they are trying to take away their right to pray"; the outsiders' critique of female circumcision seemed more like a critique of

Islam than of FGM. Second, "even the Mandinga woman who refused to *toma faca* [literally, 'take up the knife' and become a traditional circumciser] so as to start up her own clothing business made it clear to me that clitoridectomy is crucial for being Mandinga and for becoming a Muslim and that the government and foreigners have no business telling Mandinga women otherwise." Third, "religious affiliation is perhaps the most readily apparent factor in the debate surrounding female 'circumcision' in Guinea-Bissau. . . . All the women with whom I spoke who were opposed to 'circumcision' for women were non-Muslims."[24]

Thorough analysis of local notions about rights is essential for comprehending the daily negotiations of these rights in light of African conditions and environmental, economic, social, and political challenges. Positioning the debates on reproductive rights within the frame of gender justice enables us to excavate local articulations and ideologies around questions of religion and cultural difference. In the context of Muslim societies, Adila Abusharaf calls for understanding the religious institutions' jurisprudential grounds for women's roles and rights and the enforceability of principles mandating gender equality from Islamic perspectives.[25] Gender justice regarding sexuality and reproduction cannot be realized without sustained explications of how women negotiate power and effect decisions in the family and society at large through deep understanding of their rights and responsibilities as citizens.

Women's Human Rights Politics in the African Union

The attainment of gender justice must be situated and understood within the broader framework of local and supra-local politics as well as within African states' politics and trajectories.[26] Grave breaches of women's human rights as a whole escalate under circumstances of political violence and civil or interstate warfare, especially when coupled with demographic, economic, and environmental stresses.[27] Many contraventions of women's human rights arise from policies that ostensibly have nothing to do with gender and are justified by a range of political ideologies.

By portraying women as guardians of moral principles and cultural tradition, African political leaders have appropriated gender in ways that are extraordinarily inauspicious to equal citizenship and opportunity. From Mubutu's promotion of *authenticité* to the El-Bashir government's enforcement of *hijab* in Sudan, women were made to acquiesce not only to male kin but also to patriarchal nationalist projects regardless of their own cultural orientation and religious affiliation. In some nations, women's rights activists have advocated structural transformation in state politics. Other African leaders have recognized the promotion of women's interests as part of the advancement of the nation as a whole. For example, historians Cheryl Johnson-Odim and Margaret

Strobel emphasized that women's liberation was part and parcel of revolutionary ideology in Guinea-Bissau during the 1960s and 1970s.[28] State-sanctioned discriminatory practices cannot be overhauled without reforms promoting good governance, accountability, democratization, and gender mainstreaming that entail the direct involvement of women's organizations and programs for capacity building, as well as social and economic mobilization.

The African Charter on Human and Peoples' Rights (formerly known as the Banjul Charter) adopted in 1981 has had a powerful influence on the realization of human rights in sub-Saharan Africa. The charter of the African Union, which entered into force on October 21, 1986, after its unanimous ratification, provides a strong endorsement of what Burns Weston, Robin Lukes, and Kelly Hnatt identify as "first generation" civil and political rights and "second generation" economic, social, and cultural rights.[29] The charter recognizes human rights "without distinction of any kind" and details individual duties as well as individual rights in "the family, society, the State, and the international African community."[30]

The charter's Protocol on the Rights of Women in Africa, adopted by the 2nd Ordinary Session of the Assembly of the African Union in Maputo on July 11, 2003, has been one of the most important tools for considering gender as a central element in development and in implementing the principles of equality enshrined in the Constitutive Act of the African Union, which refers to the observance of human and peoples' rights in its Charter, which was signed by Heads of States and Government member states of the Organization for African Unity/African Union. Article 1 of the Maputo Protocol defines discrimination against women as "any distinction, exclusion or restriction or any differential treatment based on sex and whose objectives or effects compromise or destroy the recognition, enjoyment or the exercise by women, regardless of their marital status, of human rights and fundamental freedoms in all spheres of life." Recognizing that cultural traditions and social policies have infringed on women's economic, social, civil, and political rights, the protocol urges African states to consider women's rights to dignity, integrity, and security, equality in marriage, protection before the law, political participation, promotion of peace, protection during armed conflicts, education, social welfare, reproductive rights, and health. The African Union recognizes the importance of having the tools required to build and enforce the regimes of rights expertly crafted as part of the charter.

In sub-Saharan Africa, the eradication of FGM and the institutionalization of rights are key measures for effecting gender-specific reproductive health policies that include safe motherhood and the prevention of sexually transmitted diseases (STDs) and human immunovirus/acquired immunodeficiency syndrome (HIV/AIDS). In focusing on the particularities of women's reproductive lives, the African Charter surpasses the UN Convention on the Elimination of All Forms of Discrimination against Women (CEDAW). The charter's advocacy of women's rights through various "informational, educational, prescriptive, and cooperative means" registers the importance of regional human rights regimes.[31]

Providing the tools for enshrining women's rights in African societies, the AU made explicit its view of FGM as a form of gender-based violence affecting women and girls. In Addis Ababa, February 6, 2004 was designated the first "International Day of Zero Tolerance of Female Genital Mutilation." The African Union address was delivered by its Commissioner for Social Affairs, Advocate Bience Gawanas. The AU has embarked on extensive campaigns to ratify protocols for incorporation in national laws. Among many significant actions addressing violence against women, the AU adopted the 1999–2009 African Decade for People with Disabilities, which labels FGM a disability; the Abuja Declaration and Plan of Action on HIV/AIDS; and the recommendations of the Tripoli Meeting of Ministers on FGM and gender-based violence. The African Union pressed its member states in June 2006 to end the practice of FGM, citing the trauma experienced by women and girls who undergo these procedures and the violation of human rights and dignity that accompanies them. Calling FGM an "atrocity" with serious consequences for women's health, Alpha Omar Konare, chairman of the African Union Commission, said, "We need to mobilize our communities, religious leaders, traditional leaders, women and men through education and information to change their mindset and involve them in combating FGM." Several countries that have ratified the Maputo Protocol are seeking to create a social and cultural atmosphere that supports ending the practice by forging cooperative relationships between governmental bodies and civil society organizations so as to share information, best practices, and successful experiences.[32]

Amid the rising awareness across sub-Saharan Africa of the necessity for change to alleviate women's suffering, women's groups, religious leaders, and civil society organizations have been empowered to voice their opposition to gender-based violence and other forms of discrimination against women. Mindful of the vital role of religion in the lives of people across ethnic, cultural, and linguistic boundaries, increasing numbers of international NGOs started tapping into the authority of religious leaders. Nowhere has this been more plainly demonstrated than in the case of Planned Parenthood Federation (PPF) Youth Programs. The Planned Parenthood Federation's International Youth Program has Sudanese partners who cooperate in the implementation of its programs, including Ahfad University for Women, the Sudanese Red Crescent Society, and youth from member organizations of the Network for Adolescents and Youth of Africa (NAYA). The program has also been active in Benin, Cameroon, Kenya, Nigeria, and Uganda.

Planned Parenthood's coordinated efforts with local groups, including imams, church leaders, and other religious figures, were essential in finding ways to address youth who are particularly susceptible to HIV/AIDS and other sexually transmitted diseases. The Network for Adolescents and Youth of Africa is an exemplary program directed at disentangling the contradictions that may otherwise exist between PPF's overall agenda promoting reproductive and sexual rights and local religious interpretations of that agenda. By focusing on safe motherhood and healthy childhood, PPF managed to craft consensus in favor of change. It conceded the futility of attempting to impose its vision on local communities without the full cooperation and encouragement of opinion leaders and activists. Using culturally accepted ideas about health and conveying information in an unintimidating manner, this and other international networks have helped create a productive space for contemplating health and human rights and interacting with local activists on equal terms.[33] Recently, greater emphasis has been put on human development, redressing poverty, and promoting equal citizenship through empowerment and the strengthening of women's capacities and creativity. According to Martinez, harmful traditions may be tackled more effectively by expanding women's access to locally important political and economic resources.[34]

Religious Leaders and FGM

When the British sought the support of prestigious Sudanese religious figures for the anticircumcision ban of 1946, they were acutely aware of the enormous impact religious leaders' views had on their followers. Relying heavily on the authority of religious clerics, the colonial government employed religion as one of the most practicable instruments for the obliteration of what they deemed an abominable evil.[35] Imam Abdel Rahman Almahdi of the Ansar sect and Ali El Merghani of the Khatmiya, who wielded considerable power in Sudanese society because of their social positions, wealth, and piety, were asked to approach their followers and others who invoked religious arguments in support of circumcision. The imams contested the authenticity of the most famous sayings of Prophet Muhammed that appeared to condone, if not recommend, female circumcision.

In colonial Kenya, John W. Arthur, a medical missionary and minister of the Church of Scotland stationed among the Kikuyu, searched for ways to bolster the mission's opposition to clitoridectomy and in 1929 demanded that Presbyterian Christians abstain from the practice because it entailed unnecessary suffering. In both Kenya and Sudan, female genital cutting emerged as a major site of highly charged conflicts over nationalism, sovereignty, colonial intrusion in cultural life, and prospects for self-government. These controversies continue today, but in the postcolonial context this debate can be conducted on more focused grounds having to do with women's lives rather than their significance as a symbol of "authentic" national traditions.

For Imam Demba Diawara, a prominent Muslim leader in Simbara, Senegal, promoting women's human rights is not an agenda imposed by foreign powers but a fundamental expression of his value system and religious beliefs. His remarkable involvement in the campaign against ritualized genital surgeries on girls and women was featured in reports on activities conducted by Tostan, an African NGO that focuses on women's reproductive health.

> Imam Demba Diawara, a 76 year-old local religious leader, first
> grappled with the issue of female genital cutting [FGC] when women
> of his village asked him (if the practice) were a religious obligation.
> The women had learned about the negative health consequences of
> FGC through the Tostan education program in their village and
> thought to abandon the practice if, and only if, the Quran did not
> require the cutting. The Imam read, reflected, and consulted reli-
> gious colleagues before telling them that FGC is not an obligation of
> Islam. For three months, the elderly Imam walked from village to
> village—engaging extended family members in discussions on FGC
> and persuading them to join Keur Simbara [his own village] in
> ending the practice. His efforts culminated in a public declaration
> ceremony that ended the practice in ten villages.[36]

The positive response to Imam Diawara's message demonstrates the importance of religion in African sociopolitical and cultural life.

The field of human rights activism in sub-Saharan Africa is bursting with exemplary efforts aiming at constructing conditions that are favorable to valuing women's dignity and entitlement to freedom from violence and abuse. Religious leaders have been indispensable partners in this grassroots movement. They have been committed to propagating the recognition of gender justice as part of a larger, homegrown critique of patriarchal notions of tradition, gender, and kinship. Considering the many obstacles to attaining women's human rights, including their right to bodily integrity, the participation of the community's most respected teachers is often crucial.

The active involvement of male clerics is a key part of the process of localizing human rights and gender justice. In Sudan, Sheikh Ahmed Hassan Abu Sabib, like his counterparts in Senegal, Mali, and Gambia, has mobilized his enormous moral authority to affirm and reiterate important clarifications that figured in the Banjul Declaration. This learned Muslim jurist deliberately dissociated the practice from orthodox Islam. In a workshop led by the Babikir Bedri Association, he responded to a set of questions that Muslims frequently ask.

> Is female circumcision a *"makrama,"* a pious act that was sanctioned
> by Islam, or a cultural invention that has no relationship to religion?
> How can you explain the fact that there is no linguistic distinction
> between *"tahara"* as purification and *"tahara"* as used to signify

ritualized genital cutting? And does the prospective husband have the
right to make inquiries about whether the woman he is about to
marry is circumcised "*mukhafada*" or not? On the first topic, Sheikh
Abu Sabib reaffirmed that female circumcision is not obligatory and
is exceedingly detrimental to women's right to health and freedom
from harm, and *tahara* as cleanliness should not be confused with
violence against the body. As for the last question, he illuminated a
widely held view in Islam, that the partner has the right to know
about any malady or "*aib*," imperfection, so as to resolve for herself
or himself whether she or he wishes to marry. Certain kinds of
diseases are perceived as grounds for marriage annulment, and
circumcision is the mutilation of a woman's body that can be seen as
a major flaw.

The most exceptional aspect of this statement is that Sheikh Abu Sabib declared
genital mutilation a condition that might, instead of rendering a woman marriageable, be taken as disqualifying her for marriage to a man who seeks a bride
whose body is inviolate.

The blending of local, national, regional, and international forces is clear in
the activities of the Sudanese Committee on Traditional Harmful Practices Affecting the Health of Women and Children (SCTNP). This organization has
made religion central to its efforts to persuade fervent supporters of female circumcision that the practice is contrary to Muslim teachings about the body. With
support from The United Nations Children's Fund (UNICEF), SCTNP has prepared "an appeal to the family" headlined "*El-Din Yanhi*," Religion Prohibits:

FGM destroys one's physical and bodily integrity, thus it is a cruel
injury of the human body, which Allah has produced, in a perfect,
unblemished form. The practice is barbaric and therefore disallowed
by major world religions. It is not a Sunna or a prophet's tradition
but instead it is a remnant of *jahilia* or the days of ignorance that
preceded Islam. It is not obligatory and has no links to the safeguard-
ing of chastity and honor, which can only be promoted through
proper Islamic education and ethics.

These views are articulated in various forums in Khartoum, such as *Al-Muntada
El-Fiqhi li Khifad El-Inath*, the Juridical Forum on Female Circumcision.

Current efforts in sub-Saharan Africa to promote the endorsement of
women's rights to bodily integrity and sexual rights illuminate the dynamic
intersections of religion with human rights politics. This aspect of the religious
argument is significant since it challenges the perception that the right to cor-
poreal and sexual integrity relies solely on liberal notions of autonomy and
individuality and that those who invoke them are proponents of a universalized
discourse on sexuality, the body, and subjectivity.[37] Although these connections

have only recently emerged as a subject of sustained scholarly analysis, the issues figured prominently in a range of sociocultural and historical contexts across Africa. It is important to note that the role of religious leaders who support women's rights is significant precisely because it often rises above the romanticization and exaltation of ideas of tradition and nationalism by showing exactly how these hierarchical forces of domination conspire to obstruct the struggle for human rights. Living under state violence left no alternative for these leaders but to call a spade a spade, even if they had to fall back on the language of human rights.

The struggle against FGM has both led to and been facilitated by the promulgation of several declarations against the continuation of the practice, including those adopted in Djibouti, Abuja, Ouagadougou, Burkina Faso, Addis Ababa, and Banjul. These declarations have enormous symbolic power, especially in their capacity to tackle the tenacious dilemma of individual versus group rights. These rights are not mutually exclusive. Because female circumcision is a transformative rite of passage that ensures marriageability and future social security, FGM is widely safeguarded by particular communities and subgroups within them, such as the Bundo and Sande secret societies of Sierra Leone. These collective declarations empower individual families to make decisions that were previously unimaginable. In many situations, they helped to prevent the impending cutting because the justifications behind it were subjected to critical reflection.

The Banjul Declaration, issued by religious leaders and medical practitioners who attended a workshop on FGM, typifies this approach to the indissoluble character of women's rights and their compatibility with cultural rights.

On Violence against Women

We the participants at the Symposium for Religious Leaders and Medical Personnel on FGM as a Form of Violence, organized by the Inter-African Committee on Traditional Practices/GAMCOTRAP, held in Banjul, The Gambia July 20–23, 1998, declare as follows:

* Having examined and appreciated the health and human rights implications of violence against women and girls, particularly female genital mutilation;

* Having recognized that in Africa over 100 million women and girls are victims of FGM;

* Having confirmed that FGM has neither Islamic nor Christian origin or justifications;

* Seriously concerned by the incorrect interpretations and misuse of Islamic teachings to perpetuate violence against women, particularly FGM;

* Upholding the principle of equality and justice for all, without discrimination between men and women;

* Reaffirming the universality of human rights principles and their indivisibility;

Hereby strongly condemn the continuation of female genital mutilation.

Condemn the misuse of religious argument to perpetuate FGM and other forms of violence.

Commit ourselves to clarify the misinterpretation of religion and to teach the true principles of Islam and Christianity with regard to violence against women, including FGM.

Propose:

* The setting up of a network of religious leaders and scholars to support the IAC in its campaign against harmful traditional practices.

* The establishment of family tribunals, comprising men and women, to settle family disputes.

* Family laws to be reviewed in the light of Christian and Islamic principles and human rights.

* Legislate against the continuation of the practice of FGM, stipulating penalties for offenders.

* Call on all religious leaders to spare no efforts to enhance the campaign aimed at freeing women from all forms of violence, including FGM.

The Banjul participants recognized that "harmful traditional practices" such as FGM, while popularly regarded as based on religious precepts, are in truth not justified by religious teachings and violate the principles of Islam and Christianity as well as of international human rights.

The power of religion in validating the critique of female circumcision as a breach of human rights is evidenced in the testimony of Isnino Shurie of Kenya, whose experience as a former circumciser was chronicled by Efua Dorkenoo in *Awaken*.[38] "The clerics told me that cutting off a woman's genitals is just as bad as cutting off any other body part, like a finger or an arm. . . . They told me that . . . genitals . . . are organs and . . . are part of us for a reason." Those who damaged a woman by cutting her genitals owed her compensation. Shurie realized that "I've circumcised so many girls and I knew I couldn't pay that amount. I asked if there was anything else I could do for God to forgive my sins and they said that I must go to each girl that I circumcised and ask for forgiveness. And if the girls were no longer alive I must ask forgiveness from God." Her decision to stop performing genital surgeries attests to the compelling character of religious proscription, since other programs have had difficulty persuading midwives and ritual specialists to give up this source of income.

Several gatherings organized to mobilize leaders of religious communities in support of women's human rights have issued declarations on the subject of FGM. For example, after intense debate on religious and legal issues, participants in an East Africa regional conference concluded, "FGM is not a religious or medical requirement." Religious leaders joined government officials, scholars, and representatives of NGOs, the UN, the AU, and civil society organizations in a two-day conference organized by the Sudan National Committee on Traditional Practices and Womankind. TOMRIC news agency reported that during a two-day symposium in Arusha, Tanzania, religious leaders denounced FGM and called for immediate action against the practice.[39] The symposium, organized by the Inter-African Committee, included fifty African religious and traditional leaders and representatives from the World Health Organization (WHO) and UNICEF. Participants concluded that FGM is not a religious tradition or an obligation in Islam.[40] These interfaith campaigns were prominent in Senegal, Sudan, and Mali, among other societies where the practice is nearly universal.[41]

Christian leaders have effected dramatic changes in Tanzania, Ethiopia, and Nigeria. Seventh-day Adventists, also drawing on biblical principles, issued a statement against FGM.[42] Today numerous organizations representing various institutions and religious denominations and networks have opened channels for communication to improve women's conditions through political, legal, and social reforms. The Center for Health and Social Policy report details pan-African networks and faith-based groups working in specific countries.[43]

Campaigns against FGM in sub-Saharan Africa have articulated this practice as a significant health risk. In Tanzania, where maternal mortality is a significant concern, the WHO provided support to the Ministry of Health to incorporate into its agenda education about the risks to healthy childbearing that FGM creates along with information about HIV/AIDS and STDs. The government also passed the Sexual Offenses Special Provision Act, which defines causing a "girl child under 18 years of age . . . to be genitally mutilated" as a criminal offense.[44] This governmental action was followed by campaigns led by civil society and faith-based organizations to obliterate the practice, persuading people to comply with the law before they encountered its coercive power. A variety of Christian churches played influential roles.[45] Backed by the government's ratification of important international conventions and the passage of national laws, these groups have managed to strike a balance between individual and community rights by showing that religion seeks to promote health and security.

The growing influence of male religious leaders in the struggle against FGM led Equality Now, a New York-based NGO, to devote a section of its newsletter *Awaken* to this important development in human rights advocacy. These campaigns are especially notable for their collaboration between religious leaders who promulgate the idea that the female body was created perfect and feminists who critique the gender ideologies that justify the continuation of FGM. Feminist gatherings in Sudan and other countries have begun to include clergy from a variety of faith traditions. One of the pioneering conferences was African Women Speak, held in Khartoum in October 1984. Following careful deliberations of the cultural, political, and religious factors affecting female circumcision, women's rights activists from Sudan, Gambia, Somalia, Liberia, Kenya, Ghana, Djibouti, Sierra Leone, Egypt, Togo, Ethiopia, Eritrea, and Mali drafted a Plan of Action that involved letters of appeal to all heads of state, the secretary general of the United Nations, and the secretary general of the OAU (now the African Union).[46]

In Mali, a predominantly Muslim country with an FGM prevalence rate of 91 percent across ethnic and religious boundaries, the state has coordinated campaigns with international organizations such as Plan International to advance social transformation through drama, folk songs, storytelling, and radio talk shows. The participation of prominent imams such as Alhaji Zeidi Drame in the campaign proved particularly valuable. A key participant in Islamic Action, which represents the association of progressive Muslims, Imam Drame worked assiduously to refute the popular belief that uncircumcised women are prone to sexual immorality. Pronouncing the practice of FGM "a relic from pagan times," Imam Drame has painstakingly woven discourses of Islam as a modernizing, liberating influence in Malian social life.[47]

The government of Mali adopted a National Plan for the Eradication of Excision by 2007 and has ratified numerous international treaties, including the Women's Convention, Children's Rights Convention, Civil and Political Rights Covenant, Economic, Social and Cultural Rights Covenant, Banjul Charter, and the African Charter.[48] In a society in which religion plays such a substantial role, religious leaders play a constructive role in supporting public policy and persuading the populace to uphold women's reproductive rights. However, the involvement of religion in fashioning the discourse on women's rights in Mali cannot be understood in isolation from other processes pertaining to democratization, in which segments of this society are espousing the principles of gender justice and women's mobilization across ethnic lines.[49] As a constitutional democracy, Mali has maintained a good human rights record, which resonates with its campaign for women's rights. This political framework was amenable to the acceptance of the 1994 Population and Development Conference in Cairo, in which the issue of reproductive rights was identified as the prime concern on the public policy and development agenda.

Grassroots organizations across sub-Saharan Africa are promoting change in their communities. In Chad, Sudan, Burkina Faso, and Congo-Brazzaville, activists have called on their governments to end female circumcision through a variety of measures, including the ratification of regional and international instruments. Women's groups and other civil society organizations have joined with religious leaders to implement national, regional, and international human rights agreements and disseminate knowledge about women's human rights and entitlements to health and bodily integrity. For example, in Cameroon, where all Muslims and two-thirds of Christians in the southwest and northern provinces adhere to FGM, women members of the Cameroon National Assembly have persisted in promoting a bill banning the practice and demanding the acknowledgment of women's rights to sexual enjoyment as a gender justice issue.[50] According to Mme. Toure Zenabou of the Inter-African Committee (IAC) Togo, attitudes toward the practice are shifting as sensitization of community members, excisors, traditional chiefs, and religious leaders goes hand in hand with advocacy of social and economic transformation.[51] Recognition of religion as a force in social change is evident in Uganda's Kapchorwa region, where the Sabiny Elders Association (SEA) received a major United Nations Population Fund (UNFPA) award in 1998 for initiatives leading people to abandon FGM. SEA managed to fashion a constructive dialogue about tradition and culture as open-ended categories that are subject to everyday negotiation and reconsideration.

Conclusion

Efforts to end female genital mutilation offer a unique opportunity for diverse religious communities and faith-based organizations to collaborate as citizens concerned about health and human rights. Because of their vast moral credibility, religious leaders who spoke out in this cause were not seen by the communities in question as interventionist, much less intrusive, but rather as introducing sustained strategies for promoting change and carrying out cultural critique. Muslim and Christian leaders have worked hand in hand as partners for human rights, building bridges across religious differences. Their efforts provide a compelling response to a fundamental question raised by Abdullahi An-Na'im: "Can an analysis of human rights issues through multiple view points, both cross-cultural and indigenous, help us reinterpret and reconstruct prevailing theories of human rights?"[52]

Some critics see religion as a force that legitimates discrimination against women everywhere. This view oversimplifies the complex role of religion in the growing activist networks that seek to foster women's individual and collective power. National, regional, and international organizations working to promote women's rights have recognized the value of involving religious leaders as key cultural brokers. African women have worked collaboratively to put into practice an inclusive approach to violence in all its layered complexity, addressing reproductive rights within the context of HIV/AIDS, domestic violence, structural adjustment, sex work, and trafficking.[53] Women in sub-Saharan Africa, like their counterparts elsewhere in the continent, have not accepted their subordination without objection. They have managed to mobilize collectively, construct alliances, and define empowerment in their own terms as they contest their secondary status within and beyond the household. They are cognizant that reproductive and sexual rights are closely associated with their capacity to negotiate their position and their ability to participate actively in politics. As evidenced in the work of numerous civil society organizations in sub-Saharan Africa today, the empowerment of women is within reach if policies and laws within these countries value the paramount role women are playing at all levels of state and society and find cultural validation in social institutions that are as fundamental and powerful as religion.

Close analysis of the vital roles being played by religious leaders and teachers in these multifaceted campaigns to eradicate female genital mutilation and advance women's human rights across sub-Saharan Africa illuminates a different paradox than that with which this chapter begins. Not only is religion among those forces that both uphold and subvert the practice of FGM, but change is facilitated by a double movement. Religious discourses and organizations both localize international human rights by linking them firmly to vernacular understandings of social relations and dissociate the practice of FGM and its connotations of fertility, chastity, and purity from their embeddedness in cultural traditions. Simultaneously opening prevalent practices to scrutiny in the light of ultimate values regarding the sacredness of the human body and validating alternative practices through the authority of religion is a uniquely powerful combination.

This dialectical process is especially apparent in the Alternative Rights of Passage developed in four predominantly Christian districts in Kenya. This initiative was successful because local people were central in crafting the approach to ending genital cutting. According to Mahmoud, Radeny, and Ringheim, religious leaders and ritual specialists widened community support for alternative rights of passage, promoting confidence in the program and dispelling common myths.[54] Strikingly, this program valorizes the transmission of traditional wisdom from female elders to younger generations of women while incorporating modern instruction in health promotion and disease prevention, including reproductive and sexual rights. This fusion of critique of popular practices and local engagement with women's human rights, including the right to bodily integrity, exemplifies the most constructive roles that religious communities play in advancing gender justice in sub-Saharan Africa.

NOTES

I am indebted to Tom Banchoff and Bob Wuthnow, organizers of the conference on "Religion and the Global Politics of Human Rights," for inviting me to undertake this project and for providing helpful comments on the paper I presented. Brown University student Andrea Richardson did excellent library research. Marwa Maziad has provided inestimable help with much needed technical assistance. Thanks to Grey Osterud who helped to clarify many arguments and to Adila Mustafa Abusharaf for sharing her connections on the continent.

1. Anthony Giddens, *Modernity and Self-identity* (Stanford, CA: Stanford University Press, 1991), 18.

2. Ibid., 21.

3. Sally Merry, *Human Rights and Gender Violence: Translating International Law into Local Justice* (Chicago: University of Chicago Press, 2006), 37.

4. Henrietta Moore, *Anthropological Theory Today* (Cambridge: Cambridge University Press, 2000), 16.

5. Abdullahi Ahmed An-Na'im, "Islam and Human Rights in Sahelian Africa," in *African Islam and Islam in Africa*, ed. Eva Rosander and David Westerland (Athens: Ohio University Press, 1997), 75–95.

6. Rogaia Mustafa Abusharaf, "Ina Beasley: Her Perspectives on Women's Prospects in British Sudan," Sir William Luce Fellowship Publication Series, Paper no. 8, Durham University Institute for Middle Eastern and Islamic Studies, 2007.

7. See Anika Rahman and Nahid Toubia, *Female Genital Mutilation: A Guide to Laws and Policies Worldwide* (London: Zed Books, 2000).

8. See I. O. Orubuloye, Pat Caldwell, and John Caldwell, "Female 'Circumcision' among the Yoruba of Southwestern Nigeria: Beginning of Change," in *Female Circumcision in Africa: Culture, Controversy, and Change*, ed. Bettina Shell-Duncan and Ylva Hernlund (Boulder, CO: Lynn Reinner, 2007), 3–95.

9. Rogaia Mustafa Abusharaf, "Unmasking Tradition: A Sudanese Anthropologist Confronts Female Circumcision and Its Terrible Tenacity," *The Sciences* 38:2 (1998): 34–35.

10. *Awaken*, Newsletter on Female Genital Mutilation published by Equality Now, 9 (2004).

11. Lamin Sanneh, "New Gods," in *The Africans*, ed. Ali A. Mazrui and Toby K. Levine (Westport, CT: Praeger, 1986), 83.

12. See Mazrui A. Ali and Toby K. Levine, eds., *The Africans* (Westport, CT: Praeger, 1986); and see also John Hunwick, "Sub-Saharan Africa and the Wider World of Islam," in *African Islam and Islam in Africa*, ed. David Westerlund and Eva Rosander (Athens: Ohio University Press, 1997), 28–54; and David Dickson, "Political Islam in Sub-Saharan Africa: The Need for a New Research and Diplomatic Agenda," Special Report 140 (Washington, DC: United States Institute of Peace, 2005).

13. Mazrui and Levine, eds., *The Africans*, 8.

14. Al-Sayed El-Aswad, *Religions and Folk Cosmology: Scenarios of the Visible and Invisible in Rural Egypt* (Westport, CT: Praeger, 2002), 9.

15. James Ferguson, *Global Shadows* (Durham: NC: Duke University Press, 2006), 23.

16. Cheryl Johnson-Odim and Margaret Strobel, "Conceptualizing the History of Women," in *Women in Sub-Saharan Africa*, ed. Iris Berger and Frances White (Bloomington: Indiana University Press, 1999), xxvi–ixi.

17. Iris Berger and Frances White, *Women in Sub-Saharan Africa* (Bloomington: Indiana University Press, 1999), 40–41.

18. Rosalind P. Petchesky, "Cross-country Comparisons and Political Visions," in *Negotiating Reproductive Rights: Women's Perspectives across Countries and Cultures*, ed. Rosalind P. Petchesky and Karen Judd (London: Zed Books, 1998), 305.

19. Thoraya A. Obaid, "Religion and Reproductive Health and Rights," *Journal of the American Academy of Religion* 73:4 (2005): 1159.

20. Mahnaz Afkhami, ed., *Faith and Freedom: Women's Human Rights in the Muslim World* (I. B. Tauris, 2000), 5.

21. See Fareda Banda, *Women, Law and Human Rights: An African Perspective* (Portland: Hart Publishing, 2005). See also Obioma Nnaemeka and Joy Ezeilo, eds., *Engendering Human Rights and Socioeconomic Realities in Africa* (New York: Palgrave Macmillan, 2006).

22. Caroline Bledsoe, "Reproductive Relativity: Time, Space, and Western Contraception in Rural Gambia," *Ahfad Journal* 22:1 (2005): 3–21.

23. Quoted in *San Diego Union-Tribune*, cited in *Awaken*, Newsletter on Female Genital Mutilation published by Equality Now (1997), 8.

24. Michelle Johnson, "The Internal Debate Surrounding Female 'Circumcision,'" *Awaken* 4:3 (2000): 9–11.

25. Adila M. Abusharaf, "Women in Islamic Communities: The Quest for Gender Justice Research," *Human Rights Quarterly* 28 (2006): 717–18.

26. Naomi Chazan, "Gender Perspectives on African States," in *Women and the State in Africa*, ed. Jane L. Parpart and Kathleen Staudt (Boulder, CO: Lynn Reinner, 1989), 186.

27. Caroline Delaney and Sonja Vonga, "Conflict Risk Assessment Report," Foreign Policy Project, Norman Paterson School of International Affairs, Ottawa, Canada, 2002.

28. Cheryl Johnson-Odim and Margaret Strobel, "Conceptualizing the History of Women," in *Women in Sub-Saharan Africa*, ed. Iris Berger and Frances White (Bloomington: Indiana University Press, 1999), xiv.

29. Burns Weston, Robin Ann Lukes, and Kelly M. Hnatt, "Regional Human Rights Regimes: A Comparison and Appraisal," in *Human Rights in the World Community*, ed. Richard Pierre Claude and Burns Weston (Philadelphia: University of Pennsylvania Press, 1992), 251.

30. Quoted in ibid., 251. For the full address, see Alpha Omar Konare, "Keynote Address on International Day on Zero Tolerance against Female Genital Mutilation," Addis Ababa, Febuary 6, 2004, http://www.africa-union.org/official_ documents/Speeches_&_Statements/other/Adv.%20obience%20keynote%20 address%20at%20the%20IAC%20Meeting%20on%20FGM%20-%206%20 Feb%20041.pdf.

31. Rachel Murray, *Human Rights in Africa: From the OAU to the African Union* (Cambridge: Cambridge University Press, 2004), 251.

32. No Peace without Justice Newsletter, "2004–2006 Campaign for the Ratification of the Maputo Protocol," posted on Democracy Assistance Dialogue Program, www.npwj.org/npwj_topics_fgm.

33. For critiques, see Kamran Asdar Ali, *Planning the Family in Egypt* (Austin: University of Texas Press, 2002), and also James Ferguson, *Global Shadows* (Durham: NC: Duke University Press, 2006).

34. Samuel Martinez, "Searching for a Middle Path: Rights, Capabilities, and Political Culture in the Study of Female Genital Cutting," *Ahfad Journal* 22:1 (2005): 31–45.

35. Rogaia Abusharaf, "'We Have Supped So Deep in Horrors': Understanding Colonialist Emotionality and British Responses to Female Circumcision in Northern Sudan," *History and Anthropology* 17:3 (2006b): 209–29.

36. Julia M. Masterson and Julie Swanson, *Female Genital Cutting: Breaking the Silence, Enabling Change* (Washington, DC: International Center for Research on Women and the Centre for Development and Population Activities, 2000), 12.

37. Rogaia Abusharaf, ed., *Female Circumcision: Multicultural Perspectives* (Philadelphia: University of Pennsylvania Press, 2006a), 11.

38. Efua Dorkenoo, "Reflections on Testimonies of Traditional Excisors," *Awaken* 8:2 (2004): 10.

39. *Awaken*, Newsletter on Female Genital Mutilation published by Equality Now (2000).

40. "Religious and Legal Debate on FGM Held in Khartoum," *Awaken* 9:1 (2005): 8.

41. Nafissatou Diop and Ian Askew, "Strategies for the Abandonment of Female Genital Cutting: Experiences from Senegal, Burkina Faso, and Mali," in *Female Circumcision: Multicultural Perspectives*, ed. Rogaia M. Abusharaf (Philadelphia: University of Pennsylvania Press, 2006), 125–42.

42. Adventist News Network, "Adventists Speak Out on Female Genital Mutilation," April 25, 2000, http://news.adventist.org/2000/04/avetists-speak-out-o-female-genital-mutilatio.html; IRIN News, "End Female Genital Mutilation—African Union," June 16, 2006, http://www.irinnews.org/Report.aspx?ReportId=59355.

43. Center for Health and Social Policy, "Religion and Sexual and Reproductive Health and Rights: An Inventory of Organizations, Scholars and Foundations," report for the John D. and Catherine T. MacArthur Foundation and Ford Foundation (San Francisco: The Center for Health and Social Policy, 2005) among regional organizations, the report lists African Forum of Faith-based Organizations in Reproductive Health and HIV/AIDS, African Women of Faith Network, African Women Economic Policy Network, African Council of Religious Leaders, Akina Mama WA Africa, All Africa Council of Churches, Balm in Gilead, Circle of Concerned African Women Theologians, and Ecumenical HIV/AIDS Initiative in Africa. Among networks operating in specific countries, the report includes Anglican Church of Tanzania; Christian Health Association of Kenya, Nigeria, and Zambia; Christian Relief and Development of Ethiopia; Church of Uganda; Churches Health Association of Zambia; Current Evangelical Ministries of West Africa; Positive Muslims of South Africa; Tanzania Episcopal Conference; Ugandan Protestant and Catholic Medical Bureaus; and World Conference on Religion and Peace in South Africa.

44. Parliament of the United Republic of Tanzania, *The Sexual Offences Special Provisions Act, 1998*, 2 no. 4, http://www.parliament.go.tz/Polis/PAMS/Docs/4-1998.pdf.

45. Tanzanian reports were featured in Xinhua News Agency, June 4, 1998. It is also important to note that some of the most influential groups include the Evangelical Lutheran Church of Arusha, Kilimanjaro, Mara, and Dodoma regions; Catholic

Church-Dodoma; Anglican Church; Seventh-day Adventists Church of Mara, Dodoma, and Kilimanjaro; and Lutheran Eastern Diocese of Arusha.

46. "Synopsis: Proceedings of the Workshop African Women Speak on Female Circumcision," Khartoum, October 21–25, 1984.

47. See IRIN News. "FGM in Mali connected to pre-Islamic traditions," June 15, 2004, http://www.afrol.com/articles/13372.

48. Anika Rahman and Nahid Toubia, *Female Genital Mutilation: A Guide to Laws and Policies Worldwide* (London: Zed Books, 2000), 180.

49. Women's organizations in Mali are key to the overall population and health policy. They include Malian Association for Human Rights, Promotion of Women's Associations, Association for the Progress and Defense of the Rights of Malian Women, Women's Collective of Mali, Action Committee for the Rights of the Child and the Woman. See Human Rights Library at the University of Minnesota, http://www1.umn.edu/humanrts/africa/mali.htm.

50. Rahman and Toubia, *Female Genital Mutilation*, 52. This bill was dismissed in spite of sustained campaigning by the Ministry of Women's Affairs since the 1980s; see Rahman and Toubia, 2000, and see also *Cameroon Tribune*, June 12, 2006, quoted in *Awaken* (2006): 3–4.

51. *Awaken*, Newsletter on Female Genital Mutilation published by Equality Now (2000).

52. Nigel Rapport and Joanna Overing, *Social and Cultural Anthropology: Key Concepts* (London: Routledge, 2000), 75.

53. Meredith Trushen, ed., *African Women's Health* (New Brunswick, NJ: Africa World Press, 2000).

54. Asha Mahamoud, Samson Radeny, and Karin Ringheim, "Community-based Efforts to End Female Genital Mutilation in Kenya: Raising Awareness and Organizing Alternative Rights of Passage," in *Female Circumcision: Multicultural Perspectives*, ed. Rogaia M. Abusharaf (Philadelphia: University of Pennsylvania Press, 2006), 73–104.

BIBLIOGRAPHY

Abu Sabib, Hassan. "Ask about Circumcision." Presentation at a workshop by the Babikir Bedri Association for Women's Studies, Omdurman, Sudan, 1993.

Abusharaf, Adila M. "Women in Islamic Communities: The Quest for Gender Justice Research." *Human Rights Quarterly* 28 (2006): 714–28.

Abusharaf, Rogaia Mustafa. "Ina Beasley: Her Perspectives on Women's Prospects in British Sudan." Sir William Luce Fellowship Publication Series, Paper no. 8. Durham University Institute for Middle Eastern and Islamic Studies. Durham, UK, 2007.

———, ed. *Female Circumcision: Multicultural Perspectives*. Philadelphia: University of Pennsylvania Press, 2006a.

———. "'We Have Supped So Deep in Horrors': Understanding Colonialist Emotionality and British Responses to Female Circumcision in Northern Sudan." *History and Anthropology* 17:3 (2006b): 209–29.

———. "Unmasking Tradition: A Sudanese Anthropologist Confronts Female Circumcision and Its Terrible Tenacity." *The Sciences* 38:2 (1998): 22–28.

Adventist News Network. "Adventists Speak Out on Female Genital Mutilation." April 25, 2000, http://news.adventist.org/2000/04/avetists-speak-out-o-female-geital-mutilatio.html.

Afkhami, Mahnaz, ed. *Faith and Freedom: Women's Human Rights in the Muslim World.* London, New York, and Melbourne I. B. Tauris 2000.

Ali, Kamran Asdar. *Planning the Family in Egypt.* Austin: University of Texas Press, 2002.

An–Na'im, Abdullahi Ahmed. "Islam and Human Rights in Sahelian Africa." In *African Islam and Islam in Africa,* ed. Eva Rosander and David Westerland, 75–95. Athens: Ohio University Press, 1997.

Awaken. Newsletter on Female Genital Mutilation published by Equality Now (1997), http://www.equalitynow.orglEnglish/campagins/fgm/awaken.en.html.

Awaken. Newsletter on Female Genital Mutilation published by Equality Now (1999), http://www.equalitynow.orglEnglish/campagins/fgm/awaken.en.html

Awaken. Newsletter on Female Genital Muitlation published by Equality Now (2000), http://www.equalitynow.orglEnglish/campagins/fgm/awaken.en.html.

Awaken. Newsletter on Female Genital Mutilation published by Equality Now, 9 (2004), http://www.equalitynow.orglEnglish/campagins/fgm/awaken.en.html.

Awaken. Newsletter on Female Genital Muitlation published by Equality Now (2005), http://www.equalitynow.orglEnglish/campagins/fgm/awaken.en.html.

Awaken. Newsletter on Female Genital Mutilation published by Equality Now (2006), http://www.equalitynow.orglEnglish/campagins/fgm/awaken.en.html.

Banda, Fareda. *Women, Law and Human Rights: An African Perspective.* Portland: Hart Publishing, 2005.

Berger, Iris, and Frances White. *Women in Sub-Saharan Africa.* Bloomington: Indiana University Press, 1999.

Bledsoe, Caroline. "Reproductive Relativity: Time, Space, and Western Contraception in Rural Gambia." *Ahfad Journal* 22:1 (2005): 3–21.

Center for Health and Social Policy. "Religion and Sexual and Reproductive Health and Rights: An Inventory of Organizations, Scholars and Foundations." Report for the John D. and Catherine T. MacArthur Foundation and Ford Foundation. San Francisco: The Center for Health and Social Policy 2005.

Chazan, Naomi. "Gender Perspectives on African States." In *Women and the State in Africa,* ed. Jane L. Parpart and Kathleen Staudt, 185–203. Boulder, CO: Lynn Reinner, 1989.

Delaney, Caroline, and Sonja Vonga. "Conflict Risk Assessment Report." *Foreign Policy Project,* Norman Paterson School of International Affairs, Ottawa, Canada, 2002.

Dickson, David. "Political Islam in Sub-Saharan Africa: The Need for a New Research and Diplomatic Agenda." Special Report 140. Washington, DC: United States Institute of Peace, 2005.

Diop, Nafissatou, and Ian Askew. "Strategies for the Abandonment of Female Genital Cutting: Experiences from Senegal, Burkina Faso, and Mali." In *Female Circumcision: Multicultural Perspectives,* ed. Rogaia M. Abusharaf, 125–42. Philadelphia: University of Pennsylvania Press, 2006.

Dorkenoo, Efua. "Reflections on Testimonies of Traditional Excisors." *Awaken* 8:2 (2004): 10.

El-Aswad, Al-Sayed. *Religions and Folk Cosmology: Scenarios of the Visible and Invisible in Rural Egypt*. Westport, CT: Praeger, 2002.

Ferguson, James. *Global Shadows*. Durham, NC: Duke University Press, 2006.

Giddens, Anthony. *Modernity and Self-identity*. Stanford, CA: Stanford University Press, 1991.

Hunwick, John. "Sub-Saharan Africa and the Wider World of Islam." In *African Islam and Islam in Africa*, ed. David Westerlund and Eva Rosander, 28–54. Athens: Ohio University Press, 1997.

IRIN News. "End Female Genital Mutilation–African Union." June 16, 2006. http://www.irinnews.org/Report.aspx?ReportId=59355.

IRIN News. "FGM in Mali Connected to Pre-Islamic Traditions." June 15, 2004. http://www.afrol.com/articles/13372.

Johnson-Odim, Cheryl, and Margaret Strobel. "Conceptualizing the History of Women." In *Women in Sub-Saharan Africa*, ed. Iris Berger and Frances White, xxvi–ixi. Bloomington: Indiana University Press, 1999.

Johnson, Michelle. "The Internal Debate Surrounding Female 'Circumcision.'" *Awaken* 4:3 (2000): 9–11.

Mahamoud, Asha, Samson Radeny, and Karin Ringheim. "Community-based Efforts to End Female Genital Mutilation in Kenya: Raising Awareness and Organizing Alternative Rights of Passage." In *Female Circumcision: Multicultural Perspectives*, ed. Rogaia M. Abusharaf, 73–104. Philadelphia: University of Pennsylvania Press, 2006.

Masterson, Julia M., and Julie Swanson. "Female Genital Cutting: Breaking the Silence, Enabling Change." Washington, DC: International Center for Research on Women and the Centre for Development and Population Activities, 2000. http://www.icrw.org/docs/FGCfinalpdf.pdf.

Martinez, Samuel. "Searching for a Middle Path: Rights, Capabilities, and Political Culture in the Study of Female Genital Cutting." *Ahfad Journal* 22:1 (2005): 31–45.

Mazrui, Ali A., and Toby K. Levine, eds. *The Africans*. Westport, CT: Praeger, 1986.

Merry, Sally. *Human Rights and Gender Violence: Translating International Law into Local Justice*. Chicago: University of Chicago Press, 2006.

Moore, Henrietta. *Anthropological Theory Today*. Cambridge: Cambridge University Press, 2000.

Murray, Rachel. *Human Rights in Africa: From the OAU to the African Union*. Cambridge: Cambridge University Press, 2004.

Nnaemeka, Obioma, and Joy Ezeilo, eds. *Engendering Human Rights and Socioeconomic Realities in Africa*. New York: Palgrave Macmillan, 2006.

No Peace without Justice Newsletter. "2004–2006 Campaign for the Ratification of the Maputo Protocol." Posted on Democracy Assistance Dialogue Program. www.npwj.org/npwj_topics_fgm.

Obaid, Thoraya A. "Religion and Reproductive Health and Rights." *Journal of the American Academy of Religion* 73:4 (2005): 1155–173.

Orubuloye, I.O., Pat Caldwell, and John Caldwell. "Female 'Circumcision' among the Yoruba of Southwestern Nigeria: Beginning of Change." In *Female Circumcision in Africa: Culture, Controversy, and Change*, ed. Bettina Shell-Duncan and Ylva Hernlund, 73–95. Boulder, CO: Lynn Reinner, 2000.

Parliament of the United Republic of Tanzania. *The Sexual Offences Special Provisions Act*, 1998, 2, no. 4. http://www.parliament.go.tz/Polis/PAMS/Docs/ 4-1998.pdf.

Petchesky, Rosalind P. "Cross-country Comparisons and Political Visions." In *Negotiating Reproductive Rights: Women's Perspectives across Countries and Cultures*, ed. Rosalind P. Petchesky and Karen Judd, 295–323. London: Zed Books, 1998.

Rahman, Anika, and Nahid Toubia. *Female Genital Mutilation: A Guide to Laws and Policies Worldwide*. London: Zed Books, 2000.

Rapport, Nigel, and Joanna Overing. *Social and Cultural Anthropology: Key Concepts*. London: Routledge, 2000.

Salih, Mahgouba Mohamed. "Circumcision in Shari`a and the Law." Omdurman, Sudan: Babikir Bedri Association and UNICEF, 1997.

Sanneh, Lamin. "New Gods." In *The Africans*, ed. Ali A. Mazrui and Toby K. Levine, 82–108. Westport, CT: Praeger, 1986.

Shahroor, Mohamed. *Towards a New Islamic Jurisprudence: Women, the Will, Inheritance, Guardianship, Polygamy and Dress*. Damascus, Syria: El–Ahalai, 2000.

"Synopsis: Proceedings of the Workshop African Women Speak on Female Circumcision." Ahfad University, Khartoum, Sudan, October 21–25, 1984.

Trushen, Meredith, ed. *African Women's Health*. New Brunswick, NJ: Africa World Press, 2000.

Weston, Burns, Robin Ann Lukes, and Kelly M. Hnatt. "Regional Human Rights Regimes: A Comparison and Appraisal." In *Human Rights in the World Community*, ed. Richard Pierre Claude and Burns Weston, 244–55 Philadelphia: University of Pennsylvania Press, 1992.

7

Buddhism, Human Rights, and Non-Buddhist Minorities

Charles Keyes

Of all the world religions, Buddhism is almost always characterized as being a religion of peace, tolerance, and compassion.[1] When after World War II Western, Enlightenment-derived ideas of universal human rights were introduced into societies with Buddhist majorities and minorities in South and Southeast Asia, governments there all endorsed the 1948 United Nations Universal Declaration of Human Rights. Despite this acceptance at the governmental level, there remains the question of how Buddhism as a religious tradition approaches human rights. Damien Keown, a prominent scholar of Buddhist ethics, asks "whether Buddhism would endorse the Universal Declaration of Human Rights." He notes that "the repeated calls by the Dalai Lama for respect for human rights give some reason to think that it would" and reminds us that other scholars have concluded that early Buddhist teachings are in harmony with the spirit of the Declaration. For Keown a critical issue still remains: "the philosophical presuppositions underlying these passages" and how they relate to "the overall Buddhist vision of individual and social good."[2]

Keown's article and subsequent work remain the most sustained and compelling review of doctrinal justifications for Buddhist acceptance of the principle that all humans share rights that are inherent in being human.[3] As Keown demonstrates, rights is an alien concept in what he terms "classical" Buddhism, which for him is "neither the same as nor different from Buddhism in any historical or cultural context" and is "broad enough to include both the Theravāda and Mahāyāna schools." For Keown, "the justification for this fiction lies in the belief that whatever concept of human rights we regard Buddhism as holding must be one which is universal in form."[4] I agree, and would restate his position as follows:

The fundamental Buddhist assumption about human nature that is common to all Buddhist traditions, past and present, is that all humans will, unless they have disciplined their desires (*tanhā*), act in ways that generate consequences that are manifest as *dukkha*. While *dukkha* is usually glossed in English as "suffering," it also must be understood as the cessation of pleasure (*sukkha*). The Buddha prescribed *sīla*—moral disciplining—especially if cultivated through "mindfulness" (*samādhi*), as the basic method to reduce the actions that generate *dukkha*. The essential elements of *sīla* are manifest in what are known as the "five precepts":[5] to abstain from taking life; from taking what is not given; from wrong conduct in sexual desires; from telling lies; and from intoxicating liquors that occasion heedlessness. Every Buddhist ritual begins with the laity requesting the precepts and then repeating them after a monk or monks chant them. The "discipline" that monks subject themselves to consists of rules that have been elaborated on from these basic precepts.[6]

As Keown observes, while the precepts—particularly the first four—are expressed in Buddhism as "duties" that the practitioner undertakes, they can be seen as entailing "rights" since the duties are based on the relations one has with others.[7] As he puts it, "it is in the *interrelatedness* of persons rather than in the persons themselves that the [Buddhist] justification for human rights is to be found."[8] As one has a duty to refrain from taking life, others have a right to life and freedom from actions or threats that might end their lives; as one has a duty to refrain from stealing, others have a right to their property; as one has a duty to refrain from acting lustfully, others have a right to the nonviolability of their bodies; as one has the duty to refrain from lying, others have the right to be told the truth. Overall, a compelling case can be made that a discourse on universal human rights is compatible with Buddhist beliefs.

Such a discourse is rooted in Buddhist epistemology adopted in all Buddhist societies predicated on a distinction between this-worldly (*lokiyā*) and other-worldly (*lokuttarā*).[9] The Burmese category of *lawki pyinna*,[10] "this-worldly knowledge," that subsumes not only laws for maintaining social order but also practices whereby magical and supernatural forces are evoked for social ends has equivalents in every Buddhist society. As Swearer observes, the Buddhist ruler has primary responsibility for the worldly, while the Buddha is the ultimate authority for guiding actions that lead to religious ends.[11]

Every government headed by Buddhists has instituted laws that aim to reduce threats to the social order through the imposition of punishments on those who have transgressed the laws. Such laws in all Buddhist countries include those mandating capital punishment for some types of murders, even though the implementation of such laws entails the taking of a human life.

Legal codes, including constitutions as well as laws passed by parliaments, are necessary because all people live in this world, even though those who adhere to Buddhism aspire to achieve the other-worldly goal of *Nibbāna*.

If the Buddhist-majority societies' governments' endorsement of international human rights instruments and the Buddhist tradition as a whole are broadly compatible with human rights, one might expect those rights to be protected by law as well as in practice within those societies. I will show that this is not, in fact, generally the case. While fundamental Buddhist teachings can be shown theoretically or theologically to support "universal human rights," in practice in those polities dominated by Buddhists' adherence to the principles of human rights is uneven at best. In fact, in our contemporary era, political elites in Buddhist societies and their followers have sometimes invoked Buddhism to question or even deny equal rights to non-Buddhist minorities.

Theravāda Buddhism and Traditional Sociopolitical Orders

Although Buddhism is an element of the religious traditions of most of East and mainland Southeast Asia and parts of South Asia, there are only five countries in the world in which Buddhism is the official or state religion—Sri Lanka (formerly known as Ceylon), Burma (Myanmar), Thailand (formerly known as Siam), Cambodia, and Bhutan.[12] In the first four of these, the dominant form of Buddhism, is Theravādin, while in tiny Bhutan, the Buddhist tradition is Vajrayāna, a tradition particularly associated with Tibetan Buddhism. There is no country in the world today where Mahāyāna Buddhism is the state-supported religion.[13]

Theravāda Buddhists, like all Buddhists, commit themselves to "take refuge" in the "Three Gems": the Buddha, the *dhamma* or teachings of the Buddha, and the *sangha*, the ordained followers of the Buddha. The Buddha was a historical person who began life as Prince Siddhattha Gotama and is believed by followers to have died in the sixth century B.C.E., although historians today think he probably lived two centuries earlier.[14] After discovering the way to transcend the condition of suffering that all who are born as humans experience, he taught this way to others for nearly half a century. The Buddha is remembered through images and monumental structures known as stupas which, even if they contain no actual relic, represent the mound in which his remains were enshrined after his death.

Members of the sangha are looked to both as the exemplars of the way taught by the Buddha by virtue of their adherence to the "discipline" (*vinaya*) that he laid down during his lifetime, and as the propagators of the way through their communication of the Buddha's teachings in rituals and sermons. Monks (*bhikkhu*) and novices (*samanera*) in Theravāda Buddhist societies are easily recognizable by distinctive robes that are usually yellow but sometimes brown or even red. Monks must abide not only by the basic moral precepts incumbent on all Buddhists, but also must follow a cloistered life characterized by chastity, poverty, and asceticism.[15] In Thailand, Cambodia, and Laos most monks spend only a few months in the monastery, and even in Sri Lanka and Burma many monks spend only part of their lives in the sangha.

The foundation of the *dhamma* is the doctrine of *dukkha*, by which it is understood that all who are born will experience suffering directly as pain or indirectly as the cessation of that which is pleasurable. Death, which combines both, is the culmination of *dukkha*. The Buddha taught that transcendence of *dukkha* can be attained through following the "way" or "path" that includes the practice of "morality" (*sīla*), mental concentration (*samādhi*), and cultivation of wisdom (*paññā*).

The fifth precept—a commitment to refrain from ingesting substances (notably, alcohol and drugs) that conduce heedlessness—represents a step toward the cultivation of "mindfulness." Through such cultivation as well as the practice of "mental concentration"—that is, meditation—one seeks to acquire the ability to detach oneself from those desires that lead to increased *dukkha*. If one is successful in practicing mental concentration, one will gain that insight into the self that is a basic form of wisdom.

Although monks are most assiduous in seeking to follow the path of the Buddha, Theravāda Buddhism is not a religion for monastics alone. For the sangha to exist, monks have to depend on lay persons for their main "requisites"—food, shelter, clothing, and medications. The members of the sangha, those who both exemplify the *dhamma* in their practice and teach the *dhamma* to others, have always needed the economic support of the laity and the protection offered by rulers.

For lay Buddhists, *sīla* is understood primarily as entailing the offering of alms (*dāna*) to the sangha in the form of food, clothing, shelter, and medicines and following the five precepts. In return for alms, laypersons accumulate "merit" or "positive *kamma*" (*puñña*). By adhering to the moral precepts to refrain from taking life, stealing, lying, and improper sexual relations, one avoids accumulating "demerit" or "negative *kamma*" (*pāppa*). The balance of one's *kamma* will condition the relative degree of *dukkha* one will experience in both this life and in future existences. The *kamma* one inherited at birth is understood to have generated some of the physical and social conditions of one's present life.

The followers of Theravāda Buddhism credit King Aśoka, who ruled much of India in the third century B.C.E., not only with the spread of Buddhism to Sri Lanka and Southeast Asia, where this tradition of Buddhism became dominant, but also with the establishment of a model of a Buddhist sociopolitical order. This model, known as the "Two Wheels of the *Dhamma*," makes the laity, and especially a lay ruler, as responsible as the sangha for the perpetuation and dissemination of the teachings of the Buddha.[16]

The Aśokan model was emulated in all Theravādin societies, although it only became fully institutionalized in the period between the thirteenth and nineteenth centuries.[17] During this period, rulers of Buddhist kingdoms provided an example for all laypersons in their monetary support for the sangha. The monarch also intervened from time to time to ensure that the sangha adhered properly to Buddhist discipline and to prevent schisms. In return, the sangha participated in royally sponsored rites that conferred legitimacy on the monarch.

The societies ruled by Buddhist monarchs between the thirteenth and nineteenth centuries were hardly without conflict. The island of Sri Lanka was beset by almost perpetual wars throughout this period, and on at least two occasions the political turmoil led to the nearly total disappearance of the sangha.[18] In mainland Southeast Asia, following the collapse of the empires centered on Pagan and Angkor in the thirteenth century, there was almost constant warfare between the Burman and Siamese empires and between these empires and the smaller principalities that surrounded them.[19] The conflicts in South and Southeast Asia came to an end (at least temporarily) in the nineteenth century with the British conquest of Sri Lanka and Burma and the incorporation of Laos and Cambodia into French Indochina. The colonial era proved to be the crucible for forging new relationships between Buddhism and power.

Buddhist Reformation in Response to Colonial Domination and Western Influence

Beginning in Sri Lanka in the eighteenth century, lower Burma in the early nineteenth century, and throughout the nineteenth century in South and Southeast Asia, Theravādin traditions were challenged by new political and economic influences associated with the expansion of Western colonialism and capitalism and by new cultural influences associated with Christianity and Western science. Taken together, these influences created a crisis of authority for both the rulers and the populace in the countries of this region. Responses to that crisis resituated Theravāda Buddhism within a modern world.[20]

In Sri Lanka and Burma, the traditional sociopolitical order subsumed under the "Two Wheels of the *Dhamma*" was radically devalued when British colonial governments abolished the indigenous monarchies and ended government patronage of the sangha. In both Cambodia and Laos the French colonial government retained indigenous monarchies under nominal protectorates, but the reality of rule by non-Buddhist Frenchmen reduced the relationship between monarchy and sangha to empty rituals.

In Siam, by contrast, the crisis of authority began not with colonial domination by an outside power but through a radical redefinition of the monarchy and its relationship to its subjects and the sangha to meet the colonial threat.

Following the conclusion of the Anglo-Burman war of 1824–26 Siam had to concede territory to the expanding British and French empires. By the late nineteenth century, the king and his advisors determined that the only way to retain an independent country was to promote national integration of the diverse peoples living within the boundaries of the kingdom. In 1892, beginning with sweeping administrative reforms, Siam undertook its own "internal colonialism" by extending the authority of Bangkok over what had been previously autonomous polities in several parts of the Siamese empire. Rulers of these polities were replaced by officials under a new bureaucracy modeled on that of nearby colonial domains.[21] In the pursuit of political integration, in 1902 the Siamese government also instituted a reform that placed all monks within the kingdom under the authority of a supreme patriarch appointed by the king. Prior to this reform, there were autonomous sanghas among the Siamese in central and the upper southern regions of Thailand, the Yuan in northern Thailand, the Lao in northeastern Thailand, and the Khmer-speaking people in eastern and northeastern Thailand, each with its own writing systems for transliterating the teachings of the Buddha from Pāli and other languages into the vernacular. Following the reform, only those monks authorized by the supreme patriarch could perform ordinations and all members of the sangha were required to study the same religious curriculum using standard Thai orthography.[22]

In their reaction to the crises of authority occasioned by both the threat and the reality of Western colonial domination, many people in the Theravādin countries turned to charismatic religious and political leaders whom they believed could restore the traditional sociopolitical order. In numerous cases they followed their leaders in violent reactions against the new orders. In Sri Lanka and to an even greater extent in Burma supporters of the traditional monarchies fought strongly against the British forces sent to "pacify" those countries. Violence did not end with pacification, however. In the first decades of the twentieth century in Siam, French Laos, and British Burma, thousands of people died or were injured after having joined Buddhist millenarian movements to resist—unsuccessfully—the extension of new types of authority over them.

By the 1920s the anticolonial movements that drew on Buddhist millennialist ideas had begun to be replaced by nationalisms also shaped by Buddhism. Buddhist nationalism was predicated less on traditional Buddhist ideas about the sociopolitical order than on reforms of Buddhist thought in response to Western religious and cultural influence. The first charismatic leaders of Buddhist reform movements in Sri Lanka, Burma, and Siam were Buddhist monks who found themselves confronted with challenges to their religious authority posed by Protestant missionaries. Protestant missionaries laid great emphasis on establishing schools that offered instruction not only in religion but also in secular subjects. Protestant missions also sponsored hospitals and clinics. Through both these institutions and their schools, the Protestant missionaries

exposed local elites to the distinction between religious and secular knowledge—a distinction alien to traditional thought in Buddhist societies.

What has often been called "Protestant Buddhism" emerged as a reformist
response, led by influential monks including Prince Vajirañāna, who subsequently became King Mongkut of Siam (1804–1868), Ledi Sayadaw (1846–
1923) in Burma, and the unique half-monk, half-layman, Angārika Dharmapāla
(1864–1933), in Sri Lanka.[23] The reformed Buddhists followed Protestant
Christians in recognizing that many aspects of the natural world could be
explained scientifically rather than theologically. Like Protestant Christians
they shifted the emphasis of religious practice from ritual to ethics. Unlike
Christians, however, the reform Buddhists also accentuated a distinctive Buddhist practice, namely meditation. Whereas in pre-modern Buddhism meditation had been a practice primarily engaged in by monks, in modern Buddhism
this practice has also been widely adopted by laypersons as a means to act in the
world with detachment.

Although rooted in a different theology and religious practice, reformist
Buddhism is like the modernist versions of Protestant Christianity in being as
much this-wordly as other-worldly oriented. That is, religious goals are understood with reference to actions undertaken in the everyday world in addition to
or in substitution for actions that will ensure a better existence in a future existence. This perspective has opened a space for those who make Buddhist ideals
the basis for social and political action. During the colonial period many leading
modernist monks and laymen came to advocate the establishment of a postcolonial state in which Buddhism would be fundamental to national identity.
Buddhist nationalisms, albeit some more exclusivist than others, that have
their origin in the colonial period have continued to be very significant in the
postcolonial nation-states where Theravāda Buddhism is preeminent.

Theravāda Buddhist States and Non-Buddhist Minorities

In the postcolonial world in Southeast and South Asia, four nation-states
adopted Theravāda Buddhism as the state or official religion, namely, Sri Lanka,
Burma, Thailand, and Cambodia. As there are significant minorities in each of
these countries whose members are not adherents of Buddhism, governments
have faced the question of whether non-Buddhists have the same rights as the
Buddhist majorities. The answers governments have given to this question
have shaped the politics of human rights in these societies.

Sri Lanka

When Ceylon (later renamed Sri Lanka) became independent in 1948, it was a
plural society with marked diversity. While nearly 70 percent of the populace

were speakers of Sinhala and most of these were followers of Buddhism, albeit of different orders of monks (*nikāya*), another 30 percent consisted of Tamil Hindus and Tamil Muslims and other Muslims. There was also a small but politically significant Eurasian segment known as Burghers, most of whom were Christian. In the first years of independence, the government, led by an English-educated elite of diverse backgrounds, promoted a civil order in which diversity was recognized and initially protected by the constitution. The country also ratified the Universal Declaration of Human Rights that had been adopted by the United Nations in the same year that Sri Lanka became independent. In 1956 S.W.R.D. Bandaranaike, the leader of the Sri Lanka Freedom Party (SLFP), became prime minister. He chose to guide Sri Lanka toward a more restrictive nationalism that would have lasting consequences for ethnic relations in the country.

Bandaranaike, who had been educated at Oxford, was a convert to Buddhism and, like Angārika Dharmapāla was zealous in linking religion and politics. He introduced three new policies that accorded a privileged position to the Buddhist Sinhalese. Sinhala was recognized as the only national language, to the exclusion of English and Tamil; the national history taught in government schools accentuated the history of Buddhism in the country; and the state officially embraced and supported Buddhism, beginning with the celebration of 2,500 years of Buddhism in 1955–56. Not surprisingly, Bandaranaike could count on the strong support of many Buddhist monks.[24] Bandaranaike's connection to Buddhism proved, however, to be a double-edged sword. He also was criticized by some for not promoting Buddhist nationalism vigorously enough, and in 1959 a monk assassinated him. Although the monk may have been insane, the assassination can be seen, nonetheless, to have initiated an increased association between Buddhism and political violence in Sri Lanka.

Although Sri Lanka had long been an ethnically complex society, the primary conflict linking Sinhalese nationalism and Buddhism has been that between Tamils and the Sri Lankan state. The relegation of non-Buddhists to second-class citizenship in Sri Lanka led to growing tensions within the country and finally to open conflict beginning in the 1980s. In 1983, the Sri Lankan government either backed or tolerated a pogrom-like attack by security forces and many ordinary Sinhalese aimed at Tamils living in the capital of Colombo as well as in the highlands. Tamils subsequently turned in increasing numbers to a movement led by the radical and militant Tamil Tigers ("Liberation of Tamil Eelam"). Because the Tigers were pioneers in the use of suicide bombings and have killed many more noncombatants than Sri Lankan soldiers, they were branded a terrorist organization by India, the United States, and other countries, as well as by the Sri Lankan government. The government's war with the Tamil Tigers continued for over twenty years and cost nearly 70,000 lives on both sides of the conflict.[25]

In 2002 the Tigers declared a cease-fire and entered into negotiations with the Sri Lankan government headed by President Chandrika Bandaranaike Kumaratunga, the daughter of Bandaranaike. However, the negotiations collapsed in the wake of a controversy over the distribution of aid in Tamil areas following the December 2004 tsunami and the assassination of the country's foreign minister Lakshman Kadirgamar by a Tamil sniper in August 2005.

President Kumaratunga was pressed by the National Buddhist Front (NBMF), an influential organization of monks, to continue the war and even ban non-Buddhist nongovernmental organizations (NGOs) from working in the country.[26] By 2007 members of the group had joined the government and were pressing for even more aggressive actions against the Tamil rebels.[27] The National Buddhist Front, represented in parliament by the National Heritage Party (NHP), justified such actions as a duty undertaken "in order to preserve the sacred prophecy of the Buddha about the land of Lanka."[28] James Astill, the South Asian correspondent for *The Economist*, has written that as "purveyors of an extreme brand of Sinhalese nationalism, the NHP considers Sri Lanka Sinhalese and Buddhist; the party believes that those of other faiths and ethnicities, while welcome, must behave like guests. In effect, this means a policy of zero tolerance toward the complaints of the country's Tamil minority and their self-proclaimed champions, the Liberation Tigers of Eelam (LTTE), known as the Tamil Tigers."[29] In short, Buddhist nationalism has provided a powerful foundation for a "just" war against the Tamil "terrorists."

When the Sri Lankan military succeeded in defeating the Tamil Tigers in May 2009, Athurliye Rathana Thero, the monk who headed the National Heritage Party, took credit for having earlier persuaded Mahinda Rajapaksa, the president, to abandon peace talks and press for a final victory. This party was subsequently invited to join the government, but was represented by a layman rather than a monk. In the wake of their defeat, Tamils have been relegated even more to the margins of Buddhist Sri Lanka.

Burma

In Burma (today officially known as Myanmar), as in Sri Lanka, the establishment of a colonial order by the British created a crisis of order that has yet to be fully resolved. As in Sri Lanka, those who came to power in postcolonial Burma in 1948 sought to rule over a very diverse population. About two-thirds of the populace, living mostly in the central divisions of the country are ethnically Burman (today officially called Bamar). Those living in the peripheral states belong to such different groups as the Shan, Mon, Rakhine, Karen, Karenni, Wa, Kachin, Chin, Naga, and Rohingyas.[30]

The Burmans are overwhelmingly Buddhists, as are most of the Shan, Mon, Rakhine, and some Karen. Buddhists constitute approximately 89 percent to 90 percent of the total population.[31] The term "Buddhist," however, subsumes significant differences in the religious orders (*gaing*) to which Buddhist monks belong, as well as differences in practices among the laity. The latter are succinctly noted in *Burma: International Religious Freedom Report 2002* issued by the U.S. Department of State: "in practice popular Burmese Buddhism includes veneration of many indigenous pre-Buddhist deities called 'nats,' and coexists with astrology, numerology, and fortune-telling."[32]

By contrast, the majority of the Kachin, Chin, Naga, and a substantial majority of the Karen are Protestant or Catholic Christians. The Rohingyas, living in the Rakhine (Arakan) state in an area bordering Bangladesh, are Muslims. Other Muslims are also found in Burma among the descendants of Indian migrants and Malays living in the Tenasserim Peninsula. In Burma today, Muslims and Christians each constitute at least 4 percent of the total population of the country.[33]

In addition to the indigenous peoples of Burma, thousands of Chinese and hundreds of thousands of South Asians settled in Burma during the colonial period. They settled primarily in urban areas where new job opportunities arose in the export economy promoted by the British. Although in the immediate post-independence period the new government instituted what could only be termed ethnic cleansing by compelling a large percentage of the Indian population to leave the country, about 2 percent of the Burmese population is still of Indian descent. A limited number of Chinese also settled in Burma during the colonial period, but a much larger influx of Chinese into Burma has taken place quite recently.

The leaders of successive governments in Burma since it became independent in 1948 have based their legitimacy on demonstrating public relationships with Buddhist sacred rites and sites—most notably with stupas thought to contain relics of the Buddha—as well as with the sangha. Ever since 1962, when General Ne Win took control of the government through a coup, Burmese governments have been headed by the military. There has, however, long been significant opposition to the central government. Until 1988 the most significant resistance to Burman military domination was posed by a number of ethnic insurgencies. Since 1988 there has also been strong resistance by ethnic Burmans themselves who have looked for leadership and inspiration to Daw Aung San Suu Kyi, the daughter of the assassinated leader who had guided Burma to independence from Great Britain. Although the National League for Democracy that coalesced around Aung San Suu Kyi won a convincing election in 1990, the military junta, which after 1997 took the name State Peace and Development Council, has used force to ensure its continued dominance of the polity.

Even though the military regime has maintained total control of power through the use of force, its legitimacy has been rendered deeply problematic by the involvement of Buddhist monks in protest movements, first in 1990 and then much more dramatically and in much greater numbers in 2007. Lacking the support of monks who are the latter day followers of a modernist Buddhism that first developed in the late nineteenth and early twentieth century, the junta has turned to a magical Buddhism centered on the worship of stupas and Buddha images to shore up its legitimacy.[34]

In efforts to cloak itself with a Buddhist aura, the junta has also moved in a number of ways to marginalize those residents of Burma who are non-Buddhist, especially if they are ethnically distinct from the dominant Burmans. As Monique Skidmore has observed, the junta has sought to establish a "Buddhist totalitarian utopia" in which non-Buddhist minorities are not accorded equal rights.[35] The U.S. government's 2004 human rights report concluded, "Constitutional support for religious freedom does not exist. Most religious adherents registered with the authorities generally were free to worship as they chose; however, the government imposed restrictions on certain religious activities and promoted Buddhism over other religions in some ethnic minority areas. In practice, the Government also restricted efforts by Buddhist clergy to promote human rights and political freedom."[36]

While some Christian ethnic minorities, such as the Kachin in northern Burma, have maintained spaces in which they can practice their religion without too much interference by the state, other Christians have fared less well. One report has documented how the government has undertaken sponsorship of new Buddhist shrines and images, "including on ethnic minority sacred sites. Some monuments sacred to ethnic minorities were destroyed and replaced with new structures, such as hotels, against local objections."[37] Karen Christians in particular have been targeted, as they constitute the primary support for the Karen insurrection against the Burmese state.

The most significant target of violent discrimination in Burma has been the Muslim Rohingyas living in the northwest of the country on the border between Burma and Bangladesh. Because of their religion and because of their location, the Rohingyas are considered by the Burmese government to be illegal migrants in the country, even though the vast majority claim to be descendants of the indigenous people of northern Rakhine. The government has made efforts, including as recently as 1991, to force Rohingyas to "return" to Bangladesh. An Amnesty International report issued in 2004 stated that it "is concerned that the Burma Citizenship Law of 1982 and the manner in which this law is implemented effectively denies the right to a nationality for members of the Rohingya population."[38]

The abysmal human rights record of the junta that has ruled Burma since 1988 has not gone without challenge from among the dominant Burman population. At least as significant as the challenge to the legitimacy of the junta posed by the National League for Democracy headed by Aung San Suu Kyi is that of the Buddhist sangha. Although the junta has devoted great effort to co-opting Buddhist monks and to organizing elaborate ceremonies at Buddhist monuments, the involvement of monks in the 1988 uprising, the protests initiated in 1990 by monks in Mandalay, and the even larger monk-led protests in what has been called the "Saffron Revolution" in 2007 have clearly signaled not only to the outside world but also to much of the Burmese population that the state lacks moral legitimacy.

The Saffron Revolution, despite the large number of monks who participated and the significant support they received from the populace, did not succeed in bringing fundamental change to Burma. After moving slowly at the outset to control the monk-led protestors, the government then sent a large security force to put down the demonstrations. The very repression of the demonstrators, which involved the killing of some monks and the imprisonment of hundreds more, served, however, to reinforce the lack of moral legitimacy of the junta, as did the fact that monks played a more prominent role than the government in efforts to assist the Burmese living in the Irrawaddy Delta when it was struck by a cataclysmic cyclone in May 2008.

With the government now imposing control over the public stance of monks, discussions of the relationship between Buddhism and human rights, including the rights of non-Buddhist minorities, have effectively been silenced. Given, however, the significance that Buddhism and the Buddhist sangha have in Burma, this silence can only be temporary. As Schober concluded in a recent paper on the Saffron Revolution: "Modern Buddhist conjunctures in Myanmar show that collaboration between the sangha and the state can create overwhelming social and political synergies, while their mutual contestation harbors the potential to engender divisive conflict of law and authority. These potentialities . . . illustrate how religious action continues to empower the imagination of political futures."[39]

On November 7, 2010, the government of Myanmar orchestrated an election that while entailing no true transfer of power – most of the new elected leaders are actually the same as old military ones, but without their uniforms – may nonetheless have represented a shift in the way in which power is legitimated. That Daw Aung San Suu Kyi was released from detention a few days later also may prove to be a positive change, but the fact that she has been re-arrested after previous releases makes it likely that the government will be monitoring her activities very closely. Meanwhile, the conflict between government forces and Karen rebels has intensified, signaling that ethnic minorities will continue to have problems in the country.

Cambodia

The legacy of violence in Cambodia has been even more horrendous than that of Sri Lanka and Burma. On the surface it would seem as though Cambodia's ordeal was the product not of Buddhist nationalism but of the radical secularist ideology of the Khmer Rouge led by Pol Pot. However, as I discovered when I sought to understand the origins of the Khmer Rouge, its own ideology has unequivocal roots in a version of reformist Buddhism.[40]

The first imagining of a Khmer nation was spurred by the founding of the Buddhist Institute in 1930. The French had founded the Institute "to lessen the influence of Thai Buddhism (and Thai politics) on the Cambodian sangha and to substitute more Indo-Chinese loyalties between the Lao sangha and their Cambodian counterparts."[41] Suzanne Karpelès, a French Buddhist scholar who was placed in charge of the institute, recruited as her chief associates a number of former monks. Several of them subsequently founded the Khmer Communist Party. Pol Pot, the nom de guerre of Saloth Sar, who had been a novice for a period of time, was one of the party's recruits.

Pol Pot and his close associates conceived of the Party, which they called Angkar—"the organization"—in ways that made it very similar to the sangha. Those who became members subjected themselves to a discipline that subordinated them to the organization. Alexander Hinton has shown how the Khmer Rouge concept of "revolutionary consciousness" is linked to the Buddhist conception of mindfulness.[42] Even more perversely the Khmer Rouge took the conception of "cutting off one's heart" (dach chett), which in Buddhist practice meant cultivating detachment from worldly desires, and utilized it to promote among cadres a detachment from emotion when taking the lives of those deemed to be "enemies."[43] But while the Angkar promised a future to Khmer that was an earthly Nibbāna, its actions actually led to a marked increase in suffering.

One of the first actions of Angkar after the Khmer Rouge took control of Cambodia in April 1975 was a move to eliminate the Buddhist sangha.[44] Monks and novices, even those in the base areas that the Khmer Rouge had controlled before April 1975, were compelled to disrobe. Being sent for reeducation often meant a death sentence. In 1980 it was estimated that five of every eight monks were executed during the Pol Pot regime. Major temple-monasteries were destroyed and lesser ones were converted into storage centers, prisons, or extermination camps. A very few of the individuals who remained monks survived by fleeing to southern Vietnam.

The Khmer Rouge reign of terror resulted in at least two million deaths out of a population of about nine million. Every survivor of the Khmer Rouge is haunted by the ghosts of those who died. In the late 1980s, the regime that came to power after the Vietnamese forced the Khmer Rouge to flee to the peripheries of the country erected monuments at sites of some of the worst killing—Tuol Sleng in Phnom Penh and Choeng Ek on the outskirts of the city.

Although Cambodia has very small numbers of people who are not historically followers of Buddhism, the Khmer Rouge used Buddhism to define a radically "other" within the country, separating "real" Khmer from "false" Khmer. Not only did the followers of Pol Pot invert the teachings and practice of Buddhism to justify their genocide, but they also set out to systematically eliminate Buddhist institutions from Khmer society. Although the Khmer Rouge regime ended in early 1979, the memories of this reign have continued to raise fundamental questions for many Khmer about how a Buddhist society could have spawned such violence. Ros Sotha, a leading Buddhist layperson and follower of Maha Ghosananda, the leader of the Buddhist peace movement in Cambodia, summarized what many Cambodians have asked: "It became a big question to all Cambodians how Buddhists could commit such massive crimes on humans and destroy their own religion."[45]

Maha Ghosananda (1929–2007) was renowned among Khmer monks even before the Khmer Rouge came to power. He had studied in India and Japan as well as under the leading monk of Cambodia. In 1965 he had become a disciple of the Venerable Achaan Dhammadaro, a highly respected meditation master in southern Thailand. He left this hermitage in 1978 when the first Khmer refugees began to flee their country. He subsequently became the chief spiritual mentor for Khmer refugees and he himself moved to live in the United States. In 1992 he returned to Cambodia to initiate the Dhammayietra, a peace march or pilgrimage, which entailed leading his followers across war-torn Cambodia. The Dhammayietra subsequently became an annual event in Cambodia. Maha Ghosananda saw that "the suffering of Cambodia has been deep. From this suffering comes great Compassion." If this compassion is cultivated, he maintained, it can lead to peaceful reconciliation.[46]

Ever since Cambodia rejoined the world community after a period in the early 1990s under the UN Transitional Authority in Cambodia (UNTAC), there have been pressures from opposition politicians, from NGOs, and especially from Western donor countries on the Hun Sen government to bring the remaining leaders of the Khmer Rouge to trial for war crimes and crimes against humanity. Because of his own past membership in the Khmer Rouge, Hun Sen was very slow in responding to these pressures. Although the government agreed in 1997 to the establishment of a Khmer Rouge Trial Task Force to create a legal and judicial structure to try the remaining Khmer Rouge leaders, it was not until 2003 that an agreement was finally signed between the Cambodian government and the United Nations to establish such a structure. It took another three years before a tribunal, a hybrid structure administered in part under Cambodian law by the Cambodian justice system and in part under international law through the United Nations, was formally established.

The trial of Kaing Guek Eav, better known as Duch, the commandant of the notorious Tuol Sleng prison, finally got underway in 2009. In 2010 he was found guilty of overseeing the deaths of at least 14,000 people, but was sentenced to only 19 years in prison. In September 2010 another four Khmer Rouge leaders were formally indicted. It is, however, very unlikely that any lower level cadres will ever be brought to trial.[47]

The process leading up to the trials led, as John Marston has noted, to "concepts of 'human rights' [entering] Cambodian public discourse in a way that they never had before."[48] Other scholars have shown that the translation of international human rights discourse into terms meaningful to the Khmer has been undertaken by local groups who have drawn on "Buddhist notions of moral behavior with others, non-violence and mutual respect."[49] At the same time, Ros Sotha observes that because of the legacy of the Khmer Rouge and the Hun Sen government's commitment to subordinating Buddhism to the state "not many Buddhist institutions are able to understand or translate a vision of Buddhism into practice as it applies to social and economic development." He concludes that since the death of Ghosananda in 2007, *"there is no clear movement to build spiritual peace in Cambodia."*[50]

Thailand

Of all the countries in which Theravāda Buddhism is the dominant religion, Thailand enjoys the greatest continuity with the pre-modern past. Because Thailand was never brought under colonial rule, no foreign power eliminated the Thai monarchy or interfered with the Buddhist sangha. Although a coup in 1932 resulted in the transformation of the government from an absolute to a constitutional monarchy, the monarchy not only continued to exist but would in the second half of the twentieth century become the primary pillar of Thai nationalism.

From the first constitution in 1932 to the most recent one of 2007, the King of Thailand has been required to be a Buddhist. As the "upholder of religion," to use the wording of the 1997 constitution, he is the country's chief patron of the Buddhist sangha. He appoints, on the recommendation of leading monks and with the advice of the Privy Council and the current government, a *sangha-rāja*, known in English as the Buddhist patriarch of the country. Members of the sangha in Thailand, including those belonging to Mahāyāna as well as Theravādin orders, are under an ecclesiastical structure headed by the *sangha-rāja* and organized according to laws of the state.

Despite the establishment of Buddhism as an official religion, Thai society is, nonetheless, a religiously plural society. Not all Thai are Buddhists. The 2000 census showed that 94.6 percent of the population was Buddhist, 4.6 percent was Muslim, 0.7 percent was Christian, and 0.1 percent adhered to other religions. The number of Muslims was, however, most probably under-recorded, and the category includes not only Malay-speaking Muslims who have the most problematic relationship to the Thai nation, but also Thai-speaking Muslims and a small number of Indian and Chinese Muslims as well. Buddhism is, moreover, not understood or practiced in the same way by all Thai. There are deep historical differences that have been compounded in recent decades.

Prior to the 1970s, nationalism in Thailand was predicated on both the monarchy and Buddhism, and this nationalism provided the basis for hegemonic rule by the military and bureaucracy over the vast majority of people in the country. By the early 1970s, however, this hegemony had begun to be significantly challenged by a growing student movement. In 1973, after the military used force to suppress large student protests, King Bhumipol Adulyadej intervened to halt a bloody confrontation between the student-led movement and security forces. After the then military dictators went into exile, the king chose an interim prime minister who oversaw the writing of the most democratic constitution Thailand had ever seen. But in the subsequent brief democratic period a marked division in the Thai political system developed. Right-wing forces supported by elements of the military and police began to use intimidation and death squads to regain power. Many in the student movement, on the other hand, began to see the Communist Party of Thailand (CPT) as the best vehicle for ensuring a more just distribution of wealth in the society.

These social and political divisions were exacerbated in 1975 by Thai reactions to communist takeovers in South Vietnam, Cambodia, and Laos.[51] In the mid-1970s, a very prominent Buddhist monk, Kittivuddho *Bhikkhu*, began to preach that communists were less than human and, thus, to kill them would not be a "sin"—that is, would not lead to "demerit"—in Buddhist terms.[52] Although many leading Buddhist monks and laypersons strongly denounced Kittivuddho for this position, the Ecclesiastical Council made up of the most senior monks in the Thai sangha refused to reprimand him. When the patriarch of the Buddhist sangha agreed to preside at the ordination of Thanom Kittikachorn, the former military dictator, thereby enabling him to return to the country, it seemed clear that the established sangha had sided with right-wing forces.

On October 6, 1976, right-wing paramilitary groups backed by units of the police staged a vicious attack on student protestors at one of the main universities in Bangkok. Many students were brutally killed and their bodies mutilated. In the wake of this event, the military once again took control of the government, and hundreds of students went upcountry to join the communist-led insurgency. Senior monks in the Buddhist establishment were conspicuous at rituals sponsored by the royal family and the leaders of the coup. Not all Buddhist leaders were co-opted, however. Some monks performed ordinations of a number of student activists. Several Buddhist laypersons who were strongly critical of the 1976 coup—such as Sulak Sivaraksa—felt compelled to go into exile.

By 1980 the insurgency had failed. This failure was a consequence, in part, of the rigidity of the leadership of the Communist Party of Thailand that alienated many former followers among both the students and rural population. It was even more the consequence of a decision taken by senior members of the Thai army who had taken control of the government to offer unconditional amnesty to those who had joined the CPT. These officers had come to power in what was, in effect, a counter-coup, having decided that the rigid right-wing ideology that had justified the violent crackdown on the student movement in 1976 had seriously undermined efforts to promote economic growth. Although they continued to express their loyalty to the monarchy and the state religion of Buddhism, they fostered the emergence of a new political culture that was far more tolerant and inclusive. In this new context, the appeal of the militant Buddhism advocated by Kittivuddho declined significantly.

As the economy began to grow rapidly in the 1980s, a number of new religious movements and sects attracted significant followings from among those who had been raised as Buddhists. One movement that initially drew many ranking military officers was the hybrid and heterodox sect known by the name of its headquarters as *samnak pu sawan*, "the Abode of the Heavenly Ancestors" or *hupha sawan*. The center of this sect was noted for its statues of Christ, Mahayana Buddhist saints, and Hindu deities as well as Theravādin images of the Buddha. When its leader, Suchat Kosonkitiwong, a poorly educated Sino-Thai who had begun as a small-scale spirit medium, began to style himself as a "prince" and offer unsolicited advice to the king, the government of General Prem Tinsulanond moved to restrict the activities of Suchat and his movement to the point that it effectively was suppressed.[53] While spirit cults have proliferated to an extraordinary degree in the 1980s and 1990s, none with any significant following has ever since sought to situate itself above Buddhism or the monarchy.[54]

Other movements within Buddhism have posed more of a challenge to the Buddhist establishment. As I have noted elsewhere, four significant Buddhist movements succeeded in gaining, through a contentious process, independent status alongside the established sangha. The four movements—*socially engaged Buddhism, heterodox Buddhism (Santi Asoke), Buddhist ecology*, and *evangelical Buddhism (Dhammakaya)*—do not encompass all monks and laypersons independent of the establishment that are viewed as possessing *bun barami* (Buddhist charisma) relevant to political action. But the high visibility of the four demonstrates the fragmentation of the Thai sangha.[55] Of particular relevance for our consideration of the relationship between Buddhism and human rights is socially engaged Buddhism that takes its lead from the sermons, writings, and practices of the late Buddhadāsa *Bhikkhu* (1906–1993), the most prominent Thai monk of the twentieth century. Buddhadāsa advocated a "*Dhammic* Socialism," maintaining that a Buddhist should not only seek to act in ways that will ensure a reduction in *dukkha* in future lives but should also act to help reduce suffering for all with whom one shares a social world in this life.[56] In sermons such as "Till the World Is with Peace" he urged that all live up to the ideal of being a *manuśya*, a human being in the original sense of having a "noble heart."[57] Socially engaged Buddhism, however, has had to compete with resurgent Buddhist nationalism.

In the 1980s and 1990s there was strong popular support for moves by the government and King Bhumipol to expand Thailand's civil society to be inclusive of minorities, including religious ones.[58] This inclusiveness was legitimated in a new constitution promulgated in 1997. This constitution redefined the term *sātsanā*, previously used primarily to designate Buddhism, to mean "religion" in a broader sense, so that those following Islam and Christianity could also be considered full citizens of the nation. The promotion of inclusive policies led to greater integration of Muslims, including the large Malay-speaking Muslim population of southern Thailand, into Thai society.[59] The voices of Buddhist nationalists were very muted during this period.

They reemerged, however, in the early twenty-first century. Thaksin Shinawatra became prime minister in early 2001 when his Thai Rak Thai (Thai love Thai) Party won a majority of seats in parliament. The party made even greater gains in a new election in 2005. During his five years as prime minister, he and his government instituted policies such as universal health care and government loan programs for villages that won him and the Thai Rak Thai Party wide support in the countryside. At the same time he and his government instituted other policies that alienated much of the Muslim population and led to a confrontation with the urban middle class. Many in the latter group rallied around leaders who promoted a royalist and Buddhist-centered nationalism.

The Thaksin government had to confront escalating violence in the four southern provinces of the country where most of the people are Malay-speaking Muslims.[60] Soon after coming to power, Thaksin turned his back on policies of elected governments in the 1990s that had given increasing recognition to the distinctiveness of the Malay-Muslim citizens of Thailand. Following the destruction of the World Trade Center in September 2001, Thaksin aligned his government with the United States in the "war on terror." In 2003 the Thaksin government sent a small contingent of Thai troops to participate in the war in Iraq, a move strongly protested by Thai Muslims. In early 2004 violent confrontations erupted in the Malay-speaking provinces of Thailand's far south. The violence escalated, with Thai government troops killing several hundred suspected terrorists and some noncombatants, including two incidents in 2004 during which excessive force was used. Insurgents, in turn, assassinated many police, local officials, teachers, and even Buddhist monks and novices, all deemed to be representatives of a political order they strongly rejected. The conflict in southern Thailand has been exacerbated because many Buddhist Thai consider Malay-speaking Muslims to be more alien than any other indigenous people living within the borders of Thailand.

Thaksin's government not only deployed large numbers of security forces in the far south but also began to promote a form of ultra-nationalism that entailed rejecting proposals to allow the Malay-Muslims of southern Thailand any form of autonomy. The rhetoric of the government as well as in the press led many in the country to think of all Malay-speaking Muslims as falling within this rubric. In this context, some Buddhist monks, led by Phra Thepwisutkawi of the Buddhist Protection Centre of Thailand, agitated for a constitutional change that would recognize Buddhism as not only as an official religion but as the state religion.[61]

In September 2006 a military junta staged a coup and took power from the elected government of Thaksin Shinawatra. It is noteworthy that this coup was headed by General Sonthi Boonyaratglin, who is himself a Thai-speaking Muslim but with no personal connection to the Thai-Malay minority. One of the first actions of the new government was to declare that it would reduce the use of security forces in the Malay-speaking provinces and implement the recommendations of a National Reconciliation Commission to negotiate with the insurgents. In response, the insurgents—who appear to be primarily young men who adhere to a radical form of Islam—actually increased the number of violent attacks on public facilities, schools, and businesses in the area. The murders of several monks provoked very strong public pressures on the government to protect Buddhism. The media began to write of the conflict more as a religious than an ethnic one.[62]

The junta-sponsored government oversaw the writing of a new constitution. During the drafting process a number of senior monks such as Phra Rajpanyamethi, vice-dean of Maha Chulalongkorn Buddhist University, and some leading laypersons such as General Thongchai Kuersakul organized a large movement of monks and laypersons to press for inclusion of an article in the constitution designating Buddhism the state religion.[63] In the end, however, the drafting committee resisted this pressure and refused to include such a provision.[64] The new constitution adopted through a referendum in August 2007 lacked a provision of this type.

After the new constitution was adopted, the military-backed government sponsored elections for a new parliament in December 2007. Thaksin and the Thai Rak Thai Party were banned from this election by judicial decisions reached during the time the military government was in power. A new party, the People's Action Party, was created as the successor to the Thai Rak Thai Party. This party, promoting the populist platform that the Thai Rak Thai Party had run on, won a majority of seats in parliament with backing from rural constituencies in northeastern and northern Thailand.

In January 2008 a new government was formed, led by Samak Sundaravej, a politician with a checkered history that spanned membership in right-wing groups when the student movement was suppressed in 1976 to being a controversial mayor of Bangkok. Samak proclaimed that he was a surrogate for Thaksin and soon after forming a government began to lay the groundwork through parliamentary decisions and an effort to revise the constitution to make it possible for Thaksin and the Thai Rak Thai Party to return to power. Samak soon came under attack by the People's Alliance for Democracy (PAD), a royalist-nationalist movement led by the media magnate Sonthi Limthongkun and supported primarily by members of Bangkok's middle class, but also with backing from the palace, elements in the military, and some in the Democrat Party, the main opposition party in parliament. The movement is more popularly known as the Yellow Shirts, a color adopted because of its association with the king.

Throughout 2008, there was an escalating struggle led by PAD against several successive governments led by allies of Thaksin. Thaksin himself returned to Thailand, but left again after his wife was convicted of an illegal land deal. He himself was subsequently found guilty in absentia by another court for misuse of power. His supporters held on to control of the government despite successive court decisions that stripped their leaders of power. The crisis culminated with the PAD seizing Bangkok's two international airports for over a week. In mid-December 2008, following the defection of some parliamentary supporters of the pro-Thaksin government, the Democrat Party led by Abhisit Vejjajiva formed a fragile government.

During this crisis, although the PAD presented itself as far more pro-royalist than the supporters of Thaksin, who claimed legitimacy because of their strong electoral support from upcountry people, neither side made Buddhist nationalism central to their appeal. Although some monks were present at PAD rallies, they were not at the forefront of the protests. Monks have been conspicuous, however, in the movement known officially as the United Front for Democracy Against Dictatorship, but more widely referred to as the Red Shirts, which was established to challenge the PAD. In 2009 and especially in 2010, the Red Shirts mounted prolonged demonstrations, most dramatically in Bangkok, against the government. The monks within exemplify the deep relationship between the rural followers of the movement and village-based Buddhism rather than Buddhist nationalism.

Given that the political future of Thailand continues to be uncertain and will become even more so when King Bhumipol dies, there will surely be some extreme nationalists who will again emerge to advocate that the centrality of Buddhism to Thai identity requires the marginalization of non-Buddhists within the kingdom. At the same time, there are also among the civil society groups in Thailand those who will strongly resist such advocacy.

Conclusions

The fundamental precepts of Buddhism call on adherents to refrain from actions that will cause death or loss of property, prevent violations of the body, or preclude access to the truth. Over the postwar decades, these precepts have not proved to be deterrents to governments headed by adherents to Buddhism intent on policies that deny rights to specific citizens living within their jurisdiction. Because the teaching of the Buddha accepted by all Buddhists recognizes that all humans are driven by desire (*tanhā*) for power, wealth, fulfillment of sexual urges, and control of others, Buddhist governments from the time of King Aśoka in the third century B.C.E. to the present have invoked the principles of security and stability to justify the suppression of subjects whose own drives supposedly threaten public order. In doing so, they have often adopted policies that violate widely recognized and universal rights that, as we have seen, can themselves be articulated and defended in a Buddhist idiom.

In modern times, many politicians have gone beyond the laws and practices long accepted as legitimate for Buddhist rulers. They have acted in order to gain or retain power by employing means, often violent, that deny the rights accorded to citizens to individuals or groups who live within their countries and are sometimes deemed to be threats to a Buddhist nation-state. Antiterrorist campaigns have been among the most widespread and effective means deployed by autocratic governments to marginalize ethnic and religious minorities in Buddhist-majority countries. In both Sri Lanka and Thailand recent governments have adopted laws that place "terrorists"—that is, those who use violence and killing to achieve political ends—outside the bounds of humanity. An act determined to be "terrorist" is ipso facto one that results in the denial of the right to life enjoyed by other humans. By extension, those who are deemed to support terrorists—notably, Hindu, Muslim, and Christian Tamils in Sri Lanka and Malay-speaking Muslims in southern Thailand—have also seen their rights severely compromised. In Burma, the government has adopted an even wider definition of those who pose a threat to the Buddhist state. Not only have ethnic and religious minorities been targeted, but so have ethnic Burmans who have joined the opposition to military rule. In Cambodia, the Khmer Rouge used a radical ideology that was predicated, in part, on an inversion of Buddhist ideas to justify genocidal policies toward a large segment of the population.

Because they claim to act in the name of Buddhism, autocratic regimes have felt it necessary to seek sanction for their acts from the chief representatives of the Buddha, the members of the Buddhist sangha. Not all members of the sangha have, however, proffered a religious imprimatur for such acts. In each of these countries, there are among Buddhist monks and lay leaders influential critics of efforts to promote a nationalism that allows only state-recognized Buddhists to be full citizens. These critics have contributed collectively to a Buddhist approach to human rights that intersects with universal human rights discourse.

A major challenge to this focus on government protection of stability and order has come from those who fall into the category of "socially engaged Buddhism." This challenge is predicated on a modernist variant of the tradition that rejects any radical separation of the "worldly" and the "other-worldly." Advocates of socially engaged Buddhism, including the late Buddhadāsa *Bhikkhu* in Thailand as well as the Dalai Lama and the Vietnamese monk Thích Nhất Hạnh outside of the Theravādin world, have in recent years challenged the use of violence as a means to maintain order within Buddhist societies. At a symposium titled "Religion and Peace" held in Thailand in 1987, the Venerable Prayoon Mererk (Prayoon Dhammcitto), rector of one of the two Buddhist universities in the country and a follower of Buddhadāsa, reviewed the justifications for violence against non-Buddhists that have been put forward in both Sri Lanka and Thailand. He concluded that "considering the Buddha's teaching thoroughly, we find that the advocate of Buddhistic violence is deviating from the Buddha's true teaching."[65]

In Sri Lanka, Buddhist nationalists who support the denial of human rights to Tamils and other non-Buddhists have been opposed by the Sarvodaya Shramadana Movement. This movement, founded in the 1950s by A.T. Ariyaratne, was initially focused on using Buddhist values to shape rural development, or, in his words, "to transform the Buddhist doctrines into a developmental process."[66] As the movement evolved into a major nongovernmental organization in Sri Lanka, it also became an advocate for social justice.[67] Sarvodaya Shramadana has opposed the use of violence to suppress the Tamil insurrection and, in marked contrast to Buddhist nationalists in Sri Lanka, has promoted the forging of what he calls "a national identity that transcends ethnic or religious identity and recognizes Sri Lanka's multi-ethnic, multireligious character; to create a sense of 'one nation, many cultures.'"[68]

In Cambodia the highly revered monk Mahā Ghosananda through teachings and actions—notably, his leadership of peace marches through the country— also sought to promote reconciliation and social justice on the basis of Buddhist values.[69] Buddhist monks have also been active in Burma in opposing the repressive policies of the regime, as the world witnessed most dramatically in September 2007. However, the military regime once again asserted the dominance of this-worldly power over the moral authority of the sangha through force of arms.

While there is no question that some non-Buddhists are not accorded equal rights in societies dominated by governments who base their legitimacy on Buddhist nationalism, the actions of these governments do not constitute *the* Buddhist stance regarding human rights. Influential monks and laypersons have articulated and nongovernmental organizations and social movements have promoted a distinctive Buddhist understanding of the rights of all humans to life, to security of their property, to inviolability of their bodies, and to access to truth. In every Buddhist society we find a tension between political reality and Buddhist values. In societies in which Theravāda Buddhism is dominant— Sri Lanka, Burma, Thailand, and Cambodia—the future of human rights will depend, in large part, on the course of the struggle between socially engaged Buddhism and Buddhism used as an instrument of authority by the state.

NOTES

1. I want to thank Tom Banchoff and Robert Wuthnow for inviting me to participate in this project and for their useful comments on earlier drafts. I am especially grateful to Jane Keyes who has, once again, made excellent suggestions for revisions.

2. Damien V. Keown, "Are There 'Human Rights' in Buddhism?" *Journal of Buddhist Ethics* 2 (1995): 10–11. See also Damien V. Keown, Charles S. Prebish, and Wayne R. Husted, eds., *Buddhism and Human Rights* (Richmond, Surrey: Curzon, 1998).

3. Keown reviews and critiques the work of a number of others such those by Inada L. H. H. Perera, L. P. N. Perera, and Unno who have also considered the Buddhist stance toward universal human rights. See Kenneth K. Inada, "The Buddhist Perspective on Human Rights," in *Human Rights in Religious Traditions*, ed. Arlene Swidler (New York: Pilgrims Press, 1982), 66–76; Inada, "A Buddhist Response to the Nature of Human Rights," in *Asian Perspectives on Human Rights*, ed. Claude E. Welch, Jr., and Virginia A. Leary (Boulder, CO: Westview Press, 1990), 91–103; L. H. H. Perera, ed., *Human Rights and Religions in Sri Lanka: A Commentary on the Universal Declaration of Human Rights* (Colombo: Sri Lanka Foundation, 1988); L. P. N. Perera, *Buddhism and Human Rights: A Buddhist Commentary on the Universal Declaration of Human Rights* (Colombo: Karunaratne and Sons, 1991); and Taitetsu Unno, "Personal Rights and Contemporary Buddhism," in *Human Rights in the World's Religions*, ed. Leroy S. Rouner (Notre Dame, IN: University of Notre Dame Press, 1988), 129–47.

4. Keown, "Are There 'Human Rights' in Buddhism?" 6.

5. I have given Buddhist terms in their Pāli form as this language is used in Theravāda Buddhism, the tradition of Buddhism that is practiced in the societies considered here.

6. See John C. Holt, *Discipline: The Canonical Buddhism of the Vinayapitaka* (Delhi: Moitlal Banarsidass, 1981).

7. The fifth precept should be understood as linked to "mindfulness," which is cultivated to ensure that one does not become "heedless" and act on one's desires.

8. Keown, "Are There 'Human Rights' in Buddhism?" 15.

9. Steven Collins, *Selfless Persons: Imagery and Thought in* Theravāda *Buddhism* (Cambridge: Cambridge University Press, 1982), 92, identifies the commentary to the *Sammādiṭṭhi Sutta* as a source for this distinction.

10. Keiko Tosa, "The Chicken and the Scorpion: Rumor, Counternarratives, and the Political Uses of Buddhism," in *Burma at the Turn of the Twenty-first Century*, ed. Monique Skidmore (Honolulu: University of Hawaii Press, 2005), 143–73.

11. Donald K. Swearer, *The Buddhist World of Southeast Asia* (Albany: State University of New York Press, 1995), 92. On the history of legal systems in Burma and Thailand, see Andrew Huxley, ed., *Thai Law: Buddhist Law—Essays on the Legal History of Thailand, Laos, and Burma* (Bangkok: White Orchid, 1996).

12. I use the name Ceylon when referring to the colonial period in Sri Lanka and Siam as the name of what is today Thailand for the period prior to 1939 when the name was officially changed. I follow most other Western scholars in using Burma instead of Myanmar even for the modern period because the latter term has become so connected with the military-led regime that has held power since 1988. Cambodia has also been officially known as Kampuchea, but this name has not been used officially since the late 1980s.

13. Mahāyāna Buddhism is found primarily in China, Taiwan, Japan, Korea, and Vietnam. Theravāda Buddhism is also the dominant religion in Laos, but as the ruling elite belong to the Communist Party, Buddhism in Laos does not enjoy the official

position it does in the other countries where Theravādin is dominant. Although Tibet was long a (Vajrayāna) Buddhist polity, since its incorporation into China, it has ceased to be such. Nonetheless, Tibet is sill the focus of attention for many in understanding the relationship between Buddhism and human rights. I do not consider Bhutan, where Vajrayāna Buddhism is dominant, because it not comparable in size to the Theravādin countries.

14. The Theravādin tradition places the death of the Buddha at 544–543 B.C.E. Recent scholarship strongly indicates that the Buddha's life was confined to the fourth century B.C.E.; see Heinz Bechert, ed., *The Dating of the Historical Buddha*, Numbers 189, 194, and 222 in *Abhandlungen der Akademie der Wissenschaften in Göttingen* (Göttingen: Vandenhoeck and Ruprecht, 1991–97).

15. Monks and novices are all males. In recent years there have been limited efforts in Sri Lanka and Thailand to resurrect an order of *bhikkhuni* in which females can live an ordained life. The vast majority of women who take religious roles in Theravādin societies, however, are not members of the sangha but are considered strict lay practitioners.

16. See Frank Reynolds, "The Two Wheels of Dhamma: A Study of Early Buddhism," in *The Two Wheels of Dhamma: Essays on the Theravada Tradition in India and Ceylon*, AAR Studies in Religion 3, ed. Bardwell L. Smith (Chambersburg, PA: American Academy of Religion, 1972).

17. See Richard Gombrich, *Theravada Buddhism: A Social History from Ancient Benares to Modern Colombo* (London: Routledge, 1988); S. J. Tambiah, *World Conqueror and World Renouncer: A Study of Buddhism and Polity in Thailand against a Historical Background* (Cambridge: Cambridge University Press, 1976).

18. See Gombrich, *Theravada Buddhism*; Kitsiri Malalgoda, *Buddhism in Sinhalese Society, 1750–1900* (Berkeley and Los Angeles: University of California Press, 1976).

19. Damrong Rajanubhab, *The Chronicle of Our Wars with the Burmese: Hostilities between Siamese and Burmese When Ayutthaya Was the Capital of Siam*, trans. Phra Phraison Salarak, Thein Subindu, alias U Aung Thein; ed. and intro. Chris Baker (Bangkok: White Lotus, 2001); Sunait Chutintharanond, "King Bayinnaung as Historical Hero in Thai Perspective," in *Comparative Studies on Literature and History of Thailand and Myanmar* (Bangkok: Chulalongkorn University, 1997), 9–16.

20. Much of the material in this section is adapted from Charles Keyes, "Monks, Guns and Peace: Theravada Buddhism and Political Violence," in *Belief and Bloodshed*, ed. James Wellman (Lanham, MD: Rowman and Littlefield, 2007), 147–65.

21. On Siam's implementation of a policy of national integration, see Thongchai Winichakul, *Siam Mapped: A History of the Geo-Body of a Nation* (Honolulu: University of Hawaii Press, 1994); also see Tej Bunnag, *The Provincial Administration of Siam, 1892–1915* (Kuala Lumpur: Oxford University Press, 1977).

22. The best study of the reforms that led to the integration of the sangha is Craig Reynolds, "The Buddhist Monkhood in Nineteenth Century Thailand," unpublished Ph.D. diss., Cornell University, 1973. Also see Yoneo Ishii, "Church and State in Thailand," *Asian Survey* 8.10 (1968): 864–71; Charles F. Keyes, "Buddhism and National Integration in Thailand," *Journal of Asian Studies* 3.3 (1971): 51–567; and A. Thomas Kirsch, "Modernizing Implications of 19th Century Reforms in the Thai Sangha," *Contributions to Asian Studies* 8 (1973): 8–23.

23. This term was first coined for Sri Lanka (Richard Gombrich and Gananath Obeyesekere, *Buddhism Transformed: Religious Change in Sri Lanka*. [Princeton: Princeton University Press, 1989]), but is equally applicable to Siam and Burma. For the religious reforms of the monkly Prince Vajiriñāna, see especially Craig Reynolds, "The Buddhist Monkhood in Nineteenth Century Thailand," and Craig Reynolds, "Buddhist Cosmography in Thai History, with Special Reference to Nineteenth-Century Culture Change," *Journal of Asian Studies* 35.2 (1976): 203–20. For the role of Ledi Sayadaw and the development of reformist Buddhism in Burma, see E. Michael Mendelson, *Sangha and State in Burma: A Study of Monastic Sectarianism and Leadership*, ed. John Ferguson (Ithaca, NY: Cornell University Press, 1975). For comparison of the development of reformist Buddhism in both countries, see Charles F. Keyes, "Buddhist Economics and Buddhist Fundamentalism in Burma and Thailand," in *Remaking the World: Fundamentalist Impact*, ed. Martin Marty and Scott Appleby (Chicago: University of Chicago Press, 1993), 367–409. Gombrich and Obeyesekere in *Buddhism Transformed* provide the best overview of the development of reformist Buddhism in Sri Lanka. Reform Buddhism in Cambodia and Laos was borrowed from Thailand.

24. See Heinz Bechert, "S.W.R.D. Bandaranike and the Legitimation of Power through Buddhist Ideals," in *Religion and the Legitimation of Power in Sri Lanka*, ed. Bardwell L. Smith (Chambersburg, PA: Anima, 1978), 199–211.

25. For some examination of the role of Buddhist nationalism in the Tamil-Sri Lankan conflict, see the following: James Manor, *Sri Lanka in Change and Crisis* (New York: St. Martin's Press, 1985); Stanley Jeyaraja Tambiah, *Buddhism Betrayed? Religion, Politics and Violence in Sri Lanka* (Chicago: University of Chicago Press, 1992); Tambiah, "Buddhism, Politics, and Violence in Sri Lanka," in *Fundamentalisms and the State: Remaking Polities, Economies, and Militance*, ed. Martin E. Marty and R. Scott Appleby (Chicago: University of Chicago Press, 1993), 589–619; Tessa J. Bartholomeusz and Chandra R. De Silva, eds., *Buddhist Fundamentalism and Minority Identities in Sri Lanka* (Albany: State University of New York Press, 1998); George D. Bond, "Buddhism, War and Peace: Two Perspectives from Sri Lanka," paper presented at conference, "Religion and Democratic Culture: The Problems of Violence and the Possibilities of Peace," organized by the Comparative Religion Program, University of Washington, Seattle, October 26–27, 2006; and Mahinda Degalle, "Buddhism in Sri Lanka and Its Relationship with the Modern State," paper presented at workshop, "Buddhism and the Crises of the Nation-State," organized by the Asia Research Institute and the Faculty of Arts and Social Sciences, National University of Singapore, June 19–20, 2008.

26. On the direct involvement of monks in the election of 2004 as well as the advocacy of some monks for the violent suppression of Tamil ethnonationalism, see the article "Powerful Buddhist Monks Enter Sri Lanka's Election Race," *Dow Jones News Service*, March 2, 2004, http://framehosting.dowjonesnews.com/sample/samplestory.asp?StoryID'2004030207260015&Take'1.

27. Somini Sengupta, "Sri Lankan Government Finds Support from Buddhist Monks," *New York Times*, February 25, 2007.

28. See Bond, "Buddhism, War and Peace . . ."

29. James Astill, "Monks and Tigers in Sri Lanka," *More Intelligent Life.com*, May 27, 2008, http://moreintelligentlife.com/story/monks-and-tigers-in-sri-lanka.

30. Burma has, since the colonial period, been administratively divided into divisions in the core regions of the country where the population is overwhelmingly ethnically Burman and states in the outer regions of the country where the people are mainly members of non-Burman ethnic groups.

31. It is difficult to obtain precise figures for any demographic aspect of Burma. The 89–90 percent figure reported to be Buddhist is found in most reputable sources. See, for example, the United States Department of State, Bureau of Democracy, Human Rights, and Labor, *Burma: International Religious Freedom Report 2002*, http://www.state.gov/g/drl/rls/irf/2002/13868.htm.

32. Ibid. The best work on the divisions of the sangha in Burma is that by Mendelson, *Sangha and State in Burma*. On the complexity of the religious practices by Burmans, see E. Michael Mendelson, "Buddhism and the Burmese Establishment," *Archives de Sociologie des Religions* 9.17 (1964): 85–95; John P. Ferguson, "The Symbolic Dimensions of the Burmese Sangha," unpublished Ph.D. diss., Cornell University, 1975; Melford E. Spiro, *Buddhism and Society: A Great Tradition and Its Burmese Vicissitudes* (New York: Harper and Row, 1970); Spiro, *Burmese Supernaturalism*, 2nd rev. ed. (Philadelphia: Institute for the Study of Human Issues, 1978); Juliane Schober, "Buddhist Visions of Moral Authority and Civil Society: The Search for the Post-Colonial State in Burma," in *Burma at the Turn of the Twenty-first Century*, ed. Monique Skidmore (Honolulu: University of Hawaii Press, 2005), 113–33.

33. These statistics are based on the U.S. Department of State online "Background Note: Burma," http://www.state.gov/r/pa/ei/bgn/35910.htm.

34. For some analysis of the relationship of how the military junta has shaped Buddhist politics in Burma, see, in addition to sources cited in footnote 32, Gustaaf Houtman, *Mental Culture in Burmese Crisis Politics: Aung San Suu Kyi and the National League for Democracy*, ILCAA Study of Languages and Cultures of Asia and Africa, Monograph Series No. 33 (Tokyo: Institute for the Study of Languages and Cultures of Asia and Africa, 1999). The protests led by monks in 2007 were given an extraordinary amount of press coverage; see, for example, Choe Sang-Hun, "In Myanmar, Fear Is a Constant Companion," *New York Times*, October 21, 2007; and Seth Mydans, "What Makes a Monk Mad?" *New York Times*, September 30, 2007. The best analysis to date of the sangha's challenge to the legitimacy of the junta is in a forthcoming book by Juliane Schober.

35. Monique Skidmore, "Darker than Midnight: Fear, Vulnerability, and Terror Making in Urban Burma (Myanmar)," *American Ethnologist* 30.1 (2003): 7.

36. "Country Reports on Human Rights Practices—2004," United States Department of State, Bureau of Democracy, Human Rights, and Labor, February 28, 2005, http://www.state.gov/g/drl/rls/hrrpt/2004/41637.htm.

37. Human Rights Work, *World Report, 2003*, http://hrw.org/wr2k3/asia2.html.

38. Amnesty International, "Myanmar—The Rohingya Minority: Fundamental Rights Denied," May 19, 2004, http://web.amnesty.org/library/Index/ENGASA160052004.

39. Juliane Schober, "Modern Buddhist Conjunctures in Myanmar's Global Economy," paper presented at a workshop, "Buddhism and the Crises of the Nation-State," organized by the Asia Research Institute and the Faculty of Arts and Social Sciences, National University of Singapore, June 19–20, 2008.

40. Charles F. Keyes, "Communist Revolution and the Buddhist Past in Cambodia," in *Asian Visions of Authority: Religion and the Modern States of East and Southeast Asia*, ed. Charles F. Keyes, Laurel Kendall, and Helen Hardacre (Honolulu: University of Hawaii Press, 1994), 43–73.

41. David Chandler, *The Tragedy of Cambodian History: Politics, War, and Revolution since 1945* (New Haven, CT: Yale University Press, 1991), 18.

42. Alexander Laban Hinton, *Why Did They Kill? Cambodia in the Shadow of Genocide* (Berkeley: University of California Press, 2005), 195ff.

42. Ibid., 262–63.

44. By far the most detailed account of the fate of the sangha under the Khmer Rouge is Ian Harris, *Buddhism under Pol Pot*, Documentation Series No. 13 (Phnom Penh: Documentation Center of Cambodia, 2007).

45. Ros Sotha, "National Political Violence and Buddhist Response in Cambodia," *Seeds of Peace* 21.2 (2005): 28–31. *Seeds of Peace* is the publication of the International Network of Engaged Buddhists, edited and published in Bangkok by Sulak Sivaraksa, a leader of this movement.

46. Maha Ghosananda, *Step by Step: Meditations on Wisdom and Compassion.* (Berkeley, CA: Parallax Press, 1992).

47. On the Khmer Rouge trials, see Seth Mydans, "In Khmer Rouge Trial, Victims Will Not Stand Idly By," *New York Times*, June 17, 2008 (the same article was also published under the title of "Khmer Rouge Victims Given a Voice in Cambodia Trials," *International Herald Tribune*, June 16, 2008); Peter Maguire, "Cambodia's Troubled Tribunal," *New York Times*, July 28, 2010; Seth Mydans, "Anger in Cambodia over Khmer Rouge Sentence," *New York Times*, July 26, 2010. Also see articles for which links are provided in "Special Tribunal for Cambodia," a Web site of the Global Policy Forum that "monitors policy making at the United Nations," http://www.globalpolicy. org/intljustice/camindx.htm.

48. John Marston, "Buddhism and Human Rights NGOs in Cambodia," unpublished paper for a seminar at El Colegio de México, February 14, 2006.

49. Judy Ledgerwood and Kheang Un, "Global Concepts and Local Meaning: Human Rights and Buddhism in Cambodia," *Journal of Human Rights* 2.4 (2003): 546.

50. Ros Sotha, *"National Political Violence and Buddhist Response in Cambodia,"* 31, emphasis in original.

51. There is a large literature on the political crisis in Thailand in the 1970s. Among the most relevant sources for understanding the emergence of militant Buddhism in the period are the following: John Girling, *Thailand: Society and Politics* (Ithaca, NY: Cornell University Press, 1981); David Morell and Chai-anan Samudavanija, *Political Conflict in Thailand: Reform, Reaction, Revolution* (Cambridge, MA: Oelgeschlager, Gunn and Hain, 1981); Ben Anderson, "Withdrawal Symptoms: Social and Cultural Aspects of the October 6 Coup," *Bulletin of Concerned Asian Scholars* 9.3 (1977): 13–30; and Thongchai Winichakul, "Remembering/Silencing the Traumatic Past: The Ambivalent Memories of the October 1976 Massacre in Bangkok," in *Cultural Crisis and Social Memory: Modernity and Identity in Thailand and Laos*, ed. Shigeharu Tanabe and Charles Keyes (Richmond, Surrey, UK: RoutledgeCurzon, 2002), 243–83.

52. I have discussed Kittivuddho's advocacy of militant Buddhism at some length elsewhere; see Keyes, "Political Crisis and Militant Buddhism in Contemporary

Thailand," in *Religion and Legitimation of Power in Thailand, Burma, and Laos*, ed. Bardwell Smith (Chambersburg, PA: Anima Books, 1978), 147–64. His most extended justification of militant Buddhism is found in *Khā Khômmūnit mai bāp* [Killing Communists Is Not Demeritorious] by Kittivuddho Bhikkhu (Kittiwutthō Phikkhu) (Bangkok: Abhidhamma Foundation of Wat Mahādhātu [Mūnnithi Aphitham, Wat Mahāthāt], 1976). For further details, also see Somboon Suksamran, *Buddhism and Politics in Thailand* (Singapore: Institute of Southeast Asian Studies, 1982).

53. See Shusuke Yagi, "*Samnak Puu Sawan*: Rise and Oppression of a New Religious Movement in Thailand," unpublished Ph.D. diss., University of Washington, 1988; and Peter Jackson, "The Hupphaasawan Movement: Millenarian Buddhism among the Thai Political Elite," *Sojourn* 3.2 (1988): 134–70.

54. See Pattana Kitiarsa, "'You May Not Believe but Never Offend Spirit': Spirit-Medium Cult Discourses and the Postmodernization of Thai Religion," unpublished Ph.D. diss., University of Washington, 1999.

55. Charles Keyes, "Buddhism Fragmented: Thai Buddhism and Political Order since the 1970s," keynote address presented at Seventh International Thai Studies Conference, Amsterdam, July 1999.

56. See Buddhadāsa Bhikkhu, *Thammikasangkhomniyom/Dhammic Socialism*, trans. and ed. Donald K. Swearer (Bangkok: Munnithi Komonkhimthong, b.e. 2529/c.e. 1986); and Donald K. Swearer, "Thai Buddhism: Two Responses to Modernity," *Contributions to Asian Studies* 4 (1973): 78–93.

57. Buddhadāsa, "Till the World Is with Peace," *Seeds of Peace*, trans. Pataporn Srikanchana (Bangkok) 3.1 (1987): 14.

58. I have traced the development of an inclusive pluralism in Thailand in the 1980s and 1990s in greater detail in "Cultural Diversity and National Identity in Thailand," in *Government Policies and Ethnic Relations in Asia and the Pacific*, ed. Michael Brown and Sunait Ganguly (Cambridge, MA: MIT Press, 1997), 197–232; and "Ethnicity and the Nation-States of Thailand and Vietnam," in *Challenging the Limits: Indigenous Peoples of the Mekong Region*, ed. Prasit Leepreecha, Don McCaskill, and Kwanchewan Buadaeng (Chiang Mai: Mekong Press, 2008), 13–53.

59. See Chaiwat Satha-Anand, *Islam and Violence: A Case Study of Violent Events in the Four Southern Provinces of Thailand, 1976–1981*, USF Monographs in Religion and Public Policy, no. 2 (Tampa: Department of Religious Studies, University of South Florida, 1986); Chaiwat Satha-Anand and Suwanna Satha-Anand, *Struggling Dove and Plastic Lotus: Peacemaking in Thai Society*, Occasional Papers, No. VI (Bangkok: Pridi Banomyong Institute, 1987); and Carlo Bonura, "Political Theory on Location: Formations of Muslim Political Community in Southern Thailand," unpublished Ph.D. diss., University of Washington, 2003.

60. For reasons of space, I will not here consider minorities, such as the so-called hill tribes including the Hmong, Lahu, Akha, and Lisu who live primarily in northern Thailand, who have been denied full rights of citizenship. I have, however, given them extended attention in my "Ethnicity and the Nation-States of Thailand and Vietnam."

61. Quotation taken from Web site of "The Buddhist Channel," which quotes the TNA Newservice, http://www.buddhistchannel.tv/index.php?id=52,1355,0,0,1,0.

62. See, for example, S. P. Harrish, "Ethnic or Religious Cleavage? Investigating the Nature of the Conflict in Southern Thailand," *Contemporary Southeast Asia* 1 (2006): 48–69.

63. See the *Bangkok Post*, February 10 and 16, 2007; *The Nation* (Bangkok), February 14 and April 23, 2007.

64. *The Nation*, June 29, 2007.

65. Prayoon Mererk (Prayoon Dhammcitto), "The Buddhist Way of Solving National Conflict," *Seeds of Peace* 3.2 (1987): 16–19.

66. Quoted in Bond, "Buddhism, War and Peace . . ." 13. For background on the movement, see Hans Wismeijer, *Diversity in Harmony: A Study of the Leaders of the Sarvodaya Shramadana Movement in Sri Lanka*, trans. Geoffrey Ostergaard (Utrecht: Department of Cultural Anthropology, Heidelberglaan 2, 1981).

67. See Robert Bobilin, *Revolution from Below: Buddhist and Christian Movements for Justice in Asia—Four Case Studies from Thailand and Sri Lanka* (Lanham, MD: University Press of America, 1988).

68. Quoted in Bond, "Buddhism, War and Peace . . ." 16.

69. On Maha Ghosananda, see the following Web sites: http://www.buddhanetz. org/engaged/engaged3.htm and http://www.buddhanet.net/s_img052.htm. Also see Harris (1999, 2005), and Skidmore (1996).

BIBLIOGRAPHY

Amnesty International. "Myanmar—The Rohingya Minority: Fundamental Rights Denied." http://web.amnesty.org/library/Index/ENGASA160052004).

Anderson, Ben. "Withdrawal Symptoms: Social and Cultural Aspects of the October 6 Coup." *Bulletin of Concerned Asian Scholars* 9.3 (1977): 13–30.

Astill, James. "Monks and Tigers in Sri Lanka." *More Intelligent Life.com*, May 27, 2008. http://moreintelligentlife.com/story/monks-and-tigers-in-sri-lanka.

Bartholomeusz, Tessa J., and Chandra R. De Silva, eds. *Buddhist Fundamentalism and Minority Identities in Sri Lanka* Albany: State University of New York Press, 1998.

Bechert, Heinz. "S.W.R.D. Bandaranike and the Legitimation of Power through Buddhist Ideals." In *Religion and the Legitimation of Power in Sri Lanka*, ed. Bardwell L. Smith, 199–211. Chambersburg, PA: Anima, 1978.

———, ed. *The Dating of the Historical Buddha*. Numbers 189, 194, and 222 in *Abhandlungen der Akademie der Wissenschaften in Göttingen*. Göttingen: Vandenhoeck and Ruprecht, 1991–1997.

Bobilin, Robert. *Revolution from Below: Buddhist and Christian Movements for Justice in Asia—Four Case Studies from Thailand and Sri Lanka*. Lanham, MD: University Press of America, 1988.

Bond, George D. "Buddhism, War and Peace: Two Perspectives from Sri Lanka." Paper presented at a conference, "Religion and Democratic Culture: The Problems of Violence and the Possibilities of Peace," organized by the Comparative Religion Program, University of Washington, Seattle, October 26–27, 2006.

Bonura, Carlo. "Political Theory on Location: Formations of Muslim Political Community in Southern Thailand." Unpublished Ph.D. diss., University of Washington, 2003.

Bosleigh, Robert. "Victorious War Monk Athuraliye Rathana turns on Britain," *The Times* (London), May 21, 2009.

Buddhadāsa Bhikkhu. *Thammikasangkhomniyom/Dhammic Socialism*. Ed. and trans. Donald K. Swearer. Bangkok: Munnithi Komonkhimthong, 1986 [2529].

———. "Till the World Is with Peace." *Seeds of Peace*, trans. Patraporn Srikanchana (Bangkok) 3.1 (1987): 12–15.

The Buddhist Channel. "Monks Call for Buddhism to Be Made National Religion." *TNA Newservice*. http://www.buddhistchannel.tv/index.php?id=52, 1355,0,0,1,0.

Chaiwat Satha-Anand. *Islam and Violence: A Case Study of Violent Events in the Four Southern Provinces of Thailand, 1976–1981*. USF Monographs in Religion and Public Policy, no. 2. Tampa: Department of Religious Studies, University of South Florida, 1986.

Chaiwat Satha-Anand and Suwanna Satha-Anand. *Struggling Dove and Plastic Lotus: Peacemaking in Thai Society*. Occasional Papers, No. VI. Bangkok: Pridi Banomyong Institute, 1987.

Chandler, David. *The Tragedy of Cambodian History: Politics, War, and Revolution since 1945*. New Haven, CT: Yale University Press, 1991.

Choe Sang-Hun. "In Myanmar, Fear Is a Constant Companion." *New York Times*, October 21, 2007.

Collins, Steven. *Selfless Persons: Imagery and Thought in Theravāda Buddhism*. Cambridge: Cambridge University Press, 1982.

Damrong Rajanubhab. *The Chronicle of Our Wars with the Burmese: Hostilities between Siamese and Burmese When Ayutthaya Was the Capital of Siam*. Trans. Phra Phraison Salarak, Thein Subindu, alias U Aung Thein; ed. and intro. Chris Baker. Bangkok: White Lotus, 2001.

Degalle, Mahinda. "Buddhism in Sri Lanka and Its Relationship with the Modern State." Paper presented at workshop, "Buddhism and the Crises of the Nation-State," organized by the Asia Research Institute and the Faculty of Arts and Social Sciences, National University of Singapore, June 19–20, 2008.

Dow Jones News Service. "Powerful Buddhist Monks Enter Sri Lanka's Election Race." http://framehosting.dowjonesnews.com/sample/samplestory.asp?StoryID'20040 30207260015&Take'1.

Ferguson, John P. "The Symbolic Dimensions of the Burmese Sangha." Unpublished Ph.D. diss., Cornell University, 1975.

Girling, John. *Thailand: Society and Politics*. Ithaca, NY: Cornell University Press, 1981.

Global Policy Forum. "Special Tribunal for Cambodia." http://www.globalpolicy.org/intljustice/camindx.htm.

Gombrich, Richard. *Theravada Buddhism: A Social History from Ancient Benares to Modern Colombo*. London: Routledge, 1988.

Gombrich, Richard, and Gananath Obeyesekere. *Buddhism Transformed: Religious Change in Sri Lanka*. Princeton: Princeton University Press, 1989.

Harris, Ian. *Buddhism under Pol Pot*. Documentation Series No. 13. Phnom Penh: Documentation Center of Cambodia, 2007.

———. "Truth Commission or Truth Act: A Buddhist Perspective on Reconciliation in Contemporary Cambodia." Paper presented at conference, "Religion and

Democratic Culture: The Problems of Violence and the Possibilities of Peace,"
organized by the Comparative Religion Program, University of Washington, Seattle, October 26–27, 2006.

Harrish, S. P. "Ethnic or Religious Cleavage? Investigating the Nature of the Conflict
in Southern Thailand." *Contemporary Southeast Asia* 1 (2006): 48–69.

Hinton, Alexander Laban. *Why Did They Kill? Cambodia in the Shadow of Genocide.*
Berkeley: University of California Press, 2005.

Holt, John C. *Discipline: The Canonical Buddhism of the Vinayapitaka.* Delhi: Moitlal
Banarsidass, 1981.

Houtman, Gustaaf. *Mental Culture in Burmese Crisis Politics: Aung San Suu Kyi and the
National League for Democracy.* ILCAA Study of Languages and Cultures of Asia
and Africa, Monograph Series No. 33. Tokyo: Institute for the Study of Languages
and Cultures of Asia and Africa, 1999.

Human Rights Watch. *World Report, 2003.* http://hrw.org/wr2k3/asia2.html.

Huxley, Andrew, ed. *Thai Law: Buddhist Law—Essays on the Legal History of Thailand,
Laos, and Burma.* Bangkok: White Orchid, 1996.

Inada, Kenneth K. *"The Buddhist Perspective on Human Rights."* In *Human Rights in
Religious Traditions,* ed. Arlene Swidler, 66–76. New York: Pilgrims Press, 1982.

———. "A Buddhist Response to the Nature of Human Rights." In *Asian Perspectives
on Human Rights,* ed. Claude E. Welch, Jr., and Virginia A. Leary, 91–103. Boulder,
CO: Westview Press, 1990.

Ishii Yoneo. "Church and State in Thailand." *Asian Survey* 8.10 (1968): 864–71.

Jackson, Peter. "The Hupphaasawan Movement: Millenarian Buddhism among the
Thai Political Elite." *Sojourn* 3.2 (1988): 134–70.

Keown, Damien. "Are There 'Human Rights' in Buddhism?" *Journal of Buddhist Ethics*
2 (1995): 3–27.

Keown, Damien V., Charles S. Prebish, and Wayne R. Husted, eds. *Buddhism and Human Rights.* Richmond, Surrey: Curzon, 1998.

Keyes, Charles F. "Buddhism and National Integration in Thailand." *Journal of Asian
Studies* 3.3 (1971): 51–567.

———. "Buddhism Fragmented: Thai Buddhism and Political Order since the 1970s."
Keynote address presented at Seventh International Thai Studies Conference,
Amsterdam, July 1999.

———. "Buddhist Economics and Buddhist Fundamentalism in Burma and Thailand." In *Remaking the World: Fundamentalist Impact,* ed. Martin Marty and Scott
Appleby, 367–409. Chicago: University of Chicago Press, 1993.

———. "Communist Revolution and the Buddhist Past in Cambodia." In *Asian Visions
of Authority: Religion and the Modern States of East and Southeast Asia,* ed. Charles
F. Keyes, Laurel Kendall, and Helen Hardacre, 43–73. Honolulu: University of
Hawaii Press, 1994.

———. "Cultural Diversity and National Identity in Thailand." In *Government Policies
and Ethnic Relations in Asia and the Pacific,* ed. Michael Brown and Sunait Ganguly, 197–232. Cambridge: MIT Press, 1997.

———. "Ethnicity and the Nation-States of Thailand and Vietnam." In *Challenging the
Limits: Indigenous Peoples of the Mekong Region,* ed. Prasit Leepreecha, Don Mc-
Caskill, and Kwanchewan Buadaeng, 13–53. Chiang Mai: Mekong Press, 2008.

————. "Monks, Guns and Peace: Theravada Buddhism and Political Violence." In *Belief and Bloodshed*, ed. James Wellman, 147–65. Lanham, MD: Rowman and Littlefield, 2007.

————. "Muslim 'Others' in Buddhist Thailand," *Thammasat Review* 13 (2008–2009): 19–42.

————. "Political Crisis and Militant Buddhism in Contemporary Thailand." In *Religion and Legitimation of Power in Thailand, Burma, and Laos*, ed. Bardwell Smith, 147–64. Chambersburg, Pa.: Anima Books, 1978.

Kirsch, A. Thomas. "Modernizing Implications of 19th Century Reforms in the Thai Sangha." *Contributions to Asian Studies* 8 (1973): 8–23.

Kittivuddho Bhikkhu (Kittiwutthō Phikkhu). *Khā Khômmūnit mai bāp* [Killing Communists Is Not Demeritorious]. Bangkok: Abhidhamma Foundation of Wat Mahādhātu (Mūnnithi Aphitham, Wat Mahāthāt), 1976.

Ledgerwood, Judy, and Kheang Un. "Global Concepts and Local Meaning: Human Rights and Buddhism in Cambodia." *Journal of Human Rights* 2.4 (2003): 531–49.

Ledi Sayadaw. *The Manual of Insight: Vipassanā Dīpanī*. U NyāĀa Mahā-Thera, trans. Kandy. The Wheel Publication No. 31/32. Ceylon: Buddhist Publication Society, 1961.

————. *The Requisites of Enlightment: Bodhipakkhiya Dīpanī*. Sein Nyo Tun, trans. Kandy. The Wheel Publication No. 171/74. Ceylon: Buddhist Publication Society, 1971.

Maguire, Peter. "Cambodia's Troubled Tribunal," *New York Times*, July 28, 2010.

Malalgoda, Kitsiri. *Buddhism in Sinhalese Society, 1750–1900*. Berkeley and Los Angeles: University of California Press, 1976.

Manor, James. *Sri Lanka in Change and Crisis*. New York: St. Martin's Press, 1985.

Marston, John. "Buddhism and Human Rights NGOs in Cambodia." Unpublished paper for a seminar at El Colegio de México, February 14, 2006.

Mendelson, E. Michael. "Buddhism and the Burmese Establishment." *Archives de Sociologie des Religions* 9.17 (1964): 85–95.

————. *Sangha and State in Burma: A Study of Monastic Sectarianism and Leadership*. ed. John Ferguson. Ithaca, NY: Cornell University Press, 1975.

Morell, David, and Chai-anan Samudavanija. *Political Conflict in Thailand: Reform, Reaction, Revolution*. Cambridge, MA: Oelgeschlager, Gunn, and Hain, 1981.

Mydans, Seth. "What Makes a Monk Mad?" *New York Times*, September 30, 2007.

Mydans, Seth. "Thai-Cambodian Temple Standoff Continues." *New York Times*, July 21, 2008.

Mydans, Seth. "In Khmer Rouge Trial, Victims Will Not Stand Idly By." *New York Times*, June 17, 2008.

Mydans, Seth. "Anger in Cambodia over Khmer Rouge Sentence," *New York Times*, July 26, 2010.

Pattana Kitiarsa, "'You May Not Believe but Never Offend Spirit': Spirit-Medium Cult Discourses and the Postmodernization of Thai Religion." Unpublished Ph.D. diss., University of Washington, 1999.

Perera, L. H. H., ed. *Human Rights and Religions in Sri Lanka: A Commentary on the Universal Declaration of Human Rights*. Colombo: Sri Lanka Foundation, 1988.

Perera, L. P. N. *Buddhism and Human Rights: A Buddhist Commentary on the Universal Declaration of Human Rights*. Colombo: Karunaratne and Sons, 1991.

Prayoon Mererk (Prayoon Dhammcitto). "The Buddhist Way of Solving National Conflict." *Seeds of Peace* 3.2 (1987): 16–19.

Reynolds, Craig J. "The Buddhist Monkhood in Nineteenth Century Thailand." Unpublished Ph.D. diss., Cornell University, 1973.

———. "Buddhist Cosmography in Thai History, with Special Reference to Nineteenth-Century Culture Change." *Journal of Asian Studies* 35.2 (1976): 203–20.

Reynolds, Frank. "The Two Wheels of Dhamma: A Study of Early Buddhism." In *The Two Wheels of Dhamma: Essays on the Theravada Tradition in India and Ceylon*, ed. Bardwell L. Smith, 6–30. AAR Studies in Religion 3. Chambersburg, PA: American Academy of Religion, 1972.

Roberts, Michael. "For Humanity. For the Sinhalese. Dharmapala as Crusading Bosat." *Journal of Asian Studies* 56.4 (1997): 1006–32.

Ros Sotha. "National Political Violence and Buddhist Response in Cambodia." *Seeds of Peace* 21.2 (2005): 28–31.

Schober, Juliane. "Buddhist Just Rule and Burmese National Culture: State Patronage of the Chinese Tooth Relic in Myanmar." *History of Religions* 36.3 (1997): 218–43.

———. "Buddhist Visions of Moral Authority and Civil Society: The Search for the Post-Colonial State in Burma." In *Burma at the Turn of the Twenty-first Century*, ed. Monique Skidmore, 113–33. Honolulu: University of Hawaii Press, 2005.

———. "Buddhism, Violence and the State in Burma (Myanmar) and Sri Lanka." In *Disrupting Violence: Religion and Conflict in South and Southeast Asia*, ed. Linell E. Cady and Sheldon W. Simon, 51–69. Oxon: Routledge, 2006.

———. "Modern Buddhist Conjunctures in Myanmar's Global Economy." Paper presented at a workshop, "Buddhism and the Crises of the Nation-State," organized by the Asia Research Institute and the Faculty of Arts and Social Sciences, National University of Singapore, June 19–20, 2008.

Seneviratne, H. L. "Religion and Legitimacy of Power in the Kandyan Kingdom." In *Religion and the Legitimation of Power in Sri Lanka*, ed. Bardwell L. Smith, 177–87. Chambersburg, PA: Anima, 1978.

Sirisena, W. M. *Sri Lanka and South-East Asia: Political, Religious and Cultural Relations from A.D. c. 1000 to c. 1500*. Leiden: E. J. Brill, 1978.

Skidmore, Monique. "Darker than Midnight: Fear, Vulnerability, and Terror Making in Urban Burma (Myanmar)." *American Ethnologist* 30.1 (2003): 5–21.

Somboon Suksamran. *Buddhism and Politics in Thailand*. Singapore: Institute of Southeast Asian Studies, 1982.

Somini Sengupta. "Sri Lankan Government Finds Support from Buddhist Monks." *New York Times*, February 25, 2007.

Spiro, Melford E. *Buddhism and Society: A Great Tradition and Its Burmese Vicissitudes*. New York: Harper and Row, 1970.

———. *Burmese Supernaturalism*, 2nd. rev. ed. Philadelphia: Institute for the Study of Human Issues, 1978.

Sunait Chutintharanond. "King Bayinnaung as Historical Hero in Thai Perspective." In *Comparative Studies on Literature and History of Thailand and Myanmar*, 9–16. Bangkok: Chulalongkorn University, 1997.

Swearer, Donald K. 1973. "Thai Buddhism: Two Responses to Modernity." *Contributions to Asian Studies* 4 (1973): 78–93.

———. *The Buddhist World of Southeast Asia*. Albany: State University of New York Press, 1995.

Tambiah, S. J. *Buddhism Betrayed? Religion, Politics and Violence in Sri Lanka*. Chicago: University of Chicago Press, 1992.

———. "Buddhism, Politics, and Violence in Sri Lanka." In *Fundamentalisms and the State: Remaking Polities. Economies, and Militance*, ed. Martin E. Marty and R. Scott Appleby, 589–619. Chicago: University of Chicago Press, 1993.

———. *World Conqueror and World Renouncer: A Study of Buddhism and Polity in Thailand against a Historical Background*. Cambridge: Cambridge University Press, 1976.

Tej Bunnag. *The Provincial Administration of Siam, 1892–1915*. Kuala Lumpur: Oxford University Press, 1977.

Thongchai Winichakul. *Siam Mapped: A History of the Geo-Body of a Nation*. Honolulu: University of Hawaii Press, 1994.

———. "Remembering/Silencing the Traumatic Past: The Ambivalent Memories of the October 1976 Massacre in Bangkok." In *Cultural Crisis and Social Memory: Modernity and Identity in Thailand and Laos*, ed. Shigeharu Tanabe and Charles Keyes, 243–83. Richmond, Surrey, UK: RoutledgeCurzon, 2002.

Tosa, Keiko. "The Chicken and the Scorpion: Rumor, Counternarratives, and the Political Uses of Buddhism." In *Burma at the Turn of the Twenty-first Century*, ed. Monique Skidmore, 143–73. Honolulu: University of Hawaii Press, 2005.

United States Department of State. "Country Reports on Human Rights Practices–2004." United States Department of State, United States Bureau of Democracy, Human Rights and Labor. http://www.state.gov/g/drl/rls/hrrpt/2004/41637.htm.

———. *Burma: International Religious Freedom Report 2002*. United States Department of State, Bureau of Democracy, Human Rights, and Labor. http://www.state.gov/g/drl/rls/irf/2002/13868.htm.

———. "Background Note: Burma." http://www.state.gov/r/pa/ei/bgn/35910.htm.

Unno, Taitetsu. "Personal Rights and Contemporary Buddhism." In *Human Rights in the World's Religions*, ed. Leroy S. Rouner, 129–47. Notre Dame, Indiana: University of Notre Dame Press, 1988.

Wismeijer, Hans. *Diversity in Harmony: A Study of the Leaders of the Sarvodaya Shramadana Movement in Sri Lanka*. Trans. Geoffrey Ostergaard. Utrecht: Department of Cultural Anthropology, Heidelberglaan 2, 1981.

Yagi, Shusuke. "*Samnak Puu Sawan*: Rise and Oppression of a New Religious Movement in Thailand." Unpublished Ph.D. diss., University of Washington, 1988.

PART III

Four Key Countries: India, China, Russia, and the United States

8

Hinduism and the Politics of Rights in India

Pratap Bhanu Mehta

What were the deep historical forces that moved Hinduism to become amenable to human rights–oriented discourses, apart from the fact that there were normative resources within the tradition that could be mobilized in this direction?

I will give an account of those forces and explore how they continue to shape the politics of rights in India. In the first section I will outline structural and doctrinal features of Hinduism that make it propitious for a politics of human rights. In the second section, I will argue that two challenges, colonialism and caste, have been and continue to be significant drivers in making Hindu religious groups receptive to the politics of human rights. In the third section, I argue that certain forms of Hindu self-consciousness, particularly a form of Hindu nationalism, pose threats to a discourse of human rights. All three parts of the argument posit that Hinduism's quest for recognition in the modern world has driven much of its politics. For the most part, this politics has made it receptive to internalizing human rights, but occasionally it tips over into a politics of anxiety. Drawing on the Indian case, the chapter concludes that the forms in which religious groups seek acknowledgment from others have an immeasurable impact on the values they choose to internalize and promote.

The Structure of Hinduism and the Politics of Human Rights

The question of religious support for human rights has many different aspects. Human rights are at one level a philosophical and legal construct with no direct connection with religion. On the one hand, we tend to look to some deep religious or religion-like sources to affirm their importance. For instance, the idea that we are made in God's image might be thought to sustain the authority of rights in a much deeper and more significant way than secular theories. Or Hindus might think that acknowledging the fundamental ontological unity of Atman and Brahman could be the basis for thinking that sanctioning violence toward others is also violence against oneself or creation. On the other hand, the moral claims of *human* rights rest on the thought that these are basic truths of morality that should be accessible to all human beings independently of their particular religious traditions. Allegiance to them need not depend upon adherence to any particular religion or any religion at all. It is for this reason that representatives of all major religious traditions—Jewish, Buddhist, Christian, Hindu, Muslim—were able to sign onto most aspects of the 1948 UN Universal Declaration of Human Rights, even though it is a secular document.[1] There is also often a practical recognition that human rights not only affirm our dignity, but are also practical contrivances to deal with the challenges of diversity and difference.[2]

In order to support human rights doctrines religions must therefore have a view of the relationship between moral reason and religion. There may be different ways to make religious sensibilities compatible with human rights doctrines. First, religious groups may acknowledge the fact that there are certain truths that are accessible to us by virtue of our being human; no particular religious mediation or authority is required to get to them. Second, some religions may go farther and argue that the exercise of this reason is itself the fulfillment of religious purpose. Third, they may simply accommodate themselves to the practical fact of diversity. Under conditions of diversity the best way of protecting religion may be to just agree to a set of rights that is fair to all, or go further and affirm the fact of diversity and the importance of securing all the instruments that protect it. In short, a religion may become hospitable to human rights because it acknowledges the autonomy of reason or because it seeks to protect or cherish diversity.

At this level of abstraction most of Hinduism's intellectuals and religious leaders consider it propitious for human rights discourse. Rights claims are presumptive claims against authority; they are claims that no authority may override or trump. Often religious groups turn against human rights because they are unwilling to cede this authority. Hinduism did not have this particular problem, because the idea of authority was individualized from the beginning. While the tradition has a corpus of sacred texts, there is no claim that the exercise of reason required for constructing morality has to be mediated by any religious authority. Doctrinally, there is no central authority impeding its adherents from coming to independent views about what morality requires. So the one crucial element of religious support to a human rights doctrine was already present, namely, that these doctrines were not thought to be a threat to any authority, for the simple reason that there was no authority to threaten.[3]

The second doctrinal support for human rights doctrines comes from what might be called the low level of ideologization within Hinduism. While the social practice of Hindus has often been marked by orthodoxy, the empire of orthodoxy does not extend to *belief*. Indeed, as Max Weber noted long ago, Hindus could combine extraordinary intellectual rationalism with orthodox social practice. Often there is religious resistance to particular rights doctrines because those doctrines are considered challenges to *particular beliefs*. Indeed, discourses of human rights became necessary in part because of theologically sanctioned ideologies of intolerance. Whatever its other limitations, Hinduism does not have any theologically sanctioned sources of *religiously inspired intoler-ance*. In fact, religious thinkers prepared the ground for a free society compat-ible with the recognition of human rights by emphasizing the fact that there was no religious tradition of persecuting *belief*.[4] Heresy and apostasy, two major sources of resistance to human rights, made no sense in this discourse. Rights such as freedom of religion and conscience, therefore, were compatible with inherited traditions.

But this extraordinary receptivity to freedom of religion in the sense under-stood in human rights doctrines also became, paradoxically, the source of a certain ambivalence about one particular and contentious right—the right to conversion.

Of all the rights contained in the Universal Declaration of Human Rights, only one right comes under contestation in India. This is Article 18. There is no dispute over the desirability of the claim that everyone should have the right to freedom of thought, conscience, and religion; these rights are, for the most part, well protected by the Indian constitution and have extensive support. But the way in which this right is articulated is deemed insufficient on the fol-lowing grounds. First, many Hindu movements have asserted that this article is based on a "Western" understanding of religion. Specifically, it has no provi-sions for expressing equal respect for all religions, distinct from protecting the right of individuals to choose and express their religion. In this view, the right to conversion negates the fact that for the adherents of some religions, it is possible to believe in the tenets of another religion without thereby losing your inherited religious identity. Second, the freedom of religion is not a single right but a balance between two competing rights: the right of someone to proselytize on the one hand, and the right of one not to be made an object of proselytism, on the other hand.

The issue arrived at the doors of the Indian Supreme Court, which was asked to distinguish between forced mass conversions and religious conversion. Regarding whether the right to propagate one's religion implies the right to con-vert, the Supreme Court ruled in 1977 that "there is no fundamental right to convert another person to one's own religion" and observed that such a right "would impinge on the 'freedom of conscience guaranteed to all citizens of the country alike.'"[5] Reverend Stanislaus had petitioned the court to squash the Madhya Pradesh Freedom of Religion Act 1968 and the Orissa Freedom of Religion Act 1947, which prohibited conversion through coercion or allurement or other fraudulent means. In the judgment, the court upheld the constitutionality of the two acts but also implicitly declared that forcible re-conversions are also a crime. "We have no doubt that what the Article [25] grants is not the right to convert another person to one's own religion but to transmit or spread one's religion by an exposition of its tenets," said the judge. Using the "public order" clause to justify the ruling that the states were competent to legislate on the matter, the Supreme Court observed that these statutes were framed to maintain law and order (which was a state subject). However, the vagueness of the term "inducement" remained even after this judgment. Since 1999, many state governments, headed by both the Congress Party and Hindu-nationalist Bharatiya Janata Party (BJP), have passed ironically titled "Freedom of Religion Bills" that regulate the right to proselytize and convert.

This issue is likely to continue to drive the politics of religious groups. Since Hinduism does not require adherence to a specific set of beliefs, understood in the Christian sense, it is often difficult to explain the concept of conversion within a Hindu framework. Indeed, the presumption among most Hindu religious groups is that conversion cannot be understood as a religious act. In a religion that not only self-consciously requires no particular set of beliefs but often presents itself as seeing all religions as manifestation of Divinity, the idea of conversion is hard to comprehend. Given the freedom of belief and action that is available within the tradition, the only explanation for conversion can be some extraneous political or economic motive. So paradoxically, the very ideas that make Hindu groups so receptive to the freedom of religion make them suspicious of the need to *change* religion. Even Gandhi not only could not make sense of religious conversion but was opposed to the very idea. Of course, the politics of religious conversion is considerably more complicated. But doctrinally, the right to convert is one right Hindu groups find difficult to grasp.[6]

Additional support for human rights doctrines within Hinduism comes from an acceptance of limits on state power. Indeed, modern human rights doctrines and movements derive much of their potency from the limits they place on state power. Indian religious traditions historically have had a long history of thinking about the limits of state power, drawing on two doctrinal sources. The first was the redeployment of the idea of dharma (moral law) as implying constitutional limitations on the state. On this view, any state is subject to a higher law, which is designed to protect and sustain the well-being of individuals.[7] This objective suggests limits that no state may cross.

A second source that has led religious groups to historically oppose concentration of state power is a concern for their own autonomy. Although this is a complicated historical argument, it is not too much of an exaggeration to say that political power in India has often legitimized itself by granting autonomy to different religious groups. Most political forms in India, including enduring empires, have had to accommodate religious pluralism, though not always complete religious equality. Different religious groups and sects within Hinduism carved out spaces for themselves not by claiming power over centralized authority but by protecting space for their own activity. Whatever may have been the relationship of these groups to their members, the fact that religious groups were long used to coexisting in a form of segmented toleration made them instinctively more receptive to limitations on the power of the state. Modern human rights doctrines require specific forms of limitation on state power. And in a religious culture formed by diversity and accommodation, the value of these limitations on state power was well understood. Religious groups grasped that their own existence depended upon the securities that rights doctrines granted.

In addition there was the practical fact that since Hinduism and Indic religions more generally are characterized by involuted pluralism—the tendency of multiple organizational forms to proliferate—the likelihood of any particular sect being able to monopolize power was remote. The sociological fact that the organizational form of Hinduism cannot be reduced to a few ideologically motivated sects, but instead consists of literally hundreds of thousands of organizational forms, made pluralism an almost default existential condition. What cultural referents these groups had in common can be debated. But for our purpose the fact that theological, soteriological, and social power was so fragmented made cherishing diversity easy.

I would argue that both the fact of radical pluralism within Hinduism, at least in terms of organizational authority, and the peculiar fact that politics and religion were considered autonomous social spheres made Hinduism very propitious for receiving liberal constitutional democracy, despite the tradition's social orthodoxy and hierarchical social structure.

This argument finds confirmation in how Hindu groups agreed to operate within the overall framework of a constitutional democracy. Understanding how this came about will help shed light on why Hindu religious groups have not ideologically opposed human rights doctrines or their instantiations in Indian domestic law. One Hindu self-conception that helped here was the relationship between religion and politics. It could be argued that a prerequisite for modern human rights in practice is an autonomous political realm where members of different groups can claim those rights as their own. Where politics is considered the site of sacrality, it is more difficult for diverse groups to simultaneously abide by its requirements. In some ways, human rights doctrines in the Hindu context did not have to contend with any legacy of sacred politics. Even in ancient texts that many Hindu groups claim to draw upon, politics is given its autonomy. As one of the most astute analysts of Indian political thought puts it, "Kingship remains, even theoretically, suspended between sacrality and secularity, divinity and mortal humanity, legitimate authority and arbitrary power, dharma and adharma."[8] Political power and spiritual authority were firmly separated, as exemplified by the traditional distinction between the priestly Brahmins and the Kshatriya (warrior) caste. The king inhabited the realm of necessity where politics had its own autonomy and internal logic that brooked no outside interference. At the same time, however, the king drew his legitimacy from his service to the "spiritual order," just as the priests depended upon the king for physical protection. So Hindu thought's version of the separation of church and state has never been quite stable. And yet politics, even when dependent upon religion for earthly legitimization, has never in Hindu thought taken on messianic or apocalyptic significance. The world of the political is significant, but it can never become an arena for what Eric Voegelin has called "the immanentization of the eschaton." Since the political realm was never thought to be the site of collective redemption, Hindu religious groups could not unleash a politics designed to seize state power.

In practice, this Hindu capacity to imagine the political without expecting it to give meaning to everything or comprehensively relieve the human estate has been of great service in defining the secular space that liberal democracy requires. A respect for the proper autonomy of different spheres of human action and a refusal to pine for a single moral order that can render the world whole are aspects of the Hindu moral imagination that not only reinforce democratic politics but also help to set healthy boundaries for it. When Hindus claim that democracy has been a "natural" outgrowth of Hinduism, they may be gesturing at something like this account of Hindu political prudence and moderation. The Hindu tendency to see politics as an autonomous but limited sphere obviates the need to impose a single doctrinal orthodoxy and permits a well-advised toleration of various forms of social existence. Indeed, Hindu intellectuals' discussions of democracy often seem to equate it with a kind of group pluralism: Sarvepalli Radhakrishnan's influential *Hindu View of Life* mostly sees democracy as a matter of ensuring that each group "should be allowed to develop the best in it without impeding the progress of others."[9]

Against this backdrop the Indian state not only aims to reform Hindu practices, but also has been in some sense authorized to do so by Hindus, with far-reaching consequences for the politics of human rights. In the Indian context, it is legitimate for state institutions such as the Supreme Court and the Lok Sabha (parliament) to concern themselves with reforming or eliminating invidious socioreligious practices such as second-class treatment of "untouchables." Faced with the challenge "Who shall decide?" Hindus in effect answered: "We all will, and the federal Republic of India will be our means." The point of this is to be found in the following observation, which links back to the general themes of this book. For Hindu groups in the postwar secular state, working within the confines of a democracy was almost a necessity because of the lack of any internal authority structure. Even if these groups did not have articulated commitments to human rights, understood in a technical sense, they did internalize two things: a politics of accommodation, and the fact that disputes had to be resolved democratically. Conservative religious groups often supported democracy because they did not think democratic practice would radically challenge their power and viewed democratic institutions as a potential way to augment it.

The Spur to Rights: Colonialism and Caste

While these normative resources were available to create a strong foundation for the acceptance of human rights ideas within the context of the democratic state, the force of two historical pressures must not be discounted. The first was the pressure of colonialism, which spurred critical reflection within the Hindu tradition on how to promote reform in the face of modernity. The second was pressure from below, as religious groups had to accommodate the aspirations of those it had so systematically marginalized through the caste system.

The Legacy of Colonialism

There is a long debate in Indian historiography on whether reform movements in Hinduism had indigenous roots or were simply inspired by the West and grew out of the colonial experience. The emerging consensus is that there is no simple answer to this question: religious reflection has continued to draw upon precolonial themes and ideas, even as it selectively appropriated ideas from the West.

A critical source of doctrinal support for human rights came from creative redeployments of traditional categories in the face of colonial rule.[10] It would take an extraordinarily long volume to describe the ways in which key thinkers from India's religious traditions, from Ram Mohun Roy to Tagore, from Vivekananda to Gandhi, deployed a whole range of religious categories to create a broader cultural climate that was favorable to human rights discourses.[11] There is still no definitive work on the moral categories these religious thinkers used: *ahimsa* (nonviolence), *swaraj* (self-rule), *adhikara* (rights), *shraddha* (trust), *kartavya* (duty), *shanti* (peace), and many others. It has to be remembered that these creative redeployments were often not done in the language of human rights. Indeed, often there was an implicit critique that a rights-based imagination was sidelining other duties or virtues. But they nevertheless created an environment where values conducive to human rights doctrines like equality, tolerance, freedom of expression, and cherishing of diversity became a possibility, even if they were not specifically articulated in those terms. Indeed, some thinkers went even further and tried to rearticulate Hinduism as a site of an alternative universality, where the self-identity of the religion was marked by its tolerance, respect for diversity, and reluctance to persecute. Indeed, the Indian tradition was often described as paving the way for respecting rights much earlier and much more powerfully than Western traditions had. Some of these attempts were motivated by a desire to establish the normative superiority of Hinduism. But collectively they moved Hinduism to the point where its sense of itself required a historical legitimation of rights.

The presence of the British Raj and all it signified put pressure on Hindu traditions and forced Hinduism to rearticulate its own principles. Such rethinking is a matter of active human agency, and its direction can be unpredictable. Colonial rule was legitimized by the ideas that subject peoples or societies were in some sense backward and that they were not *nations*, and hence had no claim to recognition as sovereign entities. A sense of this backdrop is crucial if one wants to understand how Hinduism has been rearticulating itself since the nineteenth century. In part, the process has been defensive: there have been attempts to show that Hinduism is the source of all that modernity prizes, from democracy to science. Whatever one thinks of such hermeneutics, the key thing politically is that they have had the effect of legitimizing new values in Hindu terms.

Here was a sense in which Western ideas of democracy and liberalism had an identifiable impact on Hindu thought. To claim, even if on dubious grounds, that one's tradition is a source of democracy is to acknowledge democracy's stature and legitimacy. In its encounter with other traditions, of which liberalism and enlightenment values were a subset, Hinduism became aware that if it failed to claim as its own certain values identified with progressive modernity, it would always remain vulnerable to both criticism by outsiders and inner defections by its own adherents. Reform may come from high principle, but it may also come from a tradition's sense of what it needs to do to survive external and internal challenges.

But there was a deeper structural way in which colonialism exerted great intellectual pressure on religious groups in India. Formally the British, for the most part, had recreated a form of indirect rule in which religious groups were often granted great autonomy. But what colonialism had subtly done was delegitimize and subordinate indigenous knowledge systems. While as a practical political matter the British were willing to accommodate religious groups, there is little doubt that a large mass of Indian religious practice was seen as a sign of India's backwardness. Indeed, it was precisely this backwardness that ideologically legitimized British rule. This fact is of cardinal psychological importance, even to this day, in how religious groups conduct their politics in relation to human rights. Many religious groups internalized the narrative that the form of religious life that existed in India was responsible for its degradation. They often argued that this degradation was not essential to their religion but a contingent historical fact. In order to reclaim legitimacy for religious traditions they had to radically recast them in forms that made them less susceptible to external critique. Many religious groups engaged in forms of revivalism. But for the most part religious groups tried to reclaim their legitimacy by showing how religion was not only compatible with modernity, but in fact required it. They engaged in a form of self-critique and reform, debating a whole range of religious practices and conventions. One way of reclaiming their ideological legitimacy, then, was to neutralize external critique by appropriating it.

This phenomenon is not of inconsiderable importance. Religious groups respond to broader social changes and challenges from rival traditions in various inventive ways. Sometimes, it is by returning to fundamentalism. But oftentimes, it is important to a religion's sense of itself that it be seen as compatible with, if not a source of, much that is largely accepted by the wider world as normatively desirable and defensible. This motive to liberalize is not without great force and still marks the politics of religious groups. Indeed, what distinguishes the politics of most religious groups is their desire to be seen as modern. Their critique of modern society might extend to market society and the instrumental view of relationships it is seen to entail. But in most areas religious groups establish their legitimacy by reclaiming modernity or its betterment.

One contemporary example of this is the change in attitudes toward sexual minorities, one important aspect of contemporary human rights doctrine. In India, homosexuality had long been criminalized. In 2009, the Delhi High Court handed down a judgment decriminalizing it. While several religious groups have objected to the ruling and have even filed an appeal to a larger constitutional bench, on the whole there has not been significant opposition. Interestingly, an argument that has proved to be particularly influential is that decriminalization has become a global norm and that to continue the practice would be a sign of backwardness.

As this example suggests, it could be argued that what makes religious groups receptive to reform and human rights is that they wish to be judged as exemplars of modernity. The crisis of legitimacy that colonialism induces unleashes a peculiar politics of self-esteem in religious groups. In part, they reform in their quest for recognition. They wish to claim not only that their tradition contains the full developmental potential for humanity but also that it does so in a way that others can recognize and acknowledge. Giving place to values that are considered to be widely approved normatively—equality, rights, toleration, and so on—is one way of demonstrating this potential. What is truly astonishing about various strands of Hindu thought in the twentieth century and down to the present day is that they embody this quest.

A revealing Indian joke says that "democracy, like cricket, is a quintessentially Indian game that just happens to have been invented elsewhere." Adopting democracy in India required a radical transformation of Hindus' self-understanding, not least because it required them to make real a polity which was, at that time, barely even imaginable. One can see that Hindus would have had to satisfy themselves that democracy was at least not against Hindu traditions. What surprises is the extent to which Hindus went beyond this: the early twentieth century on the subcontinent saw an outpouring of literature arguing that Hinduism required a positive commitment to democracy. Some arguments, including Gandhi's, sought to prove that *swaraj* (self-rule) in all its senses was at Hinduism's core.[12] Others tried to show that a certain conception of democratic practice had always been central to Indian society.[13]

The Challenge of Caste

If colonialism was the single biggest external challenge for Hinduism, the institution of caste was an internal challenge from the point of view of human rights. The origins and significance of caste as institution are complicated and the reasons for its enduring power still a matter of contention. But there is no doubt that by the nineteenth century, when the process of social reform of Indian society began in earnest, caste was one of the most egregiously hierarchical systems of rank ordering the entitlements, privileges, and even the sense of being of particular groups that human history has known, inflicting unspeakable degradation upon those who were unfortunate enough to be at the lower ends of the hierarchy, such as the untouchables. During the nineteenth century there were various apologetics on behalf of the caste system, but gradually a consensus emerged that whatever the rationale for the system, in its present forms, with the ways in which it mutilated human beings, it could not be defended. Reform of the caste system became an object of concern for some high-caste Hindus but more significantly for autonomous lower caste movements, like those led by Narayan Guru in Kerala and Phule in Maharashtra.

Many of these caste movements were religiously inspired. Much of the upper caste effort in reforming caste was and still remains motivated by the desire to consolidate Hinduism. The idea was that as the lowest castes became politically conscious they would dissociate themselves from Hinduism if it did not reform itself and give the marginalized social spaces to lead lives with dignity and self-respect. All of these movements had the effect of changing the culture beyond recognition and in ways that were more hospitable to human rights. By the time independence came, there were few apologists for the caste system left. Untouchability was abolished, and many professed to discouraging the perpetuation of caste, even though in practice the system had not been as substantially eroded as many reformers had hoped.

But it was not just the persistence of caste that remained disturbing. The modalities of social reform were themselves an object of concern. Many untouchables in particular found an upper caste concern with their plight patronizing because it did little to empower them. The agency of reform, and the terms on which it was going to be conducted, were still defined by upper caste noblesse oblige, not the agency of the oppressed themselves. Even Gandhi, for all his extraordinary personal commitment and mastery of the dramatic gestures that could symbolically undermine an oppressive ideology, increasingly began to be tainted with this suspicion, for two reasons. First, caste presented a delicate challenge for reformers ideologically. One of the impulses for social reform was a desire to restore respectability to religious traditions, but many religious groups wanted reform of the tradition without a comprehensive critique. Often reformers tried to inject egalitarian, human rights–compatible norms in ways that did not deeply challenge caste hierarchies historically linked with Hinduism. Despite a commitment to human rights, many reformers sought to mitigate the most oppressive aspects of the caste system, like untouchability, without launching a full-scale assault.

Second, the motive for reform remained first and foremost the consolidation of religious identity, not the eradication of social inequality. Gandhi, for instance, thought that granting separate electorates and representation for untouchables would divide Hinduism deeply and forever. Such a division would polarize society and impede the creation of common political projects and a sense of mutuality. Gandhi, above all, wanted upper castes to feel guilt and atone for the egregious domination and privileges they enjoyed. The untouchable leader B. R. Ambedkar, on the other hand, thought that invoking common purposes or the unity of Hindu society was simply to disguise the deep sense of oppression and fissures that existed. If Gandhi thought that emphasizing division would give rise to violence, Ambedkar powerfully argued that this would be probably no worse that the violence that already characterized Hindu society, and that in any case violence would ultimately be a result of assertion of power by the upper castes. Upper caste guilt was not good enough and was unlikely to lead to enduring change. What was required was the creation of conditions and social spaces where the untouchables and lower castes could feel empowered and act with a sense of agency.

In the subsequent democratic development of India, the extraordinary force of the reformist motive can be seen in a landmark judgment handed down by the Supreme Court in 1966, following almost two decades of litigation.[14] The Court made the Swami Narayana sect of Bombay comply with a 1947 law that had opened Hindu temples to all worshipers, including members of "untouchable" hereditary castes. The ruling denied the sect members' claim that they were non-Hindus and hence exempt from having to admit the despised castes. The Court worried that letting a Hindu sect evade the reach of progressive laws would stifle efforts to reform Hinduism at large. The Court emphasized Hinduism's historic capacity for internal reform, its progressive outlook, its flexibility, its compatibility with social equality, and its extraordinary tolerance. Hinduism, the Court taught, is not only consistent with democracy, progress, equality, and social reform but also requires a commitment to these things. The Court's opinion not only bore directly on the issue of who counts as a Hindu but also struggled with the task of defining Hinduism itself by coming up with a seven-item list of Hindu essentials.

The invidious caste distinction at the heart of the case was itself a reminder of the complicated transformations that Hinduism has had to undergo in order to become compatible with human rights. The caste system with all its interdictions, exclusions, and regulations is one of the most elaborately and egregiously hierarchical social conceptions that humans have ever entertained. Dominant interpretations of Hinduism long legitimized it. A society preoccupied with caste would hardly seem to be a promising ground for democracy, individual freedom, or equality. While it is true that freedom and equality remain subject to political contestation in India, the striking thing is that this most hierarchically ordered of societies should have so readily embraced, in principle at first and then increasingly in practice, principles compatible with human rights.

What is interesting about this judgment was the way in which it encapsulated the sources that drive religious groups to accept doctrines more compatible with human rights. It made the fact that Hinduism was compatible with, or rather required, democracy, equality, and liberty a marker of its identity and greatness. It encapsulated the drive for reform. In a nutshell, this judgment showed how religion itself had been transformed so as to be able to accept such a far-reaching ruling. It is marked deeply by the conviction that Hinduism should be seen as progressive. The force of that desire is in part an enduring response to the colonial claim that delegitimized the normative worth of indigenous religious identities.

At a political level, there have been three distinct and ongoing responses to the challenge caste poses to human rights. There are some groups who argue that the annihilation of caste is impossible within a religious framework and that the abolition of caste would require the abolition of religion. But several religious groups like the enormously influential Arya Samaj and Rashtriya Swayamsevak Sangh (RSS) have argued that Hinduism can be reformed to accommodate egalitarian aspirations, not by abolishing the high ideals of traditional religion but by making them available to hitherto excluded groups. Often religiously inspired groups are extraordinarily active in their own brand of inclusion through social work and providing access to schools. The third religious option is to use some form of conversion as a means of protesting caste exclusion, often from Hinduism to Buddhism or Christianity. Often Buddhism is preferred because in the politics of religious conversion, it is not associated with the taint of "foreign" religions like Christianity and Islam. All three strands are central in efforts to articulate the relationship between caste and politics. But it is probably fair to argue that the second and third options are the dominant framework within which much of the religious politics of caste is conducted.

The politics of caste is extremely complicated. But in relation to this volume's focus on religion and human rights, an important lesson is that caste and the psychological legacy of colonialism still remain defining markers for many influential religious groups to this day. There are three more general lessons as well. First, religions reform and accommodate human rights concerns when they are pressured from below and when denial of human rights would risk losing adherents. In this sense, religion is often pitted against existing social mores and structures; it does not legitimize them. Second, there is often an inherent limitation to this accommodation of human rights concerns. It can take the form of mitigating the worst forms of evil associated with hierarchy without radically challenging existing inequality. Third, precisely because the purpose of reform is to protect the respectability of tradition, there is a great resistance to any intervention on the issue that is seen as emanating from outside. It is not an accident that while there is a deep and vigorous debate on caste in India, among different religious sects, there is a great resistance to internationalizing the issue.

Religious Nationalism and the Politics of Human Rights

The burden of the previous section has been to argue that the particular historical circumstances in which Hinduism found itself moved its politics in the direction of reform and receptivity to human rights concerns. This section explores a potential counter movement: Hindu nationalism. A major modern phenomenon that has shaped the politics of Hindu religious groups, nationalism has served in part as a force for democratization. The imperative of creating a nation required new and more horizontal forms of mobilization. Nationalism, as Leah Greenfield points out, is the crucible of modern democracy.[15] Any articulate anticolonial critique must assume that the colonized society can be a self-governing nation. Indians could demand self-determination in their struggle against colonial rule only by appealing to the authority of a new entity in the social imaginary, "the Indian people." But this would require (1) privileging their status as members of this people—as citizens of a nation struggling to be born, in other words—over older and more restrictive forms of identification such as sect, clan, or caste; and (2) granting this people at least a modicum of participatory access. Nationalism requires some degree of horizontal solidarity, and it historically goaded religious groups into creating such forms of solidarity. Anticolonial nationalism tended to bring secular and democratic ideas along in its logical train. In some ways the pressure of creating a nation was a fillip to embracing ideals of democracy and human rights.

Given the history just recounted, the heterogeneity of Hinduism itself, and the sense in which Hinduism has made modernity its own, it is unlikely that any Hindu mass movement will be able to set up anything close to a theocracy in the usual Western sense of the word. It is not insignificant that even Hindu nationalism seems to feel an imperative to legitimize itself as a secular ideology: movement apologists typically claim that they are not against secular principles as such but declare themselves discontented that Hindus, India's majority, are asked to accept secular limits while minorities receive numerous exemptions based on their various religious identities. Nevertheless, Hindu-nationalist rhetoric should still be unpacked, since it marks the politics of many religious groups like the RSS.

What is Hindu nationalism? First and foremost it is an attempt to make Hindus self-conscious of their identity as Hindus. It seeks to create a Hindu identity that can transcend the internal social, cultural, political, and regional distinctions of people classified as Hindus. It attempts to make them self-conscious of their own history and create a common identity, to mobilize this identity to protect and glorify the claims of Hindus, and most important to assert the cultural primacy of Hindus in the territorial entity called India—to define India primarily in terms of the land belonging to Hindus.

How does Hindu nationalism create this common identity? It is important to begin by understanding the sometimes inchoate but very widespread sentiment that Hindu nationalism has tapped into and sought to address.

Many who define themselves as Hindu experience an extraordinary sense of lack. Hinduism is not sure what makes it the identity that it is. In some respects Hindu identity is inflected by a sense of injury, the idea that Hindus have been victims of history, at the receiving end of onslaughts. In this view, India is a land that has been overridden by conquerors who, whether or not they settled here, conspired to ensure that Hindus could not claim cultural hegemony over a sacred territory Hindus regard as their own. Almost as compensation Hinduism redefines itself by a sense of superiority. Hindu nationalists attempt to redefine Hinduism as the highest achievement of spirituality and uniquely tolerant in order to enlist India's spirituality into the cause of nationalism. Much of the understanding of history that sustains this sense of injury is false or oversimplified. But of greater import is that several groups like the RSS and Vishwa Hindu Parishad inculcate a form of Hindu identity that rests upon a sense of resentment and puts minorities at risk and threatens liberal democracy. There is good reason to believe that these groups no longer have the kind of influence they had on Indian politics during the nineties. During the last decade, they have come to be progressively marginalized. But elements of their ideological imagination still have some cultural resonance.[16]

At a deeper level, modern Hindu identity is also driven by a diagnostic quest. Why is it that Hinduism becomes a sign of backwardness, inviting contempt rather than admiration? Why are Hindus characterized by a sense of weakness? Why, in this view, are Hindus unable break off the shackles of subjugation or respond to those who constitute a threat to them? Modern Hindu identity is also beset by a sense of uncertainty. How will this tradition make its transition to modernity without denigrating its own past? Finally, there is a yearning for belonging, a quest for a community that can do justice to them as Hindus. This psychic baggage can express itself in many ways, sometimes benign and creative, sometimes malign and close-minded. The burdens of these anxieties often created a pressing need for resolution. This resolution looks not for intellectual clarity but symbolic totems that can both express and overcome this anxiety. It is not an accident that Hindu nationalism, as Thomas Hansen perceptively points out, is not so much a well-articulated program but a politics of "signs," the creation of a symbolic order that can stabilize this amorphous experience. Almost all the major issues on which Hindu nationalism has mobilized—Ayodhya or cow protection, nuclear bombs, or Sanskrit culture—have this feature in common. These causes serve as *symbols* of a Hindu identity that can take its rightful place in the world. Their intrinsic content is of less interest than the fact that they can serve as totems of identity.[17]

What is it that defines modern Hindu identity? What is it that all Hindus share such that they can be said to possess a common identity? Modern Hindu nationalism emerges, to use John Zavos's language, as an "identity searching for solid, even reputable parameters through which to relate to other socio-religious identities in a highly politicized context."[18] As noted earlier, some Hindu thought in the nineteenth and twentieth century used the very amorphousness of Hinduism to define its identity: Hinduism is, in this view, open and tolerant, constituted by a series of practices, giving space for different forms of salvation, with no orthodoxy, no settled religious authority, and no single deity. In its quest for public recognition, however, it is haunted by the anxiety that if Hindus do not have some form of unified identity, their interests will not be protected. This creates an opening for Hindu nationalism, which takes its bearing from its interpretation of what makes other communities thrive. Since other communities, principally Islam and Christianity, have somewhat more settled lines of authority and often have had the imprimatur of political power behind them, they constitute effective models—as well as adversaries. To deny that Hindus have a common identity and therefore common interests is, in this view, an ideological ruse to deny Hindus their rightful claims and to exploit the internal divisions within Hinduism either to gain converts or to deny that Hindus collectively have any rights.

The process of negotiation with colonialism reinforced the perceived need for a Hindu national identity. Colonial power had legitimized itself, among other things, on the claim that India was not a nation and therefore had no corporate rights. The anticolonial struggle required the forging of a national identity, and of the many competing versions of what the basis of this national identity might be, a common "Hindu heritage" turned out to be one plausible candidate. Hindu nationalism was, Hansen points out, "one of the several contingent outcomes of a protracted struggle over the definition of Indian nationhood." It was not simply an aberrant species of Hindu communalism that acts in opposition to some authoritatively correct nationalism.[19] Zavos also makes the helpful distinction between Hindu communalism and Hindu nationalism. For him, Hindu communalism is a cluster of attitudes regarding others (principally Muslims) that, although frequently associated with Hindu nationalism, can be derived independently of it as well. Hindu communalism often seeks expression through Hindu nationalism, but the two are not identical.

Hindu nationalism, then, is the outcome of the very same processes that produced other forms of nationalism: the anticolonial struggle, the quest for social reform, the need to define an identity for India and the freedom afforded by democracy to create different ways of imagining an identity, and so forth. One of the theoretical advantages of Hansen's analysis is its application of the theoretical insights developed for the study of ideology to the analysis of Hindu nationalism. Following Slavoj Zizek's analysis of ideology, Hansen argues that Hindu nationalism seeks to stabilize an otherwise amorphous social experience into a harmonious symbolic order. But this attempt is fraught with paradox. On the one hand, Hindu nationalism has to present itself as a synthetic enterprise capable of representing a variety of beliefs and practices, encompassing them into one single whole. On the other hand, this very attempt makes Hindu nationalism more like an "empty place" whose content will remain ill-defined, since any attempt to define it will diminish its synthetic aspirations. Although Hansen does not draw this conclusion himself, his analysis points to the fact that, contrary to Hindu nationalist representations, there can be no stable core to the idea of Hindu nationalism.

In my view, Hindu nationalism has two basic narrative strategies that emerge in different forms. The first is what might be called the creation of a *common narrative of subjugation*. The second is a strategy of *benchmarking* Indian identity. The locus classicus of the second strategy is Veer Savarkar's text *Hindutva*, whose style of argument, if not the actual text itself, is quite widespread among Hindu nationalists. Both these narratives are analytically distinct, although they can often be mutually supportive as well. Both aspire to create a sense of unified community that is grounded in history. The effect of these efforts is not so much an ideological critique of human rights but the creation of a politics of "othering." How this politics is produced and lived out in relation to other communities, particularly Muslim politics, is a question for a different occasion.[20] But the danger to human rights comes from the fact that ethnicization can colonize both religion and human rights.

Conclusion

The approach to religion and human rights explored in this chapter moves beyond the theological and philosophical to explore the intersection of religious tradition with a changing historical, institutional, and political context. Such an approach is essential for three reasons. First, it avoids the fallacy of supposing that just because a religion has potential normative resources to support human rights, it will necessarily do so. Second, the historical contextualization helps us better understand the ways in and reasons for which human rights discourses come to be embedded in some contexts, but not others. And third, it also provides some clues to the contexts in which religious support for human rights might break down. As Hannah Arendt reminds us, although human rights are considered universal, their recognition and articulation are always in and through specific political forms.[21]

Hinduism over the past century has scored an immense historical achievement by having found ways to cope with so many features of modernity—and in making many of them its own in remarkably creative ways. India's dominant religion has not been an obstacle to India's participation and active framing of human rights; it has positively welcomed it, with some qualifications over the issue of conversion. But now is not the time—as if there could ever be one—to rest on laurels won. Hindu nationalism still has a wide hearing. Hindus must guard against letting their sense (or more precisely, senses) of identity be hijacked by a self-pity cult that preaches chimerical tests of "Hindu-ness." Here the spiritual traditions of Hinduism may be of help—indeed may be the best or perhaps the only antidote to the tragic narrowing of Hindu horizons that the apostles of Hindutva intend. Hindu metaphysics at its best teaches that a "rage for order" of the not-so-blessed kind—a mania for making false or needless distinctions and calling oneself this rather than that—may cause one to overlook a wealth of positive possibilities that reside within the self, including its capacity to transcend the egotistical "I" and proclaim "From oneness and duality and opposites I am free. I am He."[22]

Hindus have nerved themselves for the last half-century and more to follow the allure of democracy, and they have endowed the second most populous country on Earth with a liberal constitutional order. There is reason to suppose this accommodation will continue. But the shadows of identity politics will have to be resisted. Hinduism's appeal will ultimately depend on how it wishes to legitimize itself in the modern world. What role religious groups play in relation to human rights doctrines depends ultimately on the forms of historical self-consciousness they internalize. They have to ask: what do they wish to be recognized for? What kind of legitimacy do they seek? Some of this quest for legitimacy has moved in the direction of accepting rights, democracy, and reform as valid global norms to be internalized and practiced. Some of it has also moved in the direction of establishing the claims of Hindus to form a cohesive nation in the conviction that in the modern world nationalism is the best means to international recognition. It is the contest between these two forms of recognition available in the modern world that increasingly drives the politics of human rights—in India and elsewhere.

NOTES

1. As an introduction to these themes, see Arvind Sharma, *Hinduism and Human Rights: A Conceptual Approach* (Oxford: Oxford University Press, 2004).

2. See Johannes Morsink, *The Universal Declaration of Human Rights: Origins, Drafting, and Intent* (Philadelphia: University of Pennsylvania Press, 1999).

3. See Pratap Bhanu Mehta, "Reason, Tradition and Authority: Religion and the Indian State," in *Toleration on Trial*, ed. Ingrid Creppell, Russell Hardin, and Steve Macedo (Lanham, MD: Lexington Books, 2008).

4. See S. N. Eisensdtat, Reuven Kahane, and David Shulman, eds., *Orthodoxy, Heterodoxy and Dissent in India* (Berlin: Mouton, 1984).

5. *Rev. Stanislaus v. State of Madhya Pradesh and Orissa*, AIR 1977 SC 908.

6. For a good survey of issues relating to the philosophy and politics of conversion, see Rudolph C. Heredia, *Changing Gods: Rethinking Conversion in India* (New Delhi: Penguin Books, 2007).

7. Chaturvedi Badrinath, *Dharma, India and World Order* (Edinburgh: St. Andrews Press, 1992), 39.

8. J. C. Heesterman, *The Inner Conflict of Tradition: Essays in Indian Ritual, Kingship, and Society* (Chicago: University of Chicago Press, 1985), 111.

9. Sarvepalli Radhakrishnan, *The Hindu View of Life* (London: George Allen and Unwin, 1960), 70.

10. See the essays in Thomas Pantham and V. R. Mehta, eds., *Political Ideas in Modern India: Thematic Explorations*, History of Science, Philosophy and Culture in Indian Civilization, Volume 10, Part 7, ed. D. P. Chattopadhyaya (Delhi: Sage, 2005).

11. For an accessible survey, see Amiya Sen, "The Idea of Social Reform and Its Critique among Hindus," in *Development of Modern Indian Thought and the Social Sciences*, History of Science, Philosophy and Culture in Indian Civilization, Volume 10, Part 5, ed. Sabyasachi Bhattacharya (Delhi: Oxford University Press, 2007), 107–83.

12. See Anthony J. Parel, ed., *Gandhi, Freedom, and Self Rule* (Lanham, MD: Lexington Books, 2000).

13. Bruce McCully, "The Origins of Indian Nationalism According to Native Writers," *Journal of Modern History* 7 (September 1935): 295–314.

14. *Shastri Yagna Purushdasji v Muldas Bhunadardas Vaisya*, SCC 1966.

15. Liah Greenfeld, *Nationalism: Five Roads to Modernity* (Cambridge, MA: Harvard University Press, 1992).

16. Other religions besides Hinduism are tempted by their own versions of such a narrative, of course. Alarmingly prominent versions of Islam tout feelings of resentment against the West, while more marginal yet by no means invisible Christian elements in the United States traffic in the idea that Christianity is under siege.

(Interestingly, both Muslim and Christian extremists tend to place Jews high on their lists of enemies.) These narratives of victimization and resentment bespeak a wider failure of these religions to endow everyday life under the complex conditions of modernity with a sense of meaning or purpose, and also a refusal by significant currents within each religion to accept the facts of difference.

17. Thomas Blom Hansen, *The Saffron Wave: Democracy and Hindu Nationalism in Modern India* (Princeton, NJ: Princeton University Press, 1999).

18. John Zavos, *The Emergence of Hindu Nationalism in India* (Delhi: Oxford University Press, 2000), 2.

19. Hansen, *The Saffron Wave*, 90–134.

20. I have written extensively on this. See most conveniently Pratap Bhanu Mehta, "Secularism and the Identity Trap," in *Will Secular India Survive*, ed. Mushirul Hasan (Delhi: Imprint One, 2004).

21. Hannah Arendt, *Origins of Totalitarianism* (New York: Harcourt Brace Jovanovich, 1951).

22. "Maitreya Upanishad," in *The Samnyasa Upanishads: Hindu Scriptures on Asceticism and Renunciation*, trans. Patrick Olivelle (New York: Oxford University Press, 1992), 165.

BIBLIOGRAPHY

Arendt, Hannah. *Origins of Totalitarianism.* New York: Harcourt Brace Jovanovich, 1951.
Chaturvedi, Badrinath. *Dharma, India and World Order.* Edinburgh: St. Andrews Press, 1992.
Eisensdtat, S. N., Reuven Kahane, and David Shulman, eds. *Orthodoxy, Heterodoxy and Dissent in India.* Berlin: Mouton, 1984.
Greenfeld, Liah. *Nationalism: Five Roads to Modernity.* Cambridge, MA: Harvard University Press, 1992.
Hansen, Thomas Blom. *The Saffron Wave: Democracy and Hindu Nationalism in Modern India.* Princeton, NJ: Princeton University Press, 1999.
Heesterman, J. C. *The Inner Conflict of Tradition: Essays in Indian Ritual, Kingship, and Society.* Chicago: University of Chicago Press, 1985.
Heredia, Rudolph C. *Changing Gods: Rethinking Conversion in India.* New Delhi: Penguin Books, 2007.
"Maitreya Upanishad." In *The Samnyasa Upanishads: Hindu Scriptures on Asceticism and Renunciation*, trans. Patrick Olivelle, 158–69. New York: Oxford University Press, 1992.
McCully, Bruce. "The Origins of Indian Nationalism According to Native Writers." *Journal of Modern History* 7 (1935): 295–314.
Mehta, Pratap Bhanu. "Reason, Tradition and Authority: Religion and the Indian State." In *Toleration on Trial*, ed. Ingrid Creppell, Russell Hardin, and Steve Macedo, 193–214. Lanham, MD: Lexington Books, 2008.
———. "Secularism and the Identity Trap." In *Will Secular India Survive*, ed. Mushirul Hasan. Delhi: Imprint One, 2004.
Morsink, Johannes. *The Universal Declaration of Human Rights: Origins, Drafting, and Intent.* Philadelphia: University of Pennsylvania Press, 1999.

Pantham, Thomas, and V. R. Mehta, eds. *Political Ideas in Modern India: Thematic Explorations.* History of Science, Philosophy and Culture in Indian Civilization, Volume 10, Part 7, ed. D. P. Chattopadhyaya. Delhi: Sage, 2005.

Parel, Anthony J., ed. *Gandhi, Freedom, and Self Rule.* Lanham, MD: Lexington Books, 2000.

Radhakrishnan, Sarvepalli. *The Hindu View of Life.* London: George Allen and Unwin, 1960.

Sen, Amiya. "The Idea of Social Reform and Its Critique among Hindus." In *Development of Modern Indian Thought and the Social Sciences,* History of Science, Philosophy and Culture in Indian Civilization, Volume 10, Part 5, ed. Sabyasachi Bhattacharya. Delhi: Oxford University Press, 2007.

Sharma, Arvind. *Hinduism and Human Rights: A Conceptual Approach.* Oxford: Oxford University Press, 2004.

Shastri Yagna Purushdasji v. Muldas Bhunadardas Vaisya. All India Reporter (SCC), 1966, 1119.

Rev. Stanislaus v. State of Madhya Pradesh and Orissa. AIR 1977 SC 908.

Zavos, John. *The Emergence of Hindu Nationalism in India.* Delhi: Oxford University Press, 2000.

9

Religion, State Power, and Human Rights in China

David Ownby

Although China's recent and much trumpeted "awakening" generally refers to the spectacular economic transformations of the post-Mao era, China has also experienced a religious awakening of historic proportions since the late 1970s, a revival that spans the full spectrum of religious groups, including Buddhists, Daoists, Christians, Muslims, new religious groups like the Falun Gong, and a wide array of popular religious movements.[1] As a result, China's religions are by now part and parcel of everyday life, an unexpected by-product of the greater social latitude that has accompanied China's limited liberalization under the dictates of "market socialism" and globalization—the twin forces that have underwritten China's vaunted economic growth. The question of religion and the global politics of human rights has become meaningful *for the first time* in China in this context, in large measure because the religious revival has coincided with China's opening to a rapidly globalizing world, with important consequences both for China's political leadership and for many of China's religious faithful.

Yet if the question has become meaningful, the outcome remains far from clear. China's thirty-year-old religious revival has produced many conflicts, large and small, between Chinese authorities and religious groups, but has not yet generated a robust human rights dialog on Chinese soil. One reason is the posture of the Chinese government. After three decades of reform, Chinese authorities continue to view both religion and human rights in narrowly statist terms and to dominate the discursive space necessary to a genuine dialog with religious groups. Chinese leaders see religion—properly defined and structured—as a force contributing to social harmony and are committed to a policy of state management of religion through top-down administrative law, co-opting religion and harnessing it to national purposes. The Chinese people are officially accorded the right to practice those religions that contribute to the achievement of national goals, but any conflict between individual rights to religious practice and the needs of the state is quickly decided in favor of the latter. China's reform-era government has also developed its own vision of human rights, which accords priority to economic rights of subsistence and development over civil and political rights and once again emphasizes the necessity of a strong state to the achievement and protection of these rights. Such views of human rights are most frequently aired in international forums in response to Western criticism of Chinese human rights practices and are a lesser focus in official discourse within China.

Still, Chinese authorities are unable to dominate discussion of religion and human rights as completely as they would like. For example, one side effect of China's leaders' defense of a distinctively Chinese human rights regime on the international scene has been to encourage some discussion of human rights within China. Of course, the writings of many Chinese dissidents (more readily available outside of China) illustrate that ideas of human rights are hardly new, but the dynamics of discussion are significantly changed when the state itself uses the language of human rights, even if this language is flawed from a Western perspective. In addition, certain transnational Chinese religious groups with a significant presence outside of China ground their demands for greater freedom of religion within China (as well as their lobbying efforts directed toward Western governments) explicitly in human rights discourse. This is particularly true of Tibetan Buddhists and the Falun Gong, but China's Protestants, Catholics, and even Muslims are increasingly connected to fellow believers outside of China, and, through these linkages, to Western notions of human rights and the freedom of religion. It is unclear to what extent and how quickly these notions find their way back to religious communities within China, but it would be naïve to believe that religion as practiced in the Chinese diaspora has no impact on religion as practiced within China—particularly since relations with diaspora Chinese are encouraged by China's authorities for economic reasons.

Questions of religion and the politics of human rights are thus negotiated in a complex variety of settings that extend from the village temple in rural China to the floor of the United Nations. Actors in this complicated theater include Chinese religious practitioners and professionals inside and outside of China, China's political authorities, Western political authorities, Western religious groups, Western human rights and religious lobbies, lobbies organized by diaspora Chinese (particularly diaspora Chinese religious groups), and the Western and Chinese media. Not all of these actors speak with an equal voice, and some of the most important—religious practitioners in China, for example—can hardly be heard at all. Chinese authorities and the lobbies of certain diaspora Chinese religious groups are probably the "loudest" actors, producing thousands of pages of "discourse," but the relationship of such discourse to conditions on the ground in China is rarely clear.

The complexity of the situation is compounded by the difficulty of separating the politics of the debates over religion and human rights in China from genuine convictions. Do Falun Gong activists in the Chinese diaspora embrace human rights discourse because they have come to believe it or because they know that this discourse will capture the attention of Western politicians who can use the defense of religion and human rights—and criticism of "Communist China"—in their reelection campaigns? Do "house church" Protestants within China depict their conflicts with Chinese authorities in theological rather than human rights terms because their concerns are genuinely theological or because they know that there is no point in debating human rights with a regime that is unlikely to countenance such language? None of these questions can be answered straightforwardly. In any event, the challenge Chinese authorities have set for themselves is to develop and maintain a philosophy and style of management that will not provoke demands for certain rights on the part of religious believers, even if believers are increasingly aware that such rights exist elsewhere. The difficulty of this challenge is not to be underestimated.

Religion and the Politics of Human Rights in Modern China: An Overview

Culture has often been identified as the cause for China's failures to live up to Western standards of human rights, and it is true that traditional Confucianism, with its emphasis on hierarchy and harmony, can be seen to accord more respect to groups than to individuals.[2] At the same time, recent scholarship has convincingly demonstrated that many Chinese who encountered ideas of human rights, introduced along with many other new concepts in the late nineteenth century (often via Japanese translations of Western works), readily embraced them.[3] Indeed, arguments among Chinese concerning human rights have been part of the debates concerning the modernization of Chinese politics and culture throughout the twentieth century. There was Chinese participation, for example, in the drafting of the 1948 UN Universal Declaration of Human Rights, a document the Chinese government subsequently endorsed.[4]

Throughout the course of modern Chinese political history, however, the proponents of a powerful nation-state have consistently pushed human rights concerns to the margins.[5] The People's Republic of China paid scant attention to human rights questions during the Maoist period (1949–76). True, prior to the establishment of the People's Republic in 1949, Mao Zedong occasionally criticized his political adversaries for failing to respect the basic human rights of the Chinese people, but once in power, Mao was quick to follow the Soviet Union and reject human rights as "bourgeois."[6] Nor were human rights a consistent focus of Western diplomacy during the first decades of the cold war, as evidenced by U.S. support for frequently brutal dictatorships in Latin America, Africa, and Asia in the interests of maintaining the balance of power, although the United States and other Western nations did often criticize both the Soviet Union and China for human rights abuses and failure to respect religious freedom. Although briefly challenged by democracy activists in the immediate post-Mao period, the Chinese regime's stance on human rights began to change only with the embrace of globalization under Mao's successor, Deng Xiaoping, and especially since the bloody suppression of the student movement in 1989, which earned China the near universal condemnation of the West.[7]

In order to counter this criticism—and to keep open the access to Western markets so crucial to China's export-driven economy—Chinese authorities began in the 1990s to develop their own human rights discourse that foregrounds economic rights (notably to subsistence) and national rights (China's right to develop as she chooses without interference from outside) and relegates political and civil rights to the back-burner.[8] China's leaders have provided significant funding to academic think tanks and conferences devoted to discussion of human rights, hoping to create the impression of genuine intellectual vitality, but most outside observers have concluded that the regime's goal is less to encourage genuine human rights debates within China than to attempt to defuse foreign criticism—particularly since this newfound interest in human rights issues does not seem to have been accompanied by a significant improvement in the government's domestic human rights record.[9]

Questions of religion and of human rights have proceeded on largely separate tracks in modern Chinese history. With some exceptions, Chinese human rights crusaders have seldom focused on religion—except in passing—and Chinese religious leaders have made few claims on the state on the basis of human rights. The explanation is once again related to China's decades-long history of nation building, which Chinese leaders have conceived in secular terms: China's modern state has sought to harness religion to national needs, and religions have, more often than not, decided to ally themselves with the state rather than to claim abstract rights unlikely to be honored.[10] Indeed, China's management of religion in the interests of the nation-state began early in the twentieth century, culminating in the policy adopted by the communist regime in the 1950s, when the five religions sanctioned by the Chinese authorities (Buddhism, Daoism, Islam, Protestantism, and Catholicism) were all reorganized as patriotic associations under the firm control of the state, with the mission of building strong *Chinese* (not foreign) churches that would advance China's national interests.[11] Thus the China Buddhist Association (CBA) and the Patriotic Chinese Islamic Association (PCIA) were established in 1953, the Protestant Three-Self Patriotic Movement (TSPM) in 1954, and the Chinese Patriotic Catholic Association (CPCA) and the China Daoist Association (CDA—often abbreviated CTA for "China Taoist Association") in 1957. China's Protestant, Catholic, and Islamic churches were—and remain today—vulnerable to charges of undue foreign influence, yet another reason religious leaders of these communities might hesitate to invoke a "universal" human right in the face of particular, national duties as defined by China's leadership. In addition, the People's Republic under Mao Zedong adopted a generally hostile stance to religion, particularly during the Cultural Revolution (1966–76), when temples and churches were destroyed, scriptures burned, and religious personnel imprisoned or secularized. In this period, "management" of religion meant hastening its disappearance as a remnant of "feudal society."[12]

Party authorities have conveyed mixed messages about religion in the reform era, which began in the late 1970s. The revised Constitution of the People's Republic, promulgated in 1982, restated the principle, enunciated in the PRC's first constitution of 1952, that religious freedom is a basic right, and Document 19, an important State Council document issued shortly before the promulgation of the new constitution, sharply criticized religious policy during the Cultural Revolution. At the same time, neither document marked a fundamental departure from 1950s management policies, and both insisted that freedom of religious practice was to be extended only to those belonging to the state-approved Buddhist, Daoist, Muslim, Protestant, and Catholic organizations. There was no promise to surrender party authorities' power to supervise and control religious practice or to pay less attention to the rights of China's nonreligious majority (who according to the constitution require "equal protection" with religious believers). The State Council's National Work Conference on Religion, held in December 1990, heard arguments for somewhat greater tolerance of religious activities, but Document Number 6, issued in 1991, stressed once again the importance of increased regulatory control as a guarantee that tolerance would not lead to "disruptive activities."[13]

As religion has continued to boom in the 1990s and into the new century, Chinese authorities have continued to stress *both* their arguments for limited tolerance of proper religious activities *and* the elaboration of a more tightly woven body of national regulations based in top-down exercise of administrative law and designed to control the religious sphere.[14] Since 1994 Chinese authorities have issued numerous documents and directives insisting on the need for registration and constant monitoring of all religious groups; the most recent such regulations, known as State Council Document 426, came into force in 2005 and remain a central focus of high-level officials' pronouncements on religious affairs.[15] Although such documents are full of language suggesting respect for freedom of religion—headings include the phrases "Legal Protection of the Freedom of Religious Belief," and "Support for Independence and Initiative in Management of Religious Affairs"—even a superficial reading of Document 426 clearly reveals that management is accorded a much higher priority than freedom, as every aspect of communal religious life, from the certification of personnel, to the administration of church finances, to the construction of religious sites, to the printing and circulation of religious scriptures—and much more—requires the approval of the appropriate level of authorities.[16]

In sum, China's authorities offer the promise of freedom and development to those religions who willingly submit to the statist orientation of the present regime. We might read the unfolding drama as a "tale of two religions," in which the secular vision of China's authorities of a set of subservient, patriotic, religious organizations, is set against a different vision, held by some of China's religious faithful, of a more personal, individual (or perhaps communal) faith or practice, not unrelated to national concerns, but bearing complex ties to local society and to fellow believers both within and outside of China and, in some cases, to ideas about universal human rights and religious freedom.

A comprehensive portrait of Chinese religion at the beginning of the twenty-first century is elusive, for reasons of unevenness and lack of data as well as limitations of space. The balance of this chapter provides a survey of China's complex and variegated religious landscape, focusing both on areas where religious groups yield readily to state management and on cases where such management faces obstacles. The survey points to the complexity of the nexus of religion and human rights in today's China.

Chinese Buddhism and Daoism

Chinese authorities are proud to boast about the health of reform-era Buddhism and Daoism, China's two traditional indigenous religions.[17] They typically cite the numbers of temples reopened or refurbished, and the number of monks trained in newly functioning seminaries.[18] For their part, the leaders of the China Buddhist Association (CBA) and the China Daoist Association (CDA) appear to have embraced state policy, at least in its general contours. Taiwanese scholar Zhang Jialin conducted individual and group interviews among a small number of China's religious elite in the early 2000s, including leaders of the religious establishments, university professors studying religious topics, and administrators charged with managing religion. He found that the Buddhist and Daoist officials with whom he spoke viewed the current era as a "golden age."[19] According to these leaders, the reform era marks the first in which China's leaders have genuinely honored the constitution's pronouncements on religious matters, while at the same time publicly acknowledging the existence of positive links between religion and traditional culture.

The reasons for state support of Buddhism and Daoism, and for Buddhism's and Daoism's embrace of state policy, are not hard to find. In the case of Buddhism, particularly, today's plans for "better regulation" of the community can be seen to mesh with certain long-term movements within Chinese Buddhism that predate the founding of the People's Republic. The Buddhist monk Taixu (1890–1947), one of the best-known and most controversial figures in Republican-period Buddhism, labored throughout his life to create an engaged, reformed, "twentieth-century" Buddhism that would rid itself of superstition, educate its clergy in a modern fashion, and undertake social welfare projects designed to change the world (instead of withdrawing from the world through monasticism or transcending it through meditation).[20] Some of Taixu's influence can be seen in two hugely successful Taiwanese Buddhist enterprises, the Buddhist Compassion Relief Tzu Chi Foundation (Tzu Chi gongdehui) and the Light of Buddha Mountain organization (Foguangshan), whose charitable works span the globe.[21] The CBA under Communist Party control can hardly aspire to the autonomy, wealth, and global influence of these Taiwanese Buddhist establishments, but the state provides some support (including financial support) for an educated Buddhist clergy, working under a politically well-connected hierarchy, engaged in potentially meaningful social projects. Compared to the fate of Buddhism during the Cultural Revolution, this does indeed look like a golden age, and part of the Buddhist establishment thus appears quite happy to let itself be co-opted, at least up to a certain point.

From the state point of view, Buddhism would appear to represent an ideal religion, first because the leaders of the CBA are generally pleased to work with the government, second because Chinese Buddhism is distinctly Chinese and has few troublesome ties with Buddhist establishments elsewhere in the world, and finally because Buddhism is rarely a religion of mobilization. At a doctrinal level Buddhist teachings stress individual disengagement, acceptance, and transcendence, and provide little grounding for rights-based claims. Buddhists do not proselytize, and lay Buddhists do not "join" Buddhist temples in the same way that Christians join churches. Finally, while individual Buddhist monks may develop ties with those who patronize and frequent their temples, this relationship is less pastoral than in many Christian churches, and Buddhist monks are traditionally more likely to submit to hierarchy than to attempt to represent their flock to church or political authorities.

Daoism does not quite fit the Buddhist model, but Chinese authorities and some members of the Daoist leadership have high hopes that it will evolve in that direction. Like Buddhism, Daoism is an indigenous Chinese religion with relatively few ties to religious communities outside of China. By contrast, Daoism has less history of modernizing reform in the contemporary period, is less unified as a religious establishment than Buddhism (which itself is hardly unified), and remains deeply enmeshed in local society and popular religion, as is Buddhism in many cases. The leadership of the CDA, worried that many local Daoist practices are vulnerable to charges of "superstition," has been working hard over the past few years with officials of the Religious Affairs Bureau (RAB) on issues relating to registration, certification, and control.[22]

A particular challenge are local Daoist priests whose ties with the larger Daoist establishment are often unclear or tenuous. Such priests often learn their ritual/liturgical functions and receive their scriptures from a father or other male relative and are not certified by any higher authority—which by no means calls into question the central role they often play in local religious and ritual life, particularly in Southeast China. The RAB—and much of the Daoist establishment—would like to find a way to regulate and incorporate these local Daoist priests, in part to establish clearer boundaries between the proper practice of religion and the undesirable vestiges of superstition. However, the fact that many Daoist priests are more closely tied to their community than to the CDA makes their genuine co-optation problematic. Kenneth Dean, a prominent Western scholar of Daoism in contemporary China, calls the ritual networks put together by the Daoists of Fujian province "China's second government,"[23] suggesting their importance to local society. Tensions among state authorities, a central religious establishment, and certain local personnel and practices are often managed through established political and policy channels, without overt recourse to the language of human rights, but this does not mean that such tensions do not exist or that members of local Daoist communities do not consider such ritual activities an essential part of the local social order.

Christianity in China

Christianity is undergoing a significant revival in China, posing multiple challenges for Chinese authorities.[24] In his interviews with members of the religious elite in China, Taiwanese scholar Zhang Jialin found that Chinese Protestant and Catholic leaders were less sanguine about the current situation than were members of the Buddhist and Daoist establishments, even if many members of the Christian establishment are, like their Buddhist and Daoist counterparts, willing to cooperate with RAB officials.[25] The main cause of their dissatisfaction is that Christianity has grown in a way that Buddhism and Daoism have not, an expansion that has caused difficult management problems for China's Christians and those who would regulate them. Indeed, the Christian revival represents an expansion of historic proportions in the numbers of Chinese Christians (particularly Protestants—Chinese Catholics are discussed separately below): there were at most one million Protestants in China in 1949;[26] at the beginning of the twenty-first century, conservative estimates suggest that there are fifty million, and less conservative estimates go as high as

110 million.[27] Nor is the Protestant boom a regional phenomenon. New converts are found in cities and in villages, in the north and in the south, among old and young, well educated and less educated.

Since 1979, Protestant churches under the supervision of the Three-Self Protestant Movement (TSPM) have been allowed to operate openly, and in 1982 some 6,000 Protestant ministers resumed their pastoral positions at TSPM churches after having spent time in prison, at labor camps, or in other secular occupations. By 1995, 37,000 Protestant churches had been reopened and 18,000 Protestant ministers were available to serve in them.[28] The fact that there are less than half as many ministers as churches points to problems in state management of the rapidly growing movement. Many churches are overflowing with believers, yet state authorities limit new construction; there were only eight Protestant churches in Shanghai in the late 1990s, compared to more than 200 in 1949.[29] Moreover, state authorities permit only seminary-trained ministers to serve as pastors in TSPM churches—indeed, "self-appointed" ministers are subject to arrest—and yet supply is far from keeping up with demand: there have been few graduates from seminaries since 1949, and none between 1966 and 1979. This means that many of China's Protestant ministers are aged or aging, while, at least in urban areas, many converts to Protestantism are young (as well as well educated, and middle class).

The Nanjing Union Theological Seminary, China's only national seminary, has accepted some fifty candidates per year (including both BA and MA) since the beginning of the reform period, and broke ground for the construction of a new campus in January 2005, but in general authorities have not considered the production of more trained ministers a priority, preferring to suggest that their hands are tied by unfortunate circumstances.[30] Similar attitudes prevail on such questions as the availability of Bibles and other Christian literature. Whether RAB authorities are simply unable to keep pace with the burgeoning movement or are deliberately hoping to slow the growth of Protestant Christianity through regulation is unclear, but many Chinese Christians clearly feel that the deliberate pace of Chinese religious management is part of a conscious policy to contain Christianity and are aware that Christians elsewhere in the world are not necessarily subject to the same restrictions. Such consciousness of injustice could readily give birth to demands based on rights, particularly as disgruntled citizens make use of such language in other contexts, grounding their arguments in official documents that chastise local functionaries who fail to respect the rights of peasants and workers.[31]

An important if unintended result of authorities' efforts to control the growth of Protestant Christianity has been the rise of an unofficial, nonaffiliated Protestantism known as the "house church" movement.[32] The designation "house church" comes from the fact that such groups have no officially approved place of worship and thus gather in the home of one believer or another. To some extent house church Christians occupy a structural position similar to that of local Daoist priests in that their links with the central religious establishment are unclear and often tenuous. At the same time, many house church groups are much larger and better organized than the term would lead one to believe—and certainly more organized than local Daoist priests. Indeed, the movement includes thousands of church groups and several dozen larger interprovincial networks. The ten largest networks claim eighty million followers, surely an exaggeration, but there is little doubt that the number of house church adherents exceeds the membership of state-sanctioned churches.

The Religious Affairs Bureau has sought to persuade underground churches to merge with the TSPM establishment and thus embrace the state's managerial policy. At the same time, given that some of the mainstream TSPM churches are critical of aspects of state policy, the incentives for the underground church to move toward an establishment posture are not clear. Indeed, many house churches, without being unified organizationally or doctrinally, nonetheless share a global evangelical vision that drives them to fill gaps that the TSPM, constrained by the Chinese state, cannot.[33] Leaders of house church organizations are often mobile so as to avoid detection and arrest, enabling them to build effective independent, semi-underground networks in a way that officially approved ministers and church leaders cannot. Similarly, the house church networks run a huge complex of underground seminaries and printing presses to train leaders and preachers, and to supply believers with Bibles and other votive and educational literature. Funding is supplied by church members and is apparently more than ample, particularly as the house church movement appeals to the wealthy and connected as well as the poor and marginal. Indeed, there are reports of wealthy businessmen who personally finance house church seminaries as an act of devotion.

Although local authorities intervene frequently to disperse meetings and arrest leaders, such efforts appear to have been unsuccessful so far in reducing the size of the underground churches or slowing their growth. For some, persecution has come to be seen as a Christ-like badge of honor; there are reports that some church leaders have even been chosen, at least in part, on the basis of the numbers of times they have been arrested. Some observers believe that long-term trends are toward greater interpenetration of TSPM and house church organizations—but not necessarily in the sense desired by the Religious Affairs Bureau. Indeed, some TSPM churches already send their pastors to house church seminaries and take advantage of greater house church funding, flexibility, and ties with the outside world.

One example of the self-confidence of the house church movement was an open letter by leaders of ten major unofficial Protestant house churches addressed to the Chinese government in 1998. The letter argued that by dint of their superior membership and the liberty their unaffiliated status granted them in matters of religious doctrine and practice, the house church movement, rather than the TSPM churches, represented the main current of Chinese

Protestantism. It called on Chinese authorities to release house church leaders and members from prisons and labor camps and to adjust religious policy to accord more respect to God's wishes as manifested in the house church movement. A similar statement, prepared three months later and read before foreign journalists, insisted once more on the house church movement's orthodox status—Chinese authorities regularly accuse the underground church of being "sectarian" or even "cult-like"—and declared the movement's unwillingness to affiliate itself to the Chinese regime for fear of violating the will of God.[34] Such demands are based in theological rather than human rights discourse, which may make them less objectionable to Chinese authorities. At the same time, this very theological orientation might suggest a rejection of the secular posture of the Chinese state, a kind of provocation in and of itself.

China's ten to twelve million Catholics may appear numerically unimportant next to China's booming Protestant movement, but there are still twice as many Chinese Catholics as Tibetan Buddhists.[35] Although one finds many parallels in the recent experiences of China's Catholics and Protestants—and members of other faith communities—China's Catholics nonetheless possess a particular history that has made the Catholic revival slower and more difficult than that of other Christian groups, largely because allegiance to the pope is in tension with the national organization of official religion in China. Chinese Catholics' allegiance to the pope runs afoul of the statist orientation of China's religious policy.

When Chinese authorities established the Protestant Three-Self Patriotic Movement in the early 1950s, they built in part on the prerevolutionary desires of some Protestants to establish a genuinely Chinese church, free from foreign missionary control.[36] By contrast, most Chinese Catholics understood their church to be under the direction of the Vatican, and many believers adamantly refused to recognize the authority of the Catholic Patriotic Association (founded by the Chinese state in 1957) to accomplish the same tasks as the TSPM. The Vatican, virulently anticommunist in the early 1950s, refused all efforts to find common ground with the Chinese regime, and the ensuing tensions eventually split Chinese Catholics into those eventually willing to accept the CPA and those who saw the CPA and all who followed it as traitors to the church. Chinese Catholics, much like Chinese Protestants, today find themselves divided into the officially recognized church under the CPA and an underground Catholic Church that is much smaller than the Protestant house church movement. Conflicts between the two Catholic churches run much deeper than in the case of the Protestant community, even if some limited collaboration seems to have developed recently. Chinese and Vatican leaders are gradually approaching negotiation, but difficult issues remain; the Vatican still recognizes Taiwan, for example, illustrating the complexity of the diplomatic and political obstacles to a fundamental resolution. Tensions revolve around institutional autonomy and lines of authority rather than around issues of human rights, even if the post–Vatican II church makes universal human rights part of its foreign policy.

It is not just Catholicism that gives Christianity in China a prominent international dimension. Protestantism is growing in the Chinese diaspora as well as in China itself, and the growth of Christianity in China is the focus of enormous interest on the part of the worldwide Christian community. Many churches and missionary organizations assist the official and underground churches in any way they can.[37] Similarly, numerous organizations follow cases of Christian persecution in China, some of the more important being the China Aid Association and the Church in China, which chronicle the rocky relationship between Chinese authorities and the house church movement and call for greater respect for human rights and freedom of religious belief. Other groups with a global missionary orientation, such as the Voice of the Martyrs or Christian Solidarity Worldwide, also track the development of Christianity in China.[38]

The orientation of these Christian groups is largely theological, but their concerns regarding China readily dovetail with those of secular nongovernmental organizations (NGOs) and Western governments, particularly but not exclusively that of the United States, for which human rights are a fundamental preoccupation. Amnesty International and Human Rights Watch issue annual reports on China in which religious persecution is included under the rubric of human rights abuses. Defense of freedom of religion is a popular card to play in American politics, and a very critical eye is cast on developments within China catalogued in the State Department's annual reports on international religious freedom, which have been published since 2001. High-ranking American officials visiting China often take time out to attend church services, making the same point with their actions as they do in their frequent statements: that China has much improvement to make in its defense of religious freedom.[39]

It remains nonetheless extremely difficult to determine the degree to which international criticism affects the regulation of Christianity within China's borders. Even those Chinese Christians who are aware of international opinion and who would welcome greater freedom of religion in China might still be swayed by the patriotic, state-based rhetoric of China's leaders or might share the suspicion of the outside world often expressed in state media. Rights-based claims are surely seeping into China, but the logic of such claims must still compete with the logic of local and national politics in China.

Tibetan Buddhism

If Chinese Buddhism is a successful example of China's religious management policy, Tibetan Buddhism is an ongoing challenge that illustrates the government's worst fears about religion as a force for mobilization and resistance to political authority.[40] In recent decades the Dalai Lama, Tibet's exiled God-King, has emerged as a well-loved figure on the world stage for his embodiment of spiritual values and measured support for Tibetans' human rights, as well as a source of continual irritation for the Chinese regime. The violent demonstrations in Tibet in March 2008, which provoked both widespread condemnation of China's Tibet policy and a spirited response from authorities in Beijing, were a recent illustration of this point.

Whatever the validity of China's historic claims to Tibet, an autonomous if not internationally recognized Buddhist kingdom for many centuries, the Chinese have had firm control over the region only since 1959, when Chinese troops suppressed an armed uprising and the Dalai Lama fled to India where he established a Tibetan government-in-exile in Dharamsala. These events put an end to Tibet's relative autonomy, guaranteed by the Seventeen-Point Document which, from the early 1950s, had dictated a peaceful if wary coexistence between Tibetan and Chinese authorities. Tibetan autonomy *under* Chinese rule was supposedly secured by the establishment of the Tibet Autonomous Region (TAR) in 1965, but more important was the beginning of the Cultural Revolution in 1966, which marked a brutal decade-long assault on Tibetan Buddhism, its institutions, practices, personnel, and doctrines, in the name of class revolution.

Although the legacy of the Cultural Revolution and its destruction weighs heavily on Tibet, important changes have been introduced since the reform era, granting Tibet greater local autonomy and applying the policies of openness and economic development to the region.[41] Local political autonomy has been largely limited to an increase in the number of lower level Tibetan cadres and has been accompanied by significant levels of Han Chinese migration, particularly in urban areas. On the religious front, visitors to Tibet since the beginning of the reform era have uniformly observed that Tibetan Buddhism is openly and fervently practiced. Tourists, journalists, and scholars return with pictures of large and small monasteries, tales of frequent pilgrimages, and accounts of Tibetan homes containing religious shrines or prayer rooms.

Of course, few visitors to Tibet arrive with any sense of history or proportion. Melvyn Goldstein, a leading American academic authority on Tibet, has established through his research that in 1951 there were some 115,000 monks distributed among roughly 2,500 monasteries, amounting to between 10 percent and 15 percent of Tibet's total male population.[42] Official figures for 2004 provide a figure of 46,000 monks and some 1,700 religious sites, including both monasteries and temples, suggesting that the destruction wrought between the late 1950s and the late 1970s has been only partially repaired.[43] Nor are casual observers necessarily aware of the pervasive controls on religious practice that continue to be exercised by Chinese authorities. The Dalai Lama's picture has been banned since 1996, for example, bringing into clear focus the conflict between the right to practice Tibetan Buddhism and the duty to support Chinese national unity. Major Tibetan monasteries have been rebuilt and refurbished as much to encourage the development of tourism as to respect the needs or wishes of the Tibetan religious community. Monasteries are run at least in part through "democratic management committees," party organs that answer to Chinese authorities and exercise considerable control over the ordination and activities of monks and nuns. Religious education, traditionally a prerogative of the monasteries—most if not all education in traditional Tibet was religious education—is a particular focus. Religious authorities would like to make up for the departure of many qualified monks into exile as well as for deficiencies in religious training between the late 1950s and the late 1970s, but Chinese authorities are not always cooperative, attempting for example to restrict monastic education to those eighteen years of age and older, or demanding that all monks and nuns receive instruction in "patriotic education." At the same time, in July 2004, authorities did permit the resumption of the Geshe Lharampa examinations, the highest in the Gelug sect of Tibetan Buddhism, for the first time in sixteen years.

Overall, the cultural and religious picture is one of continuous, often low-level conflict. Authorities attempt to limit the growth of Tibetan Buddhism while insisting that they respect Tibetan autonomy, and Tibetans generally have little choice but to accommodate them, even as they try to increase freedom of action that, while far greater now than under Mao, does not compare with their vision of the historical past. On occasion, the conflict has turned violent. Demonstrations for greater Tibetan autonomy occurred in Lhasa in late September and early October of 1987, led principally by Buddhist monks. Similar demonstrations occurred in March of 1988, and again on March 5, 1989, this time in commemoration of the thirtieth anniversary of the 1959 revolt. A number of demonstrators were killed in the ensuing repression, and on March 7, 1989, the government imposed martial law in Lhasa, not lifting it until May 1990. Further demonstrations occurred in 1993, even as Chinese authorities attempted to install a more effective form of policing. A dispute over the successor of the Panchen Lama in 1995 led to the imprisonment of important religious figures in Tibet, if not to widespread violence. The March 2008 demonstrations were the most recent occasion for violence. Dozens if not hundreds of similar, if lower level conflicts, occur every year, as chronicled by Amnesty International, Human Rights Watch, and Tibetan advocacy groups.

The violent suppression of the Tibetan demonstrations of the late 1980s, coinciding as it did with the crackdown on student protests in Beijing and other major cities in the summer of 1989, has largely set the tone for American policy, making Tibet a recurring issue in Chinese relations with much of the Western world.[44] This was not always the case. As late as 1979, the Dalai Lama had difficulty obtaining a visa to the United States, and the Tibetan cause was accorded little priority. The Dalai Lama's rise to international celebrity, however, coincided with the violence in Tibet in the late 1980s and 1990s, which focused considerable media and political attention on Tibet. Between 1979 and 2005, the Dalai Lama visited the United States thirty-one times and Germany twenty-eight times, and gave addresses at important venues such as the U.S. Congress, the United Nations, and the European Parliament at Strasbourg, accusing the Chinese government of "cultural genocide" and demanding Tibetan autonomy and respect for human rights.[45]

As important as his formal statements and his explicitly political activities is the Dalai Lama's name recognition as a spokesman for world peace and "new age" yearnings for a better world. His writings are widely available—at least twelve of his audio books were available on the Apple iTunes store in 2008—and speak to a vast audience with little explicit interest in Tibet, Buddhism, or China. And his cause is championed by such well-known Hollywood figures as Richard Gere and Martin Scorcese, among many others.[46] Hollywood's romance of the Tibetan cause may sometimes appear frivolous or trendy, but media worldwide pay considerable attention to the political pronouncements of celebrities, and if Westerners are less informed about the plight of China's Muslims than Tibetan Buddhists, it is in no small measure because for the moment there is no Chinese Muslim equivalent of the smiling face of the Dalai Lama, and little popular embrace of the Chinese Muslim cause.[47] At the same time, this "cause" is probably understood differently in the West and in Tibet. For Western devotees of Tibetan culture, human rights concerns readily dovetail—as freedom of religion—with Tibet's struggle for autonomy and cultural survival. The Dalai Lama, by contrast, has often sought a "middle way" that would eventuate in greater autonomy—and thus more freedom of religion—for Tibet, without consistently grounding his vision in a universal human rights discourse (at least when negotiating with Chinese authorities).

An organized Tibet lobby exists as well and takes full advantage of the cachet of His Holiness.[48] The Dalai Lama and the Tibet lobby keep the Tibetan cause in the news, making it a political issue in the West, but this may be a mixed blessing for Tibetans still in China. From a positive perspective, the plight of the Tibetans is not forgotten, and their daily struggles of accommodation are depicted, in the language of international lobbying, as stark issues of religious freedom and human rights. At the same time, China's leaders refuse to accept Western discourses concerning religious freedom and human rights, claiming that such concerns represent an assault on China's national unity by championing Tibetan autonomy. One important moment in the unfolding of this drama will be the eventual death of the Dalai Lama, born in 1935, as Chinese authorities will certainly attempt to replace him with a "reincarnation" of their choosing. Should this ploy prove unsuccessful, rights discourse coming from outside China may play a larger role in the politics of religion and human rights in Tibet. This is particularly true given journalistic reports during the 2008 violence in Tibet that many younger Tibetans, both inside and outside of the autonomous region, are increasingly dissatisfied with the Dalai Lama's "middle way" and are open to a more assertive strategy.[49]

China's Muslims

China is home to some twenty to twenty-five million Muslims—who are thus four to five times more numerous than the 5.5 million Tibetan Buddhists—but they are divided by ethnicity, language, geography, history, and sectarian affiliation within Islam.[50] China's Muslims represent a much less concentrated, homogenous group than do the Tibetan Buddhists, yet some Chinese Muslims have been similarly persecuted for reasons of culture and religion and, in some cases, for desires for greater regional autonomy.[51]

The largest single group among Chinese Muslims are the Hui, Muslims whose native language is most often Chinese and who are descendants of the waves of Muslim peoples who came to China from Central Asia and the Middle East over the centuries.[52] The Hui now number almost ten million, 48 percent of China's total Muslim population, and are found throughout China, their greatest numbers being concentrated in the northwest provinces of China proper (rather than in the more distant regions of Xinjiang and Qinghai), in the general vicinity of the Chinese terminus of the silk road that historically connected China with Central Asia and points further west.[53] All Muslims are under the supposed governance of the Patriotic Chinese Islamic Association, established in 1953, but it is unclear to what extent or under what circumstances China's Muslims conceive of themselves as a unified group. Dru Gladney, one of the few Western scholars to study China's Muslims extensively, emphasizes diversity even among the Hui, to say nothing of the broader Muslim population. Issues of religion and human rights are most often raised in the context of certain Muslim groups in China's far western region of Xinjiang rather than in that of Chinese Muslims as a whole, even if it is nonetheless clear that Muslims elsewhere in China are aware of events in the larger Muslim world and the relation of these events to Xinjiang.[54]

China's Xinjiang Uighur Autonomous Region is home to a number of groups of Turkic-speaking Muslims, the largest of which is the Uighurs, of which there are some eight million in Xinjiang, about half the total population of the autonomous region.[55] Although Chinese control came late to the far northwest, and there have been a variety of independent peoples and kingdoms in the region over the centuries, we find no historical parallel to the centuries-long rule of the Buddhist theocracy in Tibet. Still, Xinjiang has an officially autonomous status like that of Tibet and constitutes the region with the highest concentration of Muslims within China.[56]

Islam received the same treatment as other religions during the Cultural Revolution and has experienced a revival much like that of other religions in the post-Mao era.[57] Although the Muslim revival has been China-wide, its dimensions are most readily observable in Xinjiang, which now has 23,000 officially registered mosques, compared to a mere 2,000 in 1978. Similarly, many traditional Muslim practices condemned during the Cultural Revolution have been revived since the reforms of the 1980s.[58] Some 6,000 Chinese made the annual pilgrimage to Mecca in the late 1990s, for example, up from 1,400 in the mid-1980s.[59]

China's perceptions—and to some extent ours—of the Islamic revival in China have been colored by the rise of Islamic fundamentalism elsewhere in the world, initiated by the overthrow of the Shah and the Islamic revolution in Iran in 1979. The subsequent collapse of the Soviet Union in 1989–91 led to the creation of a number of independent Central Asian Republics—young secular regimes with substantial Muslim majorities in a volatile part of the world. Next door to these republics, the Taliban seized power in most of Afghanistan, holding the capital of Kabul from 1996 to 2001. In the eyes of China's leaders, Xinjiang's Muslim population is uncomfortably close to a region in turmoil.

As in the case of Tibet, Xinjiang had been promised greater regional autonomy as part of the post-Mao reforms. Such autonomy always came with limits, and these limits became increasingly restrictive as Chinese authorities' fears of possible Islamic extremism rose. Predictably, in a distant region that has long chafed under conditions of internal colonization, demonstrations and violence were the result. In 1986, Uighurs marched through the streets of Urumqi, the capital of Xinjiang, protesting against environmental degradation, nuclear testing, and increased Han immigration to the region. In 1989, there were Muslim demonstrations in Beijing and many other parts of China, protesting the publication of a book, in Chinese, entitled *Sexual Customs* that depicted Muslims in a derogatory light. In April 1990, a short-lived armed rebellion led by Zahideen Yusuf, a Muslim fundamentalist, broke out in part of Xinjiang. Throughout the summer and fall of 1993 bombs exploded in several towns in the region, allegedly the work of organizations pressing for an independent Turkestan. In February 1997, a rebellion in the city of Ili resulted in the deaths of some thirteen Uighurs and the arrests of hundreds. Eight Uighurs were executed in late May 1997 for alleged bombings in northwest China, with hundreds more arrested on suspicion of taking part in ethnic riots and engaging in separatist activities.[60]

Chinese authorities have reacted swiftly and predictably, with increased military and police presence, particularly in Kashgar and Urumqi. According to one Amnesty International estimate, Xinjiang saw 1.8 executions a week in the late 1990s, in a country known for its high execution rates. In 1998, Chinese authorities announced a plan to erect a "great wall of steel" against separatists in Xinjiang.[61] Tensions have only risen since terrorist strikes against the United States in September 2001 and the mounting of the Bush administration's "war on terrorism." China has sought to connect its own regional difficulties with such broader concerns, claiming for example to have found foreign Taliban members or even foreign-trained Chinese members of the Taliban, although human rights organizations suspect that more often than not these are young Uighurs who had returned after studying Islamic law in Pakistan.[62]

There is a Uighur exile community that attempts to lobby in a manner similar to that of the Tibetans, if with less success for the moment. The East Turkestan Information Center calls for freedom, independence, and democracy in East Turkestan—religion figures somewhat less prominently in their appeals—and maintains a list of some twenty-two Uighur organizations around the world, among the most important of which appear to be the World Uighur Congress, with headquarters in Munich, Germany, and the Uighur American Association with headquarters on Pennsylvania Avenue in Washington, D.C. The list also notes organizations based in Turkey, Kazakhstan, and Kyrgyzstan.[63] The organizations that lobby in the West hardly appear to be hotbeds of Islamic fundamentalism. The mission statement of the World Uighur Congress, for example, does not mention Islam and remains faithful to the language of international human rights. Terrorism is explicitly denounced.[64] The East Turkestan Independence Movement, believed to the most extreme of the organizations agitating for regional independence, does place more emphasis on its Islamic orientation.[65]

The Uighur lobby, based on these exile communities dispersed widely throughout Russia, Europe, and North America, has yet to find a commonly recognized charismatic leader and is divided by ideology among pan-Turkists, nationalists, secularists, and Islamist factions. The Uighur language is transcribed in Cyrillic, Arabic, and Latin alphabets—reflecting the widespread dispersal of the Uighur peoples—and this inevitably slows the exchange of information even within the Uighur community.[66] But if Uighurs do someday manage to establish a lobby with the visibility and the effectiveness of the Tibetans, they may well find themselves in the same dilemma, where outside support leads to greater internal suppression. The Bush administration's emphasis on the war on terror encouraged those within the Chinese government who would take a hard line. While Uighur groups make use of human rights discourse, they may well downplay religious freedom to avoid being branded as Islamic extremists. Like the Tibetans, Uighurs are likely to emphasize cultural autonomy and communal religious traditions as part of it, rather than individual human rights.

Falun Gong

The most controversial and most unexpected aspect of China's post-Mao religious revival has been the rise and suppression of the Falun Gong, a form of *qigong* ("the discipline of the vital breath"), a particular strain of Chinese popular religion.[67] Although *qigong* enthusiasts often rightly claim that their practice has ancient roots, its contemporary form was created in the 1950s by part of the medical establishment as an effort to maintain certain traditional Chinese healing practices in the face of the import of Western medicine.[68] In creating *qigong* they sought to remove the superstitious and religious packaging that surrounded similar practices during imperial times, identifying corporal technologies and mental disciplines useful in achieving physical and mental health. Traditionally, these practices had been purveyed by charismatic spiritual figures, whom the creators of *qigong* sought out and whose practices they transplanted into modern hospitals and sanatoria. *Qigong* received considerable high-level political support in the 1950s and became quite popular among the Chinese governing elite. During the Cultural Revolution, it was attacked by Maoist radicals as part of China's "feudal" past and suppressed.

The revival of *qigong* in the post-Mao period took on a very different form and in fact became a mass, new religious movement led by charismatic masters who took their message directly to interested practitioners, bypassing the medical establishment. These masters generally came to *qigong* from outside the safe, institutional *qigong* world of the 1950s, having learned their skills from people close to traditional religious or spiritual practices. They used the name *qigong* because it was less problematic than any other available label. A small-scale *qigong* revival beginning in the early 1970s received a major boost in 1979 when well-known Chinese scientists reported the results of laboratory experiments suggesting that *qi* energy, emitted by *qigong* masters, took the form of waves that could be measured by scientific instruments.[69] This meant that *qigong* no longer belonged to the world of magic and superstition but rather to that of science and dialectical materialism and could become part of China's quest for modernization.

A large *qigong* community rapidly emerged in the late 1970s and the early 1980s, made up of scientists working on *qi* and *qigong*; journalists who spread the word of *qigong*'s power and benefits; *qigong* masters, whose numbers increased rapidly; and—most important—party and government officials who saw in *qigong* a uniquely powerful "Chinese science" as well as a practical, economical means to achieve a healthier population. High-level official support was crucial to the development of the *qigong* boom and took the form of individual patronage by powerful members of the ruling elite of particular masters and scientists, as well as organizational efforts, such as the establishment of the Chinese *Qigong* Scientific Research Association in April 1986. Although *qigong* was never seen as a religion, this association served much the same purpose as the Three-Self Protestant Movement or the China Buddhist Association, namely, oversight, regulation, and control.

Beginning from the early 1980s, China experienced a "*qigong* boom" as millions of Chinese became devoted followers of one school of *qigong* or another and made *qigong* an important part of their daily lives. These schools were led by charismatic *qigong* masters, many of whom became national celebrities and who built large, often nationwide, *qigong* organizations. Such masters went on national and sometimes international lecture tours in which thousands of enthusiasts bought tickets for lectures, often held in a local sports stadium, which could last for several hours as the masters "emitted *qi*" while they spoke, instantly curing the sick and otherwise transforming the members of the audience. These miracle cures are symbolic of the difference between the *qigong* of the 1950s and that of the boom of the 1980s. *Qigong* in the 1950s had been a therapeutic discipline practiced by the ailing patient under the guidance of a trained professional. In the 1980s it was a magico-religious power possessed by charismatic heroes who built personal followings on the basis of their charisma and their teachings and often explained *qigong*'s power with reference to traditional spiritual discourse. According to some accounts, as many as 200 million people participated in the *qigong* boom—almost one-fifth of China's population.[70]

Falun Gong founder Li Hongzhi was a latecomer to the boom, founding his school of *qigong* in 1992 and following squarely in the footsteps of previous *qigong* masters.[71] Li and Falun Gong were quickly welcomed into the Scientific *Qigong* Research Association, which sponsored many of Li's activities between 1992 and 1994, chief among which were fifty-four lectures given throughout China to a total audience of some 60,000. Li also published books of his teachings, which achieved such success that he was soon able to offer his lectures free of charge—a significant difference from many other *qigong* schools. Li's message was also somewhat different from that of other masters. He criticized miracle cures and other "parlor tricks" and presented his teachings as *qigong* taken to a higher plane, where the practitioner's goal was to arrive at a fundamental transformation of his understanding of the universe and his role therein, as well as a physical transformation of his body. Li also accorded far more importance to scripture—that is, his writings—than did most other *qigong* masters. It was the reading, rereading, and absorption through virtual memorization of Li's written teachings that made up the core of Falun Gong practice. Although it is difficult to summarize briefly the nature of Li's message, he offered the promise of moral and physical renewal, including reversal of the aging process and spiritual enlightenment, via a combination of moral practice and "cultivation" achieved through the study of his scriptures under his supernatural guidance. Li cast his message in a language that combined lay Buddhism, claims to mastery and transcendence of modern science, and warnings of an impending apocalypse.

On the basis of these teachings, Li attracted an important following in China between 1992 and the end of 1994. Estimates of numbers range from two million to sixty million, making Falun Gong one of the larger schools of *qigong*, if probably not the largest.[72] This success was probably also the reason for Falun Gong's eventual downfall. For complex reasons, Li's organization came to be the one that drew authorities' attention to the dangers of charismatic *qigong* masters with broad powers of popular mobilization. When authorities tried to rein in Falun Gong, via media criticism, its followers responded vigorously with demands for "equal time" or retractions, a practice that immediately became political since most media outlets in China are little more than mouthpieces for the regime. Sources mention more than 300 such "reactions," between summer of 1996 and late April 1999.[73] Falun Gong practitioners argued that *qigong* practice was protected by government policy, that Falun Gong had enjoyed the same status as other *qigong* groups, and that no clearly stated government policy had removed this protection from the Falun Gong. These demands were not phrased in the universal language of human rights but did insist on practitioners' rights to practice and to protest inaccurate representations of their discipline.

The tension culminated in the events of April 29, 1999, when 10,000 Falun Gong practitioners demonstrated outside the gates of Zhongnanhai, the guarded compound in central Beijing where most of China's elite leaders live and work. Stunned and frightened by the demonstration, China's leaders reacted with a fierce campaign of suppression in which the Falun Gong was outlawed as a "heterodox cult" and likened to the Solar Temple, the Branch Davidians, or Aum Shinrikyo. Other religious groups rushed to join Chinese authorities' condemnation of Falun Gong, apparently to avoid being tarred by the same brush.

Falun Gong practitioners within China responded with consternation to the campaign, believing that the authorities had simply been misinformed. Attempts to set the record straight became peaceful demonstrations that resulted in arrests, in a rapid spiral toward brutalization. Practitioners outside of China, most of whom are recent emigrants from the People's Republic of China (PRC), quickly began to organize to lobby Western governments to bring pressure on China, and during 1999 and much of 2000 they succeeded in keeping the Falun Gong issue in the news, particularly in the United States, by foregrounding human rights and religious freedom arguments. Like the Tibetans and the Uighurs, the Falun Gong also set up a series of Web sites to keep practitioners in China and abroad informed of developments and to direct their efforts to bring the campaign of suppression to a halt.[74] In the process, a movement based on lay Buddhist renunciation of individual desires and the embrace of a spiritual master came to be defended, by Falun Gong practitioners outside of China, by reference to human rights and freedom of religion discourses that trace their roots to the Western Enlightenment.

This evolution is made clear by the advocacy organizations set up since 2000 to pursue Falun Gong goals: the Falun Dafa Information Center, an organization dedicated to "document[ing] human rights abuses specific to Falun Gong in China" and "advocat[ing] for the rights of Falun Gong adherents inside China, particularly under the continued circumstance in which they are denied legal representation or fair trials";[75] Justice for Falun Gong, a group that seeks to bring China's leaders to justice through legal measures; the Falun Gong Human Rights Working Group, which brings together information on viola-tions of the human rights of Falun Gong practitioners; the World Organization to Investigate the Persecution of Falun Gong; and the Global Mission to Rescue Persecuted Falun Gong Practitioners. Falun Gong is by now a transnational new religious movement that campaigns, in the pages of its newspaper, the *Epoch Times*, for the rights of Tibetans, Uighurs, Christians, indeed all oppressed Chinese, in the language of human rights and freedom of religion—although the language of anticommunism often stands out more clearly.

The Chinese government responds to any Falun Gong claim concerning vi-olations of human rights by claiming that as a "heterodox sect," the Falun Gong violates the basic rights of its practitioners. Thus we find no genuine dialog between the Falun Gong or its Western defenders and Chinese authorities in the thousands of pages of text produced by the conflict. The extreme reaction of the Chinese state to the Falun Gong underscores yet again the importance of state power as a context for the intersection of religion and human rights in China.

Conclusion

Consideration of the case of Falun Gong leads us to two reflections with broader implications for the future of Chinese religion in general and the relationship between religion and the politics of human rights. The first is a question of sources: how do we know how religious practitioners in China view questions of rights versus questions of state management and power? As already noted, Falun Gong is a transnational new religious movement par excellence, which, at least in its public face, has fully embraced human rights discourse in the defense of freedom of religion. The massive efforts mounted by the Chinese state to insulate China from Falun Gong pronouncements have not been a complete success. Diaspora practitioners continue to return to China, or to telephone friends, family members, and fellow practitioners; the Web filters erected by Chinese authorities are not always foolproof. We know that the Falun Gong "underground" continues to distribute pro–Falun Gong materials in China that bear the imprint of the transnational Falun Gong movement and seek to tell the "truth" about Falun Gong within China in a way that draws on human rights discourse. Yet nowhere in Chinese authorities' discussion of the Falun Gong do we find reference to human rights issues—nor to religious is-sues for that matter. Chinese authorities continue to deny that Falun Gong constitutes a religion at all. In the context of this essay, this raises a broader question: how would we know if Chinese Christians, or Buddhists or Daoists, for that matter, were articulating their concerns in a human rights idiom in negotiations with local members of the Religious Affairs Bureau?

The second issue raised by the Falun Gong case is the question of the very definition of religion, and thus the nature of the groups that could be embraced by the regime's policy of management and co-optation. One of the reasons that *qigong* and Falun Gong could become mass movements is that they were not perceived as religions and hence not regulated in the same way. At first glance, this case may appear exceptional, because the legitimizing aura of "science" that surrounded *qigong* obscured the movement's links to religion, but in fact much of Chinese popular religion is similarly situated on a complex borderland between mainstream, recognized religions and what the Chinese regime calls "feudal superstitions." Indeed, despite the Chinese state's best efforts to co-opt Chinese religious practice, vast numbers of village cults, syncretic and sectarian groups, and local practices, which for the majority of the Chinese constitute their religious reality (even if they would probably not use the word "religion") exist in an immense "gray zone" that authorities cannot decide what to do with.[76] Discussions in the mainstream press of the possibility of extending recognition, and with recognition some notion of rights to popular religion and/or to new religious movements, suggest that authorities are aware of the problem, but the tone of such discussions indicates that such recognition, even if extended, would go only to groups that agreed to submit to thoroughgoing regulation and model their behavior after, say, that of Chinese Buddhists.[77] This seems impossible, if only for logistical reasons: local religious groups do not have the capacity to put together a scriptural canon and establish seminaries, and the Chinese state does not have the manpower to regulate China's religious diversity. This means that even if China does succeed in bringing the five recognized religions into the fold of secular state management, this impressive victory would be only partial.

Many modern states manage religion, and China is in no way obligated to adopt American views about the importance of the freedom of religion or the relationship between religion and human rights. At the same time, a society cannot open itself to economic globalization without experiencing other aspects of the phenomenon. Some of China's religions are already transnational, spilling over China's borders to participate in global dialogs about religious freedom and human rights. Even if such discussions occur largely outside of China at the moment, they are seeping back into China, perhaps more rapidly than we would tend to believe. The Chinese regime's management approach to religion assumes a commonality of national interests—between the state and religious groups—which is potentially threatened by the transnational character of some religions as well as by the constant, low-level conflict that marks much of today's religious scene. Considerable state resources would be required to intervene frequently and throughout the country should the current religion policy fail.

Looking forward, the statist orientation of the current regime does not encourage human rights discourse, at least not outside of the very few topics the regime has chosen to defend its own version of human rights with Chinese characteristics. Leaders of the state-recognized Buddhist, Daoist, and Christian establishments try to conform to the image of a "good religion" and a "force for stability" celebrated in the policy documents of the Religious Affairs Bureau. Even Tibetan Buddhists and Uighurs in far west China often prefer to phrase their demands for greater religious freedom in terms of "cultural autonomy" rather than in the language of universal human rights, hoping to avoid putting Chinese authorities on the defensive. The underground Protestant church often follows a similar strategy by phrasing its demands in theological terms. Against this national backdrop, the transnationalization of certain religious and cultural communities, and their efforts to mobilize international public opinion, have brought human rights discourse into the Chinese debate, if so far only on the margin. Given the outside world's focus on China and China's continued opening to the outside world, religion and the politics of human rights is likely to remain an important issue for years to come.

NOTES

1. A Confucian revival is presently underway in China, driven both by popular enthusiasm and by the desire of China's leaders to cloak the party's authoritarianism in something more culturally palatable than socialism. The fact that Confucianism is generally not viewed as a religion in China has greatly facilitated the revival. See Sébastien Billioud and Joël Thoraval, "*Jiaohua*: The Confucian Revival Today as an Educative Project," *China Perspectives* 4 (2007): 4–20; Sébastien Billioud and Joël Thoraval, "*Anshen liming* or the Religious Dimension of Confucianism," *China Perspectives* 3 (2008): 88–106; Sébastien Billioud and Joël Thoraval, "*Lijiao*: The Return of the Ceremonies to Honour Confucius in Mainland China Today," *China Perspectives* 4 (2009): 82–100; Daniel Bell, *China's New Confucianism* (Princeton: Princeton University Press, 2008); and David Ownby, "Kang Xiaoguang: Social Science, Civil Society, and Confucian Religion," *China Perspectives* 4 (2009): 101–11.

2. Theodore De Bary has devoted considerable research to problematizing this view of Confucianism, and his work can serve as an avenue of entry to debates surrounding the question. See William Theodore de Bary, *Asian Values and Human Rights* (Cambridge: Harvard University Press, 1998); and William Theodore de Bary and Tu Wei-ming, eds., *Confucianism and Human Rights* (New York: Columbia University Press, 1998).

3. Important recent book-length studies on the history of human rights discourse in China include Marina Svensson, *Debating Human Rights in China: A Conceptual and Political History* (Lanham, MD: Rowman and Littlefield, 2002); Stephen C. Angle, *Human Rights and Chinese Thought* (Cambridge: Cambridge University Press, 2002); and Stephen C. Angle and Marina Svensson, eds., *The Chinese Human Rights Reader: Documents and Commentary, 1900–2000* (Armonk, NY: M. E. Sharpe, 2001). See also Dingding Chen, "Explaining China's Changing Discourse on Human Rights, 1978–2004," *Asian Perspective* 29.3 (2005): 155–82.

4. In addition to work on democracy and human rights activists in China proper, such as R. Randle Edwards, Louis Henkin, and Andrew J. Nathan, *Human Rights in Contemporary China* (New York: Columbia University Press, 1986); and Andrew C. Nathan, *Chinese Democracy* (Berkeley: University of California Press, 1986). See also the literature on Taiwan's democratization, for example, Joseph Wong, "Deepening Democracy in Taiwan," *Pacific Affairs* 76.2 (2003): 235–56.

5. See, for example, the remarkable reconstruction of the modern history of Chinese religion by Ye Xiaowen, director of China's State Administration of Religious Affairs, in a speech given at the Chong Chi College of the Chinese University of Hong Kong in February 2001, http://www.china.org.cn/english/features/45466.htm.

6. See Svensson, *Debating Human Rights in China*, chaps. 8 and 9.

7. See James D. Seymour, ed., *The Fifth Modernization: China's Human Rights Movement, 1978–1979* (Stanfordsville, NY: Human Rights Publishing Group, 1980).

8. These arguments are summarized in the White Papers regularly issued by the Chinese government, http://english.peopledaily.com.cn/whitepaper/home.html.

9. See Svensson, *Debating Human Rights in China*, chap. 11.

10. See Vincent Goossaert, "Le destin de la religion chinoise au 20ème siècle" [The Fate of Chinese Religion in the Twentieth Century], *Social Compass* 50.4 (2003): 429–40.

11. The religious policy of the Republic of China on Taiwan was very similar until the recent liberalization of religion following the end of martial law in 1987. See Paul R. Katz, "Religion and the State in Post-War Taiwan," *China Quarterly* 174.2 (2003): 395–412.

12. See Donald E. MacInnis, *Religion in China Today: Policy and Practice* (New York: Orbis Books, 1989).

13. See Pittman B. Potter, "Belief in Control: Regulation of Religion in China," *China Quarterly* 174.2 (2003): 317–37; Mickey Spiegel, "Control and Containment in the Reform Era," in *God and Caesar in China: Policy Implications of Church-State Tensions*, ed. Jason Kindopp and Carol Lee Hamrin (Washington, DC: Brookings Institution Press, 2004), 40–57; and Karl-Fritz Daiber, "Les associations des cinq religions officiellement reconnues en République populaire de Chine" [The Five Officially Recognized Religions in the People's Republic of China], *Social Compass* 51.2 (2004): 255–71.

14. See, for example, Ye Xiaowen, "Fahui zongjiao zai cujin shehui hexie fang-mian de jiji zuoyong" [Develop the Positive Functions of Religion in Encouraging Social Harmony], *Qiushi zazhi* 11 (2007): 37–40.

15. The original Chinese text is available on line at http://news.xinhuanet.com/zhengfu/2004-12/20/content_2356626.htm; an English-language translation can be found at http://www.amityfoundation.org/cms/user/3/docs/decree_426.pdf.

16. See Fuk-Tsang Ying, "New Wine in Old Wineskins: An Appraisal of Religious Legislation in China and the Regulations on Religious Affairs of 2005," *Religion, State and Society* 34.4 (2006): 347–73.

17. For an introduction to the state of Chinese Buddhism in contemporary China, see Raoul Birnbaum, "Buddhist China at Century's Turn," *China Quarterly* 174.2 (2003): 428–50. On Daoism in contemporary China, see Kenneth Dean, *Taoist Ritual and Popular Cults of Southeast China* (Princeton: Princeton University Press, 1993), and Lai Chi-Tim, "Daoism in China Today, 1980–2002," *China Quarterly* 174.2 (2003): 414–27.

18. See, for example, China's White Paper on Freedom of Religion Belief in China, issued by the State Council in 1997, http://english.peopledaily.com.cn/whitepaper/18.html; or Ye Xiaowen, "China's Religions: Retrospect and Prospect," address presented at Chong Chi College of the Chinese University of Hong Kong, February 19, 2001, http://www.china.org.cn/english/features/45466.htm. Western scholars generally agree that Chinese Buddhism and Daoism are undergoing a significant revival. See, among others, Birnbaum, "Buddhist China at Century's Turn"; and Lai, "Daoism in China Today, 1980–2002." At the same time, the dimensions of the revivals are difficult to measure in the sense that neither the Buddhist nor the Daoist faithful are required to register with the local temple.

19. Zhang Jialin, "Dangdai Zhongguo dalu zongjiao zhengce bianqian jiqi yingxiang: jingying tujing lunshu"[Changes in Religion Policy on Contemporary Mainland China and Their Influence, from the Perspective of China's Religious Elites], in *Guojia yu zongjiao zhengce* [State and Religion Policy], ed. Zhang Jialin, (Taibei: Wenjing shuju, 2005), 256ff.

20. See Raoul Birnbaum, "Buddhist China at Century's Turn," 434ff.

21. See Robert P. Weller, *Alternate Civilities: Democracy and Culture in China and Taiwan* (Boulder, CO: Westview Press, 1999); and André Laliberté, *The Politics of Buddhist Organizations in Taiwan, 1989–2003: Safeguard the Faith, Building a Pure Land, Helping the Poor* (New York: RoutledgeCurzon, 2004).

22. Lai Chi-Tim, "Daoism in China Today, 1980–2002," 417.

23. Kenneth Dean, "China's Second Government: Regional Ritual Systems of the Putian Plains," in *Shehui, minzu yu wenhua zhanyan guoji yantaohui lunwenji* [Collected papers from the International Conference on Social, Ethnic and Cultural Transformation] (Taipei: Centre for Chinese Studies, 2001), 77–109.

24. Among the most valuable introductions to the Protestant revival in China, see Daniel H. Bays, "Chinese Protestant Christianity Today," *China Quarterly* 174.2 (2003): 488–504; Ryan Dunch, "Protestant Christianity in China Today: Fragile, Fragmented, Flourishing," in *China and Christianity: Burdened Past, Hopeful Future*, ed. Stephen Uhally, Jr., and Xiaoxin Wu (New York: M. E. Sharpe, 2001), 195–216; Alan Hunter and Kim-Kwong Chan, *Protestantism in Contemporary China* (Cambridge, UK: Cambridge University Press, 1993); Donald E. MacInnis, *Religion in China Today: Policy and Practice* (New York: Orbis Books, 1989). On China's Catholics, see Richard Madsen, *China's Catholics: Tragedy and Hope in an Emerging Civil Society* (Los Angeles and Berkeley: University of California Press, 1998); Richard Madsen, "Catholic Revival during the Reform Era," *China Quarterly* 174.2 (2003): 468–87.

25. Philip L. Wickeri's excellent biography of K. H. Ting, the most important leader of China's Three-Self Protestant movement in the communist era, illustrates the importance of taking the religious convictions and efforts of this movement seriously. See Philip L. Wickeri, *Reconstructing Christianity in China: K. H. Ting and the Chinese Church* (Maryknoll, NY: Orbis Books, 2007).

26. See estimate in G. T. Brown, *Christianity in the People's Republic of China* (Atlanta: John Knox Press, 1986), 23.

27. The fifty million figure is in Tony Lambert, *China's Christian Millions* (London: Monarch Books, 1999); the 110 million figure comes from Yie Xiaowen, the director of the Chinese State Administration for Religious Affairs, who revealed in internal

meetings that the number of Christians in China had reached 130 million by the end of 2006, including about twenty million Catholics. See "The Annual Report on Persecution of Chinese House Churches by Province," China Aid Association, January 2007, http://chinaaid.org/pdf/2006_persecution_e.pdf. The numbers of Protestants include both those affiliated with the officially approved churches and those part of the "underground" house church movement (see later in the chapter), who constitute a large majority of Protestants.

28. Fenggang Yang, "Lost in the Market, Saved at McDonald's: Conversion to Christianity in Urban China," *Journal for the Scientific Study of Religion* 44.4 (2005): 429.

29. Ibid.

30. See http://www.amitynewsservice.org/page.php?page=1613.

31. An eloquent illustration of this important development can be found in Jean-Louis Rocca, *La condition chinoise: capitalisme, mise au travail et résistances dans la Chine des réformes* [The Chinese Condition: Capitalism, Work and Resistance in Reform-era China] (Paris: Karthala, 2006).

32. The "house church" movement is discussed in Bays, "Chinese Protestant Christianity Today," and is closely followed by many missionary groups. The following discussion is based largely on Jason Kindopp, "China's War on 'Cults,'" *Current History* 100.651 (2002): 259–66.

33. For an introduction to this vision, see http://www.backtojerusalem.com/. The more fundamentalist vision of many house churches, as opposed to the liberal worldliness of the leaders of the Three-Self Protestant movement, is another important obstacle to bringing the two movements together. See Wickeri, *Reconstructing Christianity in China.*

34. Kindopp, "China's War on 'Cults,'" 265.

35. See Richard Madsen, *China's Catholics*; and Madsen, "Catholic Revival during the Reform Era."

36. See Philip Lauri Wickeri, *Seeking the Common Ground: Protestant Christianity, the Three-Self Movement, and China's United Front* (Maryknoll, NY: Orbis Books, 1988).

37. See Fenggang Yang, *Chinese Christians in America: Conversion, Assimilation, and Adhesive Identities* (University Park, PA: Penn State University Press, 1999); and Fenggang Yang, "The Chinese Gospel Church: The Sinicization of Christianity," in *Religion and the New Immigrants: Continuities and Adaptations in Immigrant Congregations*, ed. H. R. Ebaugh and J. S. Chafetz (Walnut Creek, CA: AltaMira Press, 2000), 89–107.

38. Information on these organizations may be found on their Web sites: the China Aid Association at www.chinaaid.org; the Church in China at www.churchinchina.com; the Voice of the Martyrs at www.persecution.net; and Christian Solidarity Worldwide at www.cswusa.com.

39. These themes are developed at greater length in Jason Kindopp, "Policy Dilemmas in China's Church-State Relations: An Introduction," in *God and Caesar in China*, 1–22.

40. The reigning English-language authority on modern Tibet is Melvyn C. Goldstein, whose many books include *The Snow Lion and the Dragon: China, Tibet, and the Dalai Lama* (Berkeley: University of California Press, 1997); *Tibet, China and the*

United States: Reflections on the Tibet Question (Washington, DC: Atlantic Council of the United States, 1995); *A History of Modern Tibet, 1913–1951: The Demise of the Lamaist State* (Berkeley: University of California Press, 1989); and Melvyn C. Goldstein and Matthew T. Kapstein, eds., *Buddhism in Contemporary Tibet: Religious Revival and Cultural Identity* (Berkeley: University of California Press, 1998). For a sophisticated discussion of Tibetan Buddhism, see Robert A. F. Thurman, *Essential Tibetan Buddhism* (San Francisco: HarperSanFrancisco, 1995). For a helpful overview of the recent evolution of events in Tibet, see Colin P. Mackerras, "People's Republic of China: A Background Paper on the Situation of the Tibetan Population," commissioned by United Nations High Commissioner for Refugees, Protection Information Section (DIP), February 2005, www.unhcr.org/home/RSDCOI/423ea9094.pdf.

41. This section draws largely on Mackerras, "People's Republic of China."

42. Goldstein, "The Revival of Monastic Life in Drepung Monastery," in *Buddhism in Contemporary Tibet*, 15.

43. People's Republic of China, Information Office of the State Council, "Fifty Years of Progress in China's Human Rights," *Beijing Review* 43.9 (2000), 49; People's Republic of China, Information Office of the State Council, *Regional Ethnic Autonomy in Tibet* (Beijing, May 2004).

44. See A. T. Grunfeld, "A Brief Survey of Tibetan Relations with the United States," in *Tibet and Her Neighbours: A History*, ed. A. McKay (London: Edition Hansjörg Mayer, 2003), 22–32.

45. A partial list of his speeches can be found at http://www.tibet.com/DL/and at http://www.fpmt.org/teachers/hhdl/speeches.asp.

46. See Orville Schell, *Virtual Tibet: Searching for Shangri-La from the Himalayas to Hollywood* (New York: Henry Holt, 2000); and for a longer term perspective, Donald S. Lopez, *Prisoners of Shangri-La: Tibetan Buddhism and the West* (Chicago: University of Chicago Press, 1998).

47. See "Gere Urges Germany to Press China," news.yahoo.com/s/ap/20070212/ap_en_mo/richard_gere.

48. See Barry Sautman, "The Tibet Issue in Post-Summit Sino-American Relations," *Pacific Affairs* 72.1 (1999): 7–21; and David Sanger, "Ideas and Trends: Karma and Helms; A Stick for China, a Carrot for Tibet's Lobby," *New York Times*, July 11, 1999.

49. See Geeta Pandey, "Exiles Question Dalai Lama's Non-Violence," BBC News, March 18, 2008, http://news.bbc.co.uk/2/hi/south_asia/7302661.stm.

50. Some Muslims argue that these figures seriously undercount China's Muslim population, citing pre-1949 numbers that estimated the population of Muslims in the 1930s and 1940s as between forty-five million and fifty million, leading them to project a current population of as many as 150 million now. See, for example, http://www.islamicpopulation.com/china_muslim.html. Such estimates are rejected by most academic authorities.

51. The leading English-language scholar on China's Muslims is Dru C. Gladney; see his *Muslim Chinese: Ethnic Nationalism in the People's Republic* (Cambridge: Council on East Asian Studies, Harvard University, Harvard University Press, 1996); and *Dislocating China: Reflections on Muslims, Minorities, and Other Subaltern Subjects* (Chicago: University of Chicago Press, 2004). See also Michael Dillon, *Xinjiang:*

China's Muslim Far Northwest (New York: RoutledgeCurzon, 2004); Michael Dillon, *China's Muslim Hui Community: Migration, Settlement and Sects* (Richmond, Surrey: Curzon, 1999); Michael Dillon, *China's Muslims* (Hong Kong; New York: Oxford University Press, 1996); and Raphael Israeli, *Islam in China: Religion, Ethnicity, Culture, and Politics* (Lanham, MD: Lexington Books, 2002).

52. "Hui" was a category imposed on China's Muslims in the 1950s, inspired by ethnic minority policy in the Soviet Union.

53. http://www.china.com.cn/chinese/zhuanti/166597.htm.

54. See Dru C. Gladney, "Sino-Middle Eastern Perspectives and Relations since the Gulf War: Views from Below," *International Journal of Middle East Studies* 26.4 (1994): 677–91.

55. Colin Mackerras, "Some Issues of Ethnic and Religious Identity among China's Islamic Peoples," *Asian Ethnicity* 6.1 (February 2005): 5. Other groups include Kazaks (1.2 million), and smaller groups such as the Kirgiz, Uzbeks, Tatars, and Tajiks.

56. Justin Jon Rudelson, *Oasis Identities, Uighur Nationalism along China's Silk Road* (New York: Columbia University Press, 1997).

57. Dru C. Gladney, "Islam in China: Accommodation or Separatism?" *China Quarterly* 174.2 (2003): 461.

58. See Nicolas Becquelin, "Xinjiang in the Nineties," *China Journal* 44 (July 2000): 88.

59. Gladney, "Islam in China: Accommodation or Separatism?" 463.

60. Ibid., 455ff.

61. Ibid., 458.

62. Becquelin, 89.

63. Kazakstan has forced the disbanding of several Uighur separatist organizations, and Kyrgyzstan, home to some 80,000 Uighurs, has prohibited the establishment of a Xinjiang Uighur party-in-exile. Both countries have handed over Uighur dissidents to Chinese authorities. See Becquelin, 70–71.

64. http://www.Uighurcongress.org/En/AboutWUC.asp?mid=1095738888.

65. See "In the Spotlight: East Turkestan Independence Movement," at http://www.cdi.org/terrorism/etim.cfm, the site of the Center for Defense Information.

66. Becquelin, 71.

67. Basic sources on the Falun Gong include David Ownby, *Falun Gong and China's Future* (New York: Oxford University Press, 2008); David Ownby, "Qigong, Falun Gong, and the Body Politic in China," in *China beyond the Headlines*, ed. Lionel Jensen and Timothy Westin (Boulder, CO: Rowman and Littlefield 2006), 90–111; and Maria Hsia Chang, *Falun Gong: The End of Days* (New Haven: Yale University Press, 2004).

68. The indispensable introduction to *qigong* is David A. Palmer, *Qigong Fever: Body, Science, and Utopia in China* (New York: Columbia University Press, 2007). See also Nancy C. Chen, *Breathing Spaces: Qigong, Psychiatry, and Healing in China* (New York: Columbia University Press, 2003); and Zhu Xiaoyang and Benjamin Penny, eds., "The Qigong Boom," *Chinese Sociology and Anthropology* 27.1 (1994): 3–94.

69. These experiments are discussed in Palmer, *Qigong Fever*, chap. 2.

70. Nancy C. Chen, "Urban Spaces and Experiences of Qigong," in *Urban Spaces in Contemporary China*, ed. Deborah Davis (Washington and Cambridge: Woodrow Wilson Centre Press and Cambridge University Press, 1995), 347–61.

71. The following discussion of Falun Gong is based on Ownby, *Falun Gong and China's Future*.

72. See discussion in Palmer, *Qigong Fever*, chap. 8.

73. See Tan Songqiu, Qin Baoqi, and Kong Xiangtao, *Falungong yu minjian mimi jieshe: xiejiao Falungong neimu de da jiemi* [Falungong and Popular Secret Societies: Exposing the Inner Secrets of the Falungong Cult] (Fuzhou: Fujian renmin chubanshe, 1999), 93.

74. The most important are www.falundafa.org and www.clearwisdom.net.

75. See http://www.faluninfo.net/category/10/.

76. See Fenggang Yang's excellent essay, "The Red, Black, and Gray Markets of Religion in China," *Sociological Quarterly* 47 (2006): 93–122.

77. See, for example, Huang Xianian, "Dui dangdai xinxing zongjiao xianxiang de sikao: Jiantan xinxing zongjiao zai Zhongguo" [Thoughts on Contemporary New Religious Movements, and on New Religious Movements in China], *Shijie zongjiao wenhua* 1 (2007): 6–10.

BIBLIOGRAPHY

Angle, Stephen C. *Human Rights and Chinese Thought*. Cambridge: Cambridge University Press, 2002.

Angle, Stephen C., and Marina Svensson, eds. *The Chinese Human Rights Reader: Documents and Commentary, 1900–2000*. Armonk, NY: M. E. Sharpe, 2001.

Bays, Daniel H. "Chinese Protestant Christianity Today." *China Quarterly* 174.2 (2003): 488–504.

Becquelin, Nicolas. "Xinjiang in the Nineties." *China Journal* 44 (July 2000): 65–90.

Bell, Daniel. *China's New Confucianism*. Princeton: Princeton University Press, 2008.

Billioud, Sébastien and Joël Thoraval. "*Jiaohua*: The Confucian Revival Today as an Educative Project." *China Perspectives* 4 (2007): 4–20.

———. "*Anshen liming* or the Religious Dimension of Confucianism," *China Perspectives* 3 (2008): 88–106.

———. "*Lijiao*: The Return of the Ceremonies to Honour Confucius in Mainland China Today." *China Perspectives* 4 (2009): 82–100.

Birnbaum, Raoul. "Buddhist China at Century's Turn." *China Quarterly* 174.2 (2003): 428–50.

Brown, G. T. *Christianity in the People's Republic of China*. Atlanta: John Knox Press, 1986.

Chang, Maria Hsia. *Falun Gong: The End of Days*. New Haven: Yale University Press, 2004.

Chen, Dingding. "Explaining China's Changing Discourse on Human Rights, 1978–2004." *Asian Perspective* 29.3 (2005): 155–82.

Chen, Nancy C. *Breathing Spaces: Qigong, Psychiatry, and Healing in China*. New York: Columbia University Press, 2003.

———. "Urban Spaces and Experiences of Qigong." In *Urban Spaces in Contemporary China*, ed. Deborah Davis. 347–61. Washington, DC, and Cambridge: Woodrow Wilson Centre Press and Cambridge University Press, 1995.

Daiber, Karl-Fritz. "Les associations des cinq religions officiellement reconnues en

République populaire de Chine" [The Five Officially Recognized Religions in the People's Republic of China]. *Social Compass* 51.2 (2004): 255–71.

De Bary, William Theodore. *Asian Values and Human Rights*. Cambridge: Harvard University Press, 1998.

De Bary, William Theodore, and Tu Wei-ming, eds. *Confucianism and Human Rights*. New York: Columbia University Press, 1998.

Dean, Kenneth. *Taoist Ritual and Popular Cults of Southeast China*. Princeton: Princeton University Press, 1993.

———. "China's Second Government: Regional Ritual Systems of the Putian Plains," in *Shehui, minzu yu wenhua zhanyan guoji yantaohui lunwenji* [Collected papers from the International Conference on Social, Ethnic and Cultural Transformation], 77–109. Taipei: Centre for Chinese Studies, 2001.

Dillon, Michael. *China's Muslim Hui Community: Migration, Settlement and Sects*. Richmond, Surrey: Curzon, 1999.

———. *China's Muslims*. New York: Oxford University Press, 1996.

———. *Xinjiang: China's Muslim Far Northwest*. London: RoutledgeCurzon, 2004.

Dunch, Ryan. "Protestant Christianity in China Today: Fragile, Fragmented, Flourishing." In *China and Christianity: Burdened Past, Hopeful Future*, ed. Stephen Uhally, Jr., and Xiaoxin Wu, 195–216. New York: M. E. Sharpe 2001.

Edwards, R. Randle, Louis Henkin, and Andrew J. Nathan. *Human Rights in Contemporary China*. New York: Columbia University Press, 1986.

Gladney, Dru C. "Sino-Middle Eastern Perspectives and Relations since the Gulf War: Views from Below." *International Journal of Middle East Studies* 26.4 (1994): 677–91.

———. *Dislocating China: Reflections on Muslims, Minorities, and Other Subaltern Subjects*. Chicago: University of Chicago Press, 2004.

———. "Islam in China: Accommodation or Separatism?" *China Quarterly* 174.2 (2003): 451–67.

———. *Muslim Chinese: Ethnic Nationalism in the People's Republic*. Cambridge: Council on East Asian Studies, Harvard University: Distributed by Harvard University Press, 1996.

Goldstein, Melvyn C. *A History of Modern Tibet, 1913–1951: The Demise of the Lamaist State*. Berkeley: University of California Press, 1989.

———. *The Snow Lion and the Dragon: China, Tibet, and the Dalai Lama*. Berkeley: University of California Press, 1997.

———. *Tibet, China and the United States: Reflections on the Tibet Question*. Washington, DC: Atlantic Council of the United States, 1995.

———. "The Revival of Monastic Life in Drepung Monastery." In *Buddhism in Contemporary Tibet: Religious Revival and Cultural Identity*, ed. Melvyn C. Goldstein and Matthew T. Kapstein, 15–29. Berkeley: University of California Press, 1998.

Goldstein, Melvyn C., and Matthew T. Kapstein, eds. *Buddhism in Contemporary Tibet: Religious Revival and Cultural Identity*. Berkeley: University of California Press, 1998.

Goossaert, Vincent. "Le destin de la religion chinoise au 20ème siècle" [The Fate of Chinese Religion in the Twentieth Century]. *Social Compass* 50.4 (2003): 429–40.

Grunfeld, A.T. "A Brief Survey of Tibetan Relations with the United States." In *Tibet and Her Neighbours: A History*, ed. A. McKay, 22–32. London: Edition Hansjörg Mayer, 2003.

Huang, Xianian. "Dui dangdai xinxing zongjiao xianxiang de sikao: Jiantan xinxing zongjiao zai Zhongguo" [Thoughts on Contemporary New Religious Movements, and on New Feligious Movements in China]. *Shijie zongjiao wenhua* 1 (2007): 6–10.

Hunter, Alan, and Kim-Kwong Chan. *Protestantism in Contemporary China.* Cambridge, England: Cambridge University Press, 1993.

Israeli, Raphael. *Islam in China: Religion, Ethnicity, Culture, and Politics.* Lanham, MD: Lexington Books, 2002.

Katz, Paul R. "Religion and the State in Post-War Taiwan." *China Quarterly* 174.2 (2003): 395–412.

Kindopp, Jason. "China's War on 'Cults.'" *Current History* 100.651 (2002): 259–66.

———. "Policy Dilemmas in China's Church-State Relations: An Introduction." In *God and Caesar in China: Policy Implications of Church-State Tensions,* ed. Jason Kindopp and Carole Lee Hamrin, 1–22. Washington, DC: Brookings Institution Press, 2004.

Lai, Chi-Tim. "Daoism in China Today, 1980–2002." *China Quarterly* 174.2 (2003): 414–27.

Laliberté, André. *The Politics of Buddhist Organizations in Taiwan, 1989–2003: Safeguard the Faith, Building a Pure Land, Helping the Poor.* New York: RoutledgeCurzon, 2004.

Lambert, Tony. *China's Christian Millions.* London: Monarch Books, 1999.

Lopez, Donald S. *Prisoners of Shangri-La: Tibetan Buddhism and the West.* Chicago: University of Chicago Press, 1998.

MacInnis, Donald E. *Religion in China Today: Policy and Practice.* New York: Orbis Books, 1989.

Mackerras, Colin P. "People's Republic of China: A Background Paper on the Situation of the Tibetan Population." Paper commissioned by United Nations High Commissioner for Refugees, Protection Information Section (DIP), February 2005. www.unhcr.org/home/RSDCOI/423ea9094.pdf.

———. "Some Issues of Ethnic and Religious Identity among China's Islamic Peoples." *Asian Ethnicity* 6.1 (February 2005): 3–18.

Madsen, Richard. *China's Catholics: Tragedy and Hope in an Emerging Civil Society.* Los Angeles and Berkeley: University of California Press, 1998.

———. "Catholic Revival during the Reform Era." *China Quarterly* 174.2 (2003): 468–87.

Nathan, Andrew C. *Chinese Democracy.* Berkeley: University of California Press, 1986.

Ownby, David. "Qigong, Falun Gong, and the Body Politic in China." In *China beyond the Headlines,* ed. Lionel Jensen and Timothy Westin, 90–111. Boulder, CO: Rowman & Littlefield, 2006.

———. *Falun Gong and the Future of China.* New York: Oxford University Press, 2008.

———. "Kang Xiaoguang: Social Science, Civil Society, and Confucian Religion," *China Perspectives* 2009/4: 101-11.

Palmer, David A. *Qigong Fever: Body, Science, and Utopia in China.* New York: Columbia University Press, 2007.

Pandey, Geeta. "Exiles Question Dalai Lama's Non-Violence." *BBC News*, March 18, 2008. http://news.bbc.co.uk/2/hi/south_asia/7302661.stm.

Potter, Pittman B. "Belief in Control: Regulation of Religion in China." *China Quarterly* 174.2 (2003): 317–37.

Rocca, Jean-Louis. *La condition chinoise: capitalisme, mise au travail et résistances dans la Chine des réformes* [The Chinese Condition: Capitalism, Work and Resistance in Reform-era China]. Paris: Karthala, 2006.

Rudelson, Justin Jon. *Oasis Identities, Uighur Nationalism along China's Silk Road.* New York: Columbia University Press, 1997.

Sanger, David. "Ideas and Trends: Karma and Helms; A Stick for China, a Carrot for Tibet's Lobby." *New York Times*, July 11, 1999.

Sautman, Barry. "The Tibet Issue in Post-Summit Sino-American Relations." *Pacific Affairs* 72.1 (1999): 7–21.

Schell, Orville. *Virtual Tibet: Searching for Shangri-La from the Himalayas to Hollywood.* New York: Henry Holt, 2000.

Seymour, James D., ed. *The Fifth Modernization: China's Human Rights Movement, 1978–1979.* Stanfordsville, NY: Human Rights Publishing Group, 1980.

Spiegel, Mickey. "Control and Containment in the Reform Era." In *God and Caesar in China: Policy Implications of Church-State Tensions*, ed. Jason Kindopp and Carol Lee Hamrin, 40–57. Washington, DC: Brookings Institution Press, 2004.

State Council, People's Republic of China. *Regional Ethnic Autonomy in Tibet.* State Council Information Office: Beijing, May 2004.

———. "Fifty Years of Progress in China's Human Rights." *Beijing Review* 43.9 (2000), 49.

Svensson, Marina. *Debating Human Rights in China: A Conceptual and Political History.* Lanham, MD: Rowman and Littlefield, 2002.

Tan, Songqiu, Qin, Baoqi, and Kong Xiangtao. *Falungong yu minjian mimi jieshe: xiejiao Falungong neimu de da jiemi* [Falungong and Popular Secret Societies: Exposing the Inner Secrets of the Falungong Cult]. Fuzhou: Fujian renmin chubanshe, 1999.

Thurman, Robert A.F. *Essential Tibetan Buddhism.* San Francisco: HarperSanFrancisco, 1995.

Weller, Robert P. *Alternate Civilities: Democracy and Culture in China and Taiwan.* Boulder, CO: Westview Press, 1999.

Wickeri, Philip L. *Reconstructing Christianity in China: K. H. Ting and the Chinese Church.* Maryknoll, NY: Orbis Books, 2007.

———. *Seeking the Common Ground: Protestant Christianity, the Three-Self Movement, and China's United Front.* Maryknoll, NY: Orbis Books, 1988.

Wong, Joseph. "Deepening Democracy in Taiwan." *Pacific Affairs* 76.2 (2003): 235–56.

Yang, Fenggang. "Lost in the Market, Saved at McDonald's: Conversion to Christianity in Urban China." *Journal for the Scientific Study of Religion* 44.4 (2005): 429.

———. "The Chinese Gospel Church: The Sinicization of Christianity." In *Religion and the New Immigrants: Continuities and Adaptations in Immigrant Congregations*, ed. H. R. Ebaugh and J. S. Chafetz, 89–107. Walnut Creek, CA: AltaMira Press, 2000.

———. "The Red, Black, and Gray Markets of Religion in China." *Sociological Quarterly* 47 (2006): 93–122.

————. *Chinese Christians in America: Conversion, Assimilation, and Adhesive Identities.* University Park, PA: Penn State University Press, 1999.

Ye, Xiaowen. "China's Religions Retrospect and Prospect," address presented at Chong Chi College of the Chinese University of Hong Kong, February 19, 2001. http://www.china.org.cn/english/features/45466.htm.

————. "Fahui zongjiao zai cujin shehui hexie fangmian de jiji zuoyong" [Develop the Positive Functions of Religion in Encouraging Social Harmony]. *Qiushi zazhi* 11 (2007): 37–40.

Ying, Fuk-Tsang. "New Wine in Old Wineskins: An Appraisal of Religious Legislation in China and the Regulations on Religious Affairs of 2005." *Religion, State and Society* 34.4 (2006): 347–73.

Zhang, Jialin. "Dangdai Zhongguo dalu zongjiao zhengce bianqian jiqi yingxiang: jingying tujing lunshu." [Changes in Religion Policy on Contemporary Mainland China and Their Influence, from the Perspective of China's Religious Elites]. In *Guojia yu zongjiao zhengce* [State and Religion Policy], ed. Zhang Jialin, 247–322. Taibei: Wenjing shuju, 2005.

Zhu, Xiaoyang, and Benjamin Penny, eds. "The *Qigong* Boom." *Chinese Sociology and Anthropology* 27.1 (1994): 3–94.

10

Religious Communities and Rights in the Russian Federation

Marjorie Mandelstam Balzer

The interconnection of religion and discrimination in the post-Soviet period has been changing in often contradictory ways. Tensions concerning the definition and application of human rights are sharpened in part because of the multi-ethnic diversity and multilevel political structures of the Russian Federation. Neither the optimistic term "federation" nor the standard English "Russia" begins to capture the complexity of inter-ethnic and interreligious relations in multi-ethnic *Rossiia*. However, the short designation "Russia" is used here, especially given the efforts of President Vladimir Putin's administration and its anointed successor under Dmitri Medvedev to recentralize authority by bringing the country into a single "dictatorship of law" regime. This famous phrase itself reveals a nondemocratic approach to civil society in Russia. The focus here is on diverse social and religious conditions influencing the application of human rights standards and criminal code laws.

Vladimir Putin's populist approach to religion has set a tone for conveying to Russia's citizens the acceptability of diversity within limits. While some have termed this "managed pluralism," a more accurate designation may be "managed nationalism." A memorable politicized image has been the annual presidential Easter pilgrimage to the Church of Christ the Savior in Moscow, where Putin and Medvedev shared the light of Russian Orthodox resurrection with the late Patriarch Aleksei II and numerous other Russian politicians. Another salient, signal-sending image was Putin dancing during a folk Islam festival called Sabantui in Tatarstan several years ago. Buddhism was highlighted during Putin's 2006 visit to China, where he beamed in a sea of eager young Buddhists, watching a kung fu match. Judaism was validated as a traditional community during Putin's warm endorsement of Rabbi Beryl Lazar at the opening of a renovated synagogue in Moscow. Both presidents, in keeping with "United Russia" propaganda, have endeavored to be perceived and received as admirers of multiculturalism. But conditions enabling international standards of human rights for various religious communities at local levels have been far more problematic. To protect the power of "United Russia," explicitly religious or ethnic political parties are banned.

This chapter presents Russia's religious communities in interaction with one another, with the politics of centralizing presidential power, and with increasingly critical international scrutiny. Emphasis is on freedom of religious practice for individuals and communities, since an underlying premise is that most religious individuals thrive through the social dynamics, shared values, and networking of their communities. Formal legal support for personal freedom of conscience, amply affirmed in Russian law, is not enough.

Post–Soviet Russia's religious variety makes comparisons with other plural societies in the context of globalization especially challenging. Are sharpened religious fundamentalisms permeating Russia in patterned European ways? How do specific religious histories and international human rights values correlate with threats of reactionary Russian nationalism? To what extent do recent laws conform to United Nations and European Union standards? Potentially xenophobic trends are visible in the privileging of major religions designated as "traditional" with relative freedom to recover and stimulate their indigenous cultural practices in the nonlegally binding preamble to the Russian Federation's 1997 Law on Freedom of Conscience and Religious Associations. The favored four are Russian Orthodoxy, Islam, Judaism, and Buddhism, precisely those featured in the publicity mentioned earlier.

The 1997 law, more restrictive than the liberal and decisively democratic 1993 Constitution, has created a cumbersome, sometimes discriminatory registration and accounting process for numerous religions. It also has triggered further debate about whether Russian Orthodoxy is becoming increasingly dominant, a conservative force putting brakes on democratic momentum begun in the 1980s. Duma legislation, passed in 2005, activated in 2006, and guiding the registration of all nongovernmental and noncommercial organizations, has further threatened organizations with internationally based religious sponsorship, especially but not only Christian missions. Visa regulations have been applied selectively against religious communities. Antihate speech law—for example, the revised Article 282 of the Criminal Code prohibiting actions that "incite ethnic, racial or religious hatred"—is inconsistently applied. These tensions are played out in a chaotic post-Soviet environment where diverse congregations are competing for members.

My approach to key human rights questions and to the resonance of religious policy in various religious communities uses a political anthropology lens.[1] Debates within communities and contexts for community building are featured, in recognition of our urgent need to better understand the sometimes backfiring use of power in religious and more broadly cultural matters. My perspective highlights events and debates at various social and political levels, given the constitutional rights of ethnically based republics within Russia's "federation" to set their own cultural policies. I do not cover the whole former Soviet territory, despite some common Soviet legacies. In the twenty years since Mikhail Gorbachev's first ginger opening to *glasnost'* (frankness) and *perestroika* (restructuring), many former Soviet citizens have acquired personalized spiritual or religious orientations, looking to their own traditions, to Europe, the Middle East, and the Far East for diverse models.[2] Despite some recent, rose-colored Soviet nostalgia, most are deeply relieved at their release from antireligious Marxist propaganda and Soviet agitation, as signaled by jubilant celebrations of the Millennium of Christianity in 1988.[3]

Moscow and regional authorities increasingly privilege short-term security and stability considerations over long-term nurturing of European-standard human rights conditions that are perceived to be threatening and imposed from abroad. Putin addressed this directly when he stated at 2007 meetings with European leaders and on other occasions that human rights is "largely used as an instrument to influence political life inside Russia and as an instrument that helps some states to achieve foreign policy goals in relation to Russia with the help of some kind of demagogy." This theme has been taken up by the 2009 elected Russian Orthodox Patriarch Kirill I, and illustrates debates in and out of Russia about the cultural and shifting relativity of definitions of human rights, as Micheline Ishay's *History of Human Rights* suggests.[4]

Refined analysis of multicultural Russia must acknowledge Russian Orthodoxies, Islams, Judaisms, Buddhisms, and a range of other internally cacophonous religious views and practices, particularly when assessing human rights records and advocacy. The work of French theorist Bruno Latour is relevant, emphasizing shifting social and political networks and contexts as well as the significance of debates within communities. He uses the term "iconoclash" to describe the multiple levels of contestation that cultural changes in the twenty-first century entail, within nations and religious communities and transnationally. He thus renders religious dynamics far more complex than Samuel Huntington's "clash of civilizations," leaving open alternative possibilities for negotiations among civilizations and among cultural groups diversely defined.[5] Examples of cross-cutting religious politics include cooperation between some conservative Muslim and Russian Orthodox leaders in anti-immigrant rhetoric or joint condemnation of the efforts of the Russian gay community to organize Gay Pride parades in Moscow. More positive, but often ineffective, have been some ecumenical attempts to publicize and curtail human rights abuses in Chechnya and elsewhere, as well as the designation of official human rights ombudsmen in the regions and in Moscow.

Cases are selected here to illustrate an appropriate range conveying the daunting variety of civil rights violations that regularly occur and have been increasing in Russia, a signatory to all major international human rights conventions.[6] The Moscow Helsinki Human Rights Watch group (born to monitor the famed Helsinki Charter of 1975 signed by the Soviet Union) and the Moscow Bureau for Human Rights tend to categorize offenses in the rough division "grave" and "nongrave." A 2008 Human Rights Watch report documented the shifting of grave cases from Chechnya to neighboring Ingushetia, where violent raids, extrajudicial executions, torture, forced disappearances, and abductions have accelerated, despite denials by the republic's official "ombudsman."[7] Field data analyzed according to the Moscow-based SOVA Center for Information and Analysis, as well as European Union and United Nations definitions yield more nuanced working distinctions: Chechnya and North Caucasus war zone atrocities, additional overt illegality that goes unpunished, social bigotry cases, violence against activists, and symbolic violations. The "symbolic" violations can be quite significant, since they may well indicate emerging patterns that develop or feed into social bigotry and outright criminality. The Chechnya war and its spillover into neighboring North Caucasus republics have created cadres of disillusioned Russian youth who have returned from the war to far-flung regions often polarized and sometimes hardened into anti-Muslim gang members or corrupt local police. These categories interrelate in negative, synergistic ways. Perceptions matter: when street incidents of Islamophobia or anti-Semitism are categorized by police as mere "hooliganism," it sends a signal suggesting bigotry may be overlooked and some kinds of religious nationalism may be rewarded.

I cover here major trends of the post-Soviet period concerning religion and politics in Russia, with attention to positive and negative human rights implications. Fissures and values within religious communities are linked to international concerns and legal actions where relevant. In the process, I explore whether the Russian Orthodox Church has become "first among equals" in influencing state policies concerning religion, whether recent political dynamics annul earlier fledgling democratic trends, and whether cultural revitalization trends can be compatible with international standards of tolerance. Religion emerges as a kaleidoscope through which to see shifting democratic and authoritarian values in Russian society, their implications for human rights, and their political contestation.

A Chosen Few? Recent Trends and Their Human Rights Ramifications

Diversity and Competition

An increasing diversity of religious possibilities increases competition among religious and national communities. Rough estimates of the number of practicing Muslims in Russia, between fifteen million and twenty-five million, and practicing Christians, from sixty million to seventy-five million, indicate only relative proportions and reveal difficulties in deriving accurate statistics. Surveys show that between fifty million and seventy million out of 142 million citizens of the Russian Federation are self-identifying Russian Orthodox believers, with over 11,000 congregations registered. Protestants and Catholics together represent about 2 percent of the total population.[8] Precisely the perceived threat of this diversity has led to policies of attempted over-management of religion, as diversity becomes politicized and is sometimes misrepresented. Given Russia's admirable multicultural and multiconfessional variety, analysts must pay close attention to religious leaders and practitioners to assess whether terrorist-level thresholds of dangerous religious radicalization and chauvinism have been reached or are merely evoked for purposes of control. In a fragile social and political context, it is important not to project onto individuals or groups a distorted image of radicalization.

While increased diversity stems in part from Christian mission activism in a post-Soviet environment that missionaries perceive as a spiritual vacuum, proselytizing is not the only explanation for diversity. Local religions and new indigenous religious movements contribute to the complexity. Some religions not usually viewed in Russia as traditional have deep roots—for example, certain Protestant groups (Baptists, Evangelical-Lutherans of Ingria near Finland) and Catholics (including Polish Catholics of Siberia and Pskov). My fieldwork confirms British sociologist David Lewis's conclusions that converts to Protestantism, Islam, and other religions are not necessarily the main potential parishioners for Russian Orthodox revival. Non-Orthodox converts are often the children of mixed ethnic marriages, or people drifting spiritually and looking for alternative community moorings.[9]

Increased diversity in the context of competition for congregation members changes the dynamics and contexts for human rights at the group and individual levels. By 1996, alarmed security organs, including the Federal Security Bureau that succeeded the notorious KGB, had published a list of religions deemed to be potential havens for spies and brainwashers of vulnerable youth. This broadly defined list of "cults and sects," including the Reverend Moon's Unification Church, Falun Gong, Hari Krishnaites, Mormons, Jehovah's Witnesses, Christian Scientists, the Salvation Army, Baha'i, and many more, has been periodically updated. Propaganda concerning these lists contributed to the atmosphere surrounding the passage of the restrictive 1997 Law on Freedom of Conscience and Religious Associations. The law requires complex registration procedures for groups with less than fifteen consecutive years of state-recognized residence in Russia. Duma deputies and analysts, including some liberals who opposed the law, have confirmed that it was in part passed due to stirred-up fear of avowedly violent "cults" like Aum Shinrikyo well before any focus on Islamic terrorism.[10]

Many international observers have criticized its fifteen-year probation period for religions deemed nontraditional, and some internal critique marked its ten-year anniversary.[11] During probation, religions are restricted from attaining church property, pursuing regular youth educational programs, printing religious materials, training clergy, or inviting other clergy from abroad. On the basis of this law, fifty-six religious organizations, representing Protestants, Catholics, Muslims, Buddhists, and others, were given liquidation notices in 2008.[12]

The Russian government uses religion to further state sovereignty as well as diplomatic interests, sometimes choosing favorite leaders from within religious communities, similar to the reasoning behind governor appointments in regions and republics. What Nikolas Gvosdev has termed presidential "managed pluralism" in religious affairs has had ripple effects.[13] Favoritism famously appears to mean the singling out of one main loyal religious leader per major "traditional" religion, whether or not that leader is a paragon of moral virtue. This plays on and distorts already existing fissures and competitions within religious communities. It can make some communities wealthy, and impoverish others.

For the Muslim *umma* (broad community of believers), differentiations between Muslims of the "radicalized North Caucasus" and the more moderate rest are far too simple. Religious distinctions between Sunni and Shi'ites are overlaid with a huge and complex political spectrum only partially correlated to particular ethnic groups or foreign (Saudi vs. Turkish vs. Iranian) influences. The strictest adherents of Sunni Islam are associated with exclusivist and "fundamentalist" Saudi Salafi groups, often (mis)identified as Wahhabi, and railed against in the mainstream Russian press. At another end of the multi-rayed spectrum are the followers of "neo-Jadidism," Euro-Islam or "moderate Islam," sometimes also (mis)identified as "Russian Islam." Advocates such as the Tatar historian Rafael Khakimov explain that Muslims are expected to be actively engaged in political life, but that this does not make them Islamists advocating a Caliphate.[14] On one ray of the spectrum, with its base firmly in the middle, are various Sufi groups, including some in the North Caucasus, whose religious practices have roots in mysticism and pre-Islamic practice. At the radical edge of violence advocacy is the homegrown Caucasus Emirate founded by Chechen leader Doku Umar(ov) in 2007. Another ray, similar to Salafi groups but not condoned by them, features minority, radical Islamic cells using structures akin to those of terrorist organizations, associated with global movements such as Hizb ut-Tahrir, which is outlawed in Russia.[15]

Russian authorities have tried to penetrate and control Muslim diversity using structures inherited in part from the Soviet period. The government organizes some 3,700 Muslim communities into geographical Spiritual Directorates, with some competition between the European and Asian divisions. A separate Council of Muftis of Russia (SMR) is headed by Tatar moderate Ravil

Gainutdin. Its co-director, mufti Nafigulla Ashirov, in February 2007 called Israel a "malignant tumor" at a Moscow rally protesting excavations near the Al-Aqsa mosque in Jerusalem, but these remarks were retracted later by the Council, with apologies.[16] The Spiritual Board of Muslims of European Russia was led until 2009 by the controversial Tatar, Talgat Tadzhuddin (Tajetdin), based for many years in Ufa (Bashkortostan) and known for waving a sword while declaring "jihad" on the United States in a moment of passion in 2003. He has been allowed to pass on leadership to his son, although potential candidates included the head mufti of Kazan, Usman Khasret Iskhakov. The Spiritual Board has been used for propaganda against perceived threats to Muslim dignity, including U.S. entry into Afghanistan and Iraq, and meddling in Iran. The Spiritual Board supports official efforts to claim Russian membership in the Organization of the Islamic Conference.[17]

Recent Jewish political history in Russia is linked to an earlier international campaign during the 1970s and 1980s to allow Jews to leave the Soviet Union. The prolonged campaign, highlighted in human rights controversies dividing the United States and the Soviet Union, did permit about 1.2 million to emigrate, including the current Israeli politician Natan Sharansky.[18] The resulting widespread Russian-Jewish diaspora also created conditions for some internationally oriented Jewish returnees to invest literally and figuratively in the health of post-Soviet democratic society. By the Putin period, about 20,000 Jews were actively practicing their faith out of about 230,000 with some Jewish background. Registered Jewish communities numbered over 250, up from 106 a decade earlier.[19]

In post-Soviet Judaism, the culturally salient Sephardic/Ashkenazi split is overlaid by divisions between reform and conservative movements. Adjectival Jews—Jews from various homelands—often find themselves in tension and competition with each other—for example, Mountain Jews (sometimes called Tats), Georgian Jews, and more European or secular, Russified Jews.[20] Two main rabbis vie for leadership, with the conservative Beryl Lazar in presidential favor possibly because his rival Adolf Shaevich, considered the chief rabbi by many, was backed by the Russian TV magnate Vladimir Goussinsky, now living in exile in England. More positively, the president of the Holocaust Fund, Alla Gerber, is a 2007 appointee in the presidential administration's Public Chamber. After a fact-finding trip, well-known Holocaust survivor and U.S. Congressman Tom Lantos described the revival of Russian Jewry after decades of state anti-Semitism "a real miracle."[21]

In Buddhist communities, local and elite temple jurisdictions contrast with European New Age spiritual seekers. Prominent Buddhist heritage groups include followers of the Russian artist Nikolai Roerich and his family, as well as followers of the great Buryat-Tibetan Buddhist intellectual Bidiya Dandaron (1914–74). Approximately 200 Buddhist temples and *datsans* (temple complexes with schools) are registered with the state, accounting for an estimated 530,000 adherents.[22] Mongolic and Turkic groups mostly practice the eclectic, indigenous regional form of Buddhism sometimes called Lamaism, which combines features of Vajrayana and especially Mahayana Buddhism. Its lamas (monks) are usually of the Gelugpa school, associated with the Dalai Lama and his exile community in Dharamsala, India. Major tensions have developed between representatives of the Gelugpa school, based especially at the Ivolga monastery and *datsan* in Buryatia, and more European, less institutionalized Buddhists.

As with Muslims, the government attempts to exert administrative control through Soviet legacy "spiritual directorates."[23] A key issue is the degree to which indigenous Buddhist forms should be seen as national religions. Moscow authorities seem to prefer a "divide and rule" approach. Perceived European and Asian aligned groups have vied bitterly for a monastery complex called Gunzechoinei, as have local Buddhists and Buryatia authorities over other property.[24] More positively, many communities have been able to raise money for new *datsans* and new lamas. As lamas trained abroad in arduous programs in Mongolia, Tibet, and Northern India return, they have begun to head these new *datsans*. Some conflicts have developed between monks trained abroad hoping to purify traditions they see as too syncretic and elders accustomed to mixing shamanic and Buddhist practices.[25]

Religious competition often is played out symbolically in the urban geography of places of worship. In the non-Russian Republics and in Moscow, the politics of temple, synagogue, mosque, and church building, restorations, and registrations have intensified. Persecuting religious communities through constant pressure on their real estate is a major factor in undermining the social glue that has helped migrants from within Russia and from its "near-abroad" find their moorings in difficult urban environments. One high-profile case involved the eviction of a Hare Krishna congregation in Moscow. Particularly notorious has been the saga of a Muslim community in Astrakhan, where congregants surrounded their mosque in 2006 to keep it from being destroyed due to "unauthorized construction." The case went to Strasbourg's European Court of Human Rights after an unannounced Supreme Court hearing in Moscow upheld the demolition order. Mosques have been closed and destroyed in Siberian regions as well, unnecessarily antagonizing local and migrant Muslim communities. Closings and relocating of non-Orthodox churches also have become common, with some groups fined, threatened, and evicted due to local manipulations of housing safety regulations. For example, at the Pentecostal Church in Abakan an offending jar of pickles under a stairwell constituted a "fire hazard."[26] In sum, Russian Orthodox-influenced backlashes against congregations perceived to be alien have been visible in the closing or condoned demolition of non-Orthodox shrines. However, in 2008 a planned bomb attack on a complex outside Moscow symbolizing religious tolerance, with a mosque, church, and synagogue, was averted by vigilant police.

Looking West? Increasing Success of Non-Orthodox Christian Churches

A Muscovite raised in the Urals returned to his home village in 2006 and was surprised to find that Evangelical Christians had established a church there, before the local Orthodox Church had reconstructed theirs. For those who have been experimenting with diverse beliefs and memberships, Western-based Christian churches offer a nurturing community, material benefits, and ties to the outside world. As elsewhere, Evangelical Protestants are among the fastest growing congregations, with their numbers exceeding one million. Their success has come at considerable cost. Bruno Latour's iconoclash concept is exemplified by the 2002 prosecution of the Salvation Army. While Moscow registration officials eventually understood that they had taken military metaphors too seriously, the church was dragged through an expensive and emotionally draining court ordeal. The "Army" was prosecuted on a technicality: failure to reregister a religious organization that existed before the 1997 law by the 2000 deadline. Russian lawyer Vladimir Ryakhovsky saw its eventual victory in the Constitutional Court as a direct confirmation of the freedom of conscience and right to religious assembly enshrined in the 1993 Russian Federation Constitution. The only aspect of the 1997 law that was upheld was its provision against inciting religious hatred or causing harm to members of a congregation.[27] This relatively liberal interpretation provoked recent draft laws on religion in the Duma to make more explicit nationalist concerns about proselytizing Evangelicals, Pentacostals, Mormons, and others. Religious community members feel threatened by these Russian chauvinist trends in the Duma.

The Council of Churches Baptists have been prosecuted most consistently because they refuse on principle to register with state authorities, and because they tend to play orchestral instruments at street markets, attracting the attention not only of the public but the police. Local variations on police reactions have ensued. In the Sakha republic in 2007, a particularly ugly incident against Baptists distributing literature led to broken noses and a damaged car, caused by an off-duty policeman who reportedly asserted: "I'm Orthodox and I'm the boss here."[28] A problem for Baptists and other non-Orthodox denominations is a failure of the police to respond when arson is suspected or services are disrupted. For example twenty drunken youths interrupted an Easter Service at Reconciliation Pentecostal Church in Spassk, Siberia, seizing the microphone, calling the congregation "demons" and declaring: "the only Easter we have here is Orthodox."[29]

The *Kuznetsov and Others vs. the Russian Federation* case of the Jehovah's Witnesses has been particularly prolonged, beginning in 1999 in Chelyabinsk and only in 2007 winning a precedent-setting victory in the European Court of Human Rights on appeal. The Russian Federation, a 1998 signatory of the European Convention on Human Rights, was found to have violated articles 6 and 9, on the right to a fair hearing and freedom of religion. After 1999, the government imposed and the courts had upheld a ban on Jehovah's Witnesses, estimated at about 250,000 with 900 congregations, claiming that their teachings inherently incite religious discord and threaten social peace. Hearings that included testimony by psychologists stressed that the church tends to disrupt families and put pressure on members to acquire further converts, including minors. The Witnesses, also known as the Watch Tower Bible and Tract Society, have argued that they do not disrupt social order, and that they have been in Russia for over 100 years, albeit underground and persecuted during the Soviet period. Their refusal to bear arms may be at the root of official acrimony, along with their open evangelism, biblical literalism, refusal of blood transfusions, and nonecumenical approach to other religions. They have been among the groups vigilantes have targeted with arson and termed a "cult."[30] In 2009, fourteen of their Sverdlovsk congregation members were arrested for distributing "extremist" literature, in a tactic meant to set a precedent for all of Russia.[31]

For the institution of the Russian Orthodox Church, if not for individual believers, perhaps the most serious Christian rival is the Roman Catholic Church, given its association with the twin perceived threats of the Vatican and Poland. Statistics concerning self-professing Catholics vary from as high as the Vatican's figure of 500,000 to the 150,000 noted in a prominent sociological survey.[32] In 2002, the long, festering historical rivalry between these Western and Eastern Christianities burst into a publicity uproar with Orthodox Patriarchate protests over Pope John Paul II's official upgrading of Catholic dioceses in Russia. Three temporary apostolic missions became permanent dioceses and a fourth became the archdiocese of Moscow, with a newly appointed metropolitan, Tadeusz Kondrusiewicz. One of Pope John Paul II's final wishes was to say mass in Moscow. Instead, after he was repeatedly denied visas, his disembodied sermon was piped into a main Moscow cathedral in 2004. Visa problems for Catholic priests became standard procedure.[33] Protest demonstrations against a Catholic presence, ostensibly spontaneous, were organized by the Union of Orthodox Brotherhoods in several cities, including Novosibirsk, where a rally culminated in a petition left on the altar of the local Catholic cathedral. In Irkutsk, local residents explained to me in 2005 that their historical, partially renovated Catholic Church in a main city square was under pressure concerning "technicalities" of reregistration and that their bishop, Jerzy Mazur, was blocked from returning to his congregation after a trip abroad. These difficulties were particularly hard to understand, since the elegant church had harbored an exiled Polish congregation beginning in the late nineteenth century. They fit the letter of the 1997 law as a religious organization that had existed more than fifteen years, and the spirit of the law, in that their main ministry was to indigenous Polish, Lithuanian, and German communities.

Clues to the Catholic difficulties, including a protest petition organized in the state Duma, lie in their association with Western influences, perceived individualism, missionary values, and independent religious structures. In Pskov, Catholic cathedral construction was halted after the local Orthodox Archbishop Yevsevy wrote to President Putin: "taking advantage of the fruits of our current democracy, the enemies of our state are preparing a new expansion of Catholicism . . . though their vestments are bright, their deeds are dark."[34] Russian Orthodox responses to Catholics have been mixed, including a formal statement condemning perceived Catholic provocation, yet stressing the "Catholic West and the Orthodox East" could and should cooperate in "common Christian witness." Since Pope John Paul II died, a 2007 ecumenical conference offered promises of better communication, even as both sides utilize human rights discourse to insist on defending their religious communities. President Putin's visit to Pope Benedict XVI in 2007 helped defuse the tensions, reportedly by stressing common fears about secularism and Islam.[35] Metropolitan Kirill of Smolensk and Kalingrad, elected in 2009 as Patriarch of the Russian Orthodox Church, was reputedly the architect of this tentative rapprochement.

A combination of the legal environment, visa issues, and some tense on-the-ground encounters has led to increasing numbers of Christian activists being chosen for missionary work from inside Russia, rather than from outside the country. The 1990s era of mass Western mission activity is over, as variously defined "insiders" have been found more effective, due to politics, language, and broad cultural translation reasons.

Multiculturalism and Cultural Revitalization: Can Religion and Ethnicity be Delinked?

Russia's internal multiculturalism and dynamic religious syncretism renders problematic any neat linkage between ethnicity and religion, unsettling official assumptions about religious categorization being congruent with cultural communities. This in turn has implications for attempts at differentiating ethnic from religious discrimination. While some Russian sociologists and analysts interested in broad census categories have used rough correlations of particular religions with particular ethnic groups, such efforts are increasingly inaccurate. Analysis has been hindered by the failure to ask a "religious identity" question on the official 2002 census, where over 100 ethnonational groups were recorded.[36] Although it may have correlated better in the past, religion in post-Soviet and post-modern twenty-first-century Russia does not equal ethnicity or "ethnonationalism," to use Walker Connor's term. Clearly, not all ethnic Russians are Russian Orthodox—some are atheist, animist, "neo-pagan," or have converted to other Christian religions or Islam. The congruence of ethnicity and religious identity is relatively high for the Armenians of the Armenian Apostolic Church, but only about 450,000 out of approximately one million Armenians are practicing believers in Russia.[37]

Globalization does not eradicate history. The way religious traditions have changed in various communities has meant that each major religion has within it diverse variations of folk syncretism. For instance, many of the Muslim communities value *adat*, customary law, as much as or more than shari`a, Islamic law rooted in the Qur'an. Tatar communities have their own versions of Islam, merging pre-Islamic folk customs with Islamic ones. Such "folk Islam," including variants of Sufism, can be an important mitigating factor in stemming the incursion of more radical forms of Islam.[38]

In the middle Volga region, Tatarstan's renovated showcase Kazan Kremlin has a gleaming Russian Orthodox church near the republic's main mosque. President Mintimer Shamiev officially backed a moderate revivalist Islam. Whether we call this Euro-Islam or reform Islam or neo-Jadidism, it is controversial. Neo-Jadidism recalls a movement of Muslim intellectuals at the turn of the twentieth century, led by the Crimean Tatar Ismail Bey Gasprali (Gasprinsky). He advocated education for women, a synthesis of Eastern and Western philosophies, and a merging of Western technology with the wisdom of the Qur'an. His daughter edited a satirical journal called *Kha Kha Kha* that published a cartoon of unveiled, educated Muslim women as birds flying out of a birdcage, undermining numerous stereotypes. The Jadid movement means "New Way," so those who discuss its revival today advocate a "New New Way" in education and in institutional approaches to Islam. As in the past, they highlight the importance of reforming Islam from within.[39]

Tatar debates about Islam are closely tied to local, national, and international politics. President Putin used the phrase "Euro-Islam" in some of his speeches and has stressed the special, moderate nature of "Russian Islam." This has made some Muslims nervous: presidential endorsement has discredited their reform process among activist youth with access to alternative "global Islam" proselytizing on the internet. The Volga region is also known for closing certain madrassas (religious schools) deemed radical and associated with outsider mullahs, primarily but not only from Saudi Arabia. In nearby Mordva, where my 2007 fieldwork included a Tatar village near Saransk, villagers support mosques where mullahs are moderate, preaching inter-ethnic communication with local Mordvinians and Russians, and defusing problems among youths before they become serious. Long-term Russification, however, has hindered full Mordvinian and Tatar revitalization.

Buddhist communities are often associated with particular ethnic groups—Kalmyks, Buryats, and Tuvans (Tyvans). But community divisions are increasingly salient, as members of these ethnic groups have eclectic approaches to religion. Buddhists I have interviewed from Tuva, Buryatia, and Kalmykia tend to be more amused than worried that Putin has claimed in public that there is only one Buddhist republic in Russia: Kalymkia. Kalymkia is particularly unusual, in that it has a head lama, Erdne Ombadykow, who originally hails from the United States. Its Rolls Royce–driving, chess-playing, businessman-president Kursan Iliumzhinov has declared he would like to be a monk when he retires and has expressed resentment that republic boundaries were drawn in the Soviet period to ensure that one of the main Buddhist monasteries of European Russia is just outside his republic.[40]

At a magnificent new Buddhist temple in the capital of Kyzyl in the Republic of Tuva I was privileged in 2005 to meet the republic's most senior lama, Mart-ool Norbu, who affirmed his Buddhist community's appreciation of republic-level support. However, like most Buddhists I met in Tuva, he also condemned visa problems of the Fourteenth Dalai Lama, probably derived from Chinese pressure on Russian authorities. One Buddhist lama suggested the visa denial is a form of weakness, as well as denial of a religious community's rights, and that authorities should look to Mongolia for a model of a more open society.

Communities with pre-Buddhist and pre-Christian shamanic traditions are also recovering their religious pasts. However, leaders of republics associated with shamanism are sensitive about being labeled "Shamanist"—for example, in Tuva, Altai, Buryatia, Khakasia, and Sakha. Lively debates are occurring within indigenous Siberian groups concerning how best to recover traditions of folk healing and spirituality without appearing "primitive" or incurring undue scrutiny from state authorities or unwanted attention of missionaries targeting a perceived spiritual vacuum.

In the Sakha Republic of the Siberian Far East, an example of cultural revitalization is an elegant new shamanic temple on the bank of the Lena River in the capital Yakutsk. Called Archie Dieté or House of Purification, its birth is directly related to intelligentsia concern that Sakha (Yakut) spiritual traditions are being lost in the urban environment through competition with Russian Orthodoxy and other Christian proselytizing. Feeling reciprocally threatened, the local Russian Orthodox Archbishop German told me in 2003 that he was worried the new "pagan temple" was too close to his recently built Russian Orthodox church, and that the temple's steeple was higher than the church's cupolas. Russian Orthodox believers should not feel threatened, since supporters of Archie Dieté are far from radical separatist nationalists. Adding to the republic's religious tensions have been local authorities' efforts to justify evangelical Christian evictions and the cancellation of a Christian festival. A Sakha human rights lawyer insisted to me in 2007 that the fragile revitalization of Sakha traditional religion, which he traced back to ancient Scythian "tengri" worship, was jeopardized by Christian missionary "sects invading Sakha villages." For him and some Sakha in the villages, human rights should include protection from proselytizing. However, a broader perspective is provided by the Sakha republic ombudsman for human rights, Fedora Zakharova, who has assured me that few of the cases reaching her office concern religion. Most involve ethnic discrimination, tax, housing, and labor rights complaints.[41]

The human rights implications of continued popular and administrative linkage of ethnicity and religion are positive and negative. Paradoxically, official boasting about multiculturalism occurs alongside an official emphasis on individuals' religious liberty rather than on group rights. For example, Valery Tishkov, director of the Institute of Ethnology and Anthropology and head of the "Committee on Tolerance and Freedom of Conscience" in the presidential Public Chamber frames his concepts of human rights as predominantly oriented to individual freedom in a secular society.[42] He and other influential Moscow intelligentsia seem to have a Soviet legacy psychology that religious manifestations are innocuous if they are merely cultural "survivals" of a primitive past, but they are worrisome if they represent community lobbying or party-building efforts.

The complexity of human rights politics is revealed when multiple groups strive simultaneously for revitalization in the chaos of local registration and monitoring procedures, especially when the 1997 law guiding religious affiliation is combined with the 2006 law controlling nongovernmental organizations. Corruption and unevenness in the extent of cooperation between local secular authorities and local Russian Orthodox Church officials has resulted. A republic where non-Orthodox believers have faced registration problems is Mari-El. Here, in addition to Protestant missionary inroads, a revival of the ancient Finno-Ugrian Mari religion has flourished. But Mari traditionalists have been accused of nationalism and cult-like behavior by local Orthodox authorities.[43]

Local Russian Orthodox communities have rights to their own revitalization efforts, and some are pursuing these precisely in areas where they feel threatened by "pagan" revivals. Widespread church renovations have been combined with creative whistle stop trains bearing icon chapels (in Krasnoyarsk) and planes sprinkling holy water (in Irkutsk). A striking case from my fieldwork is the 1990s construction of a nunnery near Omsk in Siberia on the grounds of a former prison camp, built from tax-free donations collected within the country and abroad. Legends of miracle-working waters fed from a never frozen pond have spread, and the five-chapel complex has become a popular pilgrimage site. One nun linked a purifying natural spring with the rightness of Orthodox revival "on land so blood soaked nothing was previously able to grow." The nunnery values reveal an interesting intersection of God-ordained ecology activism with some literally grassroots Orthodox communities. However, in Russia the global ecology and human rights movements are usually connected with secular activists, and they have been facing recent pressures from government restrictions on foreign sponsors.

Cultural revitalization through religious activism can be a positive force for change, as recognized in the religious group rights provisions of many international legal instruments such as the 1981 Declaration on the Elimination of All Forms of Intolerance and of Discrimination Based on Religion or Belief. A review of the past twenty years in Russia reveals that religious vitality and the symbolism of cultural revival are often politicized in liberal, relatively nonacrimonious directions. As they look to their pasts, many in the Russian regions and the non-Russian republics are re-forming their ideas about religion and its resonance, sometimes learning that their ethnicity need not dictate religious identity. Each generation remakes its own traditions for and in new contexts, including expanding levels of globalizing access to the outside world. However, open-minded experimentation and community revitalization have been countered by less positive trends.

Increasing Extremism? Islamophobia, Anti-Semitism, Terror in the Name of Religion

Whether the discussion involves Tatars, Chechens, Russians, or others, the delicate balance between a liberal nationalism fed by moderate, tolerant religious forces and more radical nationalism exacerbated by religious extremism has been difficult to maintain. Each religious group seems to be developing its own version of fundamentalism, making claims for "purity" and gate-keeping "authenticity." Often these are minorities within a given community, but they are vocal minorities. For example, Russian Orthodox activists increasingly rail against the dangers of the pornographic internet, cell phones, or the McDonaldization of the spirit. Some are themselves using Orthodoxy sites to make radical nationalist claims. Xenophobic patterns in the way "fundamentals" have been advocated are emerging. This is relevant not only in the more publicized versions of extremist nationalist Russian Orthodoxy or radical Caliphate-oriented Islam but also in some of the indigenous minority communities. Fundamentalist leaders, who could be termed religious entrepreneurs, vie for attention among youthful followers.

Several cases serve as crucial alerts that in Russia human rights violations can escalate beyond freedom of speech or assembly issues. One example is the 2003 trashing of a Moscow art exhibit called "Caution: Religion" at the Andrei Sakharov Museum. The organizers of the exhibit, not the vandals associated with the Russian Orthodox congregation of a nationalistic priest, were charged and fined under the selectively applied antihate speech provision "Article 282." The museum subsequently featured a new exhibit challenging speech limits, although one of the original exhibit organizers, a Jewish artist, was found dead in Germany under circumstances her family claims involved Russian nationalist motivated murder.[44]

Official fear of extremism, at the cost of free speech, is illustrated by the ripple effects of the 2006 Muhammad cartoon controversies in Europe, after they spilled into bloodshed in parts of the Middle East and South Asia. Russian preemptive reactions included prohibiting the publication of any cartoons deemed to be potentially offensive to Muslims, leading to several newspapers being closed. But hate speech has been locally defined, capriciously prosecuted, and sometimes seemingly condoned, as ethnoreligious incitement against Muslim migrants has become far more egregious than the insulting cartoons.

The horrifying 2006 antimigrant pogrom of Kondopoga, Karelia, illustrates how a local riot directed against newcomer Muslim Chechens was exacerbated by Russian calls for solidarity on the internet. It reveals official mismanagement and lack of control of organized Russian nationalist neo-Nazi mobilization, as well as the difficulty of differentiating ethnic from religious enmity. Rather than using Kondopoga as a wakeup call to curtail violence, authorities have been unable or unwilling to prevent similar incidents that have occurred since, with less international publicity, across Russia in 2007–10. One of the most chilling aspects of these violent incidents is that perpetrators brag about them while soliciting reinforcements, so that what begins as a minor local incident can escalate or turn into copycat crimes. Another pattern has been light sentences for those who are caught, signaling some complicit bigotry among certain officials.[45]

. How popular are extremist Russian nationalist views? Survey results provide a mixed, incomplete picture. To the simple proposition "All religions should have equal rights in Russia," a 2005 response was 53 percent positive, down from 70 percent in 1996. The same academic survey indicated along with many other polls that Russian Orthodoxy was viewed most positively: 95 percent in 2005, up from 88 percent in 1996. Next in line in 2005 were Islam (64%), followed by Catholicism, Buddhism, Old Believers, Judaism, Lutheranism, Baptist, Krishnaite, Pentecostal, Adventist, and Jehovah's Witness faiths. The latter had a 35 percent negative rating, possibly due to massive adverse publicity.[46] Surveys sponsored by the Moscow Bureau for Human Rights, with support from the European Union, indicated an increase in xenophobic attitudes from 2005 to 2009, with specific nations, especially Chechens and Azeris, who are associated with Islam, rated negatively.[47]

Extremism becomes particularly potent when the idioms of nationalism and religious identity are joined in us/them hate language. The two most serious indicators are Islamophobia and anti-Semitism, with their alarming cultural acceptance among some ethnic Russians. Of these, the most destabilizing is Islamophobia, and the polarization that occurs when young people who are not radical Muslims are arrested with false evidence and broad crackdowns. Muslim leaders such as Dagestani Public Chamber representative Ramazan Abdulatipov warn of the counter-productivity of Islamophobia. It is one of the key tragedies in the radicalization of Chechen youths, whose movement went from advocating predominantly secular nationalist separatism to increasingly volatile Muslim solidarity by a war-torn, displaced generation poorly educated, vendetta-oriented, and self-destructive.[48] The bitter fruits of Chechnya can be seen in the regime of its youthful president, Ramzan Kadyrov, known for his personal ruthlessness, assassinations, corruption, filtration camps for those defined as disloyal, and for his switching of sides in the two recent Chechnya wars. His extreme human rights abuses were exposed in part through the valiant reporting of Anna Politkovskaia, murdered in 2006, and the national and international legal defense of Chechens by Stanislav Markelov, murdered in 2009.[49]

For Muslim communities, a grievance with international resonance has been the persecution of the Russian-Chechen Friendship Society, founded in 2000 to document and publicize human rights atrocities perpetrated by all sides in Chechnya. According to Oksana Chelysheva, a Society activist, "its staff and journalists have been threatened, beaten and even killed."[50] Based in one of the previously open, politically diverse Russian regions, Nizhny Novgorod, the group was shut down for violating one of the registration restrictions on nongovernmental organizations. The Russian Supreme Court ruled against it in January 2007, claiming that the group published the incendiary writing of the late assassinated president of Chechnya, Aslan Maskadov. They had published one of his many calls for a negotiated peace, given that an estimated 80,000 Chechens, mostly noncombatants, have died in the conflict. Their case was upheld in the European Court of Human Rights, and their new base is Helsinki. This case reveals a spectrum of concerns about the destabilization of Muslim communities in the name of stabilization, with huge implications for issues of respect for human life, freedom of speech and religion, and democracy more generally.

Across Russia, officials have used poorly researched lists of forbidden groups and banned literature to arrest "extremists." For example, possession of the inoffensive work of the Muslim Turkish philosopher Said Nursi has garnered up to three years imprisonment. Catherine Cosman of the U.S. Commission on International Religious Freedom stresses that Muslims have become "targets of widespread discrimination, media attacks, and occasional acts of violence." In 2003, she revealed, "the Russian Supreme Court reportedly met in secret and banned 15 Muslim groups because of their alleged ties to international terrorism," leading to police arrests.[51] Once arrested on sometimes fabricated criminal charges, including possession of weapons and drugs, suspects have been tortured in pre-trial detention or prisons, and starved in labor camps. The Commission's 2005–6 report estimated that 200 such cases had occurred, and subsequent reports indicate a further increase. Other reports confirmed the involvement of law enforcement officials in Ingushetia, under its appointed president Murat Zyazikov, in kidnapping, torture, and killing of civilians, including the death of a six-year-old boy accused of resisting arrest during a raid.[52]

The desperation of North Caucasus violence is epitomized by Beslan in the Republic of Ossetia. Not long ago a bastion of multiculturalism, Beslan is now famed as a nadir of terrorism in the name of Islam, after hundreds of schoolchildren and their parents were taken hostage on the first day of school in

2004. Lack of respect for human life characterized both the assailants and the official response; more than 300 hostages, mainly children, lost their lives.[53] Polarization of the whole region has since intensified, and is one aspect of dramatic events in October 2005 in Nal'chik (Kabardino-Balkaria) in the North Caucasus, where many were hoping to avoid the violence of Chechnya and Beslan. However, young armed demonstrators attempting to liberate friends and relatives they considered unfairly detained and tortured were shot by police. A detail lost in coverage of these tragic events was that some of the Muslim youth, including those killed by police, were wearing orange armbands associated with the Ukrainian revolution, not green ones associated with Islam.[54]

Within this embittering dynamic, concern about the rise of radical Islam and terrorism in Russia is legitimate. Deterring it, while respecting the rights of the law-abiding Muslim majority, is daunting, particularly in an atmosphere of mutual fear and polarization. One way to monitor a rise in more purist, fundamentalist, or "Islamist" activism is to note when signs appear at a saint's grave or other pilgrimage sites forbidding such "traditional" practices as folk healing or offerings at the site. It is already late to curtail radicalization with dialog when terrorist acts spread beyond specific war zones to planes, police stations, cafés, a school, stadium, markets, metros, and a theater. Islamist terrorism, linked to global networks and feeding international fears, thrives most readily in social environments where local conditions for polarization are already in play.

Several analysts, on the basis of survey research, have linked increasing Islamophobia and the relative decline of anti-Semitism, almost as if one dominant ethnoconfessional scapegoat group in Russia will suffice.[55] Certainly it is fair to say that official anti-Semitism has declined since the end of the Soviet period. However, anti-Semitic street crimes and propaganda have increased, with uneven prosecution and minimal jail time for some of the most serious cases.[56] One could argue that the social tensions reflected in Islamophobia and anti-Semitism are not "about religion" per se as much as they are Russian nationalist aggression in its most virulent, xenophobic terms. However, the idioms used to express this extremism are often religious. For example, the notorious "blood libel" accusations against Jews that were featured in the spurious document "The Protocols of the Elders of Zion" from the turn of the twentieth century have resurfaced in the twenty-first century. Jews are depicted as fostering "Judeo-Masonic" conspiracies to turn Russians into slaves with their brilliant science; they are blamed for the atheist Russian Revolution of 1917; they are termed a "fifth column"; and they are labeled as Christ-killers and "the antithesis of Christian virtues and spirituality."[57]

This discourse has consequences. After reading such slander on the internet in 2004, a young tough with downwardly mobile parents went on a rampage with a knife in a Moscow synagogue. In the same year, a series of grisly anti-Semitic signs appeared on roadsides across the country. Good Samaritans who tried to take them down were injured, for the signs were booby-trapped with bombs. Jewish synagogues and cemeteries have been regularly vandalized with graffiti. The case of a devastating attack that resulted in the death of a Jewish man in Ekaterinburg in 2005 was finally resolved in 2007. Five teens, aged twelve to seventeen, were found "guilty of beating a Jewish man, dragging him to a cemetery, and fatally stabbing him with a metal cross" from a grave head-stone. None received more than ten years' imprisonment.[58]

Combating extremism requires acknowledging that sociopolitical conditions for increased anti-Semitic and anti-Muslim violence have intensified in a combustible mix with racism and antimigrant sentiment. Jewish and Muslim sacred places have been defiled with vigor, organization, self-promotion, and sometimes with impunity. In 2007, officials first denounced as fraud a neo-Nazi video showing the beheading of two Muslim men, until the Dagestani family of one recognized their missing relative. Other similar videos have surfaced more recently. The accumulated effect of extremist incidents has led to increasing calls within and outside the country for more systematic prosecution of hate crimes, in order to better protect the rights of religious and ethnic minorities in Russia.

The Russian Orthodox Church's Rising Institutional Influence

Social dynamics at the level of street violence and their prosecution are only some of the conditions creating contradictory human rights trends. The changing political context of how the laws of Russia's formally federal system are enforced has laid recent presidential administrations open to accusations that the Russian Orthodox Church as an institution is increasingly influential. A valid distinction can be made between cultural dominance, due in part to the demographic majority of the Russian people in the Russian Federation, and political dominance. Yet they are interrelated and both are relevant. Under President Putin, recentralization, pulling away from negotiated federalism, meant the retraction of official and unofficial promises related to republic or local control of education, cultural programs, and values. President Medvedev's well-publicized interest in supporting Russian Orthodox values continues the trend, as did church-state discussions concerning a successor for the aging (now deceased) Patriarch of Moscow and all-Russia Alexei II.

Standardization of school curricula has downgraded local non-Russian religious histories. At the same time, the Russian Orthodox Church has successfully promulgated a "Fundamentals of Orthodoxy" program for primary and secondary schools. Introduced at first in only a few regions as a voluntary subject, a version was made mandatory in 2006 in many regions, most famously in Belgorod. On this issue, Metropolitan Kliment, to the delight of a predominantly Orthodox audience, belittled the secularly oriented minister of education: "Dear Andrei Aleksandrovich [Fursenko], do not be afraid of seeing priests in the schools. Be afraid of the fact that, without the light of faith and virtue kindled in young people's hearts, their attention will come to focus on drug abuse, tobacco-smoking, alcoholism, obsessive gambling and indifference. And preachers of chauvinism and cruelty will come to them."[59] The Russian Duma has endorsed the Fundamentals program, although the stand taken on education in the "Committee on Tolerance" of the Public Chamber has been more sensitive to the need for locally developed programs on religious history, devoid of proselytizing.[60]

Orthodoxy's institutional reach extends beyond the public schools into the placement of chaplains in hospitals, the army, and in prisons. Here the issue is not whether Orthodox priests should minister to clearly needy patients, soldiers, accused criminals, and their jailers, but rather whether the religious authorities of other denominations have equal access. The Russian Orthodox Church has signed formal contracts for activities in the army, with the border guards, and in jails, while other religious organizations are lagging behind but at least legally recognized as having the right to access. An early contract with the Ministry of Internal Affairs in 1996 guaranteed "favorable conditions" for Russian Orthodox clergy to conduct talks and church services in prisons, and news headlines blared "Priests behind Bars." Since then Muslims, Catholics, Protestants, and Buddhists have gained some access without formal contracts.[61] Positive publicity in the Russian press for "Moscow Patriarchate" activities in the army and air force, beginning in 1994 under Defense Minister Pavel Grachev, asserts that the Orthodox ministry will offer "moral-psychological, spiritual and social support."[62]

Fissures within the Russian Orthodox community are important given their clergy's access to all levels of Russian administration. Within Orthodoxy, the democracy promoted by liberal intellectual followers of the late Father Alexander Men' contrasts sharply with the legacies of the Russian nationalist Metropolitan Ioann (Snychev). This tension often prompted Patriarch Alexei II to mediate a middle path. The overwhelming 2009 vote for the conservative, wary yet worldly Patriarch Kirill I, former Metropolitan for External Church Affairs, indicates he too is a mediator. Another pragmatic, moderate religious figure, admired for peacemaking among religious communities rather than for missionary fervor, is the strategically placed Archbishop Feofan of Stavropol and North Caucasus.[63]

On the more strident nationalist end of the political spectrum, statements from the 2004 Bishop's Council and from some less authoritative Russian Orthodox priests lean heavily toward aggressive missionary activity, monarchism, fear of outside religions as sectarian and satanic, and fear of outsiders, especially migrants (read: Muslims) and Jews. Most notorious are the Resurrection Orthodox Brotherhood, the White Brotherhood, and some other brands of Orthodoxy mixed with paganism—for example, the anti-Semitic followers of

Oleg Platonov.[64] These vocal extremists have set a dangerous tone that equates Orthodoxy with chauvinist Russian patriotism. The ultra-nationalist Eurasian Union of Youths, in the name of defending their faith, attacked the headquarters of Mormons in Samara in 2007 by smashing windows and throwing smoke bombs. One activist sarcastically remarked: "we're building sovereign democracy and a healthy civil society."[65] President Putin condemned extremists, yet allowed the pro-Kremlin youth movement Nashi to march with some of the Orthodox youth groups and condoned some anti-immigrant aspects of a 2007 market labor law. The nationalist group Movement against Illegal Immigration was permitted to demonstrate on the new holiday Unity Day, November 4, which itself marks the 1612 expulsion of Polish-Lithuanian Catholics from Moscow. This leaves Vladimir Putin's personal Orthodoxy open to interpretation by those who side with the Russian nationalists. As Russian liberal commentator Masha Lipman put it, "propagation of tolerance is only a marginal policy for the Kremlin."[66]

The Orthodox Church's Social Concept, officially launched in 2000, is less xenophobic than some analysts feared. It prohibits direct church involvement in civic elections and permits civil disobedience under duress. While its paternalistic tone seems to discourage active citizen participation, Irina Papkova suggests its resonance has been more positive. Church membership, especially for youth, often correlates with relatively active voting patterns.[67]

A key patriarchate principle defining church/state relations is *symphonia*: "The state in such symphonic relationship with the Church seeks Her spiritual support, prayer for itself and blessing upon its work to achieve the goals of its citizens' welfare, while the Church enjoys support from the state in creating conditions favorable for preaching and for the spiritual care of Her children who are at the same time citizens of the state."[68] The church attempts to keep some distance from full government control, as the recent patriarchate election demonstrates. The church also has had valid grievances against specific state or local authorities. Some within the church hierarchy and laity warn that it is difficult for the church to maintain independence as a moral authority when the patriarchate is too close to Moscow and local rulers.[69]

Battles for the soul of Russian Orthodoxy have led to rapprochement with the Russian Orthodox Church Abroad.[70] Their ceremonial reunification in 2007, termed a Canonical Communion, may be a harbinger of greater openness to international "best practice" norms of human rights within the Russian Orthodox community. It was facilitated by the patriarchate's formal acceptance of Tsar Nicholas II as a martyred saint, and by reassurances concerning conflicting property claims, among other issues. In contrast, some official church policies have led to heightened tensions with dispersed "Old Believer" communities. While no longer termed "schismatics," some "Old Believers" are nursing recent wounds stemming from a widespread property transfer practice called "rebranding."[71]

The Russian Orthodox Church recently has couched its own traditions in human rights discourse. In 2006, Patriarch Alexei II announced a "Declaration of Human Rights" specific for Russia at the Tenth World Russian Congress. His introduction stressed provisions that acknowledge the specificity of "ethnic and religious traditions." But he added: "Does the country's legal system allow the people associating themselves with Orthodoxy to live in line with their tradition? Or is there a risk that we are standing on the threshold of a renaissance of paganism?" The same congress announced a new Human Rights Center to be based in Moscow to monitor the Declaration, with monitoring beginning in 2007.[72] The founding of this Human Rights Center superseded the President's Council on Human Rights and Development of Civil Society Institutions, allowed to lapse when President Medvedev came to power.[73] Such official attention to issues of human rights, as with the presidential ombudsmen program and the Committee on Tolerance of the Public Chamber, indicate shifting attempts to control civil society "from above." These window-dressing efforts run parallel to more independent monitoring groups, such as the Moscow Helsinki Human Watch Group, the Institute of Religion and Law, the beleaguered Russian-Chechen Friendship Society, the Union of Soldiers' Mothers, the SOVA Center, and the Center for Assistance in International Protection.

In 2008, Russian Orthodox Church positions were clarified at a Bishop's Council that adopted the document "Foundations of the Russian Orthodox Church teaching on Human Dignity, Freedom and Rights." Strident against political and material "selfishness," the document also warns against harm to "representatives of other cultures."[74] Guided by the future patriarch, Metropolitan Kirill, the document rejected a "secular concept of human rights." Instead, "while acknowledging that freedom of choice is a value, the Church insists that it is not an absolute value," and that the "combination of freedom of choice with moral responsibility is very important."[75] The same council dismissed the "schismatic" Bishop Diomid of Anadyr and Chukotka, calling on him to repent his criticism of the official church as too close to the Kremlin, too international, and too complicit in "satanic" rapprochement with "enemies of Christ," including the Orthodox Church Abroad and other Christian faiths. The council opened with a revealing street clash of Diomid supporters with Nashi, the youth arm of United Russia, seen by some as a ramification of church succession struggles.[76] While the patriarch's election was more decorous, it too revealed church divisions on critical issues of human rights, including Russia's intervention in Ossetia and Georgia.

Conclusions: Human Rights and State Wrongs?

Russia's religious diversity can and should be celebrated, despite its manipulation and politicization. The image of Patriarch Alexei II with other priests in 2002 exorcising the renovated St. Sophia chapel in the courtyard of the Soviet era KGB building in Moscow remains delightfully iconic. The Volga region in particular has historically been the site of multi-ethnic and multiconfessional mixing of religious tolerance and mutual respect among religious communities and practitioners. Despite some well-known pogroms, Russia has often been a good illustration of what the nationalism theorist and historian of China Prasenjit Duara calls "soft boundaries" among its ethnic groups.[77] Precisely for this reason, any trends toward the hardening of us/them boundaries that produce polarization and radicalization are disturbing.

Institutionalization of Orthodoxy is flourishing in a context of increased Russian chauvinism against indigenous non-Russians as well as migrants from the Caucasus and Central Asia. Non-Russians, well aware they are minorities in the country, often perceive their religions to be under some degree of threat. Statements by some Russian Orthodox clergy or Russian officials are perceived to be against Muslims, Jews, Shamanists, and lumped-together Christian groups that appear on lists of "satanic sects." Russian chauvinism has its own range, latent and blatant. In this context, the preamble and certain registration provisions of the 1997 Law on Freedom of Conscience and Religious Associations unfairly privilege "traditional" religions. The law places undue burden on religions that were underground or foreign in the Soviet period. Equally significant, all relevant laws are enforced unevenly, generating increased room for corruption in registration processes and increased need to appeal to a costly, unstable, and unpredictable court system. The Russian Orthodox Church correctly is perceived as first-among-equals due to its access to power brokers and social groups such as the youth movement Nashi. Whether Russian Orthodoxy should be a considered an official state religion is an open question, politically and analytically.

In Russia, ideals of religious freedom often are not fulfilled in practice. Analyzing ten years of application of the 1997 Law, Russia's human rights ombudsman, the cosmopolitan former ambassador to the United States Vladimir Lukin, was frank about its "ideological" preamble and legal deficiencies. He cited abuse of state authority to decide whose expertise may define extremism or enable religious group reregistration, and he condemned overuse of the category "sect" and overzealous banning of literature. He sided with international assessments of religious minority discrimination, such as "Catholics, Mormons, Evangelical Christians and Jehovah's Witnesses," and affirmed Russia's need to comply with Strasbourg Court decisions that have found Russia in violation concerning religious minorities.[78]

Like the Russian Orthodox bishops, historian of human rights Micheline Ishay has suggested that human rights are culturally relative and shift over time. Many anthropologists also have struggled with this issue of human rights relativity and the morality of imposing outsider priorities.[79] Seen through the prism of valuing cultural heritage and revitalization, I might have provisional sympathy for opponents of missionaries and for the compilers of the 1997 Law on Freedom of Conscience and Religious Associations. However, a slippery slope of pragmatic problems ensues, as we also must ask who speaks for communities struggling to balance degrees of freedom, individual and community rights, diverse definitions of democracy, and internal versus international public opinion. Russia's 1997 Law and subsequent nongovernmental organization and immigration control laws have been heavy-handed attempts at compromise protectionism in the name of state security and short-term appearances of social stability.[80]

In any human rights discussion sensitive to the perils of imposed Western "imperialist" values on other peoples, we need to consider how citizens within a given country respond to the state-level use of "us/them" discourse concerning "spies," "fifth column" infiltrators, and "outside agitators" for internationally connected religious groups. In Russia, these are not terms that most believers in religious communities use, although some local authorities have tried to redefine human rights to protect local religions. The continued existence of a more internationally oriented secular human rights community, with its veteran activist Lyudmila Alekseyeva as leader and model, shows that some democratic impulses are viable within Russia, despite presidential attempts to control and nationalize human rights. Public protest over noneconomic issues is rare and likely to end with arrests. An important analytic challenge becomes determining the extent to which xenophobic thinking has become mainstream in Russian society, most notably among Russians whose increasingly popular slogan has become "Russia for the Russians," with the added assumption that Russians should be Russian Orthodox.[81] Vocal Russian nationalist minorities have not prevented a formally proclaimed national agenda of tolerance and international ecumenical communication, but xenophobia is increasing. An alarming sign is that human rights lawyers themselves, after appeals in Strasbourg, have experienced official harassment or worse. The Chechnya-linked 2009 murder of Stanislav Markelov has particularly chilled human rights advocates, as have calls for arming of citizens' groups against illegal, often Muslim, migrants. Also alarming are returns to the Soviet-style use of psychiatric facilities to repress activists and believers. Given that Russia signed the European Convention on Human Rights and Fundamental Freedoms in 1998, Russia's policies, police actions, and court decisions sometimes appear dangerously hypocritical.

Timing and contingent conditions are crucial. Just prior to the Soviet Union's breakup, and afterward, throughout the cacophonous 1990s, friends and colleagues openly stated how wonderful freedom of speech, conscience, and religion felt after many years of demoralizing self-censorship, particularly in front of their children. The palpable relief as people explored diverse religious options was clear throughout the 1990s, despite bitter expectation gaps concerning standards of living and employment, once touted as a human right in Soviet propaganda. Far from blaming or crediting some unified "West," many Russians and non-Russians credited themselves as finally capable of "growing up" and taking responsibility for their material and spiritual lives, rather than letting the state do it for them. But the words "democracy" and "freedom" became tarnished from overuse and misuse by the mid-1990s under President Yeltsin and especially after President Putin came to power. A popular reaction set in, as people returned, with official encouragement, to cynical apathy, fear, or reassertion of more "traditional" cultural values, especially but not only Russian Orthodoxy. Cultural conservatism can be a form of path dependency, the appeal of security and social safety nets over freedom of choice. Nonetheless, at moments of great societal debate and upheaval, that path can be changed. A major question for Russia today is whether the recent chance for societal debate to drive change toward a more open, tolerant society is over. Ethical and practical concerns about Russia's increasingly impoverished and polarized "marginal" social and religious groups are sharpened in this context.

Russia's political binds regarding religion and human rights derive from specifics of the Soviet legacy and the explosion of religious choice that citizens have experienced after decades of antireligious propaganda and repression. But its citizens are not unique in struggling toward a balance between international definitions of human rights and concepts more tailored to indigenous "national traditions" and national identity protectionism. My fieldwork from the Volga region to the Far East reveals a tremendous striving toward cultural revitalization across a political spectrum from internationalist to liberal nationalist to fundamentalist. It confirms religion scholar Sergei Filatov's conclusions that many post-Soviet citizens, especially young people, are experimenting with flexible processes of "chop and change" in their religious community affiliations.[82] But the danger of deepening political fissures is palpable. Violence perpetrated in the name of religion tends to escalate ethnoreligious polarization and exacerbate renewed state repression in a feedback cycle especially harmful to youth.

Given the relevance of political fissures to social justice issues, the goal of both secular and religious human rights activists in Russia needs to be an all-encompassing effort toward long-term sustainable building of civil society. Religion and multiculturalism need not be brakes on this process. Rather, the efforts of multiple actors can contribute to potentially positive synergism, strengthening civil society at many interactive levels: grassroots community activism, open intelligentsia analysis, religious community networking, ecumenism in matters of war and peace, judicial and media systems that are used and respected, police trained for tolerance, consistent state protection against hate crimes, and pressures from the international community when violations occur.

NOTES

1. Data for this project come from fieldwork, legal materials, and sociological surveys, as well as local press and internet sources such as the Bigotry Monitor, the Forum 18 News Service, and the Moscow Bureau for Human Rights. Frequent,

periodic field research has been since 1986 in the Far East (Sakha Republic, also called Yakutia). I have also had field experience in diverse parts of the federation, including the Volga region (Bashkortostan, Mordva), Northwestern Caucasus, Moscow, St. Petersburg, Omsk, Krasnoyarsk, Khanty-Mansiisk District, Tyva (Tuva), Irkutsk, and Buryatia.

2. For an English translation of the 1997 Law of Freedom of Conscience and Religious Associations, see www.stetson.edu/~psteeves/relnews/relawdraft.html. Restrictive laws curtailing religious rights have been either passed or debated in post-Soviet Central Asia (Uzbekistan, Kazakstan, Kyrgystan, Turkmenistan), Azerbaijan, Belarus, and Moldova.

3. The Millennium of Christianity also highlighted tensions between Russians and Ukrainians, each claiming the heritage of ancestral Slavic conversion to Christianity in Kiev in 988.

4. "Putin against Using Human Rights as Instrument of Political Influence," Interfax, February 10, 2007. See Micheline R. Ishay, *The History of Human Rights: From Ancient Times to the Gobalization Era* (Berkeley: University of California, 2004); Peter Beyer, *Religion and Globalization* (London: Sage, 1999); Jane Cowan, M. Dembour, and R. Wilson, eds., *Culture and Rights* (Cambridge: Cambridge University Press, 2001); Mark Goodale and Sally Merry, eds., *The Practice of Human Rights: Tracking Law between the Local and the Global* (Cambridge: Cambridge University Press, 2007); Bryan Turner, *Vulnerability and Human Rights* (University Park: Penn State, 2006).

5. Bruno Latour, ed., *Iconoclash: Beyond the Image Wars in Science, Religion and Art* (Boston: MIT Press, 2002); Bruno Latour, *Reassembling the Social: An Introduction to Actor-Network-Theory* (Oxford: Oxford University Press, 2005); Samuel Huntingon, "The Clash of Civilizations," *Foreign Affairs* 72 (1993): 22–49. See also Michael M. J. Fischer, "Culture and Cultural Analysis as Experimental Systems," *Cultural Anthropology* 22:1 (2007): 1–65.

6. This includes especially the European Convention on Human Rights and Fundamental Freedoms, signed in May 1998. For an excellent review of resulting cases, see Kirill Koroteev, "The European Factor in Russian Justice," June 26, 2008, www.opendemocracy.net.

7. The Helsinki Watch Group was founded by Lyudmila Alekseyeva, Elena Bonner, Alexander Ginsberg, Yuri Orlov, and Andrei Sakharov, among other distinguished Russian voices of moral conscience. The impressive SOVA Center for Information and Analysis is led by Alexander Verkhovski (http://www.sova-center.ru). The Moscow Bureau for Human Rights (led by Alexander Brod) site is www.antirasizm.ru. See also F. Smirnov, ed., *Stranitsy, Opalennye Smert'iu* (Moscow: Vestnik Evropy, 2006). Particularly grave have been unsolved assassinations of activists Alexander Men', Galina Starovoitova, Sergei Iushenkov, Nikolai Girenko, Anna Politkovskaia, Anastasiia Baburova, Natalya Estemirova and Sviataslav Markelov.

8. Kimmo Käärnäinen and Dmitri Furman, "Religioznost' v Rossii na rubezhe XX-XXI stoletii," *Obshestvennaia Nauk i Sovremennost'* 31:1 (2007): 103–19; S. Filatov and R. Lunkin, "Statistika rossiiskoi religioznosti," *Sociologicheskoe Issledovanie* 6 (2005): 36. See also Mark Steinberg and Catherine Wanner, eds., *Religion, Morality and Community in Post-Soviet Societies* (Bloomington: Indiana University Press, 2008); Paul Goble, "Analysis From Washington: A Religious Flowering," April 19, 2001, http://

www.rferl.org/content/Article/1096239.html; Mikhail Tulsky, "Religii," *Nezavisimaia gazeta*, April 18, 2001, www.ng.ru, on "explosions" of religious groups, with group statistics gained from access to Justice Ministry files.

9. David C. Lewis, *After Atheism: Religion and Ethnicity in Russia and Central Asia* (Surrey: Curzon Press, 2000).

10. Galina Starovoitova, personal communication to author, 1997. The lists may serve as at least partial guidelines during registration checks on specific congregations. A 2003 internal report for the Ministry of Nationalities and Migration (under the relatively liberal V. Zorin) ranked the Roman Catholic Church and Protestants as dangerous "religious extremist" groups, and recommended expelling foreign clergy. For academic alarm, see E. R. Balagushkin and V. K. Shokhin, "Religioznyi pliuralizm v Sovremennoi Rossiia," *Mir Rossiia* 15:2 (2006): 62–78. See also www.moral.ru, for example, February 20, 2007, on sect proliferation. By 2010, the European Parliament's annual report on human rights condemned the way Russia's 2002 Law on Fighting Extremist Activity has been used to generate a black list of 265 religious and faith-based organizations. See http://www.hrwf.net, November 25, 2010.

11. See, for example, the excellent interview with Vladimir Lukin, Russia's liberal and openly discouraged human rights ombudsman. Mark Smirnov, "Ombudsmen upolnomochen zaiavit," *Nezavisimaia gazeta*, April 6, 2008, www.religion.ng.ru/politic/2008-06-04/4lukin.html. At local levels, use of the 1997 law is combined with the 2006 law controlling nongovernmental organizations, exacerbating corruption and favoritism in registration processes, with thousands of new workers hired to check on extensive paperwork and monitor local activities of relevant organizations.

12. For critique of the law, see Lewis, *After Atheism*, 235–37. On the 2008 Ministry of Justice crackdown, see "Institute Condemns Russia's Move to Liquidate Dozens of Religious Groups, Churches," October 28, 2008, www.religionandpolicy.org.

13. Nikolas Gvosdev, "'Managed Pluralism' and Civil Religion in Post-Soviet Russia," in *Civil Society and the Search for Justice in Russia*, ed. Christopher Marsh and Nikolas K. Gvosdev (Lanham: Lexington, 2002), 75–88.

14. Rafael Khakimov (Khakim), personal communication to the author, fall 2005. See Rafael Khakimov, "Tatars," *Anthropology and Archeology of Eurasia* 43:3 (2004–5): 45–61; *Gde Nasha Mekka?(Manifest yevroislama)* (Kazan: Magariph 2005).

15. See www.hizb-ut-tahrir.org to judge its radicalism, noting especially the fine line it walks between advocacy of violent jihad and advocacy of a more peacefully established Caliphate. See also the more moderate www.islamnews.ru/news.

16. "Russian Muslim Council Regrets Mufti's Insulting Remarks about Israelis," Interfax, February 28, 2007.

17. The Putin-Medvedev strategy is tied with energy politics, as well as maximizing cross-cutting diplomatic engagements that return Russia to world power status. See Alexei Malashenko and Sergei Filatov, eds., *Religiia i globalizatsiia na prostorakh Evrazii* (Moscow: Neostrom, 2005); Marjorie Mandelstam Balzer, ed., *Religion and Politics in Russia* (Armonk: M. E. Sharpe, 2010); the work of Eduard Ponarin, Lilia Sagitova, Rosa Musina, Shireen Hunter, and Paul Goble; plus www.islam.ru and www.azatlyk.org.

18. See his powerful memoir, Natan Sharansky, *Fear No Evil* (New York: Random House, 1988). Soon after President Putin became president, he called Sharansky for a

private meeting. See also Yuri Slezkine, *The Jewish Century* (Princeton: Princeton University Press, 2004), 358.

19. *Argumenty I Fakty* 1990 39 8/11–17/90: 8; Tulsky, April 18, 2001; Filatov and Lunkin, 2005.

20. Research of Sascha Goluboff, Semen Kozlov, and Semyon Charny analyzes the main Jewish organizations: KEROOR (Congress of Jewish Religious Communities and Organizations), and FEOR (Federation of Jewish Communities of Russia), associated with a more mystical Hassidic and popular Judaism but recently brought into established forms through presidential support of the Moscow Chorale Synagogue and the Orthodox Chad Lubavitch movement. The World Union of Progressive Judaism and the Eurasian Jewish Congress also have followers in Russia. See Semen Kozlov, "Russian Jews: The Confessional Situation in Late Twentieth Century," *Anthropology and Archeology of Eurasia* 2 40:5 (2001): 31–55; Sascha Goluboff, *Jewish Russians: Upheavals in a Moscow Synagogue* (Philadelphia: University of Pennsylvania, 2002).

21. At a joint 2007 press conference with the congressman, Rabbi Lazar also explained that valid worries about street-level anti-Semitism and anti-Zionism are being dealt with properly by law enforcement authorities, a view debated within the Jewish community. See IRPP News Update, February 21, 2007. The U.S. Congress "Jackson-Vanick amendment" kept trade and technology sharing restrictions, despite widespread views that the pressure outlasted its political context.

22. I am grateful to ethnographers Elza-bair Guchinova, Zoya Anaiban, and Natalia Zhukovskaia for insights on Buddhist communities. On statistics, see Mikhail Tulsky, April 18, 2001; Filatov and Lunkin, 2005.

23. Tensions among the groups are evident. The head of the Gelugpa school is called the Khambo Lama, a term inherited from the tsarist Russian past. The Soviet state–sponsored organization "Central Spiritual Directorate of Buddhists (TsDUB)" became in the 1990s the less encompassing "Buddhist Traditional Sangha." Gelugpa and Rime schools are both represented in Russia. The Russian Association of Buddhists, affiliated with the School of Karma Kagyu, was founded in Kalmykia in 1993. Kagyu groups are mentored by the Danish lama Øle Nydahl.

24. Buddhists won a case over prime Lake Baikal land in 2006. Acrimony over the Gunzechoinei monastery reached a low point when someone forged a letter appointing Danzan-Khaibzun Samayev, a Buryat trained in Mongolia, as abbot.

25. This was confirmed during fieldwork in Tuva and Buryatia, summer 2005. Natalia Zhukovskaia, Tatiana Pang, Elza-bair Guchinova, Elza Bakaeva, Sergei Filatov, Geraldine Fang, and Philip Waters are authorities on Buddhist politics.

26. Geraldine Fagan, "Will Church and Mosque Demolition Threats Be Carried Out?" February 8, 2007, www.forum18.org.

27. "Salvation Army Saved," *Bigotry Monitor* 2:10 (2002). On Protestants, see also Melissa Caldwell, *Not by Bread Alone: Social Support in the New Russia* (Berkeley: University of California Press, 2004); Balagushin and Shokhin, 2006.

28. Geraldine Fagan, "Sharing Faith in Public: A Fundamental Right," May 30, 2006, www.forum18.org. This occurred in the Sakha Republic, but few knew about it in 2007.

29. A melee ensued when a church member turned off the microphone; several in the congregation were injured. Geraldine Fagan, "Russia: Whose Side Are the Police

On?" June 7, 2006, www.forum18.org. Compare David Martin, *Tongues of Fire: The Explosion of Protestantism in Latin America*, foreword by Peter Berger (Oxford: B. Blackwell, 1990).

30. A Moscow case against Jehovah's Witnesses was initiated by the Committee for the Salvation of Youth from Totalitarian Sects. Representatives of the Russian Orthodox Missionary Department, the Jewish community (Beryl Lazar), and the Muslim community (Talgat Tadjutdin) joined to applaud the decision against the Witnesses. Geraldine Fagan, "Russia: Jehovah's Witness Ban Comes into Effect," June 17, 2004, www.forum18.org; G. Fagan, "Russia: Jehovah's Witnesses 'Very Glad' about European Court of Human Rights Victory," January 17, 2007, www.forum18.org; Charles Fenyvesi, "Jehovah's Witnesses Trial Drags On," *RFE/RL Watchlist*, April 1, 1999.

31. Geraldine Fagan, "Banned "Extremist" Religious Literature—Who's Next?" January 16, 2009, www.forum18.org. See also Koroteev, June 26, 2008.

32. Sergei Filatov and Lyudmila Vorontsova, "Catholic and Anti-Catholic Traditions in Russia," *Religion, State and Society* 28:1 (2000): 79; Sergei Filatov, *Religiia i Obshchestvo: Ocherki religioznoi zhizni sovremennoi Rossii* (Moscow: Letnii Sad, 2002). Numbers may be higher.

33. See Dennis Dunn, *The Catholic Church and Russia* (Aldershot: Ashgate, 2004); Ia. V. Moravitskii, "The Catholic Community of St. Petersburg," *Anthropology and Archeology of Eurasia* 47:4 (2009), 35-57.

34. Steven Lee Myers, "New Russian Cathedral Stymied by Interfaith Rift," *New York Times*, February 20, 2002, A3; Compare Zoe Knox, *Russian Society and the Orthodox Church* (London: Curzon, 2005), 5.

35. Victor Yasmann, "Russia: Why Putin Is Going to the Vatican," *RFE/RL* March 13, 2007.

36. See official census www.2002perepis.ru; Marjorie Mandelstam Balzer, ed., "Framing the Census in Russia (Rossiia)," *Anthropology and Archeology of Eurasia* 44: 1-2 (2005). The preamble of the 1997 law acknowledges religions that are part of the "historical heritage of Russia's peoples," mentioning "ancient pagan cults, which have been preserved or are being revived in the republics of Komi, Mari-El, Udmurtia, Chuvashia, Chukotka and several other subjects of the Russian Federation."

37. See Walker Connor, *Ethnonationalism* (Princeton: Princeton University Press, 1994); Marjorie Mandelstam Balzer, *The Tenacity of Ethnicity* (Princeton: Princeton University Press, 1999). On Armenian and other statistics that differentiate ethnic and explicit religious identities, see Filatov and Lunkin, 2005.

38. A. O. Bulatov, *Sufizm na Severo-Vostochnom Kavkaze* (Moscow: Akademiia Nauk, 2006).

39. Compare Abdeeb Khalid, *The Politics of Muslim Cultural Reform: Jadidism in Central Asia* (Berkeley: University of California Press, 1998); Edward Ponarin and Irina Kouznetsova-Morenko, "Russia's Islamic Challenge," *Georgetown Journal* 7:2 (2006): 21-28; Shireen Hunter, *Islam in Russia* (Armonk, NY: M. E. Sharpe, 2004), and the work of Edward Lazzerini.

40. Seth Mydans, "An Ex-Telemarketer's Other Life as a Buddhist Saint," *New York Times*, December 12, 2004. See www.savetibet.ru for interviews with Russian Federation lamas—for example, Choi-Dorzhi Budayev, who worries believers are too "ethnic religion" oriented, and not international enough.

41. Personal communication to the author, June 4, 2007. Her bulletin is *Informat-sionnyi Builleten' Upolnomochennogo po pravam cheloveka v Respubliki Sakha (Yakutia)*. See Marjorie Mandelstam Balzer, "Whose Steeple Is Higher? Religious Competition in Siberia," *Religion State and Society* 33:1 (2005): 57–70; Afanasii Nikolaev, "Sovremnnaia religioznaia situatsiia v Respubliki Sakha," July 19, 2007, www.religare.ru. Nikolaev, a Sakha official, admits "non-traditional" religious organizations have "caused concern among authorities of the republic." The leader Uhhaan was charged with extremism in 2008.

42. Valery Tishkov interview on Mayak Radio, February 22, 2006, www.fednews.ru; and personal communication to the author, September 19, 2007. See V. Tishkov, ed., *Edinstvo i Mnogoobrazie Rossii* (Moscow: Obshestvennaia palata RF, 2007).

43. A local Russian Orthodox priest blames high suicide rates on "local paganism." Mari revivalists have about twenty ritual ceremonies annually, with approximately 120 "karts," or priests, for a population of about 600,000 Mari. Their values of patriarchy, return to nature, antiglobalization and technology have made them controversial. See Geraldine Fagan, "Mari Paganism-Historical Confession without Privileges," *Keston News Service*, July 21, 2002, www.forum18.org; Sonia Luehrmann, "Recycling Cultural Construction: Desecularisation in Postsoviet Mari El," *Religion, State and Society* 33:1 (2005): 35–56; Filatov, 2002.

44. The original vandals were caught but soon released. The head of the Sakharov Museum was nearly jailed for "blasphemy," partially provoked by the exhibit poster depicting an icon with an international road sign for warning replacing the face. During the circus trial, Russian toughs called "skinheads" taunted attendees with anti-Semitic slogans, and clashing demonstrators nearly came to blows.

45. Summarizing extremist crimes of 2006, a deputy prosecutor announced that 263 had been committed, with rates of solving and prosecuting those cases sometimes low, depending on the locality, and with no differentiation between religious and ethnic or race-based hate crimes, *Bigotry Monitor* 7:6, February 21, 2007. By 2008, the SOVA Center for Information and Analysis estimated that the number of hate crimes had increased by 15 percent to 20 percent in the previous two years (depending on how they are defined), with prosecution somewhat improved. Compare June 23, 2008, www.gazeta.ru; *Bigotry Monitor* 8:24, June 13, 2008; Galina Kozhevnikova, "Iazyk vrazhdi posle Kondopogi," in *Iazyk vrazhdi protiv obshchestva*, ed. A. Verkhovskii (Moscow: Sova, 2007), 10–71.

46. Kimmo Käärnäinen and Dmitri Furman 2007, 111.

47. Semyon Charny, "Racism, xenophobia, Ethnic Discrimination and Anti-Semitism in Russia," *Moscow Bureau for Human Rights*, 2005, www.antirasizm.ru; Nickolai Butkevich, "Russian Neo-Nazis Follow Tactics of Al-Qaeda," September 28, 2007, www.haaretz.com; Nickolai Butkevich, "Not Exactly Zero Tolerance," January 13, 2009, www.transitionsonline.org.

48. Ramazon Abdulatipov's address to the Congress of Russian Ethnologists, Ufa, Bashkortostan, 1997, and to the Assembly of the Peoples of Russia, Yakutsk, Sakha, June 2007 (field notes); Lyoma Usmanov, personal communication to the author, July 2001. See also Khasan Baiev with Ruth and Nicholas Danilloff, *The Oath* (New York: Walker, 2003); Ann Nivat, *Chienne de guerre*, trans. Susan Darnton (New York: Public Affairs, 2001).

49. Anna Politkovskaia, *Putin's Russia* (London: Harvill, 2004). On Markelov's murder, along with the murder of journalist Anastasiia Baburova, see the human rights community protest statement, Lyudmila Alekseyeva et al., "Pravozashchitniki: Ubiistvo advokata Kungaevykh—pravokatsiia," January 21, 2009, www.annews.ru/news/detail.php?ID=176048.

50. On Chechnya atrocities, Oksana Chelysheva spoke at the National Endowment for Democracy, February 23, 2007. See Claire Bigg, "Council of Europe: Moscow Confronted with More Cases from Caucasus," *RFE/RL* January 23, 2007; Vyacheslav Izmailov, "Russia Has Lost the War to Ichkeria," *Novaya Gazeta* 12, February 19–21, 2007; Nickolai Butkevich, "Human Rights Groups Snub Kadyrov's Forum in Chechnya," February 23, 2007, www.ucsj.org/bigotry-monitor.

51. Catherine Cosman, "Individual Freedom and Faith in Russia," in *Religion in Russian Society: Woodrow Wilson International Center for Scholars Conference June 8–9, 2006*, Kennan Institute Occasional Papers, 298; See U.S. Commission on International Religious Freedom reports for 2006-2010, www.uscirf.gov; and http://www.uscirf.gov/images/united%20states%20mission%20to%20the%20osce.pdf

52. Commission on Security and Cooperation in Europe: United States Helsinki Commision Congressional Briefing, "Ingushetia: The New Hot Spot in Russia's North Caucasus," June 19, 2008, www.csce.gov; Tatiana Lokshina 2008 report for Moscow Human Rights Watch, www.hrw.ru. Zyazikov was finally dismissed in 2008.

53. On Beslan, see the stunning film by Jonathan Sanders, "Beslan: Three Days in September," produced for CBS, 2005.

54. Sufian Zhemukov, resident of Nal'chik, personal communication to the author, November 8, 2005; confirmed by Fatima Tlisova, journalist and former resident of Nal'chik, personal communication to the author, June 3, 2008.

55. Norman Pereira, "Negative Images of Jews in Recent Russian Literature," *Canadian Slavonic Papers* 48:1–2 (2006): 64. See also Dmitri Furman, "Pri nalichii dobroi voli problemy legko razreshiny," *Izvestiia*, April 21, 2005.

56. See especially *Bigotry Monitor*; Mihai Varga, "How Political Opportunities Strengthen the Far Right: Understanding the Rise of Far-Right Militancy in Russia," *Europe-Asia Studies* 60:4 (2008): 561–80; Alexander Verkhovskii, ed., *Russkii natsional-izm* (Moscow: SOVA, 2006).

57. Pereira, 2006, 48. For Russian nationalist sites, see www.zavtra.ru and www.dpni.org.

58. The ringleader was sentenced to ten years in a prison colony, with the others allotted five to seven years, *Bigotry Monitor* 7:6, February 9, 2007, from Associated Press. Eleven other extremist gangs have been rounded up in 2008 in Moscow and St. Petersburg regions, associated with ethnoreligious hate crimes, including seventeen murders. *Bigotry Monitor* 8:24, June 13, 2008.

59. Mikhail Pozdnyayev, "Krest' na shkole," *Noviye Izvestia*, August 30, 2006: 1, 7, and August 31, 2006: 7. A huge response to the article generated further support by Patriarch Alexei II. See also S. S. Savva, "Klerikalizatsiia svetskogo obrazovanie v Rossii," *Religiovedenie* 5:4 (2006): 76–87; Geraldine Fagan, "Russia: Compulsory Orthodox Lessons to Continue," September 25, 2007, www.forum18.org; J. D. Basil, "Church-State Relations in Russia: Orthodoxy and Federation Law, 1990–2004," *Religion, State and Society* 33:2 (2005): 151–63.

60. Valery Tishkov, personal communication to the author, September 19, 2007.

61. Again religious architecture becomes an index of access, for over 100 Russian Orthodox chapels have been built in regional prisons and military compounds but far fewer mosques or other religious shrines are permitted. In Kalmykia, an Orthodox chapel and a Buddhist temple were constructed in a prison, and the Muslim community has been assured that a mosque can follow. Geraldine Fagan, "Russia: Orthodox Becoming First among Equals," May 27, 2003, www.forum18.org.

62. Roman Kirillov, "Voenno-Vozdushnyi sily stali eshe blizhe k bogu," *Izvestiia*, June 19, 2004, 1.

63. Valery Tishkov, interview, February 22, 2006, www.fednews.ru.

64. Victor Shnirelman, "Perun, Svarog and Others: Russian Neo-Paganism in Search of Itself," *Cambridge Anthropology* 21:3 (1999/2000): 18–36; Alexander Verkhovskii, ed., *Iazyk vrazhdy protiv obshchestva* (Moscow: SOVA, 2007).

65. *Bigotry Monitor* 7:6 (February 21, 2007), from SOVA Center for Information and Analysis.

66. Masha Lipman, "Russian Retail Politics," *Washington Post*, February 5, 2007, A15. On Orthodoxy and change, see Father Georgi Chistiakov, "In Search of the 'Russian Idea': A View from Inside the Russian Orthodox Church," in *Religion and Identity in Modern Russia*, ed. J. Johnson et al. (Aldershot: Ashgate 2005), 53–64. Experts on Orthodoxy include Nikolas Gvosdev, Sergei Filatov, Kira Tsekhanskaia, Dmitrii Dudko, Dmitri Furman, Nikolai Petro, and Elizabeth Prodromou.

67. See Irina Papkova, "Is Orthodox Christianity Compatible with Democracy? Russia as a Test Case," Ph.D. diss., Georgetown University, 2006. Papkova terms Putin's spiritual advisor, the abbot of Sretenskii monastery Archmandrite Tikhon Shevkunov, a "conservative pragmatic." Zoe Knox, 2005, takes a more hard-line position on the Archimandrite's role, linking him explicitly with chauvinist Russian nationalism. For relevant surveys, see Moscow State University sociologist Igor Ryazantsev, discussed in Interfax, June 5, 2006.

68. Lee Trepanier, "Nationalism and Religion in Russian Civil Society: An Inquiry into the 1997 Law 'On Freedom of Conscience,'" in *Civil Society and the Search for Justice in Russia*, ed. C. Marsh and N. Gvosdev (Lanham: Lexington, 2002), 69; Michael A. Meerson, "The Doctrinal Foundations of Orthodoxy," in *Eastern Christianity and Politics in the Twentieth Century*, ed. P. S. Ramet (Durham: Duke University Press, 1988), 20–36.

69. Corruption undermines the church's moral authority on human rights issues. See veteran religion analyst Lawrence Uzzell, "Religious Freedom in Russia," Testimony for the Commission on Security and Cooperation in Europe Congressional Briefing, January 14, 1997, on church corruption in its relations with the state, especially regarding church property and commercial activities. Moscow Mayor Luzhkov's renowned sponsorship enabling resurrection of the gold and marble Church of Christ the Saviour is one of many cases where church and secular authorities have both cooperated and clashed.

70. Despite some Orthodox critics, many Russian Orthodox priests and congregants within and outside Russia have celebrated this expanded community solidarity. My perspective derives from interviews with several priests and informal conversations with Russian Orthodox believers. See also "Patriarch Discusses Contents of

Russian Human Rights Declaration," *ITAR-TASS*, April 4, 2006. For a sample in the Russian press on the unification of the estranged churches, see Stanislav Minin, "Ob'edinenie Tserkvei neobratimo," *Nezavisimaia gazeta*, November 2, 2006, 1.

71. "Rebranding" involves local authorities' misguided or mistaken return of Old Believer churches and icons to the official Russian Orthodox Church in places like Samara, Cheboksary (Chuvash Republic), Morshansk (Mordova), Pugachev (Saratov), and Siberia. See Irina Budkina, "Religious Freedom since 1905—Any Progress in Russia?" www.forum18.org, May 26, 2005; and the site Irina Budkina edits, www. samstar.ru. Anthropologist Douglas Rogers confirms complicity of local administrators with Russian Orthodox authorities in "rebranding" (e-mail communication to the author, February 17, 2007).

72. "Patriarch Discusses Contents of Russian Human Rights Declaration," *ITAR-TASS*, April 4, 2006. Metropolitan Kirill addressed the conference "Evolution of Moral Values and Human Rights in Multicultural Society" in Strasbourg, October 30, 2006 (reported by *IRPP News Update*, November 6, 2006): "It is . . . too early to say that a universal vision of human rights exists. . . . I believe this to be one of the priority tasks of dialogue between civilizations."

73. Mikhail Moshkin, "Raspuskanyie," *Vremia novostei*, May 7, 2008, 2. A relatively more independent nongovernmental organization, All-Rossiia Civic Network, was founded in 2008 to monitor human rights and the judicial system, and the group Civic Assistance has funding from the European Union.

74. Grigorii Tumanov, "Pravoslavnaia deklaratsiia prav cheloveka," *Itar-Tass*, June 26, 2008, www.gazeta.ru.

75. Metropolitan Kirill explaining the council to journalists, *RIA-Novosti*, June 26, 2008.

76. The Nashi youth movement has been called "Putin's brown-shirts" and the Putsomol. See www.novayagazeta.ru/data/2008/46/16.html. The ideologically similar group "Mestnie" (Locals) has less formal affiliation.

77. Prasenjit Duara, "Historicizing National Identity, or Who Imagines What and When," in *Becoming National*, ed. Geoff Eley and Ronald Suny (New York: Oxford, 1996), 152–77.

78. Smirnov, 2008.

79. Mike Brown stresses Native American communities' concerns about preservation of their endangered religions and languages. Compare Ishay, 2004; Michael F. Brown, *Who Owns Native Culture?* (Cambridge: Harvard University Press, 2003).

80. Edwin Bacon, using Marc Howard's definitions of civil society, has provocatively argued that the 1997 law has the potential to improve Russia's weak civil society by enabling those religious groups that pass registration hurdles to be formally protected, with their own regularized administrative and social structures. However, this ignores the cumulative chill effects of the law and more recent Duma legislation. Compare Edwin Bacon, "The Church and Civil Society in Russia," in *Russian Civil Society: A Critical Assessment*, ed. A. B. Evans (Armonk, NY: M. E. Sharpe, 2005), 110–25; Marc M. Howard, *The Weakness of Civil Society in Postcommunist Europe* (Cambridge: Cambridge University Press, 2003). President Putin's February 1, 2007, press conference statements correlating the need for a nuclear shield for his state's material security and the protection of "traditional faiths" for its spiritual security are revealing.

81. Levada-zentr, press release August 3, 2005, suggested that 50–60 percent of Russians support the slogan. The prominent human rights lawyer Karinna Moskalenko of Moscow's Center for Assistance in International Protection is a practicing Russian Orthodox believer who recuses herself from religion cases. She sees religious discrimination cases as relatively easy to prosecute under European Union and Russian Federation law (personal communication to the author, September 28, 2007, at Carnegie Endowment, Washington, DC). However, in 2008 a list of rights activists was posted on a Russian nationalist Web site, www.vdesyatku.ru, sending fear through their community and leading them to request recourse through the prosecutor general's office.

82. Filatov, 2002. Compare Robert Wuthnow, *After the Baby-Boomers* (Princeton: Princeton University Press, 2007), especially the discussion of youth tinkering with religious options.

BIBLIOGRAPHY

Alekseyeva, Lyudmila et al. "Pravozashchitniki: Ubiistvo advokata Kungaevykh—pravokatsiia." January 21, 2009. www.annews.ru/news/detail.php?ID=176048.

Bacon, Edwin. "The Church and Civil Society in Russia." In *Russian Civil Society: A Critical Assessment*, ed. Alfred B. Evans, 110–25. Armonk: M. E. Sharpe, 2005.

Balagushkin, E. R., and V. K. Shokhin. "Religioznyi pliuralizm v Sovremennoi Rossiia." *Mir Rossiia* 15:2 (2006): 62–78.

Baiev, Khasan, with Ruth and Nicholas Danilloff. *The Oath.* New York: Walker, 2003.

Balzer, Marjorie Mandelstam. *The Tenacity of Ethnicity.* Princeton: Princeton University Press, 1999.

———. "Whose Steeple Is Higher? Religious Competition in Siberia." *Religion State and Society* 33:1 (2005): 57–70.

———, ed. *Religion and Politics in Russia.* Armonk: M. E. Sharpe, 2009.

———, ed. "Framing the Census in Russia (*Rossiia*)." *Anthropology and Archeology of Eurasia* 44:1–2 (2005).

Basil, John D. "Church-State Relations in Russia: Orthodoxy and Federation Law, 1990–2004." *Religion, State and Society* 33:2 (2005): 151–63.

Beyer, Peter. *Religion and Globalization.* London: Sage, 1999.

Brown, Michael F. *Who Owns Native Culture?* Cambridge: Harvard University Press, 2003.

Bulatov, A. O. *Sufizm na Severo-Vostochnom Kavkaze.* Moscow: Akademiia Nauk, 2006.

Butkevich, Nickolai. "Not Exactly Zero Tolerance." January 13, 2009. www.transitionsonline.org.

Butkevich, Nickolai. "Human Rights Groups Snub Kadyrov's Forum in Chechnya." February 23, 2007. www.ucsj.org/bigotry-monitor.

Caldwell, Melissa. *Not by Bread Alone: Social Support in the New Russia.* Berkeley: University of California Press, 2004.

Charny, Semyon. "Racism, Xenophobia, Ethnic Discrimination and Anti-Semitism in Russia." *Moscow Bureau for Human Rights 2005 Report.* www.antirasizm.ru.

Chistiakov, Georgi. "In Search of the 'Russian Idea': A View from Inside the Russian Orthodox Church." In *Religion and Identity in Modern Russia*, ed. J. Johnson et al., 53–64. Aldershot: Ashgate 2005.

Connor, Walker. *Ethnonationalism.* Princeton: Princeton University Press, 1994.

Cosman, Catherine. "Individual Freedom and Faith in Russia." In *Religion in Russian Society: Woodrow Wilson International Center for Scholars Conference, June 8–9, 2006,* ed. Joseph Dresen. Kennan Institute Occasional Papers, 298.

Cowan, Jane, M. Dembour, and R.Wilson, eds. *Culture and Rights.* Cambridge: Cambridge University Press, 2001.

Duara, Prasenjit. "Historicizing National Identity, or Who Imagines What and When." In *Becoming National,* ed. Geoff Eley and Ronald Suny, 152–77. New York: Oxford University Press, 1996.

Dunn, Dennis. *The Catholic Church and Russia.* Aldershot: Ashgate, 2004.

Fagan, Geraldine. "Will Church and Mosque Demolition Threats Be Carried Out?" February 8, 2007. www.forum18.org.

Filatov, Sergei. *Religiia i Obshchestvo: Ocherki religioznoi zhizni sovremennoi Rossii.* Moscow: Letnii Sad, 2002.

Filatov, Sergei B., and Roman H. Lunkin. "Statistika rossiiskoi religioznosti." *Sociologicheskoe Issledovanie* 6 (2005): 35–45.

Filatov, Sergei, and Lyudmila Vorontsova. "Catholic and Anti-Catholic Traditions in Russia." *Religion, State and Society* 28:1 (2000): 79.

Fischer, Michael M.J. "Culture and Cultural Analysis as Experimental Systems." *Cultural Anthropology* 22:1 (2007): 1–65.

Furman, Dmitri. "Pri nalichii dobroi voli problemy legko razreshiny." *Izvestiia,* April 21, 2005, News.

Goble, Paul. "Analysis from Washington: A Religious Flowering." April 19, 2001. http://www.rferl.org/content/Article/1096239.html.

Goluboff, Sascha. *Jewish Russians: Upheavals in a Moscow Synagogue.* Philadelphia: University of Pennsylvania, 2002.

Goodale, Mark, and Sally Merry, eds. *The Practice of Human Rights: Tracking Law between the Local and the Global.* Cambridge: Cambridge University Press, 2007.

Gvosdev, Nikolas. "'Managed Pluralism' and Civil Religion in Post-Soviet Russia." In *Civil Society and the Search for Justice in Russia,* ed. Christopher Marsh and Nikolas K. Gvosdev, 75–88. Lanham: Lexington, 2002.

Khalid, Abdeeb. *The Politics of Muslim Cultural Reform: Jadidism in Central Asia.* Berkeley: University of California Press, 1998.

Howard, Marc M. *The Weakness of Civil Society in Postcommunist Europe.* Cambridge: Cambridge University Press, 2003.

Hunter, Shireen. *Islam in Russia.* Armonk: M. E. Sharpe, 2004.

Huntingon, Samuel. "The Clash of Civilizations." *Foreign Affairs* 72 (1993): 22–49.

Ishay, Micheline R. *The History of Human Rights: From Ancient Times to the Gobalization Era.* Berkeley: University of California Press. 2004.

Käärnäinen, Kimmo, and Dmitri Furman. "Religioznost' v Rossii na rubezhe XX-XXI stoletii." *Obshestvennaia Nauk i Sovremennost'* 31:1 (2007): 103–19.

Khakimov, Rafael. "Tatars." *Anthropology and Archeology of Eurasia* 43:3(2004–5): 45–61.

Kirillov, Roman. "Voenno-Vozdushnyi sily stali eshe blizhe k bogu." *Izvestiia,* June 19, 2004, 1.

Koroteev, Kirill. "The European Factor in Russian Justice." June 26, 2008. www.opendemocracy.net.

Kozhevnikova, Galina. "Iazyk vrazhdi posle Kondopogi." In *Iazyk vrazhdi protiv obshchestva*, ed. A. Verkhovskii, 10–71. Moscow: SOVA, 2007.

Kozlov, Semen. "Russian Jews: The Confessional Situation in Late Twentieth Century." *Anthropology and Archeology of Eurasia* 40:3 (2001–2): 31–55.

Knox, Zoe. *Russian Society and the Orthodox Church*. London: Curzon, 2005.

Latour, Bruno, ed. *Iconoclash: Beyond the Image Wars in Science, Religion and Art*. Boston: MIT Press, 2002.

———. *Reassembling the Social: An Introduction to Actor-Network-Theory*. Oxford: Oxford University Press, 2005.

Lewis, David C. *After Atheism: Religion and Ethnicity in Russia and Central Asia*. Surrey: Curzon Press, 2000.

Lipman, Masha. "Russian Retail Politics." *Washington Post*, February 5, 2007, A15.

Lokshina, Tatiana. "2008 Report for Moscow Human Rights Watch." www.hrw.ru.

Luehrmann, Sonia. "Recycling Cultural Construction: Desecularisation in Postsoviet Mari El." *Religion, State and Society* 33:1 (2005): 35–56.

Malashenko, Alexei, and Sergei Filatov, eds. *Religiia i globalizatsiia na prostorakh Evrazii*. Moscow: Neostrom, 2005.

Martin, David. *Tongues of Fire: The Explosion of Protestantism in Latin America*. Foreword by Peter Berger. Oxford: B. Blackwell, 1990.

Meerson, Michael A. "The Doctrinal Foundations of Orthodoxy." In *Eastern Christianity and Politics in the Twentieth Century*, ed. P. S. Ramet, 20–36. Durham: Duke University Press, 1988.

Minin, Stanislav. "Ob'edinenie Tserkvei neobratimo." *Nezavisimaia gazeta*, November 2, 2006, 1.

Moshkin, Mikhail. "Raspuskanyie" *Vremia novostei*, May 7, 2008, 2.

Mydans, Seth. "An Ex-Telemarketer's Other Life as a Buddhist Saint." *New York Times*, December 12, 2004, News: Saturday profile.

Myers, Steven Lee. "New Russian Cathedral Stymied by Interfaith Rift." *New York Times*, February 20, 2002, A3.

Moravitskii, Ia. V. "The Catholic Community of St. Petersburg." *Anthropology and Archeology of Eurasia* 47:4 (2009), 35–57.

Nikolaev, Afanasii. "Sovremnnaia religioznaia situatsiia v Respubliki Sakha." July 19, 2007. www.religare.ru.

Nivat, Ann. *Chienne de guerre*. Trans. Susan Darnton. New York: Public Affairs, 2001.

Papkova, Irina. "Is Orthodox Christianity Compatible with Democracy? Russia as a Test Case." Ph.D. diss., Georgetown University, 2006.

Pereira, Norman. "Negative Images of Jews in Recent Russian Literature." *Canadian Slavonic Papers* 48:1–2 (2006): 47–64.

Politkovskaia, Anna. *Putin's Russia*. London: Harvill, 2004.

Ponarin, Edward, and Irina Kouznetsova-Morenko. "Russia's Islamic Challenge." *Georgetown Journal* 7:2 (2006): 21–28.

Pozdnyayev, Mikhail. "Krest' na shkole." *Noviye Izvestia*, August 30, 2006: 1, 7 and August 31, 2006: 7.

Savva, S. S. "Klerikalizatsiia svetskogo obrazovanie v Rossii." *Religiovedenie* 5:4 (2006): 76–87.

Sharansky, Natan. *Fear No Evil*. New York: Random House, 1988.

Shnirelman, Victor. "Perun, Svarog and Others: Russian Neo-Paganism in Search of Itself." *Cambridge Anthropology* 21:3 (1999/2000): 18–36.

Slezkine, Yuri. *The Jewish Century.* Princeton: Princeton University Press, 2004.

Smirnov, F., ed. *Stranitsy, Opalennye Smert'iu.* Moscow: Vestnik Evropy, 2006.

Smirnov, Mark. "Ombudsmen upolnomochen zaiavit." *Nezavisimaia gazeta,* April 6, 2008. www.religion.ng.ru/politic/2008-06-04/4 lukin.html.

Steinberg, Mark, and Catherine Wanner, eds. *Religion, Morality and Community in Post-Soviet Societies.* Bloomington: Indiana University Press, 2008.

Tishkov, Valery, ed. *Edinstvo i Mnogoobrazie Rossii.* Moscow: Obshestvennaia palata RF, 2007.

Trepanier, Lee. "Nationalism and Religion in Russian Civil Society: An Inquiry into the 1997 Law 'On Freedom of Conscience.'" In *Civil Society and the Search for Justice in Russia,* ed. C. Marsh and N. Gvosdev, 57–73. Lanham: Lexington, 2002.

Tulsky, Mikhail. "Religii." *Nezavisimaia gazeta,* April 18, 2001. www.ng.ru.

Turner, Bryan. *Vulnerability and Human Rights.* University Park: Penn State, 2006.

Varga, Mihai. "How Political Opportunities Strengthen the Far Right: Understanding the Rise of Far-Right Militancy in Russia." *Europe-Asia Studies* 60:4 (2008): 561–79.

Verkhovskii, Alexander, ed. *Russkii natsionalizm.* Moscow: SOVA, 2006.

———, ed. *Iazyk vrazhdy protiv obshchestva.* Moscow: SOVA, 2007.

Wuthnow, Robert. *After the Baby-Boomers.* Princeton: Princeton University Press, 2007.

11

Human Rights, the Catholic Church, and the Death Penalty in the United States

Thomas Banchoff

For most Americans and Europeans the politics of human rights is about established democracies criticizing rights violations elsewhere. It is an international, not a domestic matter. However reassuring to many, such a view no longer captures the politics of human rights in today's world. While the United States and Western Europe drove the construction of the postwar international human rights agenda, they are now part of a more global and diverse constellation. More states with multiple perspectives on civil, political, social, and economic rights have created and contested a wide variety of international conventions governing the rights of workers, prisoners, women, children, ethnic and religious minorities, and other groups.[1] The global politics of human rights no longer revolves exclusively around democracies criticizing the failures of nondemocracies. It also features struggles within and across democracies about what counts as human rights and how best to secure them. In the Atlantic area, as in the other regions, religious communities are key players in that political contestation.

The death penalty provides a prominent example. Capital punishment has emerged, gradually and unevenly, as an international human rights issue since the late 1940s.[2] After centuries of executing criminals with the blessing of both religious and secular authorities, Western Europe completely abandoned the practice by the early 1980s. The Roman Catholic Church, the world's largest religious organization, turned against the death penalty in the 1990s. And after several failed efforts, the United Nations General Assembly passed a declaration condemning capital punishment as a human rights violation in 2007. Over most of this period, the United States resisted these trends in the global politics of the death penalty. The U.S. Supreme Court upheld its constitutionality in 1976 and thirty-five of fifty states subsequently incorporated it into law. More than 1,100 prisoners were executed in the country over the three decades. At the dawn of the new century, however, the American politics of the death penalty shifted. The Supreme Court limited its application, states executed fewer prisoners, and two states abolished it altogether—New Jersey in 2007 and New Mexico in 2009.[3] In 2010 public support for capital punishment still ran significantly higher in the United States than in Europe. But the gap had narrowed.

To what extent were these shifts in the U.S. politics of the death penalty a response to broader international trends—the rise of capital punishment as a human rights issue and the historic shift in the position of the Catholic Church? On balance, other national and local factors were more decisive. U.S. opponents of capital punishment are more likely to invoke a national civil rights rather than an international human rights frame. They tend to be more concerned about injustice—the execution of the innocent or discrimination against minorities—than about the human dignity or right to life of criminals highlighted in contemporary Catholic moral teaching. While acknowledging the primacy of national and local politics, this chapter first describes the international human rights regime and the policies of the Roman Catholic Church and then traces their influence on the U.S. politics of capital punishment. Global and religious forces, it argues, have highlighted the increasing global isolation of the United States, influenced public opinion and jurisprudence, and strengthened coalitions pressing for abolition at the state level.

International Human Rights, the Church, and the Death Penalty

The rise of capital punishment as an international human rights issue unfolded in two phases: from the eighteenth century through 1945, and from 1945 through the start of the twenty-first century. Each phase was marked by different national and international politics and by changes in the stance of the Roman Catholic Church.

From the Enlightenment through the Second World War

Well into the eighteenth century, capital punishment was a virtually unquestioned universal norm in Europe. From ancient Greece and Rome through the Middle Ages and into the Early Modern Period, debates raged about *when, not whether,* political and religious authorities might demand and carry out the ultimate penalty. Murder, treason, rebellion, apostasy, and witchcraft were made capital offenses in different ways in different polities, as were a host of other crimes. Whatever controversy over the proper application of the death penalty might have divided political and military leaders, legal experts, and churchmen, consensus persisted about its basic legitimacy. It was deemed necessary in order to punish wrongdoers and maintain social and political order, a rationale evident in Greek and Roman law and Hebrew and Christian scriptures, as well as in the writings of the church fathers, medieval scholastics, and leading Protestant reformers. (Over the centuries, principled pacifism remained a minority current within Christianity.) The Catholic Church's Trent Catechism (1566) expressed the dominant church-state consensus: "The power of life and death is permitted to certain civil magistrates because theirs is the responsibility under law to punish the guilty and protect the innocent."[4]

Only with the eighteenth-century Enlightenment and the transition to modernity did cracks appear in this consensus. Three related developments—support for constitutionalism, the rise of science, and the cultural decline of established churches—transformed the social and political context. The drive to limit arbitrary state power through constitutional reform went hand in hand with a more critical approach to the use of the executioner. A new scientific and materialist worldview denied the immortality of the soul and construed death as the final end of human existence, casting capital punishment in a more terrible light. And the established Catholic and Protestant churches, long supporters of the death penalty as a way to protect the social order while affording repentant criminals some hope of eternal salvation, lost some of their cultural influence to more secular scholarly, scientific, and political elites. These trends, traceable from the Early Modern Period through the early nineteenth century, prepared the ground for a rethinking of the death penalty. But one author and one book almost single-handedly reframed the issue.

The Italian philosopher Cesare Beccaria published his influential and widely cited *Essay on Crimes and Punishments* in 1764. It was a carefully argued blanket indictment of the death penalty from a rationalist perspective. Drawing on the social contract theory of John Locke and Jean-Jacques Rousseau, Beccaria cast the death penalty as a human rights issue. "Did any one ever give to others the right of taking away his life?" he asked. "Is it not absurd that the laws, which detest and punish homicide, should, in order to prevent murder, publicly commit murder themselves?" Beccaria questioned the motive of retribution and revenge that had sustained the execution of lawbreakers from ancient times. He found the public spectacle of executions particularly abhorrent. Laws "intended to moderate the ferocity of mankind," he argued, "should not increase it by examples of more barbarity." He also argued in a utilitarian vein that executions had no significant deterrent effects on violent criminals and proposed long prison terms instead. None of these arguments were new to

Beccaria, but his presentation was particularly forceful and influential. Voltaire and Thomas Jefferson were among his admirers.[5]

The Roman Catholic Church took notice, too. *Essay on Crimes and Punishments* was placed on the Index of Forbidden Books. At issue were not only its conclusions—opposition to a practice the church had long endorsed—but the manner of argument. Beccaria argued from secular premises and reached secular conclusions. His opposition to capital punishment was at one with a belief in the universal rights of man, discernible through reason. For the church, support for abolition was thus a reprehensible endorsement of the secular ideals of the French Enlightenment—and an attack on the church's tradition and authority. The strong anticlerical stance of abolitionists—Voltaire scorned the burning of "so-called witches" and the "immolation of heretics" as "juridical massacres"—hardened the fronts and reinforced the church's stance. A survey of Catholic thinkers in the late eighteenth and nineteenth centuries reveals only isolated examples of opposition to the death penalty. The rejection of Enlightenment arguments for abolition resonated with the blanket condemnation of democracy and liberalism made most famous in Pope Pius IX's 1864 *Syllabus of Errors*.[6]

Into the twentieth century, the coalition of death penalty proponents in Europe as well as the United States remained robust. It included not only the Catholic but also the major Protestant churches; Quakers and Mennonites were the best established of the smaller, pacifist groups committed to abolition. For most conservatives in the aristocracy, the military, or civil service the death penalty was sacrosanct as a matter of law, order, and the administration of justice. Against this backdrop, slow and uneven progress toward abolition only began with the rise of liberal and socialist parties and the advance of constitutionalism and representative democracy. Over the course of the nineteenth century, legal reforms on both sides of the Atlantic limited the range of capital crimes, typically to treason and murder. Some jurisdictions banned the death penalty altogether. Michigan became the first U.S. state to do so in 1847, followed by Rhode Island and Wisconsin. Internationally, Venezuela abolished the death penalty in 1863, followed by several other Latin American republics. In Europe, Portugal led the way in 1867, followed by others in the run up to World War II, including Norway, Sweden, Denmark, and the Netherlands. In the United States and other leading Atlantic powers including Britain, France, Germany, Italy, and Spain, the death penalty remained law.

The Postwar International Human Rights Regime

Only after the cataclysmic destruction of World War II and revelations about the Holocaust did an international human rights regime come into shape. The barbarity of Nazism catalyzed a discussion within the new United Nations that culminated in the 1948 Universal Declaration of Human Rights. The declaration's drafters discussed the addition of an anti–capital punishment provision but could not reach any consensus. Article 3 left the issue open, declaring simply that "everyone has the right to life, liberty and security of person." Over the next several decades, this blanket formulation served to cover over national differences on the issue. Article 6 of the International Covenant on Civil and Political Rights, adopted in 1966, also invoked "the inherent right to life," but added more on the death penalty itself, noting that "no one shall be arbitrarily deprived of his life," but also that capital punishment remained licit "for the most serious crimes" in "countries which have not abolished the death penalty." Opponents could point to the "have not abolished" as a hopeful "not yet," but sharp divisions among UN member states continued to prevent progress toward abolition at the level of international law.[7]

Over time, the abolition of the death penalty within major European democracies generated more international momentum. The 1949 Constitution of the Federal Republic of Germany (Basic Law) succinctly stated that "capital punishment is abolished"—in part an explicit reaction against Nazism's state-sanctioned mass murder. Two years earlier Italy abolished the death penalty for all crimes during peacetime in its new constitution. In the United Kingdom, the Abolition of Death Penalty Act of 1965 imposed a moratorium that Parliament made permanent in 1969, with some exceptions for treason and terrorism eventually outlawed in 1998. After Franco's fall, Spain's 1978 constitution abolished capital punishment outside of wartime, an exception that was also eventually dropped. France was the last Western European country to sentence a criminal to death—in 1977. Soon after his election in 1981, François Mitterrand and his socialist-led government outlawed the death penalty. Abolition was written into the French constitution in 2007.

This trend toward abolition at the national level was reinforced by transnational efforts within the Council of Europe and the European Union (EU). The 1950 European Convention on Human Rights enshrined the right to life but, like the 1948 UN Declaration, did not take a stand on capital punishment. As European states moved toward abolition at the domestic level, European institutions adapted. A key juncture was the Sixth Protocol to the European Convention, adopted in 1983, which declared unequivocally: "The death penalty shall be abolished. No-one shall be condemned to such penalty or executed"—with exceptions in wartime. In 2002 the subsequent Thirteenth Protocol was ratified, eliminating any and all exceptions, and asserting, in a spirited preamble, that "everyone's right to life is a basic value in a democratic society and that the abolition of the death penalty is essential for the protection of this right and for the full recognition of the inherent dignity of all human beings." Parallel to these developments at the level of the Council of Europe, the European Union made abolition a prerequisite for the accession of Central and East European states after the fall of communism. The Union's 2000 Charter of Fundamental Rights included an abolition clause. Under the heading "Right to

Life," Article 2 stated that "no one shall be condemned to the death penalty, or executed."[8]

This movement on the European continent, at both the national and European level, was a primary driver of global efforts to anchor abolition as part of the international human rights regime. As early as 1971, the UN General Assembly passed a declaration that noted "the desirability of abolishing this punishment in all countries."[9] But it was not for almost two more decades that, on the initiative of European governments, a formal legal instrument was approved by the UN's Economic and Social Committee. The preamble to the 1989 Second Optional Protocol to the International Covenant on Civil and Political Rights (ICCPR) asserted that the "abolition of the death penalty contributes to enhancement of human dignity and progressive development of human rights." It noted that the ICCPR itself had referred to the death penalty "in terms that strongly suggest that abolition is desirable." The Second Protocol bound signatories to endorse "an international commitment to abolish the death penalty" and to recognize a role for UN institutions in monitoring the compliance. Some seventy countries were party to the protocol by 2009.[10]

The 1990s saw further growth in abolitionist sentiment around the world, reinforced by a global democratization trend. In 1990 the Organization of American States approved a protocol to the American Convention on Human Rights on the European model (which the United States, not surprisingly, did not endorse). The collapse of the Soviet bloc saw the emergence of new democracies banning capital punishment—in part out of an eagerness to join the EU, which insisted on it. Still, there was nothing like consensus at a global level. In 1994 a strongly worded General Assembly declaration that called on states to ratify the second protocol failed by eight votes. Invoking the millennium, the declaration draft had floated the idea of "a moratorium on pending executions with a view to ensuring that the principle that no State should dispose of the life of any human being be affirmed in every part of the world by the year 2000."[11] Retentionist states maintained that the issue was one of law and order and national sovereignty and, as the Singapore representative put it in the General Assembly debate, "not a human rights issue." While lacking a majority in the General Assembly in 1999, the UN Commission on Human Rights, encouraged by Italy and other European states, pressed the issue with repeated resolutions in 1997, 1998, and 1999, insisting that the "abolition of the death penalty contributes to the enhancement of human dignity and to the progressive development of human rights."[12]

It took another decade before a proposal for a death penalty moratorium secured majority support in the UN. In December 2007 the EU-backed resolution was debated and endorsed by the General Assembly by a vote of 104 to 54 with 29 abstentions. The text was milder than in 1994; it did not openly call on states to endorse the Second Optional Protocol to the ICCPR. It did insist, though, that they "progressively restrict the use of the death penalty and reduce the number of offences for which it may be imposed" and that they take steps to "establish a moratorium on executions with a view to abolishing the death penalty." In contrast to earlier resolutions, the text went beyond general human rights rhetoric to details of the issue, dismissing the deterrent value of the death penalty and decrying its unequal application across justice systems. But human rights concerns remained central. According to the preamble, "the use of the death penalty undermines human dignity" and "a moratorium on the use of the death penalty contributes to the enhancement and progressive development of human rights."[13]

This slow and uneven extension of the international human rights regime to cover the death penalty provided no direct constraints on national governments. Its treaties and conventions bind only signatory nations. What is more, if a signatory contravenes a treaty, there is no international enforcement mechanism available. National sovereignty reigns supreme—at least in a strict legal sense. At a political level, international norms shape expectations in relations among states and, to some extent, in the politics within them. In the case of capital punishment they provide political ammunition for political supporters of abolition and one way to hold governments to the promises they have made. The global political trend was clear. As of 2009, 139 states had abolished the death penalty in law or practice. At the time of the adoption of the Universal Declaration of Human Rights in 1948, there had been only fifteen abolitionist states.

The Shift of the Catholic Church

The gradual shift of the Roman Catholic Church against the death penalty contributed to its global emergence as a human rights issue. While the Second Vatican Council (1962–1965) was an important turning point, one can trace the origins of the transformation back to the 1930s and 1940s and the influence of Jacques Maritain, the French theologian and Christian humanist. In an effort to cast Christianity as a middle way between totalitarianism, on the one hand, and democratic capitalism, on the other, Maritain developed the notion that human dignity and human rights were part of the Christian tradition, rightly understood.[14] While the importance of human dignity in social and political affairs could be traced back to Leo XIII and his 1891 encyclical *Rerum Novarum*, Pius XI (1922–39)—an admirer of Maritain—was the first pope explicitly to raise the issue of human *rights*. His 1937 anti-Nazi encyclical, *Mit brennender Sorge*, insisted that "man as a person possesses rights he holds from God, and which any collectivity must protect against denial, suppression or neglect." Pius made the human rights connection even clearer a year later. "Christian teaching alone gives full meaning to the demands of human rights and liberty," he wrote in a little-noticed missive to American Catholics, "because it alone gives worth and dignity to human personality."[15]

The church's full embrace of the human rights agenda would have to wait until the 1960s—and its opposition to capital punishment, even longer. While Maritain played an influential role as an advisor in the drafting of the 1948 Universal Declaration, he and other progressive theologians, including the American Jesuit John Courtney Murray, were marginalized throughout the pontificate of Pius XII (1939–58). The Second Vatican Council proved a critical juncture. In his 1963 encyclical *Pacem in Terris*, Pope John XXIII hailed the 1948 Universal Declaration as "a solemn recognition of the personal dignity of every human being."[16] On the death penalty issue, however, he and the council remained silent. The 1965 "Pastoral Constitution on the Church in the Modern World" (*Gaudium et Spes*) elaborated a string of "violations of human dignity" including abortion and euthanasia but did not include capital punishment. Official church teaching remained that the state was justified in taking the life of a criminal in defense of law and order. In fact, the death penalty remained on the books in Vatican City itself until 1969.[17]

A key juncture in the development of the church's position was 1976, when American bishops asked Rome for guidance on how to respond to the unfolding U.S. capital punishment controversy. In its response the Pontifical Council for Justice and Peace noted: "The U.S. bishops have spoken out and acted firmly in defense of life against abortion and euthanasia," and Council further suggested "an inner logic that would call Catholics, with their sense of the sacredness of life, to be consistent in this defense and extend it to the practice of capital punishment."[18] This idea of a consistent ethic of life encompassing convicted felons would be developed within the U.S. church, particularly by Cardinal Joseph Bernadin of Chicago, over the next two decades. Pope John Paul II did not initially press the issue. For example, his first major encyclical on social and political issues, *Sollicitudino rei socialis* (1987), praised the Universal Declaration of Human Rights and addressed abortion and euthanasia as life issues, but made no direct mention of capital punishment.[19]

Only in 1995 did Pope John Paul II make opposition to the death penalty the official stance of the worldwide church. His encyclical *Evangelium vitae* noted "growing public opposition to the death penalty, even when such a penalty is seen as a kind of 'legitimate defence' on the part of society." The pope continued: "Modern society in fact has the means of effectively suppressing crime by rendering criminals harmless without definitively denying them the chance to reform."[20] The pope recognized the theoretical possibility of such punishment "when it would not be possible otherwise to defend society." But he added: "Today however, as a result of steady improvements in the organization of the penal system, such cases are very rare, if not practically nonexistent." The new Church Catechism finalized in 1997 was revised to fit the new policy. While not ruling out capital punishment categorically, it insisted that "non-lethal means" of punishment were "more in conformity to the dignity of the human person."[21]

The Vatican did not leave the matter at the level of moral teaching. It used its official high-level representation at the UN to join actively in the international human rights campaign to ban the death penalty in the run up to the new millennium. Before the UN's Social and Economic Committee in November 1999, for example, the Vatican's Permanent Observer to the United Nations, Cardinal Renato Martino, articulated a rationale centered on the dignity and rights of the condemned. "Let me say clearly: anyone whose life is terminated in a gas chamber, by hanging, by lethal injection or by a firing squad is one of us—a human person, a brother or sister, however cruel and inhumane his or her actions may appear." The lessons of history, Martino insisted, required opposition to the death penalty at the historic juncture of the new millennium. "At the end of a century which has seen unimaginable atrocities against the dignity of the human person and his or her inviolable rights, giving serious consideration to the abolition of the death penalty will be a remarkable undertaking for humanity."[22]

John Paul II's successor, Pope Benedict XVI (2005–) carried this policy forward, if in a less emphatic way. Some conservative capital punishment supporters had looked upon his election with hope. In a 2004 intervention in the U.S. presidential campaign, which saw pro-choice Catholic John Kerry as the democratic nominee, then Cardinal Ratzinger had contrasted abortion with the death penalty, noting a "a legitimate diversity of opinion among Catholics" on the latter issue: "While the Church exhorts civil authorities to seek peace, not war, and to exercise discretion and mercy in imposing punishment on criminals, it may still be permissible to take up arms to repel an aggressor or to have recourse to capital punishment."[23] Once in office as Benedict XVI, however, Ratzinger did not depart from John Paul II's line. While he avoided the theme of capital punishment in his first three encyclicals (2006–9), he did publicly welcome the December 2007 UN moratorium resolution: "Recalling the appeal made by Pope John Paul II on the occasion of the Jubilee Year 2000," Benedict rejoiced that the UN had "adopted a resolution calling upon States to institute a moratorium" on the use of the death penalty and expressed his "hope that this initiative will lead to public debate on the sacred character of human life."[24]

The Politics of the Death Penalty in the United States

For most of the post–World War II period, American politics of the death penalty have been decoupled from broader international trends. For a time, during the late 1960s, it looked as if the United States might join the movement toward abolition. Amid the civil rights movement and Vietnam War, support for capital punishment dropped to an all-time low in 1966—according to Gallup, only 42 percent in favor as opposed to 47 percent against. Most mainline Christian denominations, including Methodist, Lutheran, Episcopal, and Presbyterian, called for abolition at the time, as did leading Reform Jewish organizations.[25] The high-water mark for the anti–death penalty movement was the landmark Supreme Court case *Furman v. Georgia* (1972), which ruled that the death penalty, as applied, violated the Eighth Amendment's injunction against cruel and unusual punishment. But this amounted to a legal moratorium, not abolition—and it was short-lived. Thirty-five state legislatures and the U.S. Congress rewrote statutes aimed at eliminating the arbitrary infliction of death sentences, the Court's main concern. The constitutionality of capital punishment was reaffirmed in *Gregg v. Georgia* (1976), and executions recommenced in the country in 1977.[26]

The revival of the death penalty proved politically popular, particularly in the South. The late 1980s and early 1990s saw the greatest public backing for the death penalty in recent history, with surveys showing as much as 80 percent support. The 1988 presidential campaign was a political watershed. Democratic candidate Michael Dukakis's opposition to capital punishment proved unpopular with voters. He was pilloried in particular for his insistence during a presidential debate that he would not press for the death penalty even if his wife were raped and murdered.[27] In 1988 and again in 1994 Congress expanded the federal death penalty to encompass a broader range of capital crimes, including killings in connection with the large-scale drug trade. If mainline churches and Jewish organizations did not waver in their opposition to the death penalty, the country's largest Protestant denomination, the Southern Baptist Convention, continued to support it, as did the Christian Coalition and other newly mobilized evangelical organizations. Moreover, while U.S. Catholic bishops were increasingly critical of the death penalty through the 1980s and into the 1990s—a development discussed in the next section—the church had not yet officially changed its position.

How to account for such strong American support for the death penalty—a striking contrast with Western Europe? Most explanations center on a different historical trajectory and political culture. The United States, some scholars have pointed out, was spared the immediate experience of dictatorship, war, and Holocaust that turned so many Europeans against state-sponsored executions. For other observers the persistence of the death penalty is evidence of entrenched racism, given the overrepresentation of blacks on death row. Others point to high violent crime rates and the fear it induces as a reason for American exceptionalism. Still others draw a link back to the focus on retributive justice in pervasive American readings of the Old Testament. A striking example of the persistence of retribution as a motivating force was then senator Barack Obama's 2006 claim that some crimes are "so heinous, so beyond the pale, that the community is justified in expressing the full measure of its outrage by meting out the ultimate punishment." It would be politically damaging and practically unthinkable for a leading European politician to endorse vengeance as a reason for executing criminals.[28]

The contrast between American and European public sentiment is not as great as the political cleavage would suggest. When asked, close to half or more European citizens express support for capital punishment—a number considerably below the comparable U.S. figure, but nevertheless significant. It is European political institutions, in part, that keep the issue from moving back onto the political agenda. The leaders of more hierarchical European parties of the center left and center right, less directly beholden to the general population than their U.S. counterparts, took the initiative on abolition over the postwar decades without paying any significant political price. National courts generally followed in their wake, upholding abolition as a constitutional norm. And Council of Europe and EU legal guidelines against the death penalty were eventually mirrored in national law. The more participatory character of U.S. electoral politics and the Supreme Court's insistence on the constitutionality of the death penalty help to explain the closer relationship between public opinion and policy outcomes in the American politics of capital punishment.

Starting in the late 1990s, those politics shifted in significant ways. Public support for the death penalty began to drift below the 70 percent mark, reaching 64 percent in 2008 according to the annual Gallup survey.[29] In two landmark cases, the Supreme Court affirmed the death penalty but limited its range of application. *Atkins v. Virginia* (2002) ruled it unconstitutional to execute the mentally disabled, and *Roper v. Simmons* (2005) took the same step in the case of juvenile offenders. Executions all but stopped for two years in 2006–7, as the Court addressed the constitutionality of the lethal injection method (eventually affirming it). The number of inmates executed declined for eight straight years, dwindling from a high of ninety-eight in 1999 to only thirty-seven in 2008, and the number of new capital sentences went through a similar decline.[30] Several junctures in state politics reinforced this overall trend. Illinois Governor George Ryan removed all 167 inmates from death row and declared a moratorium on capital punishment in 2000. Five years later the New York High Court struck down the state's capital punishment statute, and the legislature did not subsequently reinstate it. The most striking evidence of a new politics of the death penalty were successful efforts to legislate abolition in New Jersey in 2007 and New Mexico in 2009—the first two states since the 1960s to take that step.[31]

The trend should not be exaggerated—and may not continue. At the end of the first decade of the twenty-first century, two out of three Americans still support the death penalty. And the trend might tick back upward as it did from the late 1970s through the early 1990s. Still, the unmistakable shift that set in during the late 1990s requires explanation. Three factors were particularly critical. First, advances in DNA testing that led to the exonerations of death row inmates—as many as seventeen, by one count—raised political and public anxiety about the possibility of executing the innocent.[32] A second, related factor was persistent overrepresentation of blacks and Hispanics on death row, which stoked concerns about racism and unequal access to legal resources. A third

factor was the rising cost of capital punishment linked to the legal and administrative burdens of long appeals processes. Another contributing factor may
have been the media attention given to studies casting doubt on the deterrence
function of the death penalty.[33]

The balance of this chapter examines the impact of global and religious
factors on U.S. developments: the incorporation of the death penalty into the
international human rights regime and the about-face of the Catholic Church
on the issue. The idea of capital punishment as a human rights issue—long a
staple of European and UN-level political discourse—has been historically
marginal to the U.S. debate. Through the continual criticism and frequent intervention of foreign governments and transnational and international organizations, and the mobilization of nongovernmental organizations (NGOs)
including Amnesty International and the American Civil Liberties Union
(ACLU), the human rights connection has gradually entered U.S. legal and
political discourse—in a limited way. The engagement of the Catholic Church
against the death penalty has probably had more of a political impact. The U.S.
bishops, organized nationally and at the state level, have made the abolition of
the death penalty a major policy initiative, impacting the attitudes of a cross
section of American Catholics (20–25 percent of the U.S. population) and contributing to the formation of successful abolition coalitions in the New Jersey
and New Mexico cases. Through the late 1990s, international norms and the
Catholic Church had little significant impact on U.S. death penalty politics. At
the start of the new century that was no longer the case.

The Global Context of U.S. Death Penalty Politics

As capital punishment arose as an international human rights issue, the United
States increasingly became a target of foreign criticism. Beginning in the
1980s, the EU began to censure the death penalty in America more openly and
to protest its application in particular cases. Both the European Commission
and individual European governments addressed appeals to state governors,
particularly in cases deemed to demonstrate racial or ethnic bias. They also
took up the cause of their nationals convicted of capital crimes who faced
potential execution in the United States.[34] In at least one case EU officials even
threatened economic sanctions. In a 1998 letter to then governor of Texas
George W. Bush, the head of the European Parliament's delegation for relations with the United States underscored "the almost universal repugnance"
that other countries felt toward the application of the death penalty (Texas had
executed more criminals than any other state). There followed a thinly veiled
threat: "Europe is the foremost foreign investor in Texas. Many companies,
under pressure from shareholders and public opinion to apply ethical business
practices, are beginning to consider the possibility of restricting investment in
the U.S. to states that do not apply the death penalty."[35] Disinvestment did not

materialize, but its very mention pointed to the Atlantic gulf on the issue at the time.

The EU has even provided material support to death penalty supporters in the United States. In 2003 the European Initiative for Democracy and Human Rights program made two multiyear grants designed to support the anti–death penalty campaign in the United States, one to the American Bar Association (ABA), and the other to the Death Penalty Information Center. While the ABA, a powerful organization with a large base, took no official stance on the death penalty, it used EU support to lobby for a moratorium to allow time for a more thorough study of complex legal and constitutional issues. The grant to the Death Penalty Information Center was designed to raise media awareness and provide "training and advice to local and national groups working on the death penalty."[36] European democracies investing in U.S.-based NGOs to press a human rights agenda in American politics was a clear illustration of the new global politics of human rights.

The run up to the millennium and Bush's election in 2000 further heightened European criticism. The UN Special Rapporteur's report on the United States, published in January 1998, attacked a "lack of awareness of United States international obligations" and noted that the United States was "one of the few countries, together with the Islamic Republic of Iran, Pakistan, Saudi Arabia and Yemen, to execute persons who were under 18 years of age at the time they committed the crime."[37] An anti–death penalty petition spearheaded by the Rome-based Catholic Community of Sant'Egidio and presented to the UN Secretary General in New York in December 2000, one month after George W. Bush's election to the presidency, included 3.2 million signatures from 146 countries, and had the endorsement of prominent global figures including the Dalai Lama and the Archbishop of Canterbury. Several months earlier members of the French National Assembly had sent a letter to the U.S. Congress, warning that "maintaining the death penalty in your country profoundly affects the friendship which we feel for you."[38] Even the normally U.S.-friendly *Economist* referred to the United States as "the most glaring exception to the emerging international consensus on the death penalty."[39]

The growth of the international human rights regime and the efforts of external actors—and the EU in particular—to shape the U.S. debate did not have obvious direct effects. There appears to be no clear case of such effects— for example, of a U.S. governor granting clemency to a death row inmate primarily on the basis of international appeals. It does not follow, however, that the global context had no impact. One can trace its effects on two levels: in the discourse of nongovernmental organizations and in the jurisprudence of the Supreme Court itself. In both cases, the international human rights regime was a resource for death penalty opponents.

The clearest connection between international discourse and U.S. politics was the work of Amnesty International. Founded in London in 1961, Amnesty opened a U.S. office in 1964. Its rapid growth in the 1970s was spurred by citizen participation in advocacy campaigns on behalf of prisoners of conscience. Starting in 1989, the same year that the UN General Assembly adopted the Second Optional Protocol to the ICCPR, Amnesty made capital punishment a key part of its human rights campaign. Over the next two decades it threw its support behind calls for moratoria and abolition espoused by foreign governments, the UN, and other NGOs such as the France-based World Coalition against the Death Penalty.[40] Amnesty's position within the United States, articulated nationally and by local chapters across the states, combined an international human rights frame with American legal discourse. A position statement called the death penalty "the ultimate denial of human rights" and a violation of the "right to life as proclaimed in the Universal Declaration of Human Rights" as well as "the ultimate cruel, inhuman and degrading punishment"—a reference to the Eighth Amendment to the U.S. Constitution.[41]

The American Civil Liberties Union, too, adapted human rights language in its campaign against the death penalty in the United States. Not surprisingly, given its focus on civil rights, the ACLU concentrated its efforts on the due process and equal protection clauses of the Constitution. Its slogan—"The death penalty is the ultimate denial of civil liberties"—informed a campaign centered on the exoneration of prisoners on death row with insufficient evidence or poor legal representation. But the ACLU, too, linked its efforts back to the international human rights context. In a position statement the director of its capital punishment project, John Holdridge, underscored that "the United States is the only advanced Western democracy that does not view capital punishment as a profound human rights violation and as a frightening abuse of governmental power." In addition to emphasizing the danger of arbitrary application and the possibility of error, the ACLU pointed to international reputation costs. The death penalty, Holdridge argued, "greatly diminishes the worldwide stature of the United States and its ability to work to end human rights violations in other countries."[42]

The human rights frame had little purchase within the U.S. legal system, at least up to the start of the new century. In the 1972 *Furman v. Georgia* case that placed a moratorium on the application of the death penalty, Justice William Brennan was one of only two advocates of abolition, and the only one to refer to "evolving standards of decency" in making his case. While he referred to "human dignity," Brennan did not cast his opposition to capital punishment in international terms but remained focused on constitutional provisions against cruel and unusual punishment. When noting that the executed had "lost the right to have rights," Brennan was referencing civil rights under the law, not human rights more broadly.[43] In the *Gregg* case that reinstated capital punishment in 1976, Brennan's dissent was pitched in more universal terms. He highlighted "the primary moral principle that the State, even as it punishes, must treat its citizens in a manner consistent with their intrinsic worth as human beings—a punishment must not be so severe as to be degrading to human dignity."[44] But here too, all explicit references to international law and human rights were missing. American "evolving standards of decency" were the critical ones.

This national frame had been broadened by 2002–5, when the Court took up the cases of mentally disabled and juvenile offenders. The Court's traditional insistence that it was constitutional to execute both kinds of criminals had long been an object of international criticism. When the Court took up the plight of the mentally disabled in *Atkins v. Virginia* (2002), Harold Koh of Yale Law School submitted an amicus curiae (friend of the court) brief signed by former diplomats that emphasized the international isolation of the United States. To execute Atkins, the letter argued, would "strain diplomatic relations with close American allies, provide diplomatic ammunition to countries with demonstrably worse human rights records, increase U.S. diplomatic isolation, and impair other United States foreign policy interests." Its core contention: one could not meaningfully evaluate "evolving standards of decency that mark the progress of a maturing society" without weighing international as well as domestic opinion.[45]

In declaring the execution of the mentally disabled unconstitutional, the Supreme Court majority drew on some of these arguments. Justice John Paul Stevens noted that "within the world community, the imposition of the death penalty for crimes committed by mentally retarded offenders is overwhelmingly disapproved"—and provided the European Union brief as support. Chief Justice William Rehnquist responded in his minority opinion that the views of other countries were irrelevant. Three years later, in *Roper v. Simmons* (2005), which ruled the execution of juvenile offenders unconstitutional, Justice Anthony Kennedy addressed this objection head-on. "It does not lessen fidelity to the Constitution or pride in its origins," he insisted, "to acknowledge that the express affirmation of certain fundamental rights by other nations and peoples underscores the centrality of those same rights within our own heritage of freedom."[46] This time it was Justice Antonin Scalia who insisted on the irrelevance of international opinion. The rulings in both cases—and the reaction against them—showed that global politics and international law did increasingly matter. Thirty years after the first seminal cases on capital punishment, international human rights had emerged as one frame—though not the dominant one—for U.S. jurisprudence.

The Catholic Church and Capital Punishment in U.S. Politics

At the level of national and local politics, the Catholic Church had more of an impact than the international human rights regime. Estimates of the Catholic population in the United States vary between 20 percent and 25 percent, and

Catholic bishops are organized nationally as the U.S. Conference of Catholic Bishops (USCCB) and in state conferences. During the two decades before John Paul II completed the church's turn against the death penalty in *Evangelium vitae*, Archbishop and later Cardinal Bernadin of Chicago folded the issue into the idea of a "consistent ethic of life." As early as January 1977, Bernadin called on U.S. politicians to "seek methods of dealing with crime that are more consistent with the vision of respect for life and the Gospel message of God's healing love."[47] In its first official statement on the subject in 1980, the USCCB opposed the death penalty more explicitly.[48] And in his 1983 speech at Fordham University, Bernadin more fully articulated the idea of respect for life from conception until death. "We have also opposed the death penalty because we do not think its use cultivates an attitude of respect for life in society," he told his listeners. "The purpose of proposing a consistent ethic of life is to argue that success on any one of the issues threatening life requires a concern for the broader attitude in society about respect for human life."[49]

While these ideas influenced Vatican thinking and contributed to *Evangelium vitae*, the Pope's turn against capital punishment had a particular impact on the United States. During his January 1999 visit to the United States he called publicly "for a consensus to end the death penalty, which is both cruel and unnecessary."[50] And in a broader message to the church in the Americas, he held that a society that upholds the death penalty "bears the stamp of the culture of death, and is therefore in opposition to the Gospel message."[51] This more definitive line, taken up by the USCCB and amplified in an official statement published on Good Friday in 1999, placed the defenders of the church's traditional teaching on the defensive.[52] Scalia was among the most articulate. In a footnote to his dissenting opinion in *Atkins v. Virginia* in 2002 he scorned the bishops' views as "far from being representative."[53] And in a public speech he recalled that John Paul II had not ruled out the death penalty altogether, while criticizing him for going as far as he did. Scalia echoed the old Catholic critique of the secular Enlightenment. Anti–death penalty sentiment in the church was for him "the handiwork of Napoleon, Hegel and Freud rather than of St. Thomas and St. Augustine."[54]

Despite this resistance, there was evidence of some shifts among the laity in response to new official teaching. Most polls showed that a majority of U.S. Catholics supported the death penalty, although at a lower rate than non-Catholics. A widely cited 2004 poll suggested that only about half of Catholics (48%) supported the death penalty, down from two-thirds (68%) just three years earlier, and that churchgoers were more likely to be opposed. Its most interesting conclusion: a third of those Catholics who once supported the death penalty now reported that they had since changed their minds. The downward trend was not, of course, simply a function of changes in the church's official stance. But there is no doubt that the shift in position, combined with the active campaigning of the pope, bishops, and lay Catholic activists, contributed to a new politics of the death penalty. "You have this Catholic voice coming in, and coming in loudly, and saying, 'This is our issue, too, and we are firmly against it,'" noted Richard Dieter of the Death Penalty Information Center. "The polarization between secular liberals and their mainline allies, on the one hand, and conservative Christians on the other, began to break down, opening space for new arguments." One of the most effective activists in this space was Sister Helen Prejean, author of the 1993 book *Dead Man Walking*, who crisscrossed the country in support of state abolitionist campaigns.[55]

The Cases of New Jersey and New Mexico

The effects of international and religious forces were evident in successful abolition drives in both New Jersey and New Mexico. In December 2007 New Jersey became the first state since 1966 to abolish the death penalty in law. In 2006, after several failed attempts, the state legislature passed a capital punishment moratorium and instituted a commission to study the issue. In January 2007 the committee published its report and core recommendation, supported by thirteen of its fourteen members, that New Jersey abolish the death penalty. In March 2007 a key committee of the state Senate backed legislation calling for abolition with the alternative of life imprisonment without parole. The bill was debated and then passed in December, by one vote in the Senate and a wider majority in the General Assembly. That same month Governor Jon Corzine signed the bill and commuted the death sentences of eight inmates. The signing ceremony took place one day before the UN passed its December 2007 declaration against capital punishment.

The timing was coincidental. The political struggle in New Jersey focused on the potential for miscarriages of justice, on discrimination on the basis of race and ethnicity, and on the cost of death row to the taxpayer. International human rights norms played only a minor role. Amnesty International chapters across the state had participated in the lobbying drive for legislation, as had the ACLU, but neither had emphasized the international dimension. The commission report that led to the legislation completely ignored the global frame. In an emotional speech at the bill signing ceremony, Corzine did place New Jersey in an international context, calling it "a momentous day—a day of progress—for the State of New Jersey and for the millions of people across our nation and around the globe who reject the death penalty as a moral or practical response to the grievous, even heinous, crime of murder." While he did not mention human rights directly, Corzine referred to the sanctity of life: "I believe society must first determine if its endorsement of violence begets violence, and if violence undermines our commitment to the sanctity of life."[56]

The church had a greater impact than the international rights regime. While Corzine was not Catholic, his reference to "the sanctity of life" was a nod to his Catholic supporters. Catholics accounted for 44 percent of New Jersey's population—the third highest percentage of any state and twice the national average. Bishop John Smith of Trenton led the state's Catholic conference in lending its support to the abolition campaign. Lay Catholics played a prominent role in New Jerseyans for Alternatives to the Death Penalty, a coalition of some 200 different groups formed in 1999 that served as the engine for the lobbying campaign. According to the group's director, Celeste Fitzgerald, a 2005 USCCB statement on the death penalty was a critical milestone in mobilizing the church on the issue and getting the attention of Catholic legislators.[57] Fitzgerald herself came to the abolition campaign through her work with the Catholic social justice group Pax Christi.

Further evidence of the church's impact was the role played by Raymond Lesniak, the pivotal figure in the state Senate in drafting and passing the legislation. For most of his career, Lesniak had supported the death penalty, like most other members of the Senate. For example, he had voted for its reinstatement in 1982. More than two decades later, he shifted his position after wrestling with the change in the church's teaching. In a press release around the signing ceremony he underscored that "the support of the New Jersey Bishops lead [sic] by Archbishop Smith and the Catholic Conference was of particular significance to me" and asserted: "Pope John Paul II would be proud." In a retrospective book, Lesniak later noted that after the bill signing ceremony the lay Community of Sant'Egidio had "lit up the Roman Coliseum to celebrate this victory for human rights."[58] Not all legislators with Catholic backgrounds made the shift to abolition; some insisted, echoing Scalia, that the pro-life agenda stop short of opposition to the death penalty. But enough did change their views to enable the ban.

The case of New Mexico also shows the primacy of national and local political concerns alongside a role for international and religious factors. Like New Jersey, New Mexico had a long history of political contestation around the death penalty. Legislators had tried but failed to pass bans every year from 1999 to 2007, falling only two votes short in the state Senate in 2001. After the 2008 elections delivered solid Democratic majorities, legislation to replace the death penalty with life imprisonment without parole passed the Senate and House in March 2009 by comfortable margins. Governor Bill Richardson, who had supported the death penalty during his unsuccessful run for the 2008 democratic presidential nomination, signed the legislation and commuted the sentences of two men on death row.

As in the case of New Jersey, concerns about justice, discrimination, and cost drove the creation of the winning coalition for abolition. The leading grassroots lobby, the New Mexico Coalition to Repeal the Death Penalty, was formed in 1997 and had grown to some 140 organizations by 2009. Like Amnesty International chapters and the ACLU, it emphasized civil liberties, as opposed to human rights, and fairness under the law. Richardson, too, did not emphasize the international angle, although he mentioned it more prominently than had Corzine. "From an international human rights perspective," he stated at the signing of the bill, "there is no reason the United States should be behind the rest of the world on this issue. Many of the countries that continue to support and use the death penalty are also the most repressive nations in the world. That's not something to be proud of."[59] In foreign policy terms, he maintained, the death penalty "did not seem to me to be good moral leadership and good foreign policy."[60]

Whatever his acknowledgment of the international context, Richardson certainly made his decision on domestic political grounds. As in New Jersey, the church played a significant role. About a third of New Mexicans were Catholic, and the New Mexico Catholic Conference was an influential political force. In 2005, the year the USCCB reiterated its opposition to capital punishment, Archbishop Michael Sheehan of Santa Fe made the issue one of the conference's top priorities and began to lobby Richardson personally. The fact that Richardson was Catholic helped. Sheehan later recounted: "We were able to help him understand our opposition to the death penalty and he did indeed change his view and signed the law." Among those who shaped his decision, Richardson later recounted, was "the archbishop and the Catholic Church, because they are very, very influential in a Catholic state like New Mexico. My archbishop, a man who I deeply respect, was very active on this issue." The chair of the (nondenominational) New Mexico Coalition to Repeal the Death Penalty made the same point: the "Catholic Church was wonderful here in New Mexico and literally got us the votes we needed."[61]

The most colorful sign of the church's influence was a trip that Richardson and Sheehan made to Rome after the legislation passed on the invitation of the Community of Sant'Egidio. Both men were honored at a light ceremony at the Roman Coliseum, and Sheehan introduced Richardson to the pope.[62] One should be careful not to overemphasize the church's influence on the New Mexico outcome. Richardson's conversion to abolition, it should be recalled, came only after he had dropped out of the U.S. presidential race. Had a bill passed the New Mexico House and Senate earlier in his tenure, he might well have vetoed it. A glance at other states confirms this ambiguity. During the first decade of the new century, Maryland governor Martin O'Malley, a Catholic, campaigned against the death penalty, while Bobby Jindal, the Catholic governor of Louisiana, favored extending it to noncapital crimes, such as child rape. Regional and political variations are critical to any understanding of the shifting politics of capital punishment in the United States. But the church's turn against it has certainly altered the political landscape in favor of death penalty opponents.

Conclusion

The case of the death penalty in the United States demonstrates both the significance and limits of the global and religious dimensions of human rights struggles. For a variety of reasons, human rights discourse has not made many inroads in U.S. domestic politics. The postwar emergence of international human rights norms has not displaced a deeply entrenched civil rights frame grounded in a long constitutional tradition. The centrality of that tradition for American national identity creates further resistance to a global human rights perspective, as does the unrivaled power of the United States in world affairs, which encourages the use of human rights as a rhetorical weapon directed outward against autocratic regimes deemed hostile to American interests. International uproar over the torture of terror suspects under the Bush administration sensitized U.S. popular and political opinion to human rights criticisms from abroad in the decade after September 11, 2001. But the idea that American law and American justice should be subject to international standards or scrutiny remains foreign to most.

Against this backdrop, the rise of international human rights norms has had a modest impact on the shifting American politics of the death penalty. The persistent criticism of European governments, the European Union, and the UN may have had some indirect influence on dropping levels of support for capital punishment from the late 1990s onward. The most influential NGO in the anti–death penalty campaign, Amnesty International, cast the death penalty as a human rights issue starting in the 1980s. And the Supreme Court majorities in 2002 and 2005 who ruled the execution of the mentally disabled and of juvenile offenders unconstitutional were cognizant of the near universal international opposition to both practices. Taken together, these international effects were overshadowed by domestic factors: concern about the execution of innocents, about racial disparities, and about the legal and administrative costs of death row. But the global context increasingly mattered.

The religious impact on the politics of the death penalty was probably more significant. The United States is the most religious of the leading Atlantic democracies; contested moral and ethical issues are often articulated in a religious idiom. A powerful actor in many public policy controversies, the Roman Catholic Church is the country's largest religious denomination and among its most highly organized. The global church's turn against the death penalty, itself largely a response to the rise of the international human rights regime, altered the American political constellation. The church is not a monolith, and its turn on the issue, slow and incomplete, did not reach down to all the clergy or laity. But the idea that the deliberate taking of a human life is contrary to human dignity and human rights gained traction with bishops' conferences and growing numbers of believers, altering the ethical and political landscape of the issue. The abolition drives in New Jersey and New Mexico in 2007–9 demonstrated the political force of religious engagement. In states where abolition remained on the political agenda—including New Hampshire, Colorado, Montana, Kansas, and Maryland—the church was part of the effort. The Catholic Church is, of course, one political actor among many. But its size, level of institutionalization, and interest in public policy issues make it a key player in the politics of human rights and the death penalty, both in the United States and around the world.

Ultimately, capital punishment in the United States illustrates the persistence of national and local institutions as arenas for the politics of human rights. The rise of international human rights norms is one of the most striking and enduring elements of the postwar era. But on the death penalty, as on other issues such as minority rights and gender equality, that regime provides context more than content. It provides moral and rhetorical resources for human rights advocates in national and local settings but cannot guarantee the rights themselves. The fate of human rights within states depends on shifting constellations of national political forces, including religious communities concerned about issues of justice, ethics, and the common good. The outcome of national and political struggles in turn shapes the global constellation.

These dynamics are clearly evident in the U.S. case. Still the world's dominant power, the United States has an unparalleled ability to shape the global political agenda in military, political, and economic terms. Over the past several decades power has meant the ability to resist and counter international pressures—including the force of international human rights norms. U.S. leaders have appropriated the language of human rights, but almost exclusively as a matter of foreign policy. As American power declines in relative terms, and a unipolar world gives way to multipolarity, the constraints of the international balance of power and of international law will likely increase. As those constraints are felt in U.S. politics, human rights may become more of a domestic as well as a foreign policy issue; controversy surrounding the use of torture in the "war on terror" suggests such a development. To the extent that political actors and faith communities draw international human rights norms into their national and local struggles—to embrace, oppose, or recast them—capital punishment will turn out to have been the first, but not the last American domestic issue influenced by the global and religious politics of human rights.

NOTES

1. Recent treatments of the global politics of human rights include Thomas Risse-Kappen, Steve C. Ropp, and Kathryn Sikkink, *The Power of Human Rights: International Norms and Domestic Change* (New York: Cambridge University Press, 1999); and Beth A. Simmons, *Mobilizing for Rights: International Law in Domestic Politics* (New York: Cambridge University Press, 2009).

2. For overviews, see Roger G. Hood and Carolyn Hoyle, *The Death Penalty: A Worldwide Perspective* (New York: Oxford University Press, 2008); and William Schabas, *The Abolition of the Death Penalty in International Law* (Cambridge, UK: Grotius, 1993).

3. On the United States, see Raymond Paternoster, Robert Brame, and Sarah Bacon, *The Death Penalty: America's Experience with Capital Punishment* (New York: Oxford University Press, 2008); Franklin E. Zimring, *The Contradictions of American*

Capital Punishment (New York: Oxford University Press, 2003); and Stuart Banner, *The Death Penalty: An American History* (Cambridge, MA: Harvard University Press, 2002).

4. Catholic Church, *The Catechism of the Council of Trent* (New York: Catholic Publication Society, 1929), Part III, 5, n. 4. The Catechism was originally published in 1566.

5. Cesare Beccaria, *On Crimes and Punishments* (Indianapolis: Hackett, 1986). For background on Beccaria and his impact in the United States and Europe, see John D. Bessler, "Revisiting Beccaria's Vision: The Enlightenment, America's Death Penalty, and the Abolition Movement," *Northwestern Journal of Law and Social Policy* 4, no. 2 (Fall 2009): 195–328.

6. For religious responses to Beccaria, see James J. Megivern, *The Death Penalty: An Historical and Theological Survey* (New York: Paulist Press, 1997), chapter 6.

7. *International Covenant on Civil and Political Rights*, General Assembly Resolution 2200A(XXI), December 16, 1966, http://www2.ohchr.org/english/law/ccpr.htm.

8. Council of Europe, Protocol No. 6 to the Convention for the Protection of Human Rights and Fundamental Freedoms concerning the abolition of the death penalty as amended by Protocol No. 11, April 28, 1983, http://conventions.coe.int/Treaty/En/Treaties/html/114.htm; Council of Europe, Protocol No. 13 to the Convention for the Protection of Human Rights and Fundamental Freedoms, concerning the abolition of the death penalty in all circumstances, May 3, 2002, http://conventions.coe.int/Treaty/En/Treaties/html/187.htm; European Parliament, Council of the European Union, and the Commission of the European Union, Charter of Fundamental Rights of the European Union, December 18, 2000, http://www.europarl.europa.eu/charter/pdf/text_en.pdf.

9. UN General Assembly, 26th Session, "Resolution 2857 (XXVI): Capital Punishment," December 20, 1971, http://www.un.org/documents/ga/res/26/ares26.htm.

10. UN General Assembly, 44th Session, "Resolution 44/128: Second Optional Protocol to the International Covenant on Civil and Political Rights, aiming at the abolition of the death penalty," December 15, 1989, http://www2.ohchr.org/english/law/ccpr-death.htm; United Nations, "Chapter IV: 12. Second Optional Protocol to the International Covenant on Civil and Political Rights, aiming at the abolition of the death penalty," *United Nations Treaty Collection homepage*, October 30, 2009, http://treaties.un.org/Pages/ViewDetails.aspx?src=TREATY&mtdsg_no=IV-12&chapter=4&lang=en.

11. UN General Assembly Third Committee, "Draft Resolution: Capital Punishment," A/C.3/49/L.32, December 1, 1994, in UN General Assembly, 49th Session, *Human Rights Questions: Capital Punishment, Report of the Third Committee (VI)*, A/49/610/Add.5, December 16, 1994, http://documents.un.org/welcome.asp?language=E.

12. UN Commission on Human Rights, 37th Meeting, "Resolution 1997/12: Question of the death penalty," April 3, 1997, in UN Commission on Human Rights, *Draft Report of the Commission: Commission on Human Rights, 53rd Session*, E/CN.4/1997/L.11/Add.1, April 3, 1997, http://documents.un.org/welcome.asp?language=E; UN Commission on Human Rights, 31st Meeting, "Resolution 1998/8: Question of the death penalty," April 3, 1998, in UN Commission on Human

Rights, *Draft Report of the Commission: Commission on Human Rights, 54th Session*, E/CN.4/1998/L.11/Add.1, April 3, 1998, http://documents.un.org/welcome.asp?language=E; UN Commission on Human Rights, 58th Meeting, "Resolution 1999/61: Question of the death penalty," April 28, 1999, in UN Commission on Human Rights, *Report on the Fifty-Fifth Session, Part I*, E/CN.4/1999/167, http://documents.un.org/welcome.asp?language=E.

13. Text of the December 2007 declaration: UN General Assembly, "62/149. Moratorium on the use of the death penalty," A/RES/62/149, February 26, 2008, http://documents.un.org/welcome.asp?language=E. The European Union emphasized its own role: "The European Union actively participated in the cross-regional alliance which successfully led and guided this initiative through the General Assembly and all EU partners co-sponsored this initiative." European Union, "EU Guidelines on the Death Penalty: Revised and Updated Version," *European Union: Delegation of the European Commission to the USA homepage*, 2008, http://www.eurunion.org/DPGuidelines-10-08.pdf.

14. Maritain laid out a full exposition of his argument about the compatibility of philosophy, revelation, tradition, and human rights in Jacques Maritain, *The Natural Law and Human Rights* (Windsor, Ontario: Christian Culture Press, 1942).

15. Pius XI, *Mit brennender Sorge*, March 14, 1937, http://www.vatican.va/holy_father/pius_xi/encyclicals/documents/hf_p-xi_enc_14031937_mit-brennender-sorge_en.html; Pius XI, *Letter of Pius XI to the US Catholic Hierarchy on the Occasion of the Golden Jubilee of the Catholic University of America*, cited in "Catholics Urged to Uphold Catholic Liberty Theory," *St. Petersburg Times*, October 14, 1938.

16. John XXIII, *Pacem in Terris*, April 11, 1963, http://www.vatican.va/holy_father/john_xxiii/encyclicals/documents/hf_j-xxiii_enc_11041963_pacem_en.html.

17. Paul VI, *Pastoral Constitution of the Church in the Modern World: Gaudium et Spes*, December 7, 1965, http://www.vatican.va/archive/hist_councils/ii_vatican_council/documents/vat-ii_cons_19651207_gaudium-et-spes_en.html.

18. Cited in Megivern, *The Death Penalty*, 391.

19. John Paul II, *Sollicitudino Rei Socialis*, December 30, 1987, http://www.vatican.va/holy_father/john_paul_ii/encyclicals/documents/hf_jp-ii_enc_30121987_sollicitudo-rei-socialis_en.html.

20. John Paul II, *Evangelium vitae*, March 25, 1995, http://www.vatican.va/holy_father/john_paul_ii/encyclicals/documents/hf_jp-ii_enc_25031995_evangelium-vitae_en.html.

21. *Catechism of the Catholic Church* (Washington, DC: United States Catholic Conference, 1997), 546.

22. Renato R. Martino, "Abolition of the Death Penalty" (Speech to the Third Committee of the 54th Session of the UN General Assembly, November 2, 1999), http://www.vatican.va/roman_curia/secretariat_state/documents/rc_seg-st_doc_02111999_death-penalty_en.html.

23. Never officially published, the letter was from Cardinal Ratzinger to Theodore Cardinal McCarrick, chairman of the Task Force on Catholic Bishops and Catholic Politicians, in the context of the U.S. election. Cited in Sandro Magister, "The Kerry Affair: What Ratzinger Wanted from the American Bishops," *L'espresso online*, July 3, 2004, http://chiesa.espresso.repubblica.it/articolo/7055?eng=y.

24. Benedict XVI, "Address of His Holiness Pope Benedict XVI to the Diplomatic Corps," *The Vatican homepage*, January 7, 2008, http://www.vatican.va/holy_father/benedict_xvi/speeches/2008/january/documents/hf_ben-xvi_spe_20080107_diplomatic-corps_en.html.

25. Banner, *The Death Penalty*, 241.

26. *Furman v. Georgia*, 408 U.S. 238 (1972) (per curiam), http://www.law.cornell.edu/supct/html/historics/USSC_CR_0408_0238_ZO.html; *Gregg v. Georgia*, 429 U. S. 1301 (1976), http://www.law.cornell.edu/supct/html/historics/USSC_CR_0428_0153_ZO.html.

27. Commission on Presidential Debates, "Debate Transcript: The Second Bush-Dukakis Presidential Debate," October 13, 1988, http://www.debates.org/pages/trans88b.html. In 2004, John Kerry adapted his general opposition to the death penalty for his presidential run, allowing exceptions for some forms of killing, and mentioning terrorism in particular.

28. Barack Obama, *The Audacity of Hope: Thoughts on Reclaiming the American Dream* (New York: Random House, 2006), 70. For controversy surrounding the roots of American exceptionalism, see Zimring, *The Contradictions of American Capital Punishment*, and Hood and Hoyle, *The Death Penalty*, 125–28.

29. A related question about preference for capital punishment or life imprisonment showed greater support for the latter in 2008 for the first time since the question was asked in 1985. See Gallup Poll, "Crime Survey 2009," *Gallup.com*, October 2009, http://www.gallup.com/poll/1606/death-penalty.aspx. The General Social Survey also shows a decline in support for capital punishment since the late 1990s, though not as steep.

30. Statistics available at Death Penalty Information Center, "The Death Penalty in 2008: Year End Report," *The Death Penalty Information Center homepage*, December 2008, http://www.deathpenaltyinfo.org/2008YearEnd.pdf; Robert Ruby and Allison Pond, "An Enduring Majority: Americans Continue to Support the Death Penalty," *Pew Forum on Religion and Public Life homepage*, December 19, 2007, http://pewforum.org/docs/?DocID=272.

31. Illinois Governor's Office, "Governor Ryan Declares Moratorium on Executions, Will Appoint Commission to Review Capital Punishment System," *Illinois Government News Network homepage*, January 31, 2000, http://www.illinois.gov/PressReleases/ShowPressRelease.cfm?SubjectID=3&RecNum=359; "People v. LaValle and People v. Taylor," *New York Capital Defender Office homepage*, http://www.nycdo.org/index.html; "Death Penalty Is Repealed in New Mexico," Associated Press, March 18, 2009, http://www.nytimes.com/2009/03/19/us/19execute.html.

32. The Death Penalty Information Center lists the death row inmates exonerated by DNA evidence. See Death Penalty Information Center, "The Innocence List," October 6, 2009, http://www.deathpenaltyinfo.org/innocence-list-those-freed-death-row.

33. The ABA took no official position on abolition but backed a moratorium to study the issue in 2001, noting that more than 100 prisoners had been released from death row since the reinstatement of the death penalty in 1976. See American Bar Association, "Death Penalty Moratorium Implementation Project," *American Bar Association homepage*, http://www.abanet.org/moratorium/. For discussions of U.S. political shifts and their causes, Paternoster et al., *The Death Penalty*, and Hood and Hoyle, *The Death Penalty*, 112–25.

34. An effort to incorporate a ban on capital punishment into the workings of the International Court of Justice failed. Germany, Mexico, and Paraguay have filed suits against the United States in the International Court of Justice to prevent the execution of their citizens.

35. European Parliament Delegation for Relations with the US, "Letter to Governor George W. Bush from the European Parliament Delegation for Relations with the US," *European Union: Delegation of the European Commission to the USA homepage*, June 25, 1998, http://www.eurunion.org/eu/index.php?option=com_content&task=vie w&id=1832&Itemid=74. EU guidelines were first published in 1998 and outlined a series of policies for integrating the death penalty into relations with non-EU states, including the United States. See European Union, "EU Guidelines on Human Rights," *European Union: Delegation of the European Commission to Japan homepage*, 2008, http://www.deljpn.ec.europa.eu/union/showpage_en_union.human.php.

36. European Initiative for Democracy and Human Rights: Evaluation on the Abolition of Death Penalty Projects, "Final Report," EUROPEAID/116548/C/SV, *EuropeAid homepage*, April 4, 2007, http://ec.europa.eu/europeaid/what/human-rights/documents/eidhr_evaluation_death_penalty_final_report_4april07_en.pdf.

37. UN Commission on Human Rights, *Extrajudicial, Summary or Arbitrary Executions: Report of the Special Rapporteur on Extrajudicial, Summary or Arbitrary Executions, Mr. Bacre Waly Ndiaye, Submitted Pursuant to Commission Resolution 1997/61*, E/CN.4/1998/68/Add.3, January 22, 1998, http://documents.un.org/welcome.asp?language=E.

38. "Letter to Members of the United States Congress from Members of the French National Assembly," July 2000, quoted in American Civil Liberties Union, "How the Death Penalty Weakens U.S. International Interests," December 6, 2004, http://www.aclu.org/FilesPDFs/idp_report.pdf.

39. "The Cruel and Ever More Unusual Punishment," *Economist*, May 13, 1999.

40. UN General Assembly, "Resolution 44/128: Second Optional Protocol," 1989. Amnesty International hailed the passage of the protocol in the general assembly by a vote of 59 to 26 with 48 abstentions. IPS-Inter Press Service, "United Nations: General Assembly Rebuffs Death Penalty," December 15, 1989.

41. Amnesty International, "The Death Penalty: Questions and Answers," *Amnesty International homepage*, April 2007, http://www.amnesty.org/en/library/asset/ACT50/010/2007/en/f14c87db-d3a2-11dd-a329-2f46302a8cc6/act500102007en.pdf.

42. John Holdridge, "End the Death Penalty: Statement of John Holdridge, Director, ACLU Capital Punishment Project," *American Civil Liberties Union homepage*, http://www.aclu.org/capital/general/30135res20070614.html. On the occasion of the 2009 World Day against the Death Penalty, the ACLU issued a statement insisting that "the U.S. needs to end this practice, in order to restore our country's standing and image in the world as a beacon for human rights and democratic values." Cited in "World Day against the Dealth Penalty," *American Civil Liberties Union Blog of Rights*, October 9, 2009, http://blog.aclu.org/2009/10/09/world-day-against-the-death-penalty/.

43. Brennan, J., Concurring Opinion, *Furman v. Georgia*, 408 U. S. 238 (1972) (per curiam), http://www.law.cornell.edu/supct/html/historics/USSC_CR_0408_0238_ZC1.html. Interestingly, Brennan was the only Catholic on the court at the time.

44. Brennan, J., Dissenting Opinion, *Gregg v. Georgia*, 429 U. S. 1301 (1976), http://www.law.cornell.edu/supct/html/historics/USSC_CR_0428_0153_ZD.html.

45. Brief of *Amici Curiae* Morton Abramowitz, Stephen W. Bosworth, Stuart E. Eizenstat, John C. Kornblum, Phyllis E. Oakley, Thomas R. Pickering, Felix G. Rohatyn, J. Stapleton Roy, and Frank G. Wisner in Support of Petitioner, *McCarver v. North Carolina*, O.T. 2001, No. 00–8727, p 5, 7, http://www.internationaljusticeproject.org/pdfs/FormerUSDiplomatBrief.pdf.

46. *Atkins v. Virginia*, 536 U.S. 304 (2002), http://www.law.cornell.edu/supct/html/00-8452.ZO.html; *Roper v. Simmons*, 543 U. S. 551 (2005), http://www.law.cornell.edu/supct/html/03-633.ZO.html.

47. Joseph L. Bernardin, "Statement on Capital Punishment," *United States Conference of Catholic Bishops homepage*, January 26, 1977, http://www.usccb.org/sdwp/national/criminal/death/uscc76.shtml.

48. "USCCB Statement, 1980," *United States Conference of Catholic Bishops homepage*, 1980, http://www.usccb.org/sdwp/national/criminal/death/uscc80.shtml.

49. Joseph L. Bernardin, *The Seamless Garment: Writings on the Consistent Ethic of Life* (Maryknoll, NY: Orbis Books, 2008), 12.

50. John Paul II, "Homily in St. Louis, January 27, 1999," *The Vatican homepage*, January 27, 1999, http://www.vatican.va/holy_father/john_paul_ii/travels/documents/hf_jp-ii_hom_27011999_stlouis_en.html.

51. John Paul II, "Ecclesia in America," *The Vatican homepage*, January 22, 1999, http://www.vatican.va/holy_father/john_paul_ii/apost_exhortations/documents/hf_jp-ii_exh_22011999_ecclesia-in-america_en.html.

52. "A Statement of the Administrative Board of the United States Conference of Catholic Bishops," *United States Conference of Catholic Bishops homepage*, April 2, 1999, http://www.usccb.org/sdwp/national/criminal/appeal.shtml.

53. *Atkins v. Virginia*, 536 U.S. 304 (2002), http://www.law.cornell.edu/supct/html/00-8452.ZD1.html.

54. E. J. Dionne, Jr. et al., "Transcript: Session Three: Religion, Politics, and the Death Penalty" (A Call for Reckoning: Religion and the Death Penalty Conference, January 25, 2002), http://pewforum.org/deathpenalty/resources/transcript3.php.

55. United States Conference of Catholic Bishops Office of Media Relations, "Catholic Bishops Launch Major Catholic Campaign to End the Use of the Death Penalty," *United States Conference of Catholic Bishops homepage*, March 21, 2005, http://www.usccb.org/comm/archives/2005/05-064.shtml; Helen Prejean, *Dead Man Walking: An Eyewitness Account of the Death Penalty in the United States* (New York: Random House, 1993). For background, see Thoroddur Bjarnason and Michael R. Welch, "Father Knows Best: Parishes, Priests, and American Catholic Parishioners' Attitudes Toward Capital Punishment," *Journal for the Scientific Study of Religion* 43, no. 1 (2003): 103–18.

56. Jon S. Corzine, "Remarks—Elimination of the Death Penalty," *The State of New Jersey Office of the Governor homepage*, December 17, 2007, http://www.state.nj.us/governor/news/speeches/elimination_death_penalty.html.

57. Nancy Solomon, "New Jersey's Death Penalty Moratorium," *National Public Radio homepage*, January 15, 2006, http://www.npr.org/templates/story/story.php?storyId=5158551.

58. "Lesniak Statement on the Signing of the Death Penalty Ban," *New Jersey State Democrats homepage,* December 17, 2007, http://www.njsendems.com/release. asp?rid=1694; Raymond Lesniak, "The Road to Justice and Peace," *NJ Voices: Opinions from New Jersey—Raymond Lesniak blog,* February 1, 2009, http://blog.nj.com/njv_raymond_lesniak/2009/02/the_road_to_justice_and_peace.html. See also Raymond Lesniak, *The Road to Abolition: How New Jersey Abolished the Death Penalty* (Linden, NJ: The Road to Justice and Peace, 2008).

59. Cited in Amnesty International, "New Mexico Abolishes the Death Penalty," *Amnesty International homepage,* March 19, 2009, http://www.amnesty.org/en/news-and-updates/good-news/new-mexico-abolishes-death-penalty-20090319.

60. Deborah Baker, "New Mexico Governor Agrees to Abolish Death Penalty after Visit to State's Death Chamber," Associated Press, March 19, 2009, http://abcnews.go.com/US/wireStory?id=7119135.

61. Cindy Wooden, "State's Decision to Abolish Death Penalty Marked at Rome's Colosseum," *Catholic News Service,* April 15, 2009, http://www.catholicnews.com/data/stories/cns/0901704.htm; Catholics against Capital Punishment, "CACP News Notes, Vol. 8, No. 1," *Catholics against Capital Punishment homepage,* June 15, 2009, http://www.cacp.org/cacpsnewsletter.html; Colin Wark and John F. Galliher, "Abolition of Capital Punishment in New Jersey and New Mexico: The Role of Religion and the Law" (2009), 15, http://works.bepress.com/context/colin_wark/article/1000/type/native/viewcontent/.

62. Office of New Mexico Governor Bill Richardson, "Roman Coliseum to Be Lit in Honor of New Mexico," *New Mexico Office of the Governor homepage,* April 10, 2009, http://www.governor.state.nm.us/press/2009/april/041009_01.pdf.

BIBLIOGRAPHY

Atkins v. Virginia, 536 U.S. 304 (2002). http://www.law.cornell.edu/supct/html/00-8452.ZD1.html.

Baker, Deborah. "New Mexico Governor Agrees to Abolish Death Penalty after Visit to State's Death Cchamber." Associated Press. March 19, 2009.

Banner, Stuart. *The Death Penalty: An American History.* Cambridge, MA: Harvard University Press, 2002.

Beccaria, Cesare. *On Crimes and Punishments.* 1st ed. Indianapolis: Hackett, 1986.

Bernardin, Joseph L. *The Seamless Garment: Writings on the Consistent Ethic of Life.* Maryknoll, NY: Orbis Books, 2008.

Bessler, John D. "Revisiting Beccaria's Vision: The Enlightenment, America's Death Penalty, and the Abolition Movement." *Northwestern Journal of Law and Social Policy* 4, no. 2 (Fall 2009): 195–328.

Bjarnason, Thoroddur, and Michael R. Welch. "Father Knows Best: Parishes, Priests, and American Catholic Parishioners' Attitudes Toward Capital Punishment." *Journal for the Scientific Study of Religion* 43, no. 1 (2003): 103–18.

Brennan, J., Concurring Opinion, *Furman v. Georgia,* 408 U.S. 238 (1972) (per curiam). http://www.law.cornell.edu/supct/html/historics/USSC_CR_0408_0238_ZC1.html.

Brennan, J., Dissenting Opinion, *Gregg v. Georgia,* 429 U.S. 1301 (1976). http://www.law.cornell.edu/supct/html/historics/USSC_CR_0428_0153_ZD.html.

Brief of *Amici Curiae* Morton Abramowitz, Stephen W. Bosworth, Stuart E. Eizenstat, John C. Kornblum, Phyllis E. Oakley, Thomas R. Pickering, Felix G. Rohatyn, J. Stapleton Roy, and Frank G. Wisner in Support of Petitioner. *McCarver v. North Carolina*, O.T. 2001, No. 00–8727, p 5, 7. http://www.internationaljusticeproject. org/pdfs/FormerUSDiplomatBrief.pdf.

Catechism of the Catholic Church. Washington, DC: United States Catholic Conference, 1997.

Catholics against Capital Punishment. "CACP News Notes, Vol. 8, No. 1." *Catholics against Capital Punishment homepage.* June 15, 2009. http://www.cacp.org/cacp-snewsletter.html.

Catholic Church. *The Catechism of the Council of Trent.* New York: Catholic Publication Society, 1929.

Council of Europe. *Protocol No. 6 to the Convention for the Protection of Human Rights and Fundamental Freedoms concerning the abolition of the death penalty as amended by Protocol No. 11.* April 28, 1983. http://conventions.coe.int/Treaty/en/Treaties/Html/114.htm.

Council of Europe. *Protocol No. 13 to the Convention for the Protection of Human Rights and Fundamental Freedoms, concerning the abolition of the death penalty in all circumstances.* May 3, 2002. http://conventions.coe.int/Treaty/En/Treaties/html/187. htm.

"The Cruel and Ever More Unusual Punishment." *Economist.* May 13, 1999.

Death Penalty Information Center. "The Death Penalty in 2008: Year End Report." *The Death Penalty Information Center homepage.* December 2008. http://www.death-penaltyinfo.org/2008YearEnd.pdf.

"Death Penalty Is Repealed in New Mexico." Associated Press. March 18, 2009. http:// www.nytimes.com/2009/03/19/us/19execute.html.

European Initiative for Democracy and Human Rights: Evaluation on the Abolition of Death Penalty Projects. "Final Report." EUROPEAID/116548/C/SV, *EuropeAid homepage.* April 4, 2007. http://ec.europa.eu/europeaid/what/human-rights/documents/eidhr_evaluation_death_penalty_final_report_4april07_en.pdf.

European Parliament, Council of the European Union, and the Commission of the European Union. *Charter of Fundamental Rights of the European Union.* December 18, 2000. http://www.europarl.europa.eu/charter/pdf/text_en.pdf.

Furman v. Georgia, 408 U.S. 238 (1972) (per curiam). http://www.law.cornell.edu/supct/html/historics/USSC_CR_0408_0238_ZO.html.

Gregg v. Georgia, 429 U.S. 1301 (1976). http://www.law.cornell.edu/supct/html/historics/USSC_CR_0428_0153_ZO.html.

Hood, Roger G., and Carolyn Hoyle. *The Death Penalty: A Worldwide Perspective.* 4th rev. and expanded ed. New York: Oxford University Press, 2008.

International Covenant on Civil and Political Rights. General Assembly Resolution 2200A(XXI). December 16, 1966. http://www2.ohchr.org/english/law/ccpr.htm.

IPS-Inter Press Service. "United Nations: General Assembly Rebuffs Death Penalty." December 15, 1989.

John XXIII. *Pacem in Terris.* April 11, 1963. http://www.vatican.va/holy_father/john_xxiii/encyclicals/documents/hf_j-xxiii_enc_11041963_pacem_en.html.

John Paul II. "Ecclesia in America." *The Vatican homepage,* January 22, 1999. http://

www.vatican.va/holy_father/john_paul_ii/apost_exhortations/documents/
hf_jp-ii_exh_22011999_ecclesia-in-america_en.html

John Paul II. *Evangelium vitae.* March 25, 1995. http://www.vatican.va/holy_father/
john_paul_ii/encyclicals/documents/hf_jp-ii_enc_25031995_evangelium-vitae_
en.html.

John Paul II. *Sollicitudino Rei Socialis.* December 30, 1987. http://www.vatican.va/
holy_father/john_paul_ii/encyclicals/documents/hf_jp-ii_enc_30121987_sollici-
tudo-rei-socialis_en.html.

Lesniak, Raymond. *The Road to Abolition: How New Jersey Abolished the Death Penalty.*
Linden, NJ: The Road to Justice and Peace, 2008.

"Letter to Members of the United States Congress from Members of the French National Assembly." July 2000. Quoted in American Civil Liberties Union. "How the
Death Penalty Weakens U.S. International Interests." December 2004. 6. http://
www.aclu.org/FilesPDFs/idp_report.pdf.

Magister, Sandro. "The Kerry Affair: What Ratzinger Wanted from the American
Bishops." *L'espresso online.* July 3, 2004. http://chiesa.espresso.repubblica.it/
articolo/7055?eng=y.

Maritain, Jacques. *The Natural Law and Human Rights.* Windsor, Ontario: Christian
Culture Press, 1942.

Megivern, James J. *The Death Penalty: An Historical and Theological Survey.* New York:
Paulist Press, 1997.

Obama, Barack. *The Audacity of Hope: Thoughts on Reclaiming the American Dream.*
New York: Random House, 2006.

Office of New Mexico Governor Bill Richardson. "Roman Coliseum to Be Lit in Honor
of New Mexico." *New Mexico Office of the Governor homepage.* April 10, 2009.
http://www.governor.state.nm.us/press/2009/april/041009_01.pdf.

Paul VI. *Pastoral Constitution of the Church in the Modern World: Gaudium et Spes.*
December 7, 1965. http://www.vatican.va/archive/hist_councils/ii_vatican_council/
documents/vat-ii_cons_19651207_gaudium-et-spes_en.html.

Paternoster, Raymond, Robert Brame, and Sarah Bacon. *The Death Penalty: America's
Experience with Capital Punishment.* New York: Oxford University Press, 2008.

Pius XI. *Mit brennender Sorge.* March 14, 1937. http://www.vatican.va/holy_father/pius_xi/
encyclicals/documents/hf_p-xi_enc_14031937_mit-brennender-sorge_en.html.

Pius XI. *Letter of Pius XI to the US Catholic hierarchy on the Occasion of the Golden
Jubilee of the Catholic University of America.* Cited in "Catholics Urged to Uphold
Catholic Liberty Theory." *St. Petersburg Times.* October 14, 1938.

Prejean, Helen. *Dead Man Walking: An Eyewitness Account of the Death Penalty in the
United States.* Random House, 1993.

Risse-Kappen, Thomas, Steve C. Ropp, and Kathryn Sikkink. *The Power of Human
Rights: International Norms and Domestic Change.* Cambridge Studies in International Relations 66. New York: Cambridge University Press, 1999.

Roper v. Simmons, 543 U.S. 551 (2005). http://www.law.cornell.edu/supct/html/03-633.
ZO.html.

Ruby, Robert, and Allison Pond. "An Enduring Majority: Americans Continue to
Support the Death Penalty." *Pew Forum on Religion and Public Life homepage.*
December 19, 2007. http://pewforum.org/docs/?DocID=272.

Schabas, William. *The Abolition of the Death Penalty in International Law.* Cambridge, UK: Grotius Publications, 1993.

Simmons, Beth A. *Mobilizing for Rights: International Law in Domestic Politics.* New York: Cambridge University Press, 2009.

Solomon, Nancy. "New Jersey's Death Penalty Moratorium." *National Public Radio homepage.* January 15, 2006. http://www.npr.org/templates/story/story.php?storyId=5158551.

UN Commission on Human Rights. Extrajudicial, Summary or Arbitrary Executions: Report of the Special Rapporteur on extrajudicial, summary or arbitrary executions, Mr. *Bacre Waly Ndiaye, submitted pursuant to Commission resolution 1997/61.* E/CN.4/1998/68/Add.3. January 22, 1998. http://documents.un.org/welcome.asp?language=E.

Wark, Colin, and John F. Galliher. "Abolition of Capital Punishment in New Jersey and New Mexico: The Role of Religion and the Law." 2009. http://works.bepress.com/context/colin_wark/article/1000/type/native/viewcontent/.

Wooden, Cindy. "State's Decision to Abolish Death Penalty Marked at Rome's Colosseum." *Catholic News Service*, April 15, 2009. http://www.catholicnews.com/data/stories/cns/0901704.htm.

Zimring, Franklin E. *The Contradictions of American Capital Punishment. Studies in Crime and Public Policy.* New York: Oxford University Press, 2003.

Index